CISCO

D1504160

Course Booklet

CCNA Exploration
Network Fundamentals

Version 4.0

ciscopress.com

Cisco | Networking Academy
Mind Wide Open

CCNA Exploration Course Booklet
Network Fundamentals Version 4.0
Cisco Networking Academy

Cisco Networking Academy

Copyright© 2010 Cisco Systems, Inc.

Published by:
Cisco Press
800 East 96th Street
Indianapolis, IN 46240 USA

Printed in the United States of America

Fifth Printing, May 2012

Library of Congress Cataloging-in-Publication Data is available upon request

ISBN-13: 978-1-58713-243-8

ISBN-10: 1-58713-243-5

Publisher
Paul Boger

Associate Publisher
Dave Dusthimer

Cisco Representative
Erik Ullanderson

Cisco Press
Program Manager
Anand Sundaram

Executive Editor
Mary Beth Ray

Managing Editor
Patrick Kanouse

Project Editor
Bethany Wall

Editorial Assistant
Vanessa Evans

Cover Designer
Louisa Adair

Composition
Mark Shirar

Warning and Disclaimer

This book is designed to provide information about Networking. Every effort has been made to make this book as complete and as accurate as possible, but no warranty or fitness is implied.

The information is provided on an "as is" basis. The authors, Cisco Press, and Cisco Systems, Inc. shall have neither liability nor responsibility to any person or entity with respect to any loss or damages arising from the information contained in this book or from the use of the discs or programs that may accompany it.

The opinions expressed in this book belong to the author and are not necessarily those of Cisco Systems, Inc.

Trademark Acknowledgments

All terms mentioned in this book that are known to be trademarks or service marks have been appropriately capitalized. Cisco Press or Cisco Systems, Inc., cannot attest to the accuracy of this information. Use of a term in this book should not be regarded as affecting the validity of any trademark or service mark.

Feedback Information

At Cisco Press, our goal is to create in-depth technical books of the highest quality and value. Each book is crafted with care and precision, undergoing rigorous development that involves the unique expertise of members from the professional technical community.

Readers' feedback is a natural continuation of this process. If you have any comments regarding how we could improve the quality of this book, or otherwise alter it to better suit your needs, you can contact us through email at feedback@ciscopress.com. Please make sure to include the book title and ISBN in your message.

We greatly appreciate your assistance.

Americas Headquarters
Cisco Systems, Inc.
San Jose, CA

Asia Pacific Headquarters
Cisco Systems (USA) Pte. Ltd.
Singapore

Europe Headquarters
Cisco Systems International BV
Amsterdam, The Netherlands

Cisco has more than 200 offices worldwide. Addresses, phone numbers, and fax numbers are listed on the Cisco Website at **www.cisco.com/go/offices.**

CCDE, CCENT, Cisco Eos, Cisco HealthPresence, the Cisco logo, Cisco Lumin, Cisco Nexus, Cisco StadiumVision, Cisco TelePresence, Cisco WebEx, DCE, and Welcome to the Human Network are trademarks; Changing the Way We Work, Live, Play, and Learn and Cisco Store are service marks; and Access Registrar, Aironet, AsyncOS, Bringing the Meeting To You, Catalyst, CCDA, CCDP, CCIE, CCIP, CCNA, CCNP, CCSP, CCVP, Cisco, the Cisco Certified Internetwork Expert logo, Cisco IOS, Cisco Press, Cisco Systems, Cisco Systems Capital, the Cisco Systems logo, Cisco Unity, Collaboration Without Limitation, EtherFast, EtherSwitch, Event Center, Fast Step, Follow Me Browsing, FormShare, GigaDrive, HomeLink, Internet Quotient, IOS, iPhone, iQuick Study, IronPort, the IronPort logo, LightStream, Linksys, MediaTone, MeetingPlace, MeetingPlace Chime Sound, MGX, Networkers, Networking Academy, Network Registrar, PCNow, PIX, PowerPanels, ProConnect, ScriptShare, SenderBase, SMARTnet, Spectrum Expert, StackWise, The Fastest Way to Increase Your Internet Quotient, TransPath, WebEx, and the WebEx logo are registered trademarks of Cisco Systems, Inc. and/or its affiliates in the United States and certain other countries.

All other trademarks mentioned in this document or website are the property of their respective owners. The use of the word partner does not imply a partnership relationship between Cisco and any other company. (0812R)

Contents at a Glance

Contents

Command Syntax Conventions

The conventions used to present command syntax in this book are the same conventions used in the IOS Command Reference. The Command Reference describes these conventions as follows:

- **Boldface** indicates commands and keywords that are entered literally as shown. In actual configuration examples and output (not general command syntax), boldface indicates commands that are manually input by the user (such as a show command).

- *Italic* indicates arguments for which you supply actual values.

- Vertical bars (|) separate alternative, mutually exclusive elements.

- Square brackets ([ ]) indicate an optional element.

- Braces ({ }) indicate a required choice.

- Braces within brackets ([{ }]) indicate a required choice within an optional element.

About this Course Booklet

Your Cisco® Networking Academy® Course Booklet is designed as a study resource you can easily read, highlight, and review on the go, wherever the Internet is not available or practical:

- The text is extracted directly, word-for-word, from the online course so you can highlight important points and take notes in the "Your Chapter Notes" section.

- Headings with the exact page correlations provide a quick reference to the online course for your class-room discussions and exam preparation.

- An icon system directs you to the online curriculum to take full advantage of the images, labs, Packet Tracer activities, and dynamic Flash-based activities embedded within the Networking Academy online course interface.

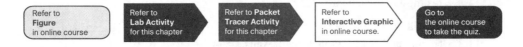

The Course Booklet is a basic, economical paper-based resource to help you succeed with the Cisco Networking Academy online course.

Welcome

Welcome to the CCNA Exploration Network Fundamentals course. The goal of this course is to introduce you to fundamental networking concepts and technologies. These online course materials will assist you in developing the skills necessary to plan and implement small networks across a range of applications. The specific skills covered in each chapter are described at the start of each chapter.

More than just information

This computer-based learning environment is an important part of the overall course experience for students and instructors in the Networking Academy. These online course materials are designed to be used along with several other instructional tools and activities. These include:

- Class presentation, discussion, and practice with your instructor
- Hands-on labs that use networking equipment within the Networking Academy classroom
- Online scored assessments and grade book
- Packet Tracer 4.1 simulation tool
- Additional software for classroom activities

A global community

When you participate in the Networking Academy, you are joining a global community linked by common goals and technologies. Schools, colleges, universities and other entities in over 160 countries participate in the program. You can see an interactive network map of the global Networking Academy community at http://www.academynetspace.com.

The material in this course encompasses a broad range of technologies that facilitate how people work, live, play, and learn by communicating with voice, video, and other data. Networking and the Internet affect people differently in different parts of the world. Although we have worked with instructors from around the world to create these materials, it is important that you work with your instructor and fellow students to make the material in this course applicable to your local situation.

Keep in Touch

These online instructional materials, as well as the rest of the course tools, are part of the larger Networking Academy. The portal for the program is located at http://cisco.netacad.net. There you will obtain access to the other tools in the program such as the assessment server and student grade book), as well as informational updates and other relevant links.

Mind Wide Open®

An important goal in education is to enrich you, the student, by expanding what you know and can do. It is important to realize, however, that the instructional materials and the instructor can only facilitate the process. You must make the commitment yourself to learn new skills. Below are a few suggestions to help you learn and grow.

1. Take notes. Professionals in the networking field often keep Engineering Journals in which they write down the things they observe and learn. Taking notes is an important way to help your understanding grow over time.

2. Think about it. The course provides information both to change what you know and what you can do. As you go through the course, ask yourself what makes sense and what doesn't. Stop and ask questions when you are confused. Try to find out more about topics that interest you. If you are not sure why something is being taught, consider asking your instructor or a friend. Think about how the different parts of the course fit together.

3. Practice. Learning new skills requires practice. We believe this is so important to e-learning that we have a special name for it. We call it e-doing. It is very important that you complete the activities in the online instructional materials and that you also complete the hands-on labs and Packet Tracer® activities.

4. Practice again. Have you ever thought that you knew how to do something and then, when it was time to show it on a test or at work, you discovered that you really hadn't mastered it? Just like learning any new skill like a sport, game, or language, learning a professional skill requires patience and repeated practice before you can say you have truly learned it. The online instructional materials in this course provide opportunities for repeated practice for many skills. Take full advantage of them. You can also work with your instructor to extend Packet Tracer, and other tools, for additional practice as needed.

5. Teach it. Teaching a friend or colleague is often a good way to reinforce your own learning. To teach well, you will have to work through details that you may have overlooked on your first reading. Conversations about the course material with fellow students, colleagues, and the instructor can help solidify your understanding of networking concepts.

6. Make changes as you go. The course is designed to provide feedback through interactive activities and quizzes, the online assessment system, and through interactions with your instructor. You can use this feedback to better understand where your strengths and weaknesses are. If there is an area that you are having trouble with, focus on studying or practicing more in that area. Seek additional feedback from your instructor and other students.

Explore the world of networking

This version of the course includes a special tool called Packet Tracer 4.1®. Packet Tracer is a networking learning tool that supports a wide range of physical and logical simulations. It also provides visualization tools to help you to understand the internal workings of a network.

The Packet Tracer activities included in the course consist of network simulations, games, activities, and challenges that provide a broad range of learning experiences.

Create your own worlds

You can also use Packet Tracer to create your own experiments and networking scenarios. We hope that, over time, you consider using Packet Tracer – not only for experiencing the activities included in the course, but also to become an author, explorer, and experimenter.

The online course materials have embedded Packet Tracer activities that will launch on computers running Windows® operating systems, if Packet Tracer is installed. This integration may also work on other operating systems using Windows emulation.

Course Overview

As the course title states, the focus of this course is on learning the fundamentals of networking. In this course, you will learn both the practical and conceptual skills that build the foundation for understanding basic networking. First, you will examine human versus network communication and see the parallels between them. Next, you will be introduced to the two major models used to plan and implement networks: OSI and TCP/IP. You will gain an understanding of the "layered" approach to networks and examine the OSI and TCP/IP layers in detail to understand their functions and services. You will become familiar with the various network devices, network addressing schemes and, finally, the types of media used to carry data across the network.

In this course, you will gain experience using networking utilities and tools, such as Packet Tracer and Wireshark®, to explore networking protocols and concepts. These tools will help you to develop an understanding of how data flows in a network. A special "model Internet" is also used to provide a test environment where a range of network services and data can be observed and analyzed.

Chapter 1 - Chapter 1 presents the basics of communication and how networks have changed our lives. You will be introduced to the concepts of networks, data, local area networks (LANs), wide area networks (WANs), quality of service (QoS), security issues, network collaboration services, and Packet Tracer activities. In the labs, you will learn how to set up a wiki and establish an instant messaging session.

Chapter 2 - Chapter 2 focuses on how networks are modeled and used. You will be introduced to the OSI and TCP/IP models and to the process of data encapsulation. You will learn about the network tool Wireshark®, which is used for analyzing network traffic, and will explore the differences between a real network and a simulated network. In the lab, you will build your first network – a small peer-to-peer network.

Chapter 3 - Using a top-down approach to teaching networking, Chapter 3 introduces you to the top network model layer, the Application layer. In this context, you will explore the interaction of protocols, services, and applications, with a focus on HTTP, DNS, DHCP, SMTP/POP, Telnet and FTP. In the labs, you will practice installing a web server/client and use Wireshark® to analyze network traffic. The Packet Tracer activities let you explore how protocols operate at the Application layer.

Chapter 4 – Chapter 4 introduces the Transport layer and focuses on how the TCP and UDP protocols apply to the common applications. In the labs and activities, you will incorporate the use of Wireshark®, the Windows utilities command netstat, and Packet Tracer to investigate these two protocols.

Chapter 5 – Chapter 5 introduces the OSI Network layer. You will examine concepts of addressing and routing and learn about path determination, data packets, and the IP protocol. By the end of this chapter, you will configure hosts to access the local network and explore routing tables.

Chapter 6 - In Chapter 6, you will focus on network addressing in detail and learn how to use the address mask, or prefix length, to determine the number of subnetworks and hosts in a network. You will also be introduced to ICMP (Internet Control Message Protocol) tools, such as ping and trace.

Chapter 7 – Chapter 7 discusses the services provided by Data Link layer. An emphasis is placed on the encapsulation processes that occur as data travels across the LAN and the WAN.

Chapter 8 – Chapter 8 introduces the Physical layer. You will discover how data sends signals and is encoded for travel across the network. You'll learn about bandwidth and also about the types of media and their associated connectors.

Chapter 9 – In Chapter 9, you will examine the technologies and operation of Ethernet. You will use Wireshark®, Packet Tracer activities, and lab exercises to explore Ethernet.

Chapter 10 – Chapter 10 focuses on designing and cabling a network. You will apply the knowledge and skills developed in the previous chapters to determine the appropriate cables to use, how to connect devices, and develop an addressing and testing scheme.

Chapter 11 –In Chapter 11, you will connect and configure a small network using basic Cisco IOS commands for routers and switches. Upon completion of this final chapter, you will be prepared you to go on to either CCNA Exploration Routing or CCNA Exploration Switching courses.

Wireshark®, is a registered trademark of Gerald Combs

CHAPTER 1

Living in a Network-Centric World

Chapter Introduction

We now stand at a critical turning point in the use of technology to extend and empower our human *network*. The globalization of the *Internet* has succeeded faster than anyone could have imagined. The manner in which social, commercial, political and personal interactions occur is rapidly changing to keep up with the evolution of this global network. In the next stage of our development, innovators will use the Internet as a starting point for their efforts - creating new products and services specifically designed to take advantage of the network capabilities. As developers push the limits of what is possible, the capabilities of the interconnected networks that form the Internet will play an increasing role in the success of these projects.

This chapter introduces the platform of *data networks* upon which our social and business relationships increasingly depend. The material lays the groundwork for exploring the services, technologies, and issues encountered by network professionals as they design, build, and maintain the modern network.

In this chapter, you will learn to:

- Describe how networks impact our daily lives.

- Describe the role of data networking in the human network.

- Identify the key components of any data network.

- Identify the opportunities and challenges posed by converged networks.

- Describe the characteristics of network architectures: fault tolerance, scalability, quality of service and security.

- Install and use IRC clients and a Wiki *server*.

1.1 Communicating in a Network-Centric World

1.1.1 Networks Supporting the Way We Live

Among all of the essentials for human existence, the need to interact with others ranks just below our need to sustain life. Communication is almost as important to us as our reliance on air, water, food, and shelter.

The methods that we use to share ideas and information are constantly changing and evolving. Whereas the human network was once limited to face-to-face conversations, *media* breakthroughs continue to extend the reach of our communications. From the printing press to television, each new development has improved and enhanced our communication.

As with every advance in communication technology, the creation and interconnection of robust data networks is having a profound effect.

Refer to
Figure
in online course

Refer to
Figure
in online course

Early data networks were limited to exchanging character-based information between connected computer systems. Current networks have evolved to carry voice, video streams, text, and graphics between many different types of devices. Previously separate and distinct communication forms have converged onto a common platform. This platform provides access to a wide range of alternative and new communication methods that enable people to interact directly with each other almost instantaneously.

The immediate nature of communications over the Internet encourages the formation of global communities. These communities foster social interaction that is independent of location or time zone.

Refer to
Figure
in online course

The Global Community

Technology is perhaps the most significant change agent in the world today, as it helps to create a world in which national borders, geographic distances, and physical limitations become less relevant, and present ever-diminishing obstacles. The creation of online communities for the exchange of ideas and information has the potential to increase productivity opportunities across the globe. As the Internet connects people and promotes unfettered communication, it presents the platform on which to run businesses, to address emergencies, to inform individuals, and to support education, science, and government.

Click PLAY to watch how the Internet, and its underlying technology, brings opportunities to people wherever they live or work.

Refer to
Figure
in online course

It is incredible how quickly the Internet became an integral part of our daily routines. The complex interconnection of electronic devices and media that comprise the network is transparent to the millions of users who make it a valued and personal part of their lives.

Data networks that were once the transport of information from business to business have been re-purposed to improve the quality of life for people everywhere. In the course of a day, resources available through the Internet can help you:

- Decide what to wear using online current weather conditions.
- Find the least congested route to your destination, displaying weather and traffic video from webcams.
- Check your bank balance and pay bills electronically.
- Receive and send *e-mail*, or make an Internet phone call, at an Internet cafe over lunch.
- Obtain health information and nutritional advice from experts all over the world, and post to a forum to share related health or treatment information.
- Download new recipes and cooking techniques to create a spectacular dinner.
- Post and share your photographs, home videos, and experiences with friends or with the world.

Many uses of the Internet would have been hard to imagine just a few years ago. Take for example, one person's experience publishing a home music video:

"My goal is to make my own movies. One day, my friend Adi and I made a video as a surprise for her boyfriend's birthday. We recorded ourselves lip-synching to a song and dancing around. Then we decided, why not post it. Well, the reaction has been huge. It's had over 9 million views so far, and the movie director Kevin Smith even did a short spoof of it. I don't know what draws people to the video. Maybe it's the simplicity of it, or the song. Maybe it's because it's spontaneous and fun, and it makes people feel good. I don't know. But I do know that I can do what I love and share it

online with millions of people around the world. All I need is my computer, digital camcorder, and some software. And that's an amazing thing."

Refer to
Lab Activity
for this chapter

Lab Activity

Use satellite imagery available through the Internet to explore your world.

Refer to
Figure
in online course

1.1.2 Examples of Today's Popular Communication Tools

The existence and broad adoption of the Internet has ushered in new forms of communication that empower individuals to create information that can be accessed by a global audience.

Instant Messaging

Instant messaging (IM) is a form of *real-time* communication between two or more people based on typed text. The text is conveyed via computers connected over either a private internal network or over a public network, such as the Internet. Developed from earlier Internet Relay Chat (IRC) services, IM also incorporates features such as file transfer, voice, and video communication. Like e-mail, IM sends a written record of the communication. However, whereas transmission of e-mail messages is sometimes delayed, IM messages are received immediately. The form of communication that IM uses is called real-time communication.

Weblogs (blogs)

Weblogs are web pages that are easy to update and edit. Unlike commercial websites, which are created by professional communications experts, blogs give anyone a means to communicate their thoughts to a global audience without technical knowledge of web design. There are blogs on nearly every topic one can think of, and communities of people often form around popular blog authors.

Wikis

Wikis are web pages that groups of people can edit and view together. Whereas a blog is more of an individual, personal journal, a *wiki* is a group creation. As such, it may be subject to more extensive review and editing. Like blogs, wikis can be created in stages, and by anyone, without the sponsorship of a major commercial enterprise. There is a public wiki, called Wikipedia, that is becoming a comprehensive resource - an online encyclopedia - of publicly-contributed topics. Private organizations and individuals can also build their own wikis to capture collected knowledge on a particular subject. Many businesses use wikis as their internal *collaboration tool*. With the global Internet, people of all walks of life can participate in wikis and add their own perspectives and knowledge to a shared resource.

Podcasting

Podcasting is an audio-based *medium* that originally enabled people to record audio and convert it for use with iPods - a small, portable device for audio playback manufactured by Apple. The ability to record audio and save it to a computer file is not new. However, *podcasting* allows people to deliver their recordings to a wide audience. The audio file is placed on a website (or blog or wiki) where others can *download* it and play the recording on their computers, laptops, and iPods.

Collaboration Tools

Collaboration tools give people the opportunity to work together on shared documents. Without the constraints of location or time zone, individuals connected to a shared system can speak to each other, share text and graphics, and edit documents together. With collaboration tools always available, organizations can move quickly to share information and pursue goals. The broad distribution of data networks means that people in remote locations can contribute on an equal basis with people at the heart of large population centers.

1.1.3 Networks Supporting the Way We Learn

Refer to
Figure
in online course

Communication, collaboration, and engagement are fundamental building blocks of education. Institutions are continually striving to enhance these processes to maximize the dissemination of knowledge. Robust and reliable networks support and enrich student learning experiences. These networks deliver learning material in a wide range of formats. The learning materials include interactive activities, assessments, and feedback.

Courses delivered using network or Internet resources are often called online learning experiences, or e-learning.

The availability of e-learning courseware has multiplied the resources available to students many times over. Traditional learning methods provide primarily two sources of expertise from which the student can obtain information: the textbook and the instructor. These two sources are limited, both in the format and the timing of the presentation. In contrast, online courses can contain voice, data, and video, and are available to the students at any time from any place. Students can follow links to different references and to subject experts in order to enhance their learning experience. Online discussion groups and message boards enable a student to collaborate with the instructor, with other students in the class, or even with students across the world. Blended courses can combine instructor-led classes with online courseware to provide the best of both delivery methods.

Access to high quality instruction is no longer restricted to students living in proximity to where that instruction is being delivered. Online distance learning has removed geographic barriers and improved student opportunity.

Refer to
Figure
in online course

The Cisco Networking Academy Program, which offers this course, is an example of a global online learning experience. The instructor provides a syllabus and establishes a preliminary schedule for completing the course content. The Academy program supplements the expertise of the instructor with an interactive curriculum that provides many forms of learning experiences. The program provides text, graphics, animations, and a simulated networking environment tool called Packet Tracer. Packet Tracer provides a way to build virtual representations of networks and emulate many of the functions of networking devices.

Students may communicate with the instructor and fellow students using online tools, like e-mail, bulletin/discussion boards, chat rooms, and *instant messaging*. Links provide access to learning resources outside of the courseware. Blended e-learning provides the benefits of computer-based training while retaining advantages of instructor-led curriculum. Students have the opportunity to work online at their own pace and skill level while still having access to an instructor and other live resources.

In addition to the benefits for the student, networks have improved the management and administration of courses as well. Some of these online functions include enrollment, assessment delivery and grade books.

Refer to
Figure
in online course

In the business world, the use of networks to provide efficient and cost-effective employee training is increasing in acceptance. Online learning opportunities can decrease time-consuming and costly travel yet still ensure that all employees are adequately trained to perform their jobs in a safe and productive manner.

Online courseware and delivery offer many benefits to businesses. Among the benefits are:

- *Current and accurate training materials.* Collaboration between vendors, equipment manufacturers and training providers ensures that the courseware is up-to-date with the latest processes and procedures. When errors in materials are found and corrected, the new courseware is immediately available to all employees.

- *Availability of training to a wide audience.* Online training is not dependent on travel schedules, instructor availability or physical class size. Employees can be given deadlines by which training is to be completed and the employees can access the courseware when it is convenient.

- *Consistent quality of instruction.* The quality of the instruction does not vary as it would if different instructors were delivering an in-person course. The online curriculum provides a consistent core of instruction to which instructors can add additional expertise.

- *Cost reduction.* In addition to reducing the cost of travel and the lost time associated with travel, there are other cost reducing factors for business related to online training. It is usually less expensive to revise and update online courseware than it is to update paper-based material. Facilities to support in-person training can also be reduced or eliminated.

Many businesses also provide customer training online. This courseware enables the customers to use the products and services provided by the business in the best manner, reducing calls to the help lines or customer service centers.

1.1.4 Networks Supporting the Way We Work

Refer to **Figure** in online course

Initially, data networks were used by businesses to internally record and manage financial information, customer information, and employee payroll systems. These business networks evolved to enable the transmission of many different types of information services, including e-mail, video, messaging, and telephony.

Intranets, private networks in use by just one company, enable businesses to communicate and perform transactions among global employee and branch locations. Companies develop *extranets*, or extended internetworks, to provide suppliers, vendors, and customers limited access to corporate data to check order status, inventory, and parts lists.

Today, networks provide a greater integration between related functions and organizations than was possible in the past.

Consider these business scenarios.

- A wheat farmer in Australia uses a laptop enabled with a Global Positioning System (GPS) to plant a crop with precision and efficiency. At harvest time, the farmer can co-ordinate harvesting with the availability of grain transporters and storage facilities. Using mobile *wireless technology*, the grain transporter can monitor the vehicle in-route in order to maintain the best fuel efficiency and safe operation. Changes in status can be relayed to the driver of the vehicle instantly.

- Remote workers, called teleworkers or telecommuters, use secure remote access services from home or while traveling. The data network enables them to work as if they were on-site, with access to all the network-based tools normally available for their jobs. Virtual meetings and conferences can be convened which include people in remote locations. The network provides audio and video capability so all participants can both see and hear each other. The information from the meetings can be recorded to a wiki or blog. The latest versions of the agenda and minutes can be shared as soon as they are created.

There are many success stories illustrating innovative ways networks are being used to make us more successful in the workplace. Some of these scenarios are available through the Cisco web site at http://www.cisco.com

1.1.5 Networks Supporting the Way We Play

Refer to **Figure** in online course

The widespread adoption of the Internet by the entertainment and travel industries enhances the ability to enjoy and share many forms of recreation, regardless of location. It is possible to explore places interactively that previously we could only dream of visiting, as well as preview the actual destinations before making a trip. The details and photographs from these adventures may be posted online for others to view.

The Internet is used for traditional forms of entertainment, as well. We listen to recording artists, preview or view motion pictures, read entire books and download material for future offline access. Live sporting events and concerts can be experienced as they are happening, or recorded and viewed on demand.

Networks enable the creation of new forms of entertainment, such as online games. Players participate in any kind of online competition that game designers can imagine. We compete with friends and foes around the world in the same manner if they were in the same room.

Even offline activities are enhanced using network collaboration services. Global communities of interest have grown rapidly. We share common experiences and hobbies well beyond our local neighborhood, city, or region. Sports fans share opinions and facts about their favorite teams. Collectors display prized collections and get expert feedback about them.

Online markets and auction sites provide the opportunity to buy, sell and trade all types of merchandise.

Whatever form of recreation we enjoy in the human network, networks are improving our experience.

1.2 Communication - An Essential Part of Our Lives

1.2.1 What is Communication?

Refer to **Figure** in online course

Communication in our daily lives takes many forms and occurs in many environments. We have different expectations depending on whether we are chatting via the Internet or participating in a job interview. Each situation has its corresponding expected behaviors and styles.

Establishing the Rules

Before beginning to communicate with each other, we establish rules or agreements to govern the conversation. These rules, or protocols, must be followed in order for the message to be successfully delivered and understood. Among the protocols that govern successful human communication are:

- An identified sender and receiver

- Agreed upon method of communicating (face-to-face, telephone, letter, photograph)

- Common language and grammar

- Speed and timing of delivery

- Confirmation or acknowledgement requirements

Communication rules may vary according to the context. If a message conveys an important fact or concept, a confirmation that the message has been received and understood is necessary. Less important messages may not require an acknowledgement from the recipient.

The techniques that are used in network communications share these fundamentals with human conversations. Because many of our human communication protocols are implicit or are ingrained in our cultures, some rules can be assumed. In establishing data networks, it is necessary to be much more explicit about how communication takes place and how it is judged successful.

1.2.2 Quality of Communications

Refer to **Figure** in online course

Communication between individuals is determined to be successful when the meaning of the message understood by the recipient matches the meaning intended by the sender.

For data networks, we use the same basic criteria to judge success. However, as a message moves through the network, many factors can prevent the message from reaching the recipient or distort its intended meaning. These factors can be either external or internal.

External Factors

The external factors affecting communication are related to the complexity of the network and the number of devices a message must pass through on its route to its final destination.

External factors affecting the success of communication include:

- The quality of the pathway between the sender and the recipient
- The number of times the message has to change form
- The number of times the message has to be redirected or readdressed
- The number of other messages being transmitted simultaneously on the communication network
- The amount of time allotted for successful communication

Refer to **Figure** in online course

Internal Factors

Internal factors that interfere with network communication are related to the nature of the message itself.

Different types of messages may vary in complexity and importance. Clear and concise messages are usually easier to understand than complex messages. Important communications require more care to ensure that they are delivered and understood by the recipient.

Internal factors affecting the successful communication across the network include:

- The size of the message
- The complexity of the message
- The importance of the message

Large messages may be interrupted or delayed at different points within the network. A message with a low importance or priority could be dropped if the network becomes overloaded.

Both the internal and external factors that affect the receipt of a message must be anticipated and controlled for network communications to be successful. New innovations in network *hardware* and software are being implemented to ensure the quality and reliability of network communications.

1.3 The Network as a Platform

1.3.1 Communicating over Networks

Refer to
Figure
in online course

Being able to reliably communicate to anyone, anywhere, is becoming increasingly important to our personal and business lives. In order to support the immediate delivery of the millions of messages being exchanged between people all over the world, we rely on a web of interconnected networks. These data or information networks vary in size and capabilities, but all networks have four basic elements in common:

- Rules or agreements to govern how the messages are sent, directed, received and interpreted

- The messages or units of information that travel from one device to another

- A means of interconnecting these devices - a medium that can transport the messages from one device to another

- Devices on the network that exchange messages with each other

The standardization of the various elements of the network enables equipment and devices created by different companies to work together. Experts in various technologies can contribute their best ideas on how to develop an efficient network, without regard to the brand or manufacturer of the equipment.

1.3.2 The Elements of a Network

Refer to
Figure
in online course

The diagram shows elements of a typical network, including devices, media, and services, tied together by rules, that work together to send messages. We use the word *messages* as a term that encompasses web pages, e-mail, instant messages, telephone calls, and other forms of communication enabled by the Internet. In this course, we will learn about a variety of messages, devices, media, and services that allow the communication of those messages. We will also learn about the rules, or protocols, that tie these network elements together.

Refer to
Figure
in online course

In this course, many networking devices will be discussed. Networking is a very graphically oriented subject, and icons are commonly used to represent networking devices. On the left side of the diagram are shown some common devices which often originate messages that comprise our communication. These include various types of computers (a PC and laptop icon are shown), servers, and IP phones. On local area networks these devices are typically connected by LAN media (wired or wireless).

The right side of the figure shows some of the most common intermediate devices, used to direct and manage messages across the network, as well as other common networking symbols. Generic symbols are shown for:

- Switch - the most common device for interconnecting local area networks

- Firewall - provides security to networks

- Router - helps direct messages as they travel across a network

- Wireless Router - a specific type of *router* often found in home networks

- Cloud - used to summarize a group of networking devices, the details of which may be unimportant to the discussion at hand

- Serial Link - one form of WAN interconnection, represented by the lightning bolt-shaped line

Refer to
Figure
in online course

For a network to function, the devices must be interconnected. Network connections can be wired or wireless. In wired connections, the medium is either copper, which carries electrical signals, or optical fiber, which carries light signals. In wireless connections, the medium is the Earth's atmosphere, or space, and the signals are microwaves. Copper medium includes cables, such as twisted pair telephone wire, *coaxial* cable, or most commonly, what is known as Category 5 Unshielded Twisted Pair (*UTP*) cable. Optical fibers, thin strands of glass or plastic that carry light signals, are another form of networking media. Wireless media may include the home wireless connection between a wireless router and a computer with a wireless network card, the terrestrial wireless connection between two ground stations, or the communication between devices on earth and satellites. In a typical journey across the Internet, a message may travel across a variety of media.

Refer to **Figure** in online course

Human beings often seek to send and receive a variety of messages using computer applications; these applications require services to be provided by the network. Some of these services include the World Wide Web, e-mail, instant messaging, and IP Telephony. Devices interconnected by medium to provide services must be governed by rules, or protocols. In the chart, some common services and a protocol most directly associated with that service are listed.

Protocols are the rules that the networked devices use to communicate with each other. The industry *standard* in networking today is a set of protocols called *TCP/IP* (Transmission Control Protocol/Internet Protocol). TCP/IP is used in home and business networks, as well as being the primary protocol of the Internet. It is TCP/IP protocols that specify the formatting, addressing and *routing* mechanisms that ensure our messages are delivered to the correct recipient.

Refer to **Figure** in online course

We close this section with an example to tie together how the elements of networks - devices, media, and services - are connected by rules to deliver a message. People often only picture networks in the abstract sense. We create and send a text message and it almost immediately shows up on the destination device. Although we know that between our sending device and the receiving device there is a network over which our message travels, we rarely think about all the parts and pieces that make up that infrastructure.

The Messages

In the first step of its journey from the computer to its destination, our instant message gets converted into a format that can be transmitted on the network. All types of messages must be converted to *bits*, *binary* coded digital signals, before being sent to their destinations. This is true no matter what the original message format was: text, video, voice, or computer data. Once our instant message is converted to bits, it is ready to be sent onto the network for delivery.

The Devices

To begin to understand the robustness and complexity of the interconnected networks that make up the Internet, it is necessary to start with the basics. Take the example of sending the text message using an instant messaging program on a computer. When we think of using network services, we usually think of using a computer to access them. But, a computer is only one type of device that can send and receive messages over a network. Many other types of devices can also be connected to the network to participate in network services. Among these devices are telephones, cameras, music systems, printers and game consoles.

In addition to the computer, there are numerous other components that make it possible for our instant message to be directed across the miles of wires, underground cables, airwaves and satellite stations that might exist between the *source* and destination devices. One of the critical components in any size network is the router. A router joins two or more networks, like a home network and the Internet, and passes information from one network to another. Routers in a network work to ensure that the message gets to its destination in the most efficient and quickest manner.

The Medium

To send our instant message to its destination, the computer must be connected to a wired or wireless local network. Local networks can be installed in homes or businesses, where they enable computers and other devices to share information with each other and to use a common connection to the Internet.

Wireless networks allow the use of networked devices anywhere in an office or home, even outdoors. Outside the office or home, wireless networking is available in public hotspots, such as coffee shops, businesses, hotel rooms, and airports.

Many installed networks use wires to provide connectivity. Ethernet is the most common wired networking technology found today. The wires, called cables, connect the computers and other devices that make up the networks. Wired networks are best for moving large amounts of data at high speeds, such as are required to support professional-quality multimedia.

The Services

Network services are computer programs that support the human network. Distributed on devices throughout the network, these services facilitate online communication tools such as e-mail, bulletin/discussion boards, chat rooms, and instant messaging. In the case of instant messaging, for example, an instant messaging service, provided by devices in the *cloud*, must be accessible to both the sender and recipient.

The Rules

Important aspects of networks that are neither devices nor media are rules, or protocols. These rules are the standards and protocols that specify how the messages are sent, how they are directed through the network, and how they are interpreted at the destination devices. For example, in the case of Jabber instant messaging, the XMPP, TCP, and IP protocols are all important sets of rules that enable our communication to occur.

1.3.3 Converged Networks

Multiple services-multiple networks

Refer to Figure in online course

Traditional telephone, radio, television, and computer data networks each have their own individual versions of the four basic network elements. In the past, every one of these services required a different technology to carry its particular communication signal. Additionally, each service had its own set of rules and standards to ensure successful communication of its signal across a specific medium.

Converged networks

Technology advances are enabling us to consolidate these disparate networks onto one platform - a platform defined as a *converged network*. The *flow* of voice, video, and data traveling over the same network eliminates the need to create and maintain separate networks. On a converged network there are still many points of contact and many specialized devices - for example, personal computers, phones, TVs, personal assistants, and retail point-of-sale registers - but only one common network infrastructure.

Intelligent Information Networks

Refer to Figure in online course

The role of the network is evolving. The intelligent communications platform of tomorrow will offer so much more than basic connectivity and access to *applications*. The convergence of the different types of communications networks onto one platform represents the first phase in building the intelligent information network. We are currently in this phase of network evolution. The next phase will be to consolidate not only the different types of messages onto a single network, but to also consolidate the applications that generate, transmit, and secure the messages onto integrated network devices. Not only will voice and video be transmitted over the same network, the devices that perform the telephone switching and video broadcasting will be the same devices that route the messages through the network. The resulting communications platform will provide high quality application functionality at a reduced cost.

Planning for the Future

The pace at which the development of exciting new converged network applications is occurring can be attributed to the rapid expansion of the Internet. This expansion has created a wider audience and a larger consumer base for whatever message, product or service can be delivered. The underlying mechanics and processes that drive this explosive growth have resulted in a network architecture that is both resilient and scalable. As the supporting technology platform for living, learning, working, and playing in the human network, the network architecture of the Internet must adapt to constantly changing requirements for a high quality of service and security.

1.4   The Architecture of the Internet

1.4.1   The Network Architecture

Refer to **Figure** in online course

Networks must support a wide range of applications and services, as well as operate over many different types of physical infrastructures. The term network architecture, in this context, refers to both the technologies that support the infrastructure and the programmed services and protocols that move the messages across that infrastructure. As the Internet, and networks in general, evolve, we are discovering that there are four basic characteristics that the underlying architectures need to address in order to meet user expectations: fault tolerance, scalability, quality of service, and security.

Fault Tolerance

The expectation that the Internet is always available to the millions of users who rely on it requires a network architecture that is designed and built to be fault tolerant. A fault tolerant network is one that limits the impact of a hardware or software failure and can recover quickly when such a failure occurs. These networks depend on redundant links, or paths, between the source and destination of a message. If one link or path fails, processes ensure that messages can be instantly routed over a different link transparent to the users on either end. Both the physical infrastructures and the logical processes that direct the messages through the network are designed to accommodate this redundancy. This is a basic premise of the architecture of current networks.

Scalability

A scalable network can expand quickly to support new users and applications without impacting the performance of the service being delivered to existing users. Thousands of new users and service providers connect to the Internet each week. The ability of the network to support these new interconnections depends on a hierarchical layered design for the underlying physical infrastructure and logical architecture. The operation at each layer enables users or service providers to be inserted without causing disruption to the entire network. Technology developments are constantly increasing the message carrying capabilities and performance of the physical infrastructure components at every layer. These developments, along with new methods to identify and locate individual users within an *internetwork*, are enabling the Internet to keep pace with user demand.

Refer to **Figure** in online course

Quality of Service (QoS)

The Internet is currently providing an acceptable level of fault tolerance and scalability for its users. But new applications available to users over internetworks create higher expectations for the quality of the delivered services. Voice and live video transmissions require a level of consistent quality and uninterrupted delivery that was not necessary for traditional computer applications. Quality of these services is measured against the quality of experiencing the same audio or video presentation in person. Traditional voice and video networks are designed to support a single type of transmission, and are therefore able to produce an acceptable level of quality. New requirements to support this quality of service over a converged network are changing the way network architectures are designed and implemented.

Security

The Internet has evolved from a tightly controlled internetwork of educational and government organizations to a widely accessible means for transmission of business and personal communications. As a result, the security requirements of the network have changed. The security and privacy expectations that result from the use of internetworks to exchange confidential and business critical information exceed what the current architecture can deliver. Rapid expansion in communication areas that were not served by traditional data networks is increasing the need to embed security into the network architecture. As a result, much effort is being devoted to this area of research and development. In the meantime, many tools and procedures are being implemented to combat inherent security flaws in the network architecture.

1.4.2 A Fault Tolerant Network Architecture

Refer to
Figure
in online course

The Internet, in its early inception, was the result of research funded by the United States Department of Defense (DoD). Its primary goal was to have a communications medium that could withstand the destruction of numerous sites and transmission facilities without disruption of service. It only follows that fault tolerance was the focus of the effort of the initial internetwork design work. Early network researchers looked at the existing communication networks, which were primarily for the transmission of voice traffic, to determine what could be done to improve the fault tolerance level.

Circuit Switched Connection-oriented Networks

To understand the challenge that the DoD researchers were faced with, it is necessary to look at how early telephone systems work. When a person makes a call using a traditional telephone set, the call first goes through a setup *process*, where all of the telephone switching locations between the person and the phone set that they are calling are identified. A temporary path, or circuit, is created through the various switching locations to use for the duration of the telephone call. If any link or device participating in the circuit fails, the call is dropped. To reconnect, a new call must be made, and a new circuit created between the source telephone set and the destination. This type of connection-oriented network is called a circuit-switched network. Early circuit switched networks did not dynamically recreate dropped circuits. In order to recover from failure, new calls had to be initiated and new circuits built *end-to-end*.

Many circuit switched networks give priority to maintaining existing circuit connections, at the expense of new circuit requests. In this type of connection-oriented network, once a circuit is established, even if no communication is occurring between the persons on either end of the call, the circuit remains connected and resources reserved until one of the parties disconnects the call. Since there is a finite capacity to create new circuits, it is possible to occasionally get a message that all circuits are busy and a call cannot be placed. The cost to create many alternate paths with enough capacity to support a large number of simultaneous circuits, and the technologies necessary to dynamically recreate dropped circuits in the event of a failure, led the DoD to consider other types of networks.

Refer to
Figure
in online course

Packet Switched Connectionless Networks

In the search for a network that could withstand the loss of a significant amount of its transmission and switching facilities, the early Internet designers reevaluated early research regarding *packet* switched networks. The premise for this type of networks is that a single message can be broken into multiple message blocks. Individual blocks containing addressing information indicate both their origination point and their final destination. Using this embedded information, these message blocks, called packets, can be sent through the network along various paths, and can be reassembled into the original message upon reaching their destination.

Utilizing Packets

The devices within the network itself are unaware of the content of the individual packets, only visible is the address of the final destination and the next device in the path to that destination. No reserved circuit is built between sender and receiver. Each packet is sent independently from one switching location to another. At each location, a routing decision is made as to which path to use to forward the packet towards its final destination. If a previously used path is no longer available, the routing function can dynamically choose the next best available path. Because the messages are sent in pieces, rather than as a single complete message, the few packets that may be lost in the advent of a failure can be retransmitted to the destination along a different path. In many cases, the destination device is unaware that any failure or rerouting has occurred.

Packet-switched Connectionless Networks

The DoD researchers realized that a packet switched connectionless network had the features necessary to support a resilient, fault tolerant network architecture. The need for a single, reserved circuit from end-to-end does not exist in a packet switched network. Any piece of a message can be sent through the network using any available path. Packets containing pieces of messages from different sources can travel the network at the same time. The problem of underutilized or idle circuits is eliminated — all available resources can be used at any time to deliver packets to their final destination. By providing a method to dynamically use redundant paths, without intervention by the user, the Internet has become a fault tolerant, scalable method of communications.

Connection-oriented Networks

Although packet-switched connectionless networks met the needs of the DoD, and continue to be the primary infrastructure for today's Internet, there are some benefits to a connection-oriented system like the circuit-switched telephone system. Because resources at the various switching locations are dedicated to providing a finite number of circuits, the quality and consistency of messages transmitted across a connection-oriented network can be guaranteed. Another benefit is that the provider of the service can charge the users of the network for the period of time that the connection is active. The ability to charge users for active connections through the network is a fundamental premise of the telecommunication service industry.

1.4.3 A Scalable Network Architecture

Refer to
Figure
in online course

The fact that the Internet is able to expand at the rate that it is, without seriously impacting the performance experienced by individual users, is a function of the design of the protocols and underlying technologies on which it is built. The Internet, which is actually a collection of interconnected private and public networks, has a hierarchical layered structure for addressing, for naming and for connectivity services. At each level or layer of the hierarchy, individual network operators maintain peering relationships with other operators at the same level. As a result, network traffic that is destined for local or regional services does not need to traverse to a central point for distribution. Common services can be duplicated in different regions, thereby keeping traffic off the higher level backbone networks.

Although there is no single organization that regulates the Internet, the operators of the many individual networks that provide Internet connectivity cooperate to follow accepted standards and protocols.

The adherence to standards enables the manufacturers of hardware and software to concentrate on product improvements in the areas of performance and capacity, knowing that the new products can integrate with and enhance the existing infrastructure.

The current Internet architecture, while highly scalable, may not always be able to keep up with the pace of user demand. New protocols and addressing structures are under development to meet the increasing rate at which Internet applications and services are being added.

1.4.4 Providing Quality of Service

Refer to
Figure
in online course

Networks must provide secure, predictable, measurable, and, at times, guaranteed services. The packet-switched network architecture does not guarantee that all packets that comprise a particular message will arrive on time, in their correct in order, or even that they will arrive at all.

Networks also need mechanisms to manage congested network traffic. Congestion is caused when the demand on the network resources exceeds the available capacity.

If all networks had infinite resources, there would not be a need to use QoS mechanisms to ensure quality of service. Unfortunately, that is not the case. There are some constraints on network resources that cannot be avoided. Constraints include technology limitations, costs, and the local availability of high-bandwidth service. Network bandwidth is the measure of the data carrying capacity of the network. When simultaneous communications are attempted across the network, the demand for network bandwidth can exceed its availability. The obvious fix for this situation is to increase the amount of available bandwidth. But, because of the previously stated constraints, this is not always possible.

In most cases, when the volume of packets is greater than what can be transported across the network, devices queue the packets in memory until resources become available to transmit them. Queuing packets causes delay. If the number of packets to be queued continues to increase, the memory queues fill up and packets are dropped.

Refer to
Figure
in online course

Achieving the required Quality of Service (QoS) by managing the delay and packet loss parameters on a network becomes the secret to a successful end-to-end application quality solution. Thus, ensuring QoS requires a set of techniques to manage the utilization of network resources. In order to maintain a high quality of service for applications that require it, it is necessary to prioritize which types of data packets must be delivered at the expense of other types of packets that can be delayed or dropped.

Classification

Ideally, we would like to assign a precise priority for each type of communication. Currently, this is neither practical nor possible. Therefore, we classify applications in categories based on specific quality of service requirements.

To create QoS classifications of data, we use a combination of communication characteristics and the relative importance assigned to the application. We then treat all data within the same classification according to the same rules. For example, communication that is time-sensitive or important would be classified differently from communication that can wait or is of lesser importance.

Assigning priorities

The characteristics of the information being communicated also affect its management. For example, the delivery of a movie uses a relatively large amount of network resources when it is delivered continuously without interruption. Other types of service - e-mail, for example - are not nearly as demanding on the network. In one company, an administrator might decide to allocate the greatest share of the network resources to the movie, believing that this is the priority for his customers. This administrator may decide that the impact will be minimal if e-mail users have to wait a few additional seconds for their e-mail to arrive. In another company, the quality of a video *stream* is not as important as critical process control information that operates the manufacturing machinery.

Refer to
Figure
in online course

QoS mechanisms enable the establishment of queue management strategies that enforce priorities for different classifications of application data. Without properly designed and implemented QoS mechanisms, data packets will be dropped without consideration of the application characteristics or priority. Examples of priority decisions for an organization might include:

- Time-sensitive communication - increase priority for services like telephony or video distribution.

- Non time-sensitive communication - decrease priority for web page retrieval or e-mail.

- High importance to organization - increase priority for production control or business transaction data.

- Undesirable communication - decrease priority or block unwanted activity, like peer-to-peer file sharing or live entertainment.

The Quality of Service a network can offer is a vital issue, and in some situations, it is crucial. Imagine the consequences of a dropped distress call to an emergency response center, or of a lost control signal to an automated piece of heavy machinery. A key responsibility for the network managers in an organization is to establish a Quality of Service policy and ensure that the mechanisms are in place to meet that goal.

1.4.5 Providing Network Security

Refer to
Figure
in online course

The network infrastructure, services, and the data contained on network attached computers are crucial personal and business assets. Compromising the integrity of these assets could have serious business and financial repercussions.

Consequences of a network security breach could include:

- Network outage that prevents communications and transactions occurring, with consequent loss of business

- Misdirection and loss of personal or business funds

- Company intellectual property (research ideas, patents or designs) that is stolen and used by a competitor

- Customer contract details that become known to competitors or made public, resulting in a loss of market confidence in the business

A lack of public trust in the business's privacy, confidentiality, and integrity levels may lead to loss of sales and eventual company failure. There are two types of network security concerns that must be addressed to prevent serious consequences: network infrastructure security and content security.

Securing a network infrastructure includes the physical securing of devices that provide network connectivity and preventing unauthorized access to the management software that resides on them.

Content security refers to protecting the information contained within the packets being transmitted over the network and the information stored on network attached devices. When transmitting information over the Internet or other network, the content of the individual packets is not readily known to the devices and facilities through which the packets travel. Tools to provide security for the content of individual messages must be implemented on top of the underlying protocols which govern how packets are formatted, addressed and delivered. Because the reassembly and interpretation of the content is delegated to programs running on the individual source and destination systems, many of the security tools and protocols must be implemented on those systems as well.

Refer to
Figure
in online course

Security measures taken in a network should:

- Prevent unauthorized disclosure or theft of information
- Prevent unauthorized modification of information
- Prevent Denial of Service

Means to achieve these goals include:

- Ensuring confidentiality
- Maintaining communication integrity
- Ensuring availability

Ensuring Confidentiality

Data privacy is maintained by allowing only the intended and authorized recipients - individuals, processes, or devices - to read the data.

Having a strong system for user *authentication*, enforcing passwords that are difficult to guess, and requiring users to change them frequently helps restrict access to communications and to data stored on network attached devices. Where appropriate, encrypting content ensures confidentiality and minimizes unauthorized disclosure or theft of information.

Maintaining Communication Integrity

Data integrity means having the assurance that the information has not been altered in transmission, from origin to destination. Data integrity can be compromised when information has been corrupted - willfully or accidentally - before the intended recipient receives it.

Source integrity is the assurance that the identity of the sender has been validated. Source integrity is compromised when a user or device fakes its identity and supplies incorrect information to a recipient.

The use of *digital signatures*, *hashing algorithms* and *checksum* mechanisms are ways to provide source and data integrity across a network to prevent unauthorized modification of information.

Ensuring Availability

Ensuring confidentiality and integrity are irrelevant if network resources become over burdened, or not available at all. Availability means having the assurance of timely and reliable access to data services for authorized users. Resources can be unavailable during a Denial of Service (DoS) attack or due to the spread of a *computer virus*. Network *firewall* devices, along with desktop and server anti-virus software can ensure system reliability and the robustness to detect, repel, and cope with such attacks. Building fully redundant network infrastructures, with few single *points of failure*, can reduce the impact of these threats.

The result of the implementation of measures to improve both the quality of service and the security of network communications is an increase in the complexity of the underlying network platform. As the Internet continues to expand to offer more and more new services, its future depends on new, more robust network architectures being developed that include all four characteristics: fault tolerance, scalability, quality of service, and security.

Refer to
Lab Activity
for this chapter

Upon completion of this activity, you will be able to:

Use the SANS site to quickly identify Internet security threats and explain how threats are organized.

1.5 Trends in Networking

1.5.1 Where Is It All Going?

Refer to
Figure
in online course

The convergence of the many different communication media onto a single network platform is fueling exponential growth in network capabilities. There are three major trends that are contributing to the future shape of complex information networks:

- Increasing number of mobile users

- Proliferation of network capable devices

- Expanding range of services

Mobile Users

With the increase in the numbers of mobile workers and the increased use of hand-held devices, we are necessarily demanding more mobile connectivity to data networks. This demand has created a market for wireless services that have greater flexibility, coverage, and security.

New and More Capable Devices

The computer is only one of many devices on today's information networks. We have a proliferation of exciting new technologies that can take advantage of available network services.

The functions performed by cell phones, Personal Digital Assistants (PDAs), organizers, and pagers are converging into single hand-held devices with continuous connectivity to providers of services and content. These devices, once thought of as "toys" or luxury items, are now an integral part of how people communicate. In addition to mobile devices, we also have Voice over IP (VoIP) devices, gaming systems, and a large assortment of household and business gadgets that can connect and use network services.

Increased Availability of Services

The widespread acceptance of technology and the fast pace of innovation in network delivered services create a spiraling dependence. To meet user demands, new services are introduced and older services are enhanced. As the users come to trust these expanded services, they want even more capabilities. The network then grows to support the increasing demand. People depend on the services provided over the network, and therefore depend on the availability and reliability of the underlying network infrastructure.

The challenge of keeping pace with an ever expanding network of users and services is the responsibility of trained network and IT professionals.

1.5.2 Networking Career Opportunities

Refer to
Figure
in online course

Information Technology and networking careers are growing and evolving as fast as the underlying technologies and services. As networks increase in sophistication, the demand for people with networking skills will continue to grow.

Traditional IT positions like programmers, software engineers, data base administrators and network technicians are now joined by new titles, such as network architect, e-Commerce site designer, information security officer, and home integration specialist. Opportunities for forward thinking entrepreneurs are unlimited.

Even non-IT jobs, like manufacturing management or medical equipment design, now require a significant amount of knowledge about network operation in order to be successful.

Chief Technology Officers in many large organizations list the lack of qualified personnel as the primary factor delaying the implementation of innovative new services.

As students of networking technology, we examine the components of data networks and the roles they play in enabling communication. This course, as well as others in the Network Academy series, is designed to empower you with the networking knowledge to build and manage these evolving networks.

1.6   Chapter Labs

1.6.1   Using Collaboration Tools - IRC and IM

Refer to
Lab Activity
for this chapter

In this lab, you will define Internet Relay Chat (IRC) and Instant Messaging (IM). You will also list several misuses and data security issues involving IM.

1.6.2   Using Collaboration Tools - Wikis and Web Logs

Refer to
Lab Activity
for this chapter

In this lab, you will define the terms wiki and blog. You will also explain the purpose of a wiki and blog and how these technologies are used for collaboration.

Summary and Review

Refer to
Figure
in online course

This chapter explained the importance of data networks as the platform for supporting business communication and the tasks of everyday life.

Data networks play a vital role in facilitating communication within the global human network.

Data networks support the way we live, learn, work, and play. They provide the platform for the services that enable us to connect - both locally and globally - with our families, friends, work, and interests. This platform supports using text, graphics, video, and speech.

Data networks and human networks use similar procedures to ensure that their communication gets to the destination accurately and on time. Agreements on language, content, form, and medium that humans often implicitly use are mirrored in the data network.

The factors that ensure the delivery of our messages and information across a data network are the networking media that connect the networking devices and the agreements and standards that govern its operation. As the demand grows for more people and devices to communicate in a mobile world, data network technologies will have to adapt and develop.

Converged networks, which carry all communications types (data, voice, and video) on one infrastructure, provide an opportunity to reduce costs and offer users feature-rich services and content. However, the design and management of converged networks requires extensive networking knowledge and skills if all services are to be delivered as expected to users.

Different types of communications flowing across our data networks need to be prioritized so that the time-sensitive and important data have the first use of limited network resources.

Integrating security into data networks is essential if our private, personal, and business communications are not going to be intercepted, stolen, or damaged.

Refer to
Figure
in online course

Refer to **Packet Tracer Activity** for this chapter

Packet Tracer 4.1 ("PT 4.1") is a standalone simulation and visualization program. PT 4.1 activities are integrated throughout this course. While formal activities using Packet Tracer begin in the next chapter, if time allows please launch the program now, and explore the Help resources, which include "My First PT Lab" and a variety of tutorials to teach you various aspects of the software. Also, please ask your instructor how obtain a copy of PT 4.1 for your personal use. Every chapter will have a Packet Tracer Skills Integration Challenge: an activity that allows you to practice most skills learned to that point in the course in a cumulative fashion. PT Skills Integration Challenges will allow you to build your practical skills for such things as hands-on performance exams and Certification exams.

Packet Tracer Skills Integration Instructions (PDF)

Refer to
Figure
in online course

To learn more about a milestone in the history of communications, read about Claude Shannon and his famous paper, "A Mathematical Theory of Communication."

Chapter Quiz

Go to
the online course
to take the quiz.

Take the chapter quiz to test your knowledge.

Your Chapter Notes

CHAPTER 2

Communicating over the Network

Chapter Introduction

Refer to **Figure** in online course

More and more, it is networks that connect us. People communicate online from everywhere. Efficient, dependable technology enables networks to be available whenever and wherever we need them. As our human network continues to expand, the platform that connects and supports it must also grow.

Rather than developing unique and separate systems for the delivery of each new service, the network industry as a whole has developed the means to both analyze the existing platform and enhance it incrementally. This ensures that existing communications are maintained while new services are introduced that are both cost effective and technologically sound.

In this course, we focus on these aspects of the information network:

- Devices that make up the network

- Media that connect the devices

- Messages that are carried across the network

- Rules and processes that govern network communications

- Tools and commands for constructing and maintaining networks

Central to the study of networks is the use of generally-accepted models that describe network functions. These models provide a framework for understanding current networks and for facilitating the development of new technologies to support future communications needs.

Within this course, we use these models, as well as tools designed to analyze and simulate network functionality. Two of the tools that will enable you to build and interact with simulated networks are Packet Tracer 4.1 software and *Wireshark* network *protocol* analyzer.

This chapter prepares you to:

- Describe the structure of a network, including the devices and media that are necessary for successful communications.

- Explain the function of protocols in network communications.

- Explain the advantages of using a *layered model* to describe network functionality.

- Describe the role of each layer in two recognized network models: The TCP/IP model and the OSI model.

- Describe the importance of addressing and naming schemes in network communications.

2.1 The Platform for Communications

2.1.1 The Elements of Communication

Refer to
Figure
in online course

Communication begins with a message, or information, that must be sent from one individual or device to another. People exchange ideas using many different communication methods. All of these methods have three elements in common. The first of these elements is the message source, or sender. Message sources are people, or electronic devices, that need to send a message to other individuals or devices. The second element of communication is the destination, or receiver, of the message. The destination receives the message and interprets it. A third element, called a *channel*, consists of the media that provides the pathway over which the message can travel from source to destination.

Consider, for example, the desire to communicate using words, pictures, and sounds. Each of these messages can be sent across a data or information network by first converting them into binary digits, or bits. These bits are then encoded into a signal that can be transmitted over the appropriate medium. In computer networks, the media is usually a type of cable, or a wireless transmission.

The term *network* in this course will refer to data or information networks capable of carrying many different types of communications, including traditional computer data, interactive voice, video, and entertainment products.

2.1.2 Communicating the Messages

Refer to
Figure
in online course

In theory, a single communication, such as a music video or an e-mail message, could be sent across a network from a source to a destination as one massive continuous stream of bits. If messages were actually transmitted in this manner, it would mean that no other device would be able to send or receive messages on the same network while this data transfer was in progress. These large streams of data would result in significant delays. Further, if a link in the interconnected network infrastructure failed during the transmission, the complete message would be lost and have to be retransmitted in full.

A better approach is to divide the data into smaller, more manageable pieces to send over the network. This division of the data stream into smaller pieces is called segmentation. Segmenting messages has two primary benefits.

First, by sending smaller individual pieces from source to destination, many different conversations can be interleaved on the network. The process used to interleave the pieces of separate conversations together on the network is called *multiplexing*.

Second, segmentation can increase the reliability of network communications. The separate pieces of each message need not travel the same pathway across the network from source to destination. If a particular path becomes congested with data traffic or fails, individual pieces of the message can still be directed to the destination using alternate pathways. If part of the message fails to make it to the destination, only the missing parts need to be retransmitted.

Refer to
Figure
in online course

The downside to using segmentation and multiplexing to transmit messages across a network is the level of complexity that is added to the process. Imagine if you had to send a 100-page letter, but each envelope would only hold one page. The process of addressing, labeling, sending, receiving, and opening the entire hundred envelopes would be time-consuming for both the sender and the recipient.

In network communications, each segment of the message must go through a similar process to ensure that it gets to the correct destination and can be reassembled into the content of the original message.

Various types of devices throughout the network participate in ensuring that the pieces of the message arrive reliably at their destination.

2.1.3 Components of the Network

Refer to **Figure** in online course

The path that a message takes from source to destination can be as simple as a single cable connecting one computer to another or as complex as a network that literally spans the globe. This network infrastructure is the platform that supports our human network. It provides the stable and reliable channel over which our communications can occur.

Devices and media are the physical elements or hardware of the network. Hardware is often the visible components of the network platform such as a laptop, a PC, a *switch*, or the cabling used to connect the devices. Occasionally, some components may not be so visible. In the case of wireless media, messages are transmitted through the air using invisible radio frequency or infrared waves.

Services and processes are the communication programs, called software, that run on the networked devices. A network service provides information in response to a request. Services include many of the common network applications people use every day, like e-mail hosting services and web hosting services. Processes provide the functionality that directs and moves the messages through the network. Processes are less obvious to us but are critical to the operation of networks.

2.1.4 End Devices and their Role on the Network

Refer to **Figure** in online course

The network devices that people are most familiar with are called *end devices*. These devices form the interface between the human network and the underlying communication network. Some examples of end devices are:

- Computers (work stations, laptops, file servers, web servers)
- Network printers
- VoIP phones
- Security cameras
- Mobile handheld devices (such as wireless barcode scanners, PDAs)

In the context of a network, end devices are referred to as hosts. A host device is either the source or destination of a message transmitted over the network. In order to distinguish one host from another, each host on a network is identified by an address. When a host initiates communication, it uses the address of the destination host to specify where the message should be sent.

In modern networks, a host can act as a *client*, a server, or both. Software installed on the host determines which role it plays on the network.

Servers are hosts that have software installed that enables them to provide information and services, like e-mail or web pages, to other hosts on the network.

Clients are hosts that have software installed that enables them to request and display the information obtained from the server.

2.1.5 Intermediary Devices and their Role on the Network

Refer to **Figure** in online course

In addition to the end devices that people are familiar with, networks rely on *intermediary devices* to provide connectivity and to work behind the scenes to ensure that data flows across the network.

These devices connect the individual hosts to the network and can connect multiple individual networks to form an internetwork. Examples of intermediary network devices are:

- Network Access Devices (Hubs, switches, and wireless access points)

- Internetworking Devices (routers)

- Communication Servers and Modems

- Security Devices (firewalls)

The management of data as it flows through the network is also a role of the intermediary devices. These devices use the destination *host address*, in conjunction with information about the network interconnections, to determine the path that messages should take through the network. Processes running on the intermediary network devices perform these functions:

- Regenerate and retransmit data signals

- Maintain information about what pathways exist through the network and internetwork

- Notify other devices of errors and communication failures

- Direct data along alternate pathways when there is a link failure

- Classify and direct messages according to QoS priorities

- Permit or deny the flow of data, based on security settings

2.1.6 Network Media

Refer to
Figure
in online course

Communication across a network is carried on a medium. The medium provides the channel over which the message travels from source to destination.

Modern networks primarily use three types of media to interconnect devices and to provide the pathway over which data can be transmitted. These media are:

- Metallic wires within cables

- Glass or plastic fibers (fiber optic cable)

- Wireless transmission

The signal *encoding* that must occur for the message to be transmitted is different for each media type. On metallic wires, the data is encoded into electrical impulses that match specific patterns. Fiber optic transmissions rely on pulses of light, within either infrared or visible light ranges. In wireless transmission, patterns of electromagnetic waves depict the various bit values.

Different types of network media have different features and benefits. Not all network media has the same characteristics and is appropriate for the same purpose. Criteria for choosing a network media are:

- The distance the media can successfully carry a signal.

- The environment in which the media is to be installed.

- The amount of data and the speed at which it must be transmitted.

- The cost of the media and installation

2.2 LANs, WANs, and Internetworks

2.2.1 Local Area Networks

Refer to
Figure
in online course

Networks infrastructures can vary greatly in terms of:

- The size of the area covered

- The number of users connected

- The number and types of services available

An individual network usually spans a single geographical area, providing services and applications to people within a common organizational structure, such as a single business, campus or region. This type of network is called a *Local Area Network (LAN)*. A LAN is usually administered by a single organization. The administrative control that governs the security and access control policies are enforced on the network level.

2.2.2 Wide Area Networks

Refer to
Figure
in online course

When a company or organization has locations that are separated by large geographical distances, it may be necessary to use a telecommunications service provider (TSP) to interconnect the LANs at the different locations. Telecommunications service providers operate large regional networks that can span long distances. Traditionally, TSPs transported voice and data communications on separate networks. Increasingly, these providers are offering converged information network services to their subscribers.

Individual organizations usually lease connections through a telecommunications service provider network. These networks that connect LANs in geographically separated locations are referred to as Wide Area Networks (WANs). Although the organization maintains all of the policies and administration of the LANs at both ends of the connection, the policies within the communications service provider network are controlled by the TSP.

WANs use specifically designed network devices to make the interconnections between LANs. Because of the importance of these devices to the network, configuring, installing and maintaining these devices are skills that are integral to the function of an organization's network.

LANs and WANs are very useful to individual organizations. They connect the users within the organization. They allow many forms of communication including exchange e-mails, corporate training, and other resource sharing.

2.2.3 The Internet - A Network of Networks

Refer to
Figure
in online course

Although there are benefits to using a LAN or WAN, most of us need to communicate with a resource on another network, outside of our local organization.

Examples of this type of communication include:

- Sending an e-mail to a friend in another country

- Accessing news or products on a website

- Getting a file from a neighbor's computer

- Instant messaging with a relative in another city

- Following a favorite sporting team's performance on a cell phone

Internetwork

A global mesh of interconnected networks (internetworks) meets these human communication needs. Some of these interconnected networks are owned by large public and private organizations, such as government agencies or industrial enterprises, and are reserved for their exclusive use. The most well-known and widely used publicly-accessible internetwork is the Internet.

The Internet is created by the interconnection of networks belonging to Internet Service Providers (ISPs). These ISP networks connect to each other to provide access for millions of users all over the world. Ensuring effective communication across this diverse infrastructure requires the application of consistent and commonly recognized technologies and protocols as well as the cooperation of many network administration agencies.

Intranet

The term *intranet* is often used to refer to a private connection of LANs and WANs that belongs to an organization, and is designed to be accessible only by the organization's members, employees, or others with authorization.

Note: The following terms may be interchangeable: internetwork, data network, and network. A connection of two or more data networks forms an internetwork - a network of networks. It is also common to refer to an internetwork as a data network - or simply as a network - when considering communications at a high level. The usage of terms depends on the context at the time and terms may often be interchanged.

2.2.4 Network Representations

Refer to
Figure
in online course

When conveying complex information such as the network connectivity and operation of a large internetwork, it is helpful to use visual representations and graphics. Like any other language, the language of networking uses a common set of symbols to represent the different end devices, network devices and media. The ability to recognize the logical representations of the physical networking components is critical to being able to visualize the organization and operation of a network. Throughout this course and labs, you will learn both how these devices operate and how to perform basic configuration tasks on these devices.

In addition to these representations, specialized terminology is used when discussing how each of these devices and media connect to each other. Important terms to remember are:

Network Interface Card - A NIC, or LAN adapter, provides the physical connection to the network at the PC or other *host* device. The media connecting the PC to the networking device plugs directly into the NIC.

Physical Port - A connector or outlet on a networking device where the media is connected to a host or other networking device.

Interface - Specialized *ports* on an internetworking device that connect to individual networks. Because routers are used to interconnect networks, the ports on a router are referred to network interfaces.

Refer to **Packet Tracer Activity** for this chapter

In this activity, you will gain experience with data network symbols by creating a simple *logical topology*.

2.2.5 Activity - Using NeoTrace™ to View Internetworks

Refer to
Lab Activity
for this chapter

In this activity, you will observe the flow of information across the Internet. This activity should be performed on a computer that has Internet access and access to a command line. You will use the Windows embedded `tracert` **utility and then the more enhanced NeoTrace program. This lab also assumes the installation of NeoTrace.**

2.3 Protocols

2.3.1 Rules that Govern Communications

Refer to
Figure
in online course

All communication, whether face-to-face or over a network, is governed by predetermined rules called protocols. These protocols are specific to the characteristics of the conversation. In our day-to-day personal communication, the rules we use to communicate over one medium, like a telephone call, are not necessarily the same as the protocols for using another medium, such as sending a letter.

Think of how many different rules or protocols govern all the different methods of communication that exist in the world today.

Successful communication between hosts on a network requires the interaction of many different protocols. A group of inter-related protocols that are necessary to perform a communication function is called a *protocol suite*. These protocols are implemented in software and hardware that is loaded on each host and network device.

One of the best ways to visualize how all of the protocols interact on a particular host is to view it as a stack. A protocol stack shows how the individual protocols within the suite are implemented on the host. The protocols are viewed as a layered hierarchy, with each higher level service depending on the functionality defined by the protocols shown in the lower levels. The lower layers of the stack are concerned with moving data over the network and providing services to the upper layers, which are focused on the content of the message being sent and the user interface.

Using layers to describe face-to-face communication

For example, consider two people communicating face-to-face. As the figure shows, we can use three layers to describe this activity. At the bottom layer, the Physical layer, we have two people, each with a voice that can utter words aloud. At the second layer, the Rules layer, we have an agreement to speak in a common language. At the top layer, the Content layer, we have the words actually spoken-the content of the communication.

Were we to witness this conversation, we would not actually see "layers" floating in space. It is important to understand that the use of layers is a model and, as such, it provides a way to conveniently break a complex task into parts and describe how they work.

2.3.2 Network Protocols

Refer to
Figure
in online course

At the human level, some communication rules are formal and others are simply understood, or implicit, based on custom and practice. For devices to successfully communicate, a network protocol *suite* must describe precise requirements and interactions.

Networking protocol suites describe processes such as:

- The format or structure of the message

- The method by which networking devices share information about pathways with other networks

- How and when error and system messages are passed between devices

- The setup and termination of data transfer sessions

Individual protocols in a protocol suite may be vendor-specific and proprietary. Proprietary, in this context, means that one company or vendor controls the definition of the protocol and how it functions. Some proprietary protocols can be used by different organizations with permission from the owner. Others can only be implemented on equipment manufactured by the proprietary vendor.

2.3.3 Protocol Suites and Industry Standards

Refer to **Figure** in online course

Often, many of the protocols that comprise a protocol suite reference other widely utilized protocols or industry standards. A standard is a process or protocol that has been endorsed by the networking industry and ratified by a standards organization, such as the *Institute of Electrical and Electronics Engineers* (IEEE) or the *Internet Engineering Task Force (IETF)*.

The use of standards in developing and implementing protocols ensures that products from different manufacturers can work together for efficient communications. If a protocol is not rigidly observed by a particular manufacturer, their equipment or software may not be able to successfully communicate with products made by other manufacturers.

In data communications, for example, if one end of a conversation is using a protocol to govern one-way communication and the other end is assuming a protocol describing two-way communication, in all probability, no information will be exchanged.

2.3.4 The Interaction of Protocols

Refer to **Figure** in online course

An example of the use of a protocol suite in network communications is the interaction between a *web server* and a *web browser*. This interaction uses a number of protocols and standards in the process of exchanging information between them. The different protocols work together to ensure that the messages are received and understood by both parties. Examples of these protocols are:

Application Protocol:

Hypertext Transfer Protocol (HTTP) is a common protocol that governs the way that a web server and a web client interact. HTTP defines the content and formatting of the requests and responses exchanged between the client and server. Both the client and the web server software implement HTTP as part of the application. The HTTP protocol relies on other protocols to govern how the messages are transported between client and server

Transport Protocol:

Transmission Control Protocol (TCP) is the transport protocol that manages the individual conversations between web servers and web clients. TCP divides the HTTP messages into smaller pieces, called segments, to be sent to the destination client. It is also responsible for controlling the size and rate at which messages are exchanged between the server and the client.

Internetwork Protocol:

The most common internetwork protocol is *Internet Protocol (IP)*. IP is responsible for taking the formatted segments from TCP, encapsulating them into packets, assigning the appropriate addresses, and selecting the best path to the destination host.

Network Access Protocols:

Network access protocols describe two primary functions, data link management and the physical transmission of data on the media. Data-link management protocols take the packets from IP and format them to be transmitted over the media. The standards and protocols for the physical media govern how the signals are sent over the media and how they are interpreted by the receiving clients. Transceivers on the network interface cards implement the appropriate standards for the media that is being used.

2.3.5 Technology Independent Protocols

Refer to **Figure** in online course

Networking protocols describe the functions that occur during network communications. In the face-to-face conversation example, a protocol for communicating might state that in order to signal that the conversation is complete, the sender must remain silent for two full seconds. However, this protocol does not specify *how* the sender is to remain silent for the two seconds.

Protocols generally do not describe *how* to accomplish a particular function. By describing only *what* functions are required of a particular communication rule but not *how* they are to be carried out, the implementation of a particular protocol can be technology-independent.

Looking at the web server example, HTTP does not specify what programming language is used to create the browser, which web server software should be used to serve the web pages, what *operating system* the software runs on, or the hardware requirements necessary to display the browser. It also does not describe how the server should detect errors, although it does describe what the server should do if an error occurs.

This means that a computer - and other devices, like mobile phones or PDAs - can access a web page stored on any type of web server that uses any form of operating system from anywhere on the Internet.

2.4 Using Layered Models

2.4.1 The Benefits of Using a Layered Model

Refer to **Figure** in online course

To visualize the interaction between various protocols, it is common to use a layered model. A layered model depicts the operation of the protocols occurring within each layer, as well as the interaction with the layers above and below it.

There are benefits to using a layered model to describe network protocols and operations. Using a layered model:

- Assists in protocol design, because protocols that operate at a specific layer have defined information that they act upon and a defined interface to the layers above and below.

- Fosters competition because products from different vendors can work together.

- Prevents technology or capability changes in one layer from affecting other layers above and below.

- Provides a common language to describe networking functions and capabilities.

2.4.2 Protocol and Reference Models

Refer to **Figure** in online course

There are two basic types of networking models: protocol models and reference models.

A protocol model provides a model that closely matches the structure of a particular protocol suite. The hierarchical set of related protocols in a suite typically represents all the functionality required to interface the human network with the data network. The TCP/IP model is a protocol model because it describes the functions that occur at each layer of protocols within the TCP/IP suite.

A reference model provides a common reference for maintaining consistency within all types of network protocols and services. A reference model is not intended to be an implementation specification or to provide a sufficient level of detail to define precisely the services of the network architecture. The primary purpose of a reference model is to aid in clearer understanding of the functions and process involved.

The Open Systems Interconnection (OSI) model is the most widely known internetwork reference model. It is used for data network design, operation specifications, and troubleshooting.

Although the TCP/IP and OSI models are the primary models used when discussing network functionality, designers of network protocols, services, or devices can create their own models to represent their products. Ultimately, designers are required to communicate to the industry by relating their product or service to either the OSI model or the TCP/IP model, or to both.

2.4.3 The TCP/IP Model

Refer to
Figure
in online course

The first layered protocol model for internetwork communications was created in the early 1970s and is referred to as the Internet model. It defines four categories of functions that must occur for communications to be successful. The architecture of the TCP/IP protocol suite follows the structure of this model. Because of this, the Internet model is commonly referred to as the TCP/IP model.

Most protocol models describe a vendor-specific protocol stack. However, since the TCP/IP model is an *open standard,* one company does not control the definition of the model. The definitions of the standard and the TCP/IP protocols are discussed in a public forum and defined in a publicly-available set of documents. These documents are called Requests for Comments (RFCs). They contain both the formal specification of data communications protocols and resources that describe the use of the protocols.

The RFCs also contain technical and organizational documents about the Internet, including the technical specifications and policy documents produced by the Internet Engineering Task Force (IETF).

2.4.4 The Communication Process

Refer to
Figure
in online course

The TCP/IP model describes the functionality of the protocols that make up the TCP/IP protocol suite. These protocols, which are implemented on both the sending and receiving hosts, interact to provide end-to-end delivery of applications over a network.

A complete communication process includes these steps:

Step 1. Creation of data at the Application layer of the originating source end device

Step 2. Segmentation and *encapsulation* of data as it passes down the protocol stack in the source end device

Step 3. Generation of the data onto the media at the Network Access layer of the stack

Step 4. Transportation of the data through the internetwork, which consists of media and any intermediary devices

Step 5. Reception of the data at the Network Access layer of the destination end device

Step 6. Decapsulation and reassembly of the data as it passes up the stack in the destination device

Step 7. Passing this data to the destination application at the Application layer of the destination end device

2.4.5 Protocol Data Units and Encapsulation

Refer to
Figure
in online course

As application data is passed down the protocol stack on its way to be transmitted across the network media, various protocols add information to it at each level. This is commonly known as the encapsulation process.

The form that a piece of data takes at any layer is called a Protocol Data Unit (PDU). During encapsulation, each succeeding layer encapsulates the PDU that it receives from the layer above in accordance with the protocol being used. At each stage of the process, a PDU has a different name to reflect its new appearance. Although there is no universal naming convention for PDUs, in this course, the PDUs are named according to the protocols of the TCP/IP suite.

general term for the PDU used at the Application layer

Transport Layer PDU

ternetwork Layer PDU

etwork Access Layer PDU

DU used when physically transmitting data over the medium

e Sending and Receiving Process

messages on a network, the protocol stack on a host operates from top to bottom. In
example, we can use the TCP/IP model to illustrate the process of sending an
ge to a client.

layer protocol, HTTP, begins the process by delivering the HTML formatted web
Transport layer. There the application data is broken into TCP segments. Each
given a label, called a *header*, containing information about which process run-
ination computer should receive the message. It also contains the information to
enable the destination process to reassemble the data back to its original format.

The Transport layer encapsulates the web page HTML data within the segment and sends it to the
Internet layer, where the IP protocol is implemented. Here the entire TCP segment is encapsulated
within an IP packet, which adds another label, called the IP header. The IP header contains source
and destination host IP addresses, as well as information necessary to deliver the packet to its corresponding destination process.

Next, the IP packet is sent to the Network Access layer Ethernet protocol where it is encapsulated
within a *frame* header and *trailer*. Each frame header contains a source and destination *physical
address*. The physical address uniquely identifies the devices on the local network. The trailer contains error checking information. Finally the bits are encoded onto the Ethernet media by the
server NIC.

Refer to
Figure
in online course

This process is reversed at the receiving host. The data is decapsulated as it moves up the stack toward the end user application.

2.4.7 The OSI Model

Refer to
Figure
in online course

Initially the OSI model was designed by the *International Organization for Standardization*
(ISO) to provide a framework on which to build a suite of open systems protocols. The vision was
that this set of protocols would be used to develop an international network that would not be dependent on proprietary systems.

Unfortunately, the speed at which the TCP/IP based Internet was adopted, and the rate at which it
expanded, caused the OSI Protocol Suite development and acceptance to lag behind. Although few
of the protocols developed using the OSI specifications are in widespread use today, the seven-
layer OSI model has made major contributions to the development of other protocols and products
for all types of new networks.

As a reference model, the OSI model provides an extensive list of functions and services that can
occur at each layer. It also describes the interaction of each layer with the layers directly above and
below it. Although the content of this course will be structured around the OSI Model the focus of
discussion will be the protocols identified in the TCP/IP protocol stack.

Note that whereas the TCP/IP model layers are referred to only by name, the seven OSI model layers are more often referred to by number than by name.

2.4.8 Comparing the OSI Model with the TCP/IP Model

Refer to
Figure
in online course

The protocols that make up the TCP/IP protocol suite can be described in terms of the OSI reference model. In the OSI model, the Network Access layer and the Application layer of the TCP/IP model are further divided to describe discreet functions that need to occur at these layers.

At the Network Access Layer, the TCP/IP protocol suite does not specify which protocols to use when transmitting over a physical medium; it only describes the handoff from the Internet Layer to the physical network protocols. The OSI Layers 1 and 2 discuss the necessary procedures to access the media and the physical means to send data over a network.

The key parallels between the two network models occur at the OSI model Layers 3 and 4. OSI Model Layer 3, the Network layer, almost universally is used to discuss and document the range of processes that occur in all data networks to address and route messages through an internetwork. The Internet Protocol (IP) is the TCP/IP suite protocol that includes the functionality described at Layer 3.

Layer 4, the Transport layer of the OSI model, is often used to describe general services or functions that manage individual conversations between source and destination hosts. These functions include acknowledgement, *error recovery*, and sequencing. At this layer, the TCP/IP protocols Transmission Control Protocol (TCP) and *User Datagram Protocol (UDP)* provide the necessary functionality.

The TCP/IP Application layer includes a number of protocols that provide specific functionality to a variety of end user applications. The OSI model Layers 5, 6 and 7 are used as references for application software developers and vendors to produce products that need to access networks for communications.

Refer to **Packet
Tracer Activity**
for this chapter

In this activity, you will see how Packet Tracer uses the OSI Model as a reference to display the encapsulation details of a variety of the TCP/IP protocols.

2.5 Network Addressing

2.5.1 Addressing in the Network

Refer to
Figure
in online course

The OSI model describes the processes of encoding, formatting, segmenting, and encapsulating data for transmission over the network. A data stream that is sent from a source to a destination can be divided into pieces and interleaved with messages traveling from other hosts to other destinations. Billions of these pieces of information are traveling over a network at any given time. It is critical for each piece of data to contain enough identifying information to get it to the correct destination.

There are various types of addresses that must be included to successfully deliver the data from a source application running on one host to the correct destination application running on another. Using the OSI model as a guide, we can see the different addresses and identifiers that are necessary at each layer.

2.5.2 Getting the Data to the End Device

Refer to
Figure
in online course

During the process of encapsulation, address identifiers are added to the data as it travels down the protocol stack on the source host. Just as there are multiple layers of protocols that prepare the data for transmission to its destination, there are multiple layers of addressing to ensure its delivery.

The first identifier, the host physical address, is contained in the header of the Layer 2 PDU, called a frame. Layer 2 is concerned with the delivery of messages on a single local network. The Layer

2 address is unique on the local network and represents the address of the end device on the physical media. In a LAN using Ethernet, this address is called the Media Access Control (MAC) address. When two end devices communicate on the local Ethernet network, the frames that are exchanged between them contain the destination and source MAC addresses. Once a frame is successfully received by the destination host, the Layer 2 address information is removed as the data is decapsulated and moved up the protocol stack to Layer 3.

2.5.3 Getting the Data through the Internetwork

Refer to **Figure** in online course

Layer 3 protocols are primarily designed to move data from one local network to another local network within an internetwork. Whereas Layer 2 addresses are only used to communicate between devices on a single local network, Layer 3 addresses must include identifiers that enable intermediary network devices to locate hosts on different networks. In the TCP/IP protocol suite, every IP host address contains information about the network where the host is located.

At the boundary of each local network, an intermediary network device, usually a router, decapsulates the frame to read the destination host address contained in the header of the packet, the Layer 3 PDU. Routers use the network identifier portion of this address to determine which path to use to reach the destination host. Once the path is determined, the router encapsulates the packet in a new frame and sends it on its way toward the destination end device. When the frame reaches its final destination, the frame and packet headers are removed and the data moved up to Layer 4.

2.5.4 Getting the Data to the Right Application

Refer to **Figure** in online course

At Layer 4, information contained in the PDU header does not identify a destination host or a destination network. What it does identify is the specific process or service running on the destination host device that will act on the data being delivered. Hosts, whether they are clients or servers on the Internet, can run multiple network applications simultaneously. People using PCs often have an *e-mail client* running at the same time as a web browser, an instant messaging program, some *streaming media*, and perhaps even a game. All these separately running programs are examples of individual processes.

Viewing a web page invokes at least one network process. Clicking a hyperlink causes a web browser to communicate with a web server. At the same time, in the background, an e-mail client may be sending and receiving email, and a colleague or friend may be sending an instant message.

Think about a computer that has only one network interface on it. All the data streams created by the applications that are running on the PC enter and leave through that one interface, yet instant messages do not popup in the middle of word processor document or e-mail showing up in a game.

This is because the individual processes running on the source and destination hosts communicate with each other. Each application or service is represented at Layer 4 by a port number. A unique dialogue between devices is identified with a pair of Layer 4 source and destination port numbers that are representative of the two communicating applications. When the data is received at the host, the port number is examined to determine which application or process is the correct destination for the data.

2.5.5 Warriors of the Net

Refer to **Figure** in online course

An entertaining resource to help you visualize networking concepts is the animated movie "Warriors of the Net" by TNG Media Lab. Before viewing the video, there are a few things to consider. First, in terms of concepts you have learned in this chapter, think about when in the video you are on the LAN, on WAN, on intranet, on Internet; and what are end devices versus intermediate devices; how the OSI and TCP/IP models apply; what protocols are involved.

Second, some terms are mentioned in the video which may not be familiar. The types of packets mentioned refers to the type of upper level data (TCP, *UDP*, ICMP Ping, PING of death) that is encapsulated in the IP Packets (everything is eventually converted into IP Packets). The devices the packet encounters on its journey are router, *proxy server*, router switch, corporate intranet, the proxy, URL, firewall, *bandwidth*, hosts, web server.

Third, while port numbers 21, 23, 25, 53, and 80 are referred to explicitly in the video, IP addresses are referred to only implicitly - can you see where? Where in the video might MAC addresses have been involved?

Finally, though all animations often have simplifications in them, there is one outright error in the video. About 5 minutes in, the statement is made "What happens when Mr. IP doesn't receive an acknowledgement, he simply sends a replacement packet." As you will find out in later chapters, this is not a function of the Layer 3 Internet Protocol, which is an "unreliable", best effort delivery protocol, but rather a function of the Transport Layer TCP Protocol.

By the end of this course you will have a much better understanding of the breadth and depth of the concepts depicted in the video. We hope you enjoy it.

Download the movie from http://www.warriorsofthe.net

2.6 Chapter Labs

2.6.1 Lab: Topology Orientation and Building a Small Network

Refer to Lab Activity for this chapter

This lab begins by having you construct two small networks. It then shows how they are connected to the larger hands-on lab network used throughout the course. This network is a simplified model of a section of the Internet and will be used to develop your practical networking skills.

The following sequence of labs will introduce the networking terms below. This networking terminology will be studied in detail in subsequent chapters.

Straight-through Cable: Unshielded twisted pair (UTP) copper cable for connecting dissimilar networking devices

Crossover Cable: UTP copper cable for connecting similar networking devices

Serial Cable: Copper cable typical of wide area connections

Ethernet: Dominant local area network technology

MAC Address: **Ethernet Layer 2, physical address**

IP Address: Layer 3 *logical address*

Subnet Mask: Required to interpret the *IP address*

Default Gateway: The IP address on a router interface to which a network sends traffic leaving the local network

NIC: Network Interface Card, the port or interface that allows an end device to participate in a network

Port (hardware): An interface that allows a networking device to participate in network and to be connected via networking media

Port (software): Layer 4 protocol address in the TCP/IP suite

Interface (hardware): A port

Interface (software): A logical interaction point within software

PC: End device

Computer: End device

Workstation: End device

Switch: Intermediate device which makes decision on frames based on Layer 2 addresses (typical Ethernet MAC addresses)

Router: Layer 3, 2, and 1 device which makes decisions on packets based on Layer 3 addresses (typically *IPv4* addresses)

Bit: Binary digit, logical 1 or zero, has various physical representations as electrical, optical, or microwave pulses; Layer 1 PDU

Frame: Layer 2 PDU

Packet: Layer 3 PDU

Refer to **Packet Tracer Activity** for this chapter

In this activity, you will use Packet Tracer to complete the Topology Orientation and Building a Small Network lab.

2.6.2 Lab: Using Wireshark™ to View Protocol Data Units

Refer to **Lab Activity** for this chapter

In this lab, you will learn to use the very powerful Wireshark tool by capturing ("sniffing") traffic off of the model network.

Refer to **Packet Tracer Activity** for this chapter

In this activity, you will use Packet Tracer's Simulation mode to capture and analyze packets from a ping from a PC's command prompt and a web request using a URL.

Summary and Review

Refer to
Figure
in online course

Data networks are systems of end devices, intermediary devices, and the media connecting the devices, which provide the platform for the human network.

These devices, and the services that operate on them, can interconnect in a global and user-transparent way because they comply with rules and protocols.

The use of layered models as abstractions means that the operations of network systems can be analyzed and developed to cater the needs of future communication services.

The most widely-used networking models are OSI and TCP/IP. Associating the protocols that set the rules of data communications with the different layers is useful in determining which devices and services are applied at specific points as data passes across LANs and WANs.

As it passes down the stack, data is segmented into pieces and encapsulated with addresses and other labels. The process is reversed as the pieces are decapsulated and passed up the destination protocol stack.

Applying models allows various individuals, companies, and trade associations to analyze current networks and plan the networks of the future.

Refer to
Figure
in online course

In this activity, you will start building, testing, and analyzing a model of the Exploration lab network.

Packet Tracer Skills Integration Instructions (PDF)

Refer to **Packet Tracer Activity** for this chapter

To Learn More

Reflection Questions

Refer to
Figure
in online course

How are the classifications LAN, WAN, and Internet still useful, and how might they actually be problematic in classifying networks?

What are strengths and weaknesses of the OSI and TCP/IP models? Why are both models still used?

Metaphors and analogies can be powerful aids to learning but must be used with care. Consider issues of devices, protocols, and addressing in the following systems:

- Standard postal service
- Express parcel delivery service
- Traditional (analog) telephone system
- Internet telephony
- Containerized shipping services
- Terrestrial and satellite radio systems
- Broadcast and cable television

Discuss what you see as common factors among these systems. Apply any similarities to other networks.

How could you apply these common concepts to developing new communications systems and networks?

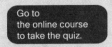
Go to
the online course
to take the quiz.

Chapter Quiz

Take the chapter quiz to test your knowledge.

Your Chapter Notes

CHAPTER 3

Application Layer Functionality and Protocols

Chapter Introduction

Most of us experience the Internet through the World Wide Web, e-mail services, and file-sharing programs. These applications, and many others, provide the human interface to the underlying network, enabling us to send and receive information with relative ease. Typically the applications that we use are intuitive, meaning we can access and use them without knowing how they work. However, for network professionals, it is important to know how an application is able to format, transmit and interpret messages that are sent and received across the network.

Visualizing the mechanisms that enable communication across the network is made easier if we use the layered framework of the *Open System Interconnection (OSI)* model. In this chapter, we will focus on the role of one layer, the Application layer and its components: applications, services, and protocols. We will explore how these three elements make the robust communication across the information network possible.

In this chapter, you will learn to:

- Describe how the functions of the three upper OSI model layers provide network services to end user applications.

- Describe how the TCP/IP Application Layer protocols provide the services specified by the upper layers of the OSI model.

- Define how people use the Application Layer to communicate across the information network.

- Describe the function of well-known TCP/IP applications, such as the World Wide Web and email, and their related services (HTTP, DNS, SMB, DHCP, SMTP/POP, and Telnet).

- Describe file-sharing processes that use peer-to-peer applications and the Gnutella protocol.

- Explain how protocols ensure services running on one kind of device can send to and receive data from many different network devices.

- Use network analysis tools to examine and explain how common user applications work.

3.1 Applications - The Interface Between the Networks

3.1.1 OSI and TCP/IP Model

Refer to
Figure
in online course

The Open Systems Interconnection reference model is a layered, abstract representation created as a guideline for network protocol design. The OSI model divides the networking process into seven logical layers, each of which has unique functionality and to which are assigned specific services and protocols.

Refer to
Figure
in online course

In this model, information is passed from one layer to the next, starting at the Application layer on the transmitting host, proceeding down the hierarchy to the Physical layer, then passing over the communications channel to the destination host, where the information proceeds back up the hierarchy, ending at the Application layer. The figure depicts the steps in this process.

The Application layer, Layer seven, is the top layer of both the OSI and TCP/IP models. It is the layer that provides the interface between the applications we use to communicate and the underlying network over which our messages are transmitted. Application layer protocols are used to exchange data between programs running on the source and destination hosts. There are many Application layer protocols and new protocols are always being developed.

Refer to
Figure
in online course

Although the TCP/IP protocol suite was developed prior to the definition of the OSI model, the functionality of the TCP/IP Application layer protocols fit roughly into the framework of the top three layers of the OSI model: Application, Presentation and Session layers.

Most TCP/IP Application layer protocols were developed before the emergence of personal computers, graphical user interfaces and multimedia objects. As a result, these protocols implement very little of the functionality that is specified in the OSI model Presentation and Session layers.

The Presentation Layer

The Presentation layer has three primary functions:

- Coding and conversion of Application layer data to ensure that data from the *source device* can be interpreted by the appropriate application on the destination device.

- Compression of the data in a manner that can be decompressed by the destination device.

- Encryption of the data for transmission and the decryption of data upon receipt by the destination.

Presentation layer implementations are not typically associated with a particular protocol stack. The standards for video and graphics are examples. Some well-known standards for video include QuickTime and Motion Picture Experts Group (MPEG). QuickTime is an Apple Computer specification for video and audio, and MPEG is a standard for video compression and coding.

Among the well-known graphic image formats are Graphics Interchange Format (GIF), Joint Photographic Experts Group (JPEG), and Tagged Image File Format (TIFF). GIF and JPEG are compression and coding standards for graphic images, and TIFF is a standard coding format for graphic images.

The Session Layer

As the name of the Session layer implies, functions at this layer create and maintain dialogs between source and destination applications. The Session layer handles the exchange of information to initiate dialogs, keep them active, and to restart sessions that are disrupted or idle for a long period of time.

Most applications, like web browsers or e-mail clients, incorporate functionality of the OSI layers 5, 6 and 7.

Refer to
Figure
in online course

The most widely-known TCP/IP Application layer protocols are those that provide for the exchange of user information. These protocols specify the format and control information necessary for many of the common Internet communication functions. Among these TCP/IP protocols are:

- Domain Name Service Protocol (DNS) is used to resolve Internet names to IP addresses.

- Hypertext Transfer Protocol (HTTP) is used to transfer files that make up the Web pages of the World Wide Web.

- *Simple Mail Transfer Protocol (SMTP)* is used for the transfer of mail messages and attachments.

- Telnet, a terminal emulation protocol, is used to provide remote access to servers and networking devices.

- File Transfer Protocol (FTP) is used for interactive file transfer between systems.

The protocols in the TCP/IP suite are generally defined by Requests for Comments (RFCs). The Internet Engineering Task Force maintains the RFCs as the standards for the TCP/IP suite.

3.1.2 Application Layer Software

Refer to **Figure** in online course

The functions associated with the Application layer protocols enable our human network to interface with the underlying data network. When we open a web browser or an instant message window, an application is started, and the program is put into the device's memory where it is executed. Each executing program loaded on a device is referred to as a process.

Within the Application layer, there are two forms of software programs or processes that provide access to the network: applications and services.

Network-Aware Applications

Applications are the software programs used by people to communicate over the network. Some end-user applications are network-aware, meaning that they implement the Application layer protocols and are able to communicate directly with the lower layers of the protocol stack. E-mail clients and web browsers are examples of these types of applications.

Application layer Services

Other programs may need the assistance of Application layer services to use network resources, like file transfer or network print spooling. Though transparent to the user, these services are the programs that interface with the network and prepare the data for transfer. Different types of data - whether it is text, graphics, or video - require different network services to ensure that it is properly prepared for processing by the functions occurring at the lower layers of OSI model.

Each application or network service uses protocols which define the standards and data formats to be used. Without protocols, the data network would not have a common way to format and direct data. In order to understand the function of various network services, it is necessary to become familiar with the underlying protocols that govern their operation.

Roll over the buttons in the figure to view examples.

3.1.3 User Applications, Services, and Application Layer Protocols

Refer to **Figure** in online course

As mentioned previously, the Application layer uses protocols that are implemented within applications and services. While applications provide people with a way to create messages and Application layer services establish an interface to the network, protocols provide the rules and formats that govern how data is treated. All three components may be used by a single executable program and may even use the same name. For example, when discussing "Telnet" we could be referring to the application, the service, or the protocol.

In the OSI model, applications that interact directly with people are considered to be at the top of the stack, as are the people themselves. Like all layers within the OSI model, the Application layer relies on the functions of the lower layers in order to complete the communication process. Within the Application layer, protocols specify what messages are exchanged between the source and destination hosts, the *syntax* of the control commands, the type and format of the data being transmitted, and the appropriate methods for error notification and recovery.

Play the animation to see the interaction between applications, services, and protocols.

3.1.4 Application Layer Protocol Functions

Refer to
Figure
in online course

Application layer protocols are used by both the source and destination devices during a communication *session*. In order for the communications to be successful, the Application layer protocols implemented on the source and destination host must match.

Protocols establish consistent rules for exchanging data between applications and services loaded on the participating devices. Protocols specify how data inside the messages is structured and the types of messages that are sent between source and destination. These messages can be requests for services, acknowledgments, data messages, status messages, or error messages. Protocols also define message dialogues, ensuring that a message being sent is met by the expected response and the correct services are invoked when data transfer occurs.

Many different types of applications communicate across data networks. Therefore, Application layer services must implement multiple protocols to provide the desired range of communication experiences. Each protocol has a specific purpose and contains the characteristics required to meet that purpose. The right protocol details in each layer must be followed so that the functions at one layer interface properly with the services in the lower layer.

Applications and services may also use multiple protocols in the course of a single conversation. One protocol may specify how to establish the network connection and another describe the process for the data transfer when the message is passed to the next lower layer.

3.2 Making Provisions for Applications and Services

3.2.1 The Client-Server Model

Refer to
Figure
in online course

When people attempt to access information on their device, whether it is a PC, laptop, PDA, cell phone, or some other device connected to a network, the data may not be physically stored on their device. If that is the case, a request to access that information must be made to the device where the data resides.

The Client/Server model

In the *client/server model*, the device requesting the information is called a client and the device responding to the request is called a server. Client and server processes are considered to be in the Application layer. The client begins the exchange by requesting data from the server, which responds by sending one or more streams of data to the client. Application layer protocols describe the format of the requests and responses between clients and servers. In addition to the actual data transfer, this exchange may also require control information, such as user authentication and the identification of a data file to be transferred.

One example of a client/server network is a corporate environment where employees use a company e-mail server to send, receive and store e-mail. The e-mail client on an employee computer issues a request to the e-mail server for any unread mail. The server responds by sending the requested e-mail to the client.

Although data is typically described as flowing from the server to the client, some data always flows from the client to the server. Data flow may be equal in both directions, or may even be greater in the direction going from the client to the server. For example, a client may transfer a file to the server for storage purposes. **Data transfer from a client to a server is referred to as an** *upload* and data from a server to a client as a download.

Roll over the tabs in the figure to view file transfer.

3.2.2 Servers

Refer to
Figure
in online course

In a general networking context, any device that responds to requests from client applications is functioning as a server. A server is usually a computer that contains information to be shared with many client systems. For example, web pages, documents, databases, pictures, video, and audio files can all be stored on a server and delivered to requesting clients. In other cases, such as a network printer, the print server delivers the client print requests to the specified printer.

Different types of server applications may have different requirements for client access. Some servers may require authentication of user account information to verify if the user has permission to access the requested data or to use a particular operation. Such servers rely on a central list of user accounts and the authorizations, or permissions, (both for data access and operations) granted to each user. When using an FTP client, for example, if you request to upload data to the FTP server, you may have permission to write to your individual folder but not to read other files on the site.

In a client/server network, the server runs a service, or process, sometimes called a server *daemon*. Like most services, daemons typically run in the background and are not under an end user's direct control. Daemons are described as "listening" for a request from a client, because they are programmed to respond whenever the server receives a request for the service provided by the daemon. When a daemon "hears" a request from a client, it exchanges appropriate messages with the client, as required by its protocol, and proceeds to send the requested data to the client in the proper format.

3.2.3 Application Layer Services and Protocols

Refer to
Figure
in online course

A single application may employ many different supporting Application layer services; thus what appears to the user as one request for a web page may, in fact, amount to dozens of individual requests. And for each request, multiple processes may be executed. For example, a client may require several individual processes to formulate just one request to a server.

Additionally, servers typically have multiple clients requesting information at the same time. For example, a **Telnet** server may have many clients requesting connections to it. These individual client requests must be handled simultaneously and separately for the network to succeed. The Application layer processes and services rely on support from lower layer functions to successfully manage the multiple conversations.

Refer to **Packet Tracer Activity** for this chapter

In this activity, you will study a simple example of client-server interaction, which can serve as a model for more complex interactions later in the course.

3.2.4 Peer-to-Peer Networking and Applications (P2P)

Refer to
Figure
in online course

The Peer-to-Peer Model

In addition to the client/server model for networking, there is also a peer-to-peer model. Peer-to-peer networking involves two distinct forms: peer-to-peer network design and peer-to-peer applications (P2P). Both forms have similar features but in practice work very differently.

Peer-to-Peer Networks

In a peer-to-peer network, two or more computers are connected via a network and can share resources (such as printers and files) without having a dedicated server. Every connected end device (known as a peer) can function as either a server or a client. One computer might assume the role of server for one transaction while simultaneously serving as a client for another. The roles of client and server are set on a per request basis.

A simple home network with two connected computers sharing a printer is an example of a peer-to-peer network. Each person can set his or her computer to share files, enable networked games, or share an Internet connection. Another example of peer-to-peer network functionality is two computers connected to a large network that use software applications to share resources between one another through the network.

Unlike the client/server model, which uses dedicated servers, peer-to-peer networks decentralize the resources on a network. Instead of locating information to be shared on dedicated servers, information can be located anywhere on any connected device. Most of the current operating systems support file and print sharing without requiring additional server software. Because peer-to-peer networks usually do not use centralized user accounts, permissions, or monitors, it is difficult to enforce security and access policies in networks containing more than just a few computers. User accounts and access rights must be set individually on each peer device.

Refer to
Figure
in online course

Peer-to-Peer Applications

A peer-to-peer application (P2P), unlike a peer-to-peer network, allows a device to act as both a client and a server within the same communication. In this model, every client is a server and every server a client. Both can initiate a communication and are considered equal in the communication process. However, peer-to-peer applications require that each end device provide a user interface and run a background service. When you launch a specific peer-to-peer application it invokes the required user interface and background services. After that the devices can communicate directly.

Some P2P applications use a hybrid system where resource sharing is decentralized but the indexes that point to resource locations are stored in a centralized directory. In a hybrid system, each peer accesses an index server to get the location of a resource stored on another peer. The index server can also help connect two peers, but once connected, the communication takes place between the two peers without additional communication to the index server.

Peer-to-peer applications can be used on peer-to-peer networks, client/server networks, and across the Internet.

3.3 Application Layer Protocols and Services Examples

3.3.1 DNS Services and Protocol

Refer to
Figure
in online course

Now that we have a better understanding of how applications provide an interface for the user and provide access to the network, we will take a look at some specific commonly used protocols.

As we will see later in this course, the Transport layer uses an addressing *scheme* called a port number. Port numbers identify applications and Application layer services that are the source and destination of data. Server programs generally use predefined port numbers that are commonly known by clients. As we examine the different TCP/IP Application layer protocols and services, we will be referring to the TCP and UDP port numbers normally associated with these services. Some of these services are:

- *Domain Name System (DNS)* - TCP/UDP Port 53

- Hypertext Transfer Protocol (HTTP) - TCP Port 80

- Simple Mail Transfer Protocol (SMTP) - TCP Port 25

- *Post Office Protocol (POP)* - TCP Port 110

- Telnet - TCP Port 23

- Dynamic Host Configuration Protocol - UDP Ports 67 and 68

- File Transfer Protocol (FTP) - TCP Ports 20 and 21

DNS

In data networks, devices are labeled with numeric IP addresses, so that they can participate in sending and receiving messages over the network. However, most people have a hard time remembering this numeric address. Hence, domain names were created to convert the numeric address into a simple, recognizable name.

On the Internet these domain names, such as www.cisco.com, are much easier for people to remember than 198.133.219.25, which is the actual numeric address for this server. Also, if Cisco decides to change the numeric address, it is transparent to the user, since the domain name will remain www.cisco.com. The new address will simply be linked to the existing domain name and connectivity is maintained. When networks were small, it was a simple task to maintain the mapping between domain names and the addresses they represented. However, as networks began to grow and the number of devices increased, this manual system became unworkable.

The Domain Name System (DNS) was created for domain name to address resolution for these networks. DNS uses a distributed set of servers to resolve the names associated with these numbered addresses.

The **DNS protocol** defines an automated service that matches resource names with the required numeric *network address*. It includes the format for queries, responses, and data formats. DNS protocol communications use a single format called a message. This message format is used for all types of client queries and server responses, error messages, and the transfer of *resource record* information between servers.

Refer to
Figure
in online course

DNS is a client/server service; however, it differs from the other client/server services that we are examining. While other services use a client that is an application (such as web browser, e-mail client), the DNS client runs as a service itself. The DNS client, sometimes called the *DNS resolver*, supports name resolution for our other network applications and other services that need it.

When configuring a network device, we generally provide one or more **DNS Server** addresses that the DNS client can use for name resolution. Usually the Internet service provider provides the addresses to use for the DNS servers. When a user's application requests to connect to a remote device by name, the requesting DNS client queries one of these name servers to resolve the name to a numeric address.

Computer operating systems also have a utility called nslookup **that allows the user to manually** *query* the name servers to resolve a given host name. This utility can also be used to troubleshoot name resolution issues and to verify the current status of the name servers.

In the figure, when the **nslookup** is issued, the default DNS server configured for your host is displayed. In this example, the DNS server is dns-sjk.cisco.com which has an address of ֽ 171.68.226.120.

We then can type the name of a host or domain for which we wish to get the address. In the first query in the figure, a query is made for www.cisco.com. The responding name server provides the address of 198.133.219.25.

The queries shown in the figure are only simple tests. The `nslookup` has many options available for extensive testing and verification of the DNS process.

Refer to
Figure
in online course

A DNS server provides the name resolution using the name daemon, which is often called named, (pronounced name-dee).

The DNS server stores different types of resource records used to resolve names. These records contain the name, address, and type of record.

Some of these record types are:

- A - an end device address

- NS - an *authoritative* name server

- CNAME - the canonical name (or Fully Qualified Domain Name) for an alias; used when multiple services have the single network address but each service has its own entry in DNS

- MX - mail exchange record; maps a *domain name* to a list of mail exchange servers for that domain

When a client makes a query, the server's "named" process first looks at its own records to see if it can resolve the name. If it is unable to resolve the name using its stored records, it contacts other servers in order to resolve the name.

The request may be passed along to a number of servers, which can take extra time and consume bandwidth. Once a match is found and returned to the original requesting server, the server temporarily stores the numbered address that matches the name in *cache*.

If that same name is requested again, the first server can return the address by using the value stored in its name cache. Caching reduces both the DNS query data network traffic and the work-loads of servers higher up the hierarchy. The DNS Client service on Windows PCs optimizes the performance of DNS name resolution by storing previously resolved names in memory, as well. The `ipconfig /displaydns` command displays all of the cached DNS entries on a Windows XP or 2000 computer system.

Refer to
Figure
in online course

The Domain Name System uses a hierarchical system to create a name database to provide name resolution. The hierarchy looks like an inverted tree with the root at the top and branches below.

At the top of the hierarchy, the root servers maintain records about how to reach the top-level domain servers, which in turn have records that point to the secondary level domain servers and so on.

The different top-level domains represent either the type of organization or the country of origin. Examples of top-level domains are:

- **.au - Australia**

- **.co - Colombia**

- **.com - a business or industry**

- **.jp - Japan**

- **.org - a non-profit organization**

After top-level domains are second-level domain names, and below them are other lower level domains.

Each domain name is a path down this inverted tree starting from the root.

For example, as shown in the figure, the root DNS server may not know exactly where the e-mail server mail.cisco.com is located, but it maintains a record for the "com" domain within the top-level domain. Likewise, the servers within the "com" domain may not have a record for mail.cisco.com, but they do have a record for the "cisco.com" domain. The servers within the cisco.com domain have a record (a MX record to be precise) for mail.cisco.com.

The Domain Name System relies on this hierarchy of decentralized servers to store and maintain these resource records. The resource records list domain names that the server can resolve and alternative servers that can also process requests. If a given server has resource records that correspond to its level in the domain hierarchy, it is said to be **authoritative** for those records.

For example, a name server in the cisco.netacad.net domain would not be authoritative for the mail.cisco.com record because that record is held at a higher domain level server, specifically the name server in the cisco.com domain.

Links

http://www.ietf.org//rfc/rfc1034.txt

http://www.ietf.org/rfc/rfc1035.txt

3.3.2 WWW Service and HTTP

Refer to
Figure
in online course

When a web address (or URL) is typed into a web browser, the web browser establishes a connection to the web service running on the server using the HTTP protocol. URLs (or Uniform Resource Locator) and URIs (Uniform Resource Identifier) are the names most people associate with web addresses.

The URL http://www.cisco.com/index.html is an example of a URL that refers to a specific resource - a web page named **index.html** on a server identified as **cisco.com** (click the tabs in the figure to see the steps used by HTTP).

Web browsers are the client applications our computers use to connect to the World Wide Web and access resources stored on a web server. As with most server processes, the web server runs as a background service and makes different types of files available.

In order to access the content, web clients make connections to the server and request the desired resources. The server replies with the resources and, upon receipt, the browser interprets the data and presents it to the user.

Browsers can interpret and present many data types, such as plain text or Hypertext Markup Language (HTML, the language in which web pages are constructed). Other types of data, however, may require another service or program, typically referred to as plug-ins or add-ons. To help the browser determine what type of file it is receiving, the server specifies what kind of data the file contains.

To better understand how the web browser and web client interact, we can examine how a web page is opened in a browser. For this example, we will use the URL: http://www.cisco.com/web-server.htm.

First, the browser interprets the three parts of the URL:

Step 1. **http** (the protocol or scheme)

Step 2. www.cisco.com (the server name)

Step 3. **web-server.htm** (the specific file name requested).

The browser then checks with a name server to convert www.cisco.com into a numeric address, which it uses to connect to the server. Using the HTTP protocol requirements, the browser sends a GET request to the server and asks for the file **web-server.htm**. The server in turn sends the HTML *code* for this web page to the browser. Finally, the browser deciphers the HTML code and formats the page for the browser window.

Refer to **Figure** in online course

The Hypertext Transfer Protocol (HTTP), one of the protocols in the TCP/IP suite, was originally developed to publish and retrieve HTML pages and is now used for distributed, collaborative information systems. HTTP is used across the World Wide Web for data transfer and is one of the most used application protocols.

HTTP specifies a request/response protocol. When a client, typically a web browser, sends a request message to a server, the HTTP protocol defines the message types the client uses to request the web page and also the message types the server uses to respond. The three common message types are GET, POST, and PUT.

GET is a client request for data. A web browser sends the **GET** message to request pages from a web server. As shown in the figure, once the server receives the **GET** request, it responds with a status line, such as HTTP/1.1 200 OK, and a message of its own, the body of which may be the requested file, an error message, or some other information.

POST and **PUT** are used to send messages that upload data to the web server. For example, when the user enters data into a form embedded in a web page, **POST** includes the data in the message sent to the server.

PUT uploads resources or content to the web server.

Although it is remarkably flexible, HTTP is not a secure protocol. The **POST** messages upload information to the server in plain text that can be intercepted and read. Similarly, the server responses, typically HTML pages, are also unencrypted.

For secure communication across the Internet, the HTTP Secure (HTTPS) protocol is used for accessing or posting web server information. HTTPS can use authentication and *encryption* to secure data as it travels between the client and server. HTTPS specifies additional rules for passing data between the Application layer and the Transport Layer.

Refer to **Packet Tracer Activity** for this chapter

In this activity, you will configure DNS and HTTP services, and then study the packets that result when a web page is requested by typing a URL.

3.3.3 E-mail Services and SMTP/POP Protocols

Refer to **Figure** in online course

E-mail, the most popular network service, has revolutionized how people communicate through its simplicity and speed. Yet to run on a computer or other end device, e-mail requires several applications and services. Two example Application layer protocols are Post Office Protocol (POP) and **Simple Mail Transfer Protocol** (SMTP), shown in the figure. As with HTTP, these protocols define client/server processes.

When people compose e-mail messages, they typically use an application called a *Mail User Agent (MUA)*, or e-mail client. The MUA allows messages to be sent and places received messages into the client's mailbox, both of which are distinct processes.

In order to receive e-mail messages from an e-mail server, the e-mail client can use POP. Sending e-mail from either a client or a server uses message formats and command strings defined by the SMTP protocol. Usually an e-mail client provides the functionality of both protocols within one application.

Refer to **Figure** in online course

E-mail Server Processes - MTA and MDA

The e-mail server operates two separate processes:

- Mail Transfer Agent (MTA)

- Mail Delivery Agent (MDA)

The Mail Transfer Agent (MTA) process is used to forward e-mail. As shown in the figure, the MTA receives messages from the MUA or from another MTA on another e-mail server. Based on the message header, it determines how a message has to be forwarded to reach its destination. If the mail is addressed to a user whose mailbox is on the local server, the mail is passed to the MDA. If the mail is for a user not on the local server, the MTA routes the e-mail to the MTA on the appropriate server.

Refer to **Figure** in online course

In the figure, we see that the Mail Delivery Agent (MDA) accepts a piece of e-mail from a Mail Transfer Agent (MTA) and performs the actual delivery. The MDA receives all the inbound mail from the MTA and places it into the appropriate users' mailboxes. The MDA can also resolve final delivery issues, such as virus scanning, *spam filtering*, and return-receipt handling. Most e-mail communications use the MUA, MTA, and MDA applications. However, there are other alternatives for e-mail delivery.

A client may be connected to a corporate e-mail system, such as IBM's Lotus Notes, Novell's Groupwise, or Microsoft's Exchange. These systems often have their own internal e-mail format, and their clients typically communicate with the e-mail server using a proprietary protocol. The server sends or receives e-mail via the Internet through the product's Internet mail *gateway*, which performs any necessary reformatting.

As another alternative, computers that do not have an MUA can still connect to a mail service on a web browser in order to retrieve and send messages in this manner. Some computers may run their own MTA and manage inter-domain e-mail themselves. If, for example, two people who work for the same company exchange e-mail with each other using a proprietary protocol, their messages may stay completely within the company's corporate e-mail system.

Refer to **Figure** in online course

As mentioned earlier, e-mail can use the protocols, POP and SMTP (see the figure for an explanation of how they each work). POP and POP3 (Post Office Protocol, version 3) are inbound mail **delivery** protocols and are typical client/server protocols. They deliver e-mail from the e-mail server to the client (MUA). The MDA listens for when a client connects to a server. Once a connection is established, the server can deliver the e-mail to the client.

The Simple Mail Transfer Protocol (SMTP), on the other hand, governs the transfer of **outbound** e-mail from the sending client to the e-mail server (MDA), as well as the transport of e-mail between e-mail servers (MTA). SMTP enables e-mail to be transported across data networks between different types of server and client software and makes e-mail exchange over the Internet possible.

The SMTP protocol message format uses a rigid set of commands and replies. These commands support the procedures used in SMTP, such as session initiation, mail transaction, forwarding mail, verifying mailbox names, expanding mailing lists, and the opening and closing exchanges.

Some of the commands specified in the SMTP protocol are:

- HELO - identifies the SMTP client process to the SMTP server process

- EHLO - Is a newer version of HELO, which includes services extensions

- MAIL FROM - Identifies the sender

- RCPT TO - Identifies the recipient
- DATA - Identifies the body of the message

3.3.4 FTP

Refer to
Figure
in online course

The File Transfer Protocol (FTP) is another commonly used Application layer protocol. FTP was developed to allow for file transfers between a client and a server. An FTP client is an application that runs on a computer that is used to push and pull files from a server running the FTP daemon (FTPd).

To successfully transfer files, FTP requires two connections between the client and the server: one for commands and replies, the other for the actual file transfer.

The client establishes the first connection to the server on TCP port 21. This connection is used for control traffic, consisting of client commands and server replies.

The client establishes the second connection to the server over TCP port 20. This connection is for the actual file transfer and is created every time there is a file transferred.

The file transfer can happen in either direction. The client can download (pull) a file from the server or, the client can upload (push) a file to the server.

3.3.5 DHCP

Refer to
Figure
in online course

The *Dynamic Host Configuration Protocol (DHCP)* service enables devices on a network to obtain IP addresses and other information from a DHCP server. This service automates the assignment of IP addresses, subnet masks, gateway and other IP networking parameters.

DHCP allows a host to obtain an IP address dynamically when it connects to the network. The DHCP server is contacted and an address requested. The DHCP server chooses an address from a configured range of addresses called a pool and assigns ("leases") it to the host for a set period.

On larger local networks, or where the user population changes frequently, DHCP is preferred. New users may arrive with laptops and need a connection. Others have new workstations that need to be connected. Rather than have the network administrator assign IP addresses for each workstation, it is more efficient to have IP addresses assigned automatically using DHCP.

DHCP distributed addresses are not permanently assigned to hosts but are only leased for a period of time. If the host is powered down or taken off the network, the address is returned to the pool for reuse. This is especially helpful with mobile users that come and go on a network. Users can freely move from location to location and re-establish network connections. The host can obtain an IP address once the hardware connection is made, either via a wired or wireless LAN.

DHCP makes it possible for you to access the Internet using wireless hotspots at airports or coffee shops. As you enter the area, your laptop DHCP client contacts the local DHCP server via a wireless connection. The DHCP server assigns an IP address to your laptop.

As the figure shows, various types of devices can be DHCP servers when running DHCP service software. The DHCP server in most medium to large networks is usually a local dedicated PC-based server.

With home networks the DHCP server is usually located at the ISP and a host on the home network receives its IP configuration directly from the ISP.

DHCP can pose a security risk because any device connected to the network can receive an address. This risk makes physical security an important factor when determining whether to use dynamic or manual addressing.

Dynamic and static addressing both have their places in network designs. Many networks use both DHCP and static addressing. DHCP is used for general purpose hosts such as end user devices, and fixed addresses are used for network devices such as gateways, switches, servers and printers.

Refer to **Figure** in online course

Without DHCP, users have to manually input the IP address, *subnet mask* and other network settings in order to join the network. The DHCP server maintains a pool of IP addresses and leases an address to any DHCP-enabled client when the client is powered on. Because the IP addresses are dynamic (leased) rather than static (permanently assigned), addresses no longer in use are automatically returned to the pool for reallocation. When a DHCP-configured device boots up or connects to the network, the client broadcasts a DHCP DISCOVER packet to identify any available DHCP servers on the network. A DHCP server replies with a DHCP OFFER, which is a lease offer message with an assigned IP address, subnet mask, DNS server, and *default gateway* information as well as the duration of the lease.

The client may receive multiple DHCP OFFER packets if there is more than one DHCP server on the local network, so it must choose between them, and broadcast a DHCP REQUEST packet that identifies the explicit server and lease offer that the client is accepting. A client may choose to request an address that it had previously been allocated by the server.

Assuming that the IP address requested by the client, or offered by the server, is still valid, the server would return a DHCP *ACK* message that acknowledges to the client the lease is finalized. If the offer is no longer valid - perhaps due to a time-out or another client allocating the lease - then the selected server will respond with a DHCP NAK message (Negative Acknowledgement). If a DHCP NAK message is returned, then the selection process must begin again with a new DHCP DISCOVER message being transmitted.

Once the client has the lease, it must be renewed prior to the lease expiration through another DHCP REQUEST message.

The DHCP server ensures that all IP addresses are unique (an IP address cannot be assigned to two different network devices simultaneously). Using DHCP enables network administrators to easily reconfigure client IP addresses without having to manually make changes to the clients. Most Internet providers use DHCP to allocate addresses to their customers who do not require a static address.

The fourth *CCNA* Exploration course will cover the operation of DHCP in greater detail.

3.3.6 File Sharing Services and SMB Protocol

Refer to **Figure** in online course

The *Server Message Block (SMB)* is a client/server file sharing protocol. IBM developed Server Message Block (SMB) in the late 1980s to describe the structure of shared network resources, such as directories, files, printers, and serial ports. It is a request-response protocol. Unlike the file sharing supported by FTP, clients establish a long term connection to servers. Once the connection is established, the user of the client can access the resources on the server as if the resource is local to the client host.

SMB file-sharing and print services have become the mainstay of Microsoft networking. With the introduction of the Windows 2000 series of software, Microsoft changed the underlying structure for using SMB. In previous versions of Microsoft products, the SMB services used a non-TCP/IP protocol to implement name resolution. Beginning with Windows 2000, all subsequent Microsoft products use DNS naming. This allows TCP/IP protocols to directly support SMB resource sharing, as shown in the figure.

The LINUX and *UNIX* operating systems also provide a method of sharing resources with Microsoft networks using a version of SMB called SAMBA. The Apple Macintosh operating systems also support resource sharing using the SMB protocol.

Refer to
Figure
in online course

The SMB protocol describes file system access and how clients can make requests for files. It also describes the SMB protocol inter-process communication. All SMB messages share a common format. This format uses a fixed-sized header followed by a variable-sized parameter and data component.

SMB messages can:

- Start, authenticate, and terminate sessions
- Control file and printer access
- Allow an application to send or receive messages to or from another device

The SMB file exchange process is shown in the figure.

3.3.7 P2P Services and Gnutella Protocol

Refer to
Figure
in online course

You learned about FTP and SMB as ways of obtaining files, here is another Application protocol. Sharing files over the Internet has become extremely popular. With **P2P applications** based on the Gnutella protocol, people can make files on their hard disks available to others for downloading. Gnutella-compatible client software allows users to connect to Gnutella services over the Internet and to locate and access resources shared by other Gnutella peers.

Many client applications are available for accessing the Gnutella network, including: BearShare, Gnucleus, LimeWire, Morpheus, WinMX and XoloX (see a screen capture of LimeWire in the figure). While the Gnutella Developer Forum maintains the basic protocol, application vendors often develop extensions to make the protocol work better on their applications.

Refer to
Figure
in online course

Many P2P applications do not use a central database to record all the files available on the peers. Instead, the devices on the network each tell the other what files are available when queried and use the Gnutella protocol and services to support locating resources. See the figure.

When a user is connected to a Gnutella service, the client applications will search for other Gnutella nodes to connect to. These nodes handle queries for resource locations and replies to those requests. They also govern control messages, which help the service discover other nodes. The actual file transfers usually rely on HTTP services.

The Gnutella protocol defines five different packet types:

- ping - for device discovery
- pong - as a reply to a ping
- query - for file location
- query hit - as a reply to a query
- push - as a download request

3.3.8 Telnet Services and Protocol

Refer to
Figure
in online course

Long before desktop computers with sophisticated graphical interfaces existed, people used text-based systems which were often just display terminals physically attached to a central computer. Once networks were available, people needed a way to remotely access the computer systems in the same manner that they did with the directly attached terminals.

Telnet was developed to meet that need. Telnet dates back to the early 1970s and is among the oldest of the Application layer protocols and services in the TCP/IP suite. Telnet provides a standard method of emulating text-based terminal devices over the data network. Both the protocol itself and the client software that implements the protocol are commonly referred to as Telnet.

Appropriately enough, a connection using Telnet is called a Virtual Terminal (VTY) session, or connection. Rather than using a physical device to connect to the server, Telnet uses software to create a virtual device that provides the same features of a terminal session with access to the server command line interface (CLI).

To support Telnet client connections, the server runs a service called the Telnet daemon. A virtual terminal connection is established from an end device using a Telnet client application. Most operating systems include an Application layer Telnet client. On a Microsoft Windows PC, Telnet can be run from the command prompt. Other common terminal applications that run as Telnet clients are HyperTerminal, Minicom, and TeraTerm.

Once a Telnet connection is established, users can perform any authorized function on the server, just as if they were using a command line session on the server itself. If authorized, they can start and stop processes, configure the device, and even shut down the system.

Click the tabs in the figure to view the Telnet example.

Refer to
Figure
in online course

Telnet is a client/server protocol and it specifies how a VTY session is established and terminated. It also provides the syntax and order of the commands used to initiate the Telnet session, as well as control commands that can be issued during a session. Each Telnet command consists of at least two bytes. The first byte is a special character called the **Interpret as Command** (IAC) character. As its name implies, the IAC defines the next byte as a command rather than text.

Some sample Telnet protocol commands include:

Are You There (AYT) - Lets the user request that something appear on the terminal screen to indicate that the VTY session is active.

Erase Line (EL) - Deletes all text from the current line.

Interrupt Process (IP) - Suspends, interrupts, aborts, or terminates the process to which the Virtual Terminal is connected. For example, if a user started a program on the Telnet server via the VTY, he or she could send an IP command to stop the program.

While the Telnet protocol supports user authentication, it does not support the transport of *encrypted* data. All data exchanged during a Telnet sessions is transported as plain text across the network. This means that the data can be intercepted and easily understood.

If security is a concern, the Secure Shell (SSH) protocol offers an alternate and secure method for server access. SSH provides the structure for secure remote login and other secure network services. It also provides stronger authentication than Telnet and supports the transport of session data using encryption. **As a best practice, network professionals should always use SSH in place of Telnet, whenever possible.**

Later in this course, we will use Telnet and SSH to access and configure network devices over the lab network.

3.4 Chapter Labs and Activities

3.4.1 Data Stream Capture

In this activity, you will use a computer that has a microphone and Microsoft Sound Recorder or Internet access so that an audio file can be downloaded.

3.4.2 Lab - Managing a Web Server

Refer to **Lab Activity** for this chapter

In this lab you will download, install, and configure the popular Apache web server. A web browser will be used to connect to the server, and Wireshark will be used to capture the communication. Analysis of the capture will aid students in understanding how the HTTP protocol operates.

3.4.3 Lab - E-mail Services and Protocols

Refer to **Lab Activity** for this chapter

In this lab, you will configure and use an e-mail client application to connect to eagle-server network services. You will then monitor the communication with Wireshark and analyze the captured packets.

Summary and Review

Refer to
Figure
in online course

The **Application layer** is responsible for directly accessing the underlying processes that manage and deliver communication to the human network. This layer serves as the source and destination of communications across data networks.

The Application layer applications, protocols, and services enable users to interact with the data network in a way that is meaningful and effective.

Applications are computer programs with which the user interacts and which initiate the data transfer process at the user's request.

Services are background programs that provide the connection between the Application layer and the lower layers of the networking model.

Protocols provide a structure of agreed-upon rules and processes that ensure services running on one particular device can send and receive data from a range of different network devices.

Delivery of data over the network can be requested from a **server** by a **client**, or between devices that operate in a **peer-to-peer** arrangement, where the client/server relationship is established according to which device is the source and destination at that time. **Messages** are exchanged between the Application layer services at each end device in accordance with the protocol specifications to establish and use these relationships.

Protocols like **HTTP**, for example, support the delivery of web pages to end devices. **SMTP/POP** protocols support sending and receiving e-mail. **SMB** enables users to share files. **DNS** resolves the human legible names used to refer to network resources into numeric addresses usable by the network.

Refer to
Figure
in online course

Refer to **Packet
Tracer Activity**
for this chapter

In this activity, you will build and analyze more complex parts of the model of the Exploration lab network.

Packet Tracer Skills Integration Instructions (PDF)

To Learn More

Refer to
Figure
in online course

Reflection Questions

Why is it important to distinguish between a particular Application layer application, the associated service, and the protocol? Discuss this in the context of network reference models.

What if it was possible to include all Application layer services with a single all-encompassing protocol? Discuss the advantages and disadvantages of having one such protocol.

How would you go about developing a new protocol for a new Application layer service? What would have to be included? Who would have to be involved in the process and how would the information be disseminated?

Links

```
http://www.ietf.org/
http://www.protocols.com/
```

Go to
the online course
to take the quiz.

Chapter Quiz

Take the chapter quiz to test your knowledge.

Your Chapter Notes

CHAPTER 4

OSI Transport Layer

Chapter Introduction

Refer to **Figure** in online course

Data networks and the Internet support the human network by supplying seamless, reliable communication between people - both locally and around the globe. On a single device, people can use multiple services such as e-mail, the web, and instant messaging to send messages or retrieve information. Applications such as e-mail clients, web browsers, and instant messaging clients allow people to use computers and networks to send messages and find information.

Data from each of these applications is packaged, transported, and delivered to the appropriate server daemon or application on the destination device. The processes described in the OSI Transport layer accept data from the Application layer and prepare it for addressing at the Network layer. The Transport layer is responsible for the overall end-to-end transfer of application data.

In this chapter, we examine the role of the Transport layer in encapsulating application data for use by the Network layer. The Transport layer also encompasses these functions:

- Enables multiple applications to communicate over the network at the same time on a single device

- Ensures that, if required, all the data is received reliably and in order by the correct application

- Employs error handling mechanisms

Learning Objectives

Upon completion of this chapter, you will be able to:

- Explain the need for the Transport layer.

- Identify the role of the Transport layer as it provides the end-to-end transfer of data between applications.

- Describe the role of two TCP/IP Transport layer protocols: TCP and UDP.

- Explain the key functions of the Transport layer, including reliability, port addressing, and segmentation.

- Explain how TCP and UDP each handle key functions.

- Identify when it is appropriate to use TCP or UDP and provide examples of applications that use each protocol.

4.1 Roles of the Transport Layer

4.1.1 Purpose of the Transport Layer

The Transport layer provides for the segmentation of data and the control necessary to reassemble these pieces into the various communication streams. Its primary responsibilities to accomplish this are:

Refer to
Figure
in online course

- Tracking the individual communication between applications on the source and destination hosts

- Segmenting data and managing each piece

- Reassembling the segments into streams of application data

- Identifying the different applications

Tracking Individual Conversations

Any host may have multiple applications that are communicating across the network. Each of these applications will be communicating with one or more applications on remote hosts. It is the responsibility of the Transport layer to maintain the multiple communication streams between these applications.

Segmenting Data

As each application creates a stream data to be sent to a remote application, this data must be prepared to be sent across the media in manageable pieces. The Transport layer protocols describe services that segment this data from the Application layer. This includes the encapsulation required on each piece of data. Each piece of application data requires headers to be added at the Transport layer to indicate to which communication it is associated.

Reassembling Segments

At the receiving host, each piece of data may be directed to the appropriate application. Additionally, these individual pieces of data must also be reconstructed into a complete data stream that is useful to the Application layer. The protocols at the Transport layer describe the how the Transport layer header information is used to reassemble the data pieces into streams to be passed to the Application layer.

Identifying the Applications

In order to pass data streams to the proper applications, the Transport layer must identify the target application. To accomplish this, the Transport layer assigns an application an identifier. The TCP/IP protocols call this identifier a port number. Each software process that needs to access the network is assigned a port number unique in that host. This port number is used in the Transport layer header to indicate to which application that piece of data is associated.

The Transport layer is the link between the Application layer and the lower layer that are responsible for network transmission. This layer accepts data from different conversations and passes it down to the lower layers as manageable pieces that can be eventually multiplexed over the media.

Applications do not need to know the operational details of the network in use. The applications generate data that is sent from one application to another, without regard to the destination host type, the type of media over which the data must travel, the path taken by the data, the *congestion* on a link, or the size of the network.

Additionally, the lower layers are not aware that there are multiple applications sending data on the network. Their responsibility is to deliver data to the appropriate device. The Transport layer then sorts these pieces before delivering them to the appropriate application.

Data Requirements Vary

Because different applications have different requirements, there are multiple Transport layer protocols. For some applications, segments must arrive in a very specific sequence in order to be processed successfully. In some cases, all of the data must be received for any of it to be of use. In other cases, an application can tolerate some loss of data during transmission over the network.

In today's converged networks, applications with very different transport needs may be communicating on the same network. The different Transport layer protocols have different rules allowing devices to handle these diverse data requirements.

Some protocols provide just the basic functions for efficiently delivering the data pieces between the appropriate applications. These types of protocols are useful for applications whose data is sensitive to delays.

Other Transport layer protocols describe processes that provide additional features, such as ensuring reliable delivery between the applications. While these additional functions provide more robust communication at the Transport layer between applications, they have additional overhead and make larger demands on the network.

Refer to
Figure
in online course

Separating Multiple Communications

Consider a computer connected to a network that is simultaneously receiving and sending e-mail and instant messages, viewing websites, and conducting a VoIP phone call. Each of these applications is sending and receiving data over the network at the same time. However, data from the phone call is not directed to the web browser, and text from an instant message does not appear in an e-mail.

Further, users require that an e-mail or web page be completely received and presented for the information to be considered useful. Slight delays are considered acceptable to ensure that the complete information is received and presented.

In contrast, occasionally missing small parts of a telephone conversation might be considered acceptable. One can either infer the missing audio from the context of the conversation or ask the other person to repeat what they said. This is considered preferable to the delays that would result from asking the network to manage and resend missing segments. In this example, the user - not the network - manages the resending or replacement of missing information.

Refer to
Figure
in online course

As explained in a previous chapter, sending some types of data - a video for example - across a network as one complete communication stream could prevent other communications from occurring at the same time. It also makes error recovery and retransmission of damaged data difficult.

Dividing data into small parts, and sending these parts from the source to the destination, enables many different communications to be interleaved (multiplexed) on the same network.

Segmentation of the data, in accordance with Transport layer protocols, provides the means to both send and receive data when running multiple applications concurrently on a computer. Without segmentation, only one application, the streaming video for example, would be able to receive data. You could not receive e-mails, chat on instant messenger, or view web pages while also viewing the video.

At the Transport layer, each particular set of pieces flowing between a source application and a destination application is known as a conversation.

To identify each segment of data, the Transport layer adds to the piece a header containing binary data. This header contains fields of bits. It is the values in these fields that enable different Transport layer protocols to perform different functions.

4.1.2 Controlling the Conversations

Refer to
Figure
in online course

The primary functions specified by all Transport layer protocols include:

Segmentation and Reassembly - Most networks have a limitation on the amount of data that can be included in a single PDU. The Transport layer divides application data into blocks of data that are an appropriate size. At the destination, the Transport layer reassembles the data before sending it to the destination application or service.

Conversation Multiplexing - There may be many applications or services running on each host in the network. Each of these applications or services is assigned an address known as a port so that the Transport layer can determine with which application or service the data is identified.

In addition to using the information contained in the headers, for the basic functions of data segmentation and reassembly, some protocols at the Transport layer provide:

- Connection-oriented conversations
- Reliable delivery
- Ordered data reconstruction
- Flow control

Refer to
Figure
in online course

Establishing a Session

The Transport layer can provide this connection orientation by creating a sessions between the applications. These connections prepare the applications to communicate with each other before any data is transmitted. Within these sessions, the data for a communication between the two applications can be closely managed.

Reliable Delivery

For many reasons, it is possible for a piece of data to become corrupted, or lost completely, as it is transmitted over the network. The Transport layer can ensure that all pieces reach their destination by having the source device to retransmit any data that is lost.

Same Order Delivery

Because networks may provide multiple routes that can have different transmission times, data can arrive in the wrong order. By numbering and sequencing the segments, the Transport layer can ensure that these segments are reassembled into the proper order.

Flow Control

Network hosts have limited resources, such as memory or bandwidth. When Transport layer is aware that these resources are overtaxed, some protocols can request that the sending application reduce the rate of data flow. This is done at the Transport layer by regulating the amount of data the source transmits as a group. Flow control can prevent the loss of segments on the network and avoid the need for retransmission.

As the protocols are discussed in this chapter, these services will be explained in more detail.

4.1.3 Supporting Reliable Communication

Refer to
Figure
in online course

Recall that the primary function of the Transport layer is to manage the application data for the conversations between hosts. However, different applications have different requirements for their data, and therefore different Transport protocols have been developed to meet these requirements.

A Transport layer protocol can implement a method to ensure reliable delivery of the data. In networking terms, reliability means ensuring that each piece of data that the source sends arrives at the destination. At the Transport layer the three basic operations of reliability are:

- tracking transmitted data

- acknowledging received data

- retransmitting any unacknowledged data

This requires the processes of the Transport layer at the source to keep track of all the data pieces of each conversation and the retransmit of any data that were not acknowledged by the destination. The Transport layer of the receiving host must also track the data as it is received and acknowledge the receipt of the data.

These reliability processes place additional overhead on the network resources due to the acknowledgement, tracking, and retransmission. To support these reliability operations, more *control data* is exchanged between the sending and receiving hosts. This control information is contained in the Layer 4 header.

This creates a trade-off between the value of reliability and the burden it places on the network. Application developers must choose which transport protocol type is appropriate based on the requirements of their applications. At the Transport layer, there are protocols that specify methods for either reliable, guaranteed delivery or best-effort delivery. In the context of networking, best-effort delivery is referred to as unreliable, because there is no acknowledgement that the data is received at the destination.

Determining the Need for Reliability

Applications, such as databases, web pages, and e-mail, require that all of the sent data arrive at the destination in its original condition, in order for the data to be useful. Any missing data could cause a corrupt communication that is either incomplete or unreadable. Therefore, these applications are designed to use a Transport layer protocol that implements reliability. The additional network overhead is considered to be required for these applications.

Other applications are more tolerant of the loss of small amounts of data. For example, if one or two segments of a video stream fail to arrive, it would only create a momentary disruption in the stream. This may appear as distortion in the image but may not even be noticeable to the user.

Imposing overhead to ensure reliability for this application could reduce the usefulness of the application. The image in a streaming video would be greatly degraded if the destination device had to account for lost data and delay the stream while waiting for its arrival. It is better to render the best image possible at the time with the segments that arrive and forego reliability. If reliability is required for some reason, these applications can provide error checking and retransmission requests.

4.1.4 TCP and UDP

Refer to
Figure
in online course

The two most common Transport layer protocols of TCP/IP protocol suite are Transmission Control Protocol (TCP) and User Datagram Protocol (UDP). Both protocols manage the communication of multiple applications. The differences between the two are the specific functions that each protocol implements.

User Datagram Protocol (UDP)

UDP is a simple, connectionless protocol, described in RFC 768. It has the advantage of providing for low overhead data delivery. The pieces of communication in UDP are called *datagrams*. These datagrams are sent as "best effort" by this Transport layer protocol.

Applications that use UDP include:

- Domain Name System (DNS)
- Video Streaming
- Voice over IP (VoIP)

Transmission Control Protocol (TCP)

TCP is a connection-oriented protocol, described in RFC 793. TCP incurs additional overhead to gain functions. Additional functions specified by TCP are the same order delivery, reliable delivery, and *flow control*. Each TCP segment has 20 bytes of overhead in the header encapsulating the Application layer data, whereas each UDP segment only has 8 bytes of overhead. See the figure for a comparison.

Applications that use TCP are:

- Web Browsers
- E-mail
- File Transfers

4.1.5 Port Addressing

Refer to
Figure
in online course

Identifying the Conversations

Consider the earlier example of a computer simultaneously receiving and sending e-mail, instant messages, web pages, and a VoIP phone call.

The TCP and UDP based services keep track of the various applications that are communicating. To differentiate the segments and datagrams for each application, both TCP and UDP have header fields that can uniquely identify these applications. These unique identifiers are the port numbers.

In the header of each segment or datagram, there is a source and destination port. The source port number is the number for this communication associated with the originating application on the local host. The destination port number is the number for this communication associated with the destination application on the remote host.

Port numbers are assigned in various ways, depending on whether the message is a request or a response. While server processes have static port numbers assigned to them, clients dynamically choose a port number for each conversation.

When a client application sends a request to a server application, the destination port contained in the header is the port number that is assigned to the service daemon running on the remote host. The client software must know what port number is associated with the server process on the remote host. This destination port number is configured, either by default or manually. For example, when a web browser application makes a request to a web server, the browser uses TCP and port number 80 unless otherwise specified. This is because TCP port 80 is the default port assigned to web-serving applications. Many common applications have default port assignments.

The source port in a segment or datagram header of a client request is randomly generated from port numbers greater than 1023. As long as it does not conflict with other ports in use on the system, the client can choose any port number from the range of default port numbers used by the operating system. This port number acts like a return address for the requesting application. The Transport layer keeps track of this port and the application that initiated the request so that when a response is returned, it can be forwarded to the correct application. The requesting application port number is used as the destination port number in the response coming back from the server.

The combination of the Transport layer port number and the Network layer IP address assigned to the host uniquely identifies a particular process running on a specific host device. This combination is called a socket. Occasionally, you may find the terms port number and socket used interchangeably. In the context of this course, the term socket refers only to the unique combination of IP address and port number. A socket pair, consisting of the source and destination IP addresses and port numbers, is also unique and identifies the conversation between the two hosts.

For example, an HTTP web page request being sent to a web server (port 80) running on a host with a Layer 3 IPv4 address of 192.168.1.20 would be destined to socket 192.168.1.20:80.

If the web browser requesting the web page is running on host 192.168.100.48 and the Dynamic port number assigned to the web browser is 49152, the socket for the web page would be 192.168.100.48:49152.

Refer to **Figure** in online course

The *Internet Assigned Numbers Authority (IANA)* assigns port numbers. IANA is a standards body that is responsible for assigning various addressing standards.

There are different types of port numbers:

Well Known Ports (Numbers 0 to 1023) - These numbers are reserved for services and applications. They are commonly used for applications such as HTTP (web server) POP3/SMTP (e-mail server) and Telnet. By defining these *well-known ports* for server applications, client applications can be programmed to request a connection to that specific port and its associated service.

Registered Ports (Numbers 1024 to 49151) - These port numbers are assigned to user processes or applications. These processes are primarily individual applications that a user has chosen to install rather than common applications that would receive a Well Known Port. When not used for a server resource, these ports may also be used dynamically selected by a client as its source port.

Dynamic or Private Ports (Numbers 49152 to 65535) - Also known as Ephemeral Ports, these are usually assigned dynamically to client applications when initiating a connection. It is not very common for a client to connect to a service using a Dynamic or Private Port (although some peer-to-peer file sharing programs do).

Using both TCP and UDP

Some applications may use both TCP and UDP. For example, the low overhead of UDP enables DNS to serve many client requests very quickly. Sometimes, however, sending the requested information may require the reliability of TCP. In this case, the well known port number of 53 is used by both protocols with this service.

Links

A current list of port numbers can be found at http://www.iana.org/assignments/port-numbers.

Refer to **Figure** in online course

Sometimes it is necessary to know which active TCP connections are open and running on a networked host. **Netstat** is an important network utility that can be used to verify those connections. **Netstat** lists the protocol in use, the local address and port number, the foreign address and port number, and the state of the connection.

Unexplained TCP connections can pose a major security threat. This is because they can indicate that something or someone is connected to the local host. Additionally, unnecessary TCP connections can consume valuable system resources thus slowing down the host's performance. **Netstat** should be used to examine the open connections on a host when performance appears to be compromised.

Many useful options are available for the **netstat** command.

4.1.6 Segmentation and Reassembly - Divide and Conquer

Refer to
Figure
in online course

A previous chapter explained how PDUs are built by passing data from an application down through the various protocols to create a PDU that is then transmitted on the medium. At the destination host, this process is reversed until the data can be passed up to the application.

Some applications transmit large amounts of data - in some cases, many gigabytes. It would be impractical to send all of this data in one large piece. No other network traffic could be transmitted while this data was being sent. A large piece of data could take minutes or even hours to send. In addition, if there were any error, the entire data file would have to be lost or resent. Network devices would not have memory buffers large enough to store this much data while it is transmitted or received. The limit varies depending on the networking technology and specific physical medium being in use.

Dividing application data into pieces both ensures that data is transmitted within the limits of the media and that data from different applications can be multiplexed on to the media.

TCP and UDP Handle Segmentation Differently.

In TCP, each segment header contains a sequence number. This sequence number allows the Transport layer functions on the destination host to reassemble segments in the order in which they were transmitted. This ensures that the destination application has the data in the exact form the sender intended.

Although services using UDP also track the conversations between applications, they are not concerned with the order in which the information was transmitted, or in maintaining a connection. There is no sequence number in the UDP header. UDP is a simpler design and generates less overhead than TCP, resulting in a faster transfer of data.

Information may arrive in a different order than it was transmitted because different packets may take different paths through the network. An application that uses UDP must tolerate the fact that data may not arrive in the order in which it was sent.

Refer to **Packet
Tracer Activity**
for this chapter

In this activity, you will "look inside" packets to see how DNS and HTTP use port numbers.

4.2 The TCP Protocol - Communicating with Reliability

4.2.1 TCP - Making Conversations Reliable

Refer to
Figure
in online course

The key distinction between TCP and UDP is reliability. The reliability of TCP communication is performed using connection-oriented sessions. Before a host using TCP sends data to another host, the Transport layer initiates a process to create a connection with the destination. This connection enables the tracking of a session, or communication stream between the hosts. This process ensures that each host is aware of and prepared for the communication. A complete TCP conversation requires the establishment of a session between the hosts in both directions.

After a session has been established, the destination sends acknowledgements to the source for the segments that it receives. These acknowledgements form the basis of reliability within the TCP session. As the source receives an acknowledgement, it knows that the data has been successfully delivered and can quit tracking that data. If the source does not receive an acknowledgement within a predetermined amount of time, it retransmits that data to the destination.

Part of the additional overhead of using TCP is the network traffic generated by acknowledgements and retransmissions. The establishment of the sessions creates overhead in the form of additional segments being exchanged. There is also additional overhead on the individual hosts created by the necessity to keep track of which segments are awaiting acknowledgement and by the re-transmission process.

This reliability is achieved by having fields in the TCP segment, each with a specific function, as shown in the figure. These fields will be discussed later in this section.

4.2.2 TCP Server Processes

Refer to **Figure** in online course

As discussed in the previous chapter, application processes run on servers. These processes wait until a client initiates communication with a request for information or other services.

Each application process running on the server is configured to use a port number, either by default or manually by a system administrator. **An individual server cannot have two services assigned to the same port number within the same Transport layer services.** A host running a web server application and a file transfer application cannot have both configured to use the same port (for example, TCP port 8080). When an active server application is assigned to a specific port, that port is considered to be "open" on the server. This means that the Transport layer accepts and processes segments addressed to that port. Any incoming client request addressed to the correct socket is accepted and the data is passed to the server application. There can be many simultaneous ports open on a server, one for each active server application. It is common for a server to provide more than one service, such as a web server and an FTP server, at the same time.

One way to improve security on a server is to restrict server access to only those ports associated with the services and applications that should be accessible to authorized requestors.

The figure shows the typical allocation of source and destination ports in TCP client/server operations.

4.2.3 TCP Connection Establishment and Termination

Refer to **Figure** in online course

When two hosts communicate using TCP, a connection is established before data can be exchanged. After the communication is completed, the sessions are closed and the connection is terminated. The connection and session mechanisms enable TCP's reliability function.

See the figure for the steps to establish and terminate a TCP connection.

The host tracks each data segment within a session and exchanges information about what data is received by each host using the information in the TCP header.

Each connection involves one-way communication streams, or sessions to establish and terminate the TCP process between end devices. To establish the connection, the hosts perform a *three-way handshake*. Control bits in the TCP header indicate the progress and status of the connection. The three-way handshake:

- Establishes that the destination device is present on the network

- Verifies that the destination device has an active service and is accepting requests on the destination port number that the initiating client intends to use for the session

- Informs the destination device that the source client intends to establish a communication session on that port number

In TCP connections, the host serving as a client initiates the session to the server. To understand how the three-way handshake used in the TCP connection process works, it is important to look at the various values that the two hosts exchange. The three steps in TCP connection establishment are:

Step 1. The initiating client sends a segment containing an initial sequence value, which serves as a request to the server to begin a communications session.

Step 2. The server responds with a segment containing an acknowledgement value equal to the received sequence value plus 1, plus its own synchronizing sequence value. The value is one greater than the sequence number because the ACK is always the next expected Byte or Octet. This acknowledgement value enables the client to tie the response back to the original segment that it sent to the server.

Step 3. Initiating client responds with an acknowledgement value equal to the sequence value it received plus one. This completes the process of establishing the connection.

Within the TCP segment header, there are six 1-bit fields that contain control information used to manage the TCP processes. Those fields are:

URG - Urgent pointer field significant

ACK - Acknowledgement field significant

PSH - Push function

RST - Reset the connection

SYN - Synchronize *sequence numbers*

FIN - No more data from sender

These fields are referred to as flags, because the value of one of these fields is only 1 bit and, therefore, has only two values: 1 or 0. When a bit value is set to 1, it indicates what control information is contained in the segment.

Using a four-step process, flags are exchanged to terminate a TCP connection.

4.2.4 TCP Three-Way Handshake

Refer to
Figure
in online course

Using the Wireshark outputs, you can examine the operation of the TCP 3-way handshake:

Step 1

A TCP client begins the three-way handshake by sending a segment with the SYN (Synchronize Sequence Number) control flag set, indicating an initial value in the sequence number field in the header. This initial value for the sequence number, known as the Initial Sequence Number (ISN), is randomly chosen and is used to begin tracking the flow of data from the client to the server for this session. The ISN in the header of each segment is increased by one for each byte of data sent from the client to the server as the data conversation continues.

As shown in the figure, output from a protocol analyzer shows the SYN control flag and the relative sequence number.

The SYN control flag is set and the relative sequence number is at 0. Although the protocol analyzer in the graphic indicates the relative values for the sequence and acknowledgement numbers, the true values are 32 bit binary numbers. We can determine the actual numbers sent in the segment headers by examining the Packet Bytes pane. Here you can see the four bytes represented in *hexadecimal*.

Refer to
Figure
in online course

Step 2

The TCP server needs to acknowledge the receipt of the SYN segment from the client to establish the session from the client to the server. To do so, the server sends a segment back to the client with the ACK flag set indicating that the Acknowledgment number is significant. With this flag set in the segment, the client recognizes this as an acknowledgement that the server received the SYN from the TCP client.

The value of the *acknowledgment* number field is equal to the client initial sequence number plus 1. This establishes a session from the client to the server. The ACK flag will remain set for the balance of the session. Recall that the conversation between the client and the server is actually two one-way sessions: one from the client to the server, and the other from the server to the client. In this second step of the three-way handshake, the server must initiate the response from the server to the client. To start this session, the server uses the SYN flag in the same way that the client did. It sets the SYN control flag in the header to establish a session from the server to the client. The SYN flag indicates that the initial value of the sequence number field is in the header. This value will be used to track the flow of data in this session from the server back to the client.

As shown in the figure, the protocol analyzer output shows that the ACK and SYN control flags are set and the relative sequence and acknowledgement numbers are shown.

Refer to
Figure
in online course

Step 3

Finally, the TCP client responds with a segment containing an ACK that is the response to the TCP SYN sent by the server. There is no user data in this segment. The value in the acknowledgment number field contains one more than the initial sequence number received from the server. Once both sessions are established between client and server, all additional segments exchanged in this communication will have the ACK flag set.

As shown in the figure, the protocol analyzer output shows the ACK control flag set and the relative sequence and acknowledgement numbers are shown.

Security can be added to the data network by:

- Denying the establishment of TCP sessions
- Only allowing sessions to be established for specific services
- Only allowing traffic as a part of already established sessions

This security can be implemented for all TCP sessions or only for selected sessions.

4.2.5 TCP Session Termination

Refer to
Figure
in online course

To close a connection, the *FIN (Finish)* control flag in the segment header must be set. To end each one-way TCP session, a two-way handshake is used, consisting of a FIN segment and an ACK segment. Therefore, to terminate a single conversation supported by TCP, four exchanges are needed to end both sessions. **Note**: In this explanation, the terms client and server are used in this description as a reference for simplicity, but the termination process can be initiated by any two hosts that complete the session:

Step 1. When the client has no more data to send in the stream, it sends a segment with the FIN flag set.

Step 2. The server sends an ACK to acknowledge the receipt of the FIN to terminate the session from client to server.

Step 3. The server sends a FIN to the client, to terminate the server to client session.

Step 4. The client responds with an ACK to acknowledge the FIN from the server.

When the client end of the session has no more data to transfer, it sets the FIN flag in the header of a segment. Next, the server end of the connection will send a normal segment containing data with the ACK flag set using the acknowledgment number, confirming that all the bytes of data have been received. When all segments have been acknowledged, the session is closed.

The session in the other direction is closed using the same process. The receiver indicates that there is no more data to send by setting the FIN flag in the header of a segment sent to the source. A return acknowledgement confirms that all bytes of data have been received and that session is, in turn, closed.

As shown in the figure, the FIN and ACK control flags are set in the segment header, thereby closing a HTTP session.

It is also possible to terminate the connection by a three-way handshake. When the client has no more data to send, it sends a FIN to the server. If the server also has no more data to send, it can reply with both the FIN and ACK flags set, combining two steps into one. The client replies with an ACK.

Refer to **Packet Tracer Activity** for this chapter

In this activity, you will study the TCP 3-way handshake for session establishment and the TCP process for session termination. Many application protocols use TCP, and visualizing the session establishment and termination processes with Packet Tracer will deepen your understanding.

4.3 Managing TCP Sessions

4.3.1 TCP Segment Reassembly

Refer to **Figure** in online course

Resequencing Segments to Order Transmitted

When services send data using TCP, segments may arrive at their destination out of order. For the original message to be understood by the recipient, the data in these segments is reassembled into the original order. Sequence numbers are assigned in the header of each packet to achieve this goal.

During session setup, an initial sequence number (ISN) is set. This initial sequence number represents the starting value for the bytes for this session that will be transmitted to the receiving application. As data is transmitted during the session, the sequence number is incremented by the number of bytes that have been transmitted. This tracking of data byte enables each segment to be uniquely identified and acknowledged. Missing segments can be identified.

Segment sequence numbers enable reliability by indicating how to reassemble and reorder received segments, as shown in the figure.

The receiving TCP process places the data from a segment into a receiving buffer. Segments are placed in the proper sequence number order and passed to the Application layer when reassembled. Any segments that arrive with noncontiguous sequence numbers are held for later processing. Then, when the segments with the missing bytes arrive, these segments are processed.

4.3.2 TCP Acknowledgement with Windowing

Refer to **Figure** in online course

Confirming Receipt of Segments

One of TCP's functions is making sure that each segment reaches its destination. The TCP services on the destination host acknowledge the data that it has received to the source application.

The segment header sequence number and acknowledgement number are used together to confirm receipt of the bytes of data contained in the segments. The sequence number is the relative number of bytes that have been transmitted in this session plus 1 (which is the number of the first data byte in the current segment). TCP uses the acknowledgement number in segments sent back to the source to indicate the next byte in this session that the receiver expects to receive. This is called *expectational acknowledgement*.

The source is informed that the destination has received all bytes in this data stream up to, but not including, the byte indicated by the acknowledgement number. The sending host is expected to send a segment that uses a sequence number that is equal to the acknowledgement number.

Remember, each connection is actually two one-way sessions. Sequence numbers and acknowledgement numbers are being exchanged in both directions.

In the example in the figure, the host on the left is sending data to the host on the right. It sends a segment containing 10 bytes of data for this session and a sequence number equal to 1 in the header.

The receiving host on the right receives the segment at Layer 4 and determines that the sequence number is 1 and that it has 10 bytes of data. The host then sends a segment back to the host on the left to acknowledge the receipt of this data. In this segment, the host sets the acknowledgement number to 11 to indicate that the next byte of data it expects to receive in this session is byte number 11. Note, the Ack. value in the source host stays 1 to indicate that the segment is part of an ongoing conversation and the number in the Acknowledgment Number field is valid.

When the sending host on the left receives this acknowledgement, it can now send the next segment containing data for this session starting with byte number 11.

Looking at this example, if the sending host had to wait for acknowledgement of the receipt of each 10 bytes, the network would have a lot of overhead. To reduce the overhead of these acknowledgements, multiple segments of data can be sent before and acknowledged with a single TCP message in the opposite direction. This acknowledgement contains an acknowledgement number based on the total number of bytes received in the session.

For example, starting with a sequence number of 2000, if 10 segments of 1000 bytes each were received, an acknowledgement number of 12000 would be returned to the source.

The amount of data that a source can transmit before an acknowledgement must be received is called the *window size*. Window Size is a field in the TCP header that enables the management of lost data and flow control.

4.3.3 TCP Retransmission

Refer to **Figure** in online course

Handling Segment Loss

No matter how well designed a network is, data loss will occasionally occur. Therefore, TCP provides methods of managing these segment losses. Among these is a mechanism to retransmit segments with unacknowledged data.

A destination host service using TCP usually only acknowledges data for contiguous sequence bytes. If one or more segments are missing, only the data in the segments that complete the stream are acknowledged.

For example, if segments with sequence numbers 1500 to 3000 and 3400 to 3500 were received, the acknowledgement number would be 3001. This is because there are segments with the sequence numbers 3001 to 3399 that have not been received.

When TCP at the source host has not received an acknowledgement after a predetermined amount of time, it will go back to the last acknowledgement number that it received and retransmit data from that point forward.

The retransmission process is not specified by the RFC, but is left up to the particular implementation of TCP.

For a typical TCP implementation, a host may transmit a segment, put a copy of the segment in a retransmission queue, and start a timer. When the data acknowledgment is received, the segment is deleted from the queue. If the acknowledgment is not received before the timer expires, the segment is retransmitted.

The animation demonstrates the retransmission of lost segments.

Hosts today may also employ an optional feature called *Selective Acknowledgements*. If both hosts support Selective Acknowledgements, it is possible for the destination to acknowledge bytes in discontinuous segments and the host would only need to retransmit the missing data.

4.3.4 TCP Congestion Control - Minimizing Segment Loss

Flow Control

Refer to **Figure** in online course

TCP also provides mechanisms for flow control. Flow control assists the reliability of TCP transmission by adjusting the effective rate of data flow between the two services in the session. When the source is informed that the specified amount of data in the segments is received, it can continue sending more data for this session.

This Window Size field in the TCP header specifies the amount of data that can be transmitted before an acknowledgement must be received. The initial window size is determined during the session startup via the three-way handshake.

TCP feedback mechanism adjusts the effective rate of data transmission to the maximum flow that the network and destination device can support without loss. TCP attempts to manage the rate of transmission so that all data will be received and retransmissions will be minimized.

See the figure for a simplified representation of window size and acknowledgements. In this example, the initial window size for a TCP session represented is set to 3000 bytes. When the sender has transmitted 3000 bytes, it waits for an acknowledgement of these bytes before transmitting more segments in this session.

Once the sender has received this acknowledgement from the receiver, the sender can transmit an additional 3000 bytes.

During the delay in receiving the acknowledgement, the sender will not be sending any additional segments for this session. In periods when the network is congested or the resources of the receiving host are strained, the delay may increase. As this delay grows longer, the effective transmission rate of the data for this session decreases. The slowdown in data rate helps reduce the resource contention.

Refer to **Figure** in online course

Reducing Window Size

Another way to control the data flow is to use dynamic window sizes. When network resources are constrained, TCP can reduce the window size to require that received segments be acknowledged more frequently. This effectively slows down the rate of transmission because the source waits for data to be acknowledged more frequently.

The TCP receiving host sends the window size value to the sending TCP to indicate the number of bytes that it is prepared to receive as a part of this session. If the destination needs to slow down the rate of communication because of limited buffer memory, it can send a smaller window size value to the source as part of an acknowledgement.

As shown in the figure, if a receiving host has congestion, it may respond to the sending host with a segment with a reduced window size. In this graphic, there was a loss of one of the segments. The receiver changed the window field in the TCP header of the returning segments in this conversation from 3000 down to 1500. This caused the sender to reduce the window size to 1500.

After periods of transmission with no data losses or constrained resources, the receiver will begin to increase the window field. This reduces the overhead on the network because fewer acknowledgments need to be sent. Window size will continue to increase until there is data loss, which will cause the window size to be decreased.

This dynamic increasing and decreasing of window size is a continuous process in TCP, which determines the optimum window size for each TCP session. In highly efficient networks, window sizes may become very large because data is not being lost. In networks where the underlying infrastructure is being stressed, the window size will likely remain small.

Links

Details of TCP's various congestion management features can be found in RFC 2581.

http://www.ietf.org/rfc/rfc2581.txt

4.4 The UDP Protocol - Communicating with Low Overhead

4.4.1 UDP - Low Overhead vs. Reliability

Refer to **Figure** in online course

UDP is a simple protocol that provides the basic Transport layer functions. It has a much lower overhead than TCP, since it is not connection-oriented and does not provide the sophisticated retransmission, sequencing, and flow control mechanisms.

This does not mean that applications that use UDP are always unreliable. It simply means that these functions are not provided by the Transport layer protocol and must be implemented elsewhere if required.

Although the total amount of UDP traffic found on a typical network is often relatively low, key Application layer protocols that use UDP include:

- Domain Name System (DNS)
- Simple Network Management Protocol (SNMP)
- Dynamic Host Configuration Protocol (DHCP)
- Routing Information Protocol (RIP)
- Trivial File Transfer Protocol (TFTP)
- Online games

Some applications, such as online games or VoIP, can tolerate some loss of some data. If these applications used TCP, they may experience large delays while TCP detects data loss and retransmits data. These delays would be more detrimental to the application than small data losses. Some applications, such as DNS, will simply retry the request if they do not receive a response, and therefore they do not need TCP to guarantee the message delivery.

The low overhead of UDP makes it very desirable for such applications.

4.4.2 UDP Datagram Reassembly

Refer to **Figure** in online course

Because UDP is connectionless, sessions are not established before communication takes place as they are with TCP. UDP is said to be transaction-based. In other words, when an application has data to send, it simply sends the data.

Many applications that use UDP send small amounts of data that can fit in one segment. However, some applications will send larger amounts of data that must be split into multiple segments. The

UDP PDU is referred to as a *datagram*, although the terms *segment* and *datagram* are sometimes used interchangeably to describe a Transport layer PDU.

When multiple datagrams are sent to a destination, they may take different paths and arrive in the wrong order. UDP does not keep track of sequence numbers the way TCP does. UDP has no way to reorder the datagrams into their transmission order. See the figure.

Therefore, UDP simply reassembles the data in the order that it was received and forwards it to the application. If the sequence of the data is important to the application, the application will have to identify the proper sequence of the data and determine how the data should be processed.

4.4.3 UDP Server Processes and Requests

Refer to
Figure
in online course

Like TCP-based applications, UDP-based server applications are assigned Well Known or Registered port numbers. When these applications or processes are running, they will accept the data matched with the assigned port number. When UDP receives a datagram destined for one of these ports, it forwards the application data to the appropriate application based on its port number.

4.4.4 UDP Client Processes

Refer to
Figure
in online course

As with TCP, client/server communication is initiated by a client application that is requesting data from a server process. The UDP client process randomly selects a port number from the dynamic range of port numbers and uses this as the source port for the conversation. The destination port will usually be the Well Known or Registered port number assigned to the server process.

Randomized source port numbers also help with security. If there is a predictable pattern for destination port selection, an intruder can more easily simulate access to a client by attempting to connect to the port number most likely to be open.

Because there is no session to be created with UDP, as soon as the data is ready to be sent and the ports identified, UDP can form the datagram and pass it to the Network layer to be addressed and sent on the network.

Remember, once a client has chosen the source and destination ports, the same pair of ports is used in the header of all datagrams used in the transaction. For the data returning to the client from the server, the source and destination port numbers in the datagram header are reversed.

Refer to **Packet Tracer Activity** for this chapter

In this activity, how DNS uses UDP is examined.

4.5 Lab Activities

4.5.1 Observing TCP and UDP using Netstat

Refer to
Lab Activity
for this chapter

In this lab, you will examine the **netstat** (network statistics utility) command on a host computer, and adjust **netstat** output options to analyze and understand TCP/IP Transport layer protocol status.

4.5.2 TCP/IP Transport Layer Protocols, TCP and UDP

Refer to
Lab Activity
for this chapter

In this lab, you will use Wireshark to capture and identify TCP header fields and operation during an FTP session and UDP header fields and operation during a TFTP session.

4.5.3 Application and Transport Layer Protocols

Refer to
Lab Activity
for this chapter

In this lab, you will use Wireshark to monitor and analyze client application (FTP and HTTP) communications between a server and clients.

Refer to **Packet Tracer Activity** for this chapter

In this activity, you will use Packet Tracer's Simulation mode to capture and analyze packets a web request using a URL.

Summary and Review

Refer to
Figure
in online course

The Transport layer provides for data network needs by:

- Dividing data received from an application into segments

- Adding a header to identify and manage each segment

- Using the header information to reassemble the segments back into application data

- Passing the assembled data to the correct application

UDP and TCP are common Transport layer protocols.

UDP datagrams and TCP segments have headers prefixed to the data that include a source port number and destination port number. These port numbers enable data to be directed to the correct application running on the destination computer.

TCP does not pass any data to the network until it knows that the destination is ready to receive it. TCP then manages the flow of the data and resends any data segments that are not acknowledged as being received at the destination. TCP uses mechanisms of handshaking, timers and acknowledgements, and dynamic windowing to achieve these reliable features. This reliability does, however, impose overhead on the network in terms of much larger segment headers and more network traffic between the source and destination managing the data transport.

If the application data needs to be delivered across the network quickly, or if network bandwidth cannot support the overhead of control messages being exchanged between the source and the destination systems, UDP would be the developer's preferred Transport layer protocol. Because UDP does not track or acknowledge the receipt of datagrams at the destination - it just passes received datagrams to the Application layer as they arrive - and does not resend lost datagrams. However, this does not necessarily mean that the communication itself is unreliable; there may be mechanisms in the Application layer protocols and services that process lost or delayed datagrams if the application has these requirements.

The choice of Transport layer protocol is made by the developer of the application to best meet the user requirements. The developer bears in mind, though, that the other layers all play a part in data network communications and will influence its performance.

Refer to
Figure
in online course

In this activity, a process which occurs every time you request a web page on Internet - the interaction of DNS, HTTP, UDP, and TCP - is examined in depth.

Refer to **Packet
Tracer Activity**
for this chapter

Packet Tracer Skills Integration Instructions (PDF)

To Learn More

Refer to
Figure
in online course

Reflection Questions

Discuss the requirements of an Application Layer application that would determine whether the developer selected UDP or TCP as the Transport Layer protocol to be used.

If a network application required its data to be delivered reliably, discuss how UDP could be used as the Transport Layer protocol and under what circumstances this would be used.

Links

Introduction to internetworking

http://www.cisco.com/en/US/docs/internetworking/technology/handbook/Intro-to-Internet.html

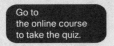

Go to
the online course
to take the quiz.

Chapter Quiz

Take the chapter quiz to test your knowledge.

Your Chapter Notes

CHAPTER 5

OSI Network Layer

Chapter Introduction

We have seen how network applications and services on one end device can communicate with applications and services running on another end device.

Next, as shown in the figure, we will consider how this data is communicated across the network - from the originating end device (or host) to the destination host - in an efficient way.

The protocols of the OSI model Network layer specify addressing and processes that enable Transport layer data to be packaged and transported. The Network layer encapsulation allows its contents to be passed to the destination within a network or on another network with minimum overhead.

This chapter focuses on the role of the Network layer - examining how it divides networks into groups of hosts to manage the flow of data packets within a network. We also consider how communication between networks is facilitated. This communication between networks is called routing.

Learning Objectives

Upon completion of this chapter, you will be able to:

- Identify the role of the Network layer as it describes communication from one end device to another end device.

- Examine the most common Network layer protocol, Internet Protocol (IP), and its features for providing connectionless and best-effort service.

- Understand the principles used to guide the division, or grouping, of devices into networks.

- Understand the *hierarchical addressing* of devices and how this allows communication between networks.

- Understand the fundamentals of routes, *next-hop* addresses, and packet forwarding to a destination network.

5.1 IPv4

5.1.1 Network Layer - Communication from Host to Host

The Network layer, or OSI Layer 3, provides services to exchange the individual pieces of data over the network between identified end devices. To accomplish this end-to-end transport, Layer 3 uses four basic processes:

- Addressing

- Encapsulation

- Routing

Refer to
Figure
in online course

■ Decapsulation

Refer to
Figure
in online course

The animation in the figure demonstrates the exchange of data.

Addressing

First, the Network layer must provide a mechanism for addressing these end devices. If individual pieces of data are to be directed to an end device, that device must have a unique address. In an IPv4 network, when this address is added to a device, the device is then referred to as a host.

Encapsulation

Second, the Network layer must provide encapsulation. Not only must the devices be identified with an address, the individual pieces - the Network layer PDUs - must also contain these addresses. During the encapsulation process, Layer 3 receives the Layer 4 PDU and adds a Layer 3 header, or label, to create the Layer 3 PDU. When referring to the Network layer, we call this PDU a packet. When a packet is created, the header must contain, among other information, the address of the host to which it is being sent. This address is referred to as the *destination address*. The Layer 3 header also contains the address of the originating host. This address is called the *source address*.

After the Network layer completes its encapsulation process, the packet is sent down to the Data Link layer to be prepared for transportation over the media.

Routing

Next, the Network layer must provide services to direct these packets to their destination host. The source and destination hosts are not always connected to the same network. In fact, the packet might have to travel through many different networks. Along the way, each packet must be guided through the network to reach its final destination. **Intermediary devices that connect the networks are called routers. The role of the router is to select paths for and direct packets toward their destination. This process is known as routing.**

During the routing through an internetwork, the packet may traverse many intermediary devices. Each route that a packet takes to reach the next device is called a *hop*. As the packet is forwarded, its contents (the Transport layer PDU), remain intact until the destination host is reached.

Decapsulation

Finally, the packet arrives at the destination host and is processed at Layer 3. The host examines the destination address to verify that the packet was addressed to this device. If the address is correct, the packet is decapsulated by the Network layer and the Layer 4 PDU contained in the packet is passed up to the appropriate service at Transport layer.

Unlike the Transport layer (OSI Layer 4), which manages the data transport between the processes running on each end host, **Network layer protocols specify the packet structure and processing used to carry the data from one host to another host**. Operating without regard to the application data carried in each packet allows the Network layer to carry packets for multiple types of communications between multiple hosts.

Refer to
Figure
in online course

Network Layer Protocols

Protocols implemented at the Network layer that carry user data include:

■ Internet Protocol version 4 (IPv4)

■ Internet Protocol version 6 (*IPv6*)

■ Novell Internetwork Packet Exchange (IPX)

- AppleTalk

- Connectionless Network Service (CLNS/DECNet)

The Internet Protocol (IPv4 and IPv6) is the most widely-used Layer 3 data carrying protocol and will be the focus of this course. Discussion of the other protocols will be minimal.

5.1.2 The IP v4 Protocol - Example Network Layer Protocol

Refer to **Figure** in online course

Role of IPv4

As shown in the figure, the Network layer services implemented by the TCP/IP protocol suite are the Internet Protocol (IP). Version 4 of IP (IPv4) is currently the most widely-used version of IP. It is the only Layer 3 protocol that is used to carry user data over the Internet and is the focus of the CCNA. Therefore, it will be the example we use for Network layer protocols in this course.

IP version 6 (IPv6) is developed and being implemented in some areas. IPv6 will operate alongside IPv4 and may replace it in the future. The services provided by IP, as well as the packet header structure and contents, are specified by either IPv4 protocol or IPv6 protocol. These services and packet structure are used to encapsulate UDP datagrams or TCP segments for their trip across an internetwork.

The characteristics of each protocol are different. Understanding these characteristics will allow you to understand the operation of the services described by this protocol.

The Internet Protocol was designed as a protocol with low overhead. It provides only the functions that are necessary to deliver a packet from a source to a destination over an interconnected system of networks. The protocol was not designed to track and manage the flow of packets. These functions are performed by other protocols in other layers.

IPv4 basic characteristics:

- Connectionless - No connection is established before sending data packets.

- Best Effort (unreliable) - No overhead is used to guarantee packet delivery.

- Media Independent - Operates independently of the medium carrying the data.

5.1.3 The IP v4 Protocol - Connectionless

Refer to **Figure** in online course

Connectionless Service

An example of connectionless communication is sending a letter to someone without notifying the recipient in advance. As shown in the figure, the postal service still takes the letter and delivers it to the recipient. Connectionless data communications works on the same principle. IP packets are sent without notifying the end host that they are coming.

Connection-oriented protocols, such as TCP, require that control data be exchanged to establish the connection as well as additional fields in the PDU header. Because IP is connectionless, it requires no initial exchange of control information to establish an end-to-end connection before packets are forwarded, nor does it require additional fields in the PDU header to maintain this connection. This process greatly reduces the overhead of IP.

Connectionless packet delivery may, however, result in packets arriving at the destination out of sequence. If out-of-order or missing packets create problems for the application using the data, then upper layer services will have to resolve these issues.

5.1.4 The IP v4 Protocol - Best Effort

Refer to
Figure
in online course

Best Effort Service (unreliable)

The IP protocol does not burden the IP service with providing reliability. Compared to a reliable protocol, the IP header is smaller. Transporting these smaller headers requires less overhead. Less overhead means less delay in delivery. This characteristic is desirable for a Layer 3 protocol.

The mission of Layer 3 is to transport the packets between the hosts while placing as little burden on the network as possible. Layer 3 is not concerned with or even aware of the type of communication contained inside of a packet. This responsibility is the role of the upper layers as required. The upper layers can decide if the communication between services needs reliability and if this communication can tolerate the overhead reliability requires.

IP is often referred to as an unreliable protocol. Unreliable in this context does not mean that IP works properly sometimes and does not function well at other times. Nor does it mean that it is unsuitable as a data communications protocol. **Unreliable means simply that IP does not have the capability to manage, and recover from, undelivered or corrupt packets.**

Since protocols at other layers can manage reliability, IP is allowed to function very efficiently at the Network layer. If we included reliability overhead in our Layer 3 protocol, then communications that do not require connections or reliability would be burdened with the bandwidth consumption and delay produced by this overhead. In the TCP/IP suite, the Transport layer can choose either TCP or UDP, based on the needs of the communication. As with all layer isolation provided by network models, leaving the reliability decision to the Transport layer makes IP more adaptable and accommodating for different types of communication.

The header of an IP packet does not include fields required for reliable data delivery. There are no acknowledgments of packet delivery. There is no error control for data. Nor is there any form of packet tracking; therefore, there is no possibility for packet retransmissions.

5.1.5 The IP v4 Protocol - Media Independent

Refer to
Figure
in online course

Media Independent

The Network layer is also not burdened with the characteristics of the media on which packets will be transported. IPv4 and IPv6 operate independently of the media that carry the data at lower layers of the protocol stack. As shown in the figure, any individual IP packet can be communicated electrically over cable, as optical signals over fiber, or wirelessly as radio signals.

It is the responsibility of the OSI Data Link layer to take an IP packet and prepare it for transmission over the communications medium. This means that the transport of IP packets is not limited to any particular medium.

There is, however, one major characteristic of the media that the Network layer considers: the maximum size of PDU that each medium can transport. This characteristic is referred to as the *Maximum Transmission Unit (MTU)*. Part of the control communication between the Data Link layer and the Network layer is the establishment of a maximum size for the packet. The Data Link layer passes the MTU upward to the Network layer. The Network layer then determines how large to create the packets.

In some cases, an intermediary device - usually a router - will need to split up a packet when forwarding it from one media to a media with a smaller MTU. This process is called *fragmenting the packet* or *fragmentation*.

Links

RFC-791 http://www.ietf.org/rfc/rfc0791.txt

5.1.6 IP v4 Packet - Packaging the Transport Layer PDU

Refer to
Figure
in online course

IPv4 encapsulates, or packages, the Transport layer segment or datagram so that the network can deliver it to the destination host. Click the steps in the figure to see this process. The IPv4 encapsulation remains in place from the time the packet leaves the Network layer of the originating host until it arrives at the Network layer of the destination host.

The process of encapsulating data by layer enables the services at the different layers to develop and scale without affecting other layers. This means that Transport layer segments can be readily packaged by existing Network layer protocols, such as IPv4 and IPv6 or by any new protocol that might be developed in the future.

Routers can implement these different Network layer protocols to operate concurrently over a network to and from the same or different hosts. The routing performed by these intermediary devices only considers the contents of the packet header that encapsulates the segment.

In all cases, the data portion of the packet - that is, the encapsulated Transport layer PDU - remains unchanged during the Network layer processes.

Links

RFC-791 http://www.ietf.org/rfc/rfc0791.txt

5.1.7 IP v4 Packet Header

Refer to
Figure
in online course

As shown in the figure, an IPv4 protocol defines many different fields in the packet header. These fields contain *binary values* that the IPv4 services reference as they forward packets across the network.

This course will consider these 6 key fields:

- IP Source Address
- IP Destination Address
- Time-to-Live (TTL)
- Type-of-Service (ToS)
- Protocol
- Fragment Offset

Key IPv4 Header Fields

Roll over each field on the graphic to see its purpose.

IP Destination Address

The IP Destination Address field contains a 32-bit binary value that represents the packet destination Network layer host address.

IP Source Address

The IP Source Address field contains a 32-bit binary value that represents the packet source Network layer host address.

Time-to-Live

The Time-to-Live (TTL) is an 8-bit binary value that indicates the remaining "life" of the packet. The TTL value is decreased by at least one each time the packet is processed by a router (that is, each hop). When the value becomes zero, the router discards or drops the packet and it is removed from the network data flow. This mechanism prevents packets that cannot reach their destination from being forwarded indefinitely between routers in a *routing loop*. If routing loops were permitted to continue, the network would become congested with data packets that will never reach their destination. Decrementing the TTL value at each hop ensures that it eventually becomes zero and that the packet with the expired TTL field will be dropped.

Protocol

This 8-bit binary value indicates the data payload type that the packet is carrying. The Protocol field enables the Network layer to pass the data to the appropriate upper-layer protocol.

Example values are:

- 01 ICMP
- 06 TCP
- 17 UDP

Type-of-Service

The Type-of-Service field contains an 8-bit binary value that is used to determine the priority of each packet. This value enables a Quality-of-Service (QoS) mechanism to be applied to high priority packets, such as those carrying telephony voice data. The router processing the packets can be configured to decide which packet it is to forward first based on the Type-of-Service value.

Fragment Offset

As mentioned earlier, a router may have to fragment a packet when forwarding it from one medium to another medium that has a smaller MTU. When fragmentation occurs, the IPv4 packet uses the Fragment Offset field and the MF flag in the IP header to reconstruct the packet when it arrives at the destination host. The *fragment offset* field identifies the order in which to place the packet fragment in the reconstruction.

More Fragments flag

The More Fragments (MF) flag is a single bit in the Flag field used with the Fragment Offset for the fragmentation and reconstruction of packets. The More Fragments flag bit is set, it means that it is not the last fragment of a packet. When a receiving host sees a packet arrive with the MF = 1, it examines the Fragment Offset to see where this fragment is to be placed in the reconstructed packet. When a receiving host receives a frame with the MF = 0 and a non-zero value in the Fragment offset, it places that fragment as the last part of the reconstructed packet. An unfragmented packet has all zero fragmentation information (MF = 0, fragment offset =0).

Don't Fragment flag

The Don't Fragment (DF) flag is a single bit in the Flag field that indicates that fragmentation of the packet is not allowed. If the Don't Fragment flag bit is set, then fragmentation of this packet is NOT permitted. If a router needs to fragment a packet to allow it to be passed downward to the Data Link layer but the DF bit is set to 1, then the router will discard this packet.

Links:

RFC 791 http://www.ietf.org/rfc/rfc0791.txt

For a complete list of values of IP Protocol Number field

Refer to
Figure
in online course

http://www.iana.org/assignments/protocol-numbers

Other IPv4 Header Fields

Roll over each field on the graphic to see its purpose.

Version - Contains the IP version number (4).

Header Length (IHL) - Specifies the size of the packet header.

Packet Length - This field gives the entire packet size, including header and data, in bytes.

Identification - This field is primarily used for uniquely identifying fragments of an original IP packet.

Header Checksum - The checksum field is used for error checking the packet header.

Options - There is provision for additional fields in the IPv4 header to provide other services but these are rarely used.

Refer to
Figure
in online course

Typical IP Packet

The figure represents a complete IP packet with typical header field values.

Ver = 4; IP version.

IHL = 5; size of header in 32 bit words (4 bytes). This header is 5*4 = 20 bytes, the minimum valid size.

Total Length = 472; size of packet (header and data) is 472 bytes.

Identification = 111; original packet identifier (required if it is later fragmented).

Flag = 0; denotes packet can be fragmented if required.

Fragment Offset = 0; denotes that this packet is not currently fragmented (there is no offset).

Time to Live = 123; denotes the Layer 3 processing time in seconds before the packet is dropped (decremented by at least 1 every time a device processes the packet header).

Protocol = 6; denotes that the data carried by this packet is a TCP segment .

5.2 Networks - Dividing Hosts into Groups

5.2.1 Networks - Separating Hosts into Common Groups

Refer to
Figure
in online course

One of the major roles of the Network layer is to provide a mechanism for addressing hosts. As the number of hosts on the network grows, more planning is required to manage and address the network.

Dividing Networks

Rather than having all hosts everywhere connected to one vast global network, it is more practical and manageable to group hosts into specific networks. Historically, IP-based networks have their roots as one large network. As this single network grew, so did the issues related to its growth. To alleviate these issues, the large network was separated into smaller networks that were interconnected. These smaller networks are often called subnetworks or subnets.

Network and subnet are terms often used interchangeably to refer to any network system made possible by the shared common communication protocols of the TCP/IP model.

Similarly, as our networks grow, they may become too large to manage as a single network. At that point, we need to divide our network. When we plan the division of the network, we need to group together those hosts with common factors into the same network.

As shown in the figure, networks can be grouped based on factors that include:

- Geographic location

- Purpose

- Ownership

Refer to
Figure
in online course

Grouping Hosts Geographically

We can group network hosts together geographically. Grouping hosts at the same location - such as each building on a campus or each floor of a multi-level building - into separate networks can improve network management and operation.

Click the GEOGRAPHIC button on the figure.

Grouping Hosts for Specific Purposes

Users who have similar tasks typically use common software, common tools, and have common traffic patterns. We can often reduce the traffic required by the use of specific software and tools by placing the resources to support them in the network with the users.

The volume of network data traffic generated by different applications can vary significantly. Dividing networks based on usage facilitates the effective allocation of network resources as well as authorized access to those resources. Network professionals need to balance the number of hosts on a network with the amount of traffic generated by the users. For example, consider a business that employs graphic designers who use the network to share very large multimedia files. These files consume most of the available bandwidth for most of the working day. The business also employs salespersons who only logged in once a day to record their sales transactions, which generates minimal network traffic. In this scenario, the best use of network resources would be to create several small networks to which a few designers had access and one larger network that all the salespersons used.

Click the PURPOSE button on the figure.

Grouping Hosts for Ownership

Using an organizational (company, department) basis for creating networks assists in controlling access to the devices and data as well as the administration of the networks. In one large network, it is much more difficult to define and limit the responsibility for the network personnel. Dividing hosts into separate networks provides a boundary for security enforcement and management of each network.

Click the OWNERSHIP button on the figure.

Links:

Network design http://www.cisco.com/en/US/docs/internetworking/design/guide/nd2002.html

5.2.2 Why Separate Hosts Into Networks? - Performance

Refer to
Figure
in online course

As mentioned previously, as networks grow larger they present problems that can be at least partially alleviated by dividing the network into smaller interconnected networks.

Common issues with large networks are:

- Performance degradation

- Security issues

■ Address Management

Improving Performance

Large numbers of hosts connected to a single network can produce volumes of data traffic that may stretch, if not overwhelm, network resources such as bandwidth and routing capability.

Dividing large networks so that hosts who need to communicate are grouped together reduces the traffic across the internetworks.

In addition to the actual data communications between hosts, network management and control traffic (overhead) also increases with the number of hosts. A significant contributor to this overhead can be network broadcasts.

A broadcast is a message sent from one host to **all** other hosts on the network. Typically, a host initiates a broadcast when information about another unknown host is required. Broadcasts are a necessary and useful tool used by protocols to enable data communication on networks. However, large numbers of hosts generate large numbers of broadcasts that consume network bandwidth. And because every other host has to process the broadcast packet it receives, the other productive functions that a host is performing are also interrupted or degraded.

Broadcasts are contained within a network. In this context, a network is also known as a *broadcast domain*. Managing the size of broadcast domains by dividing a network into subnets ensures that network and host performances are not degraded to unacceptable levels.

Roll over Optimize Grouping in the figure to see how to increase performance.

Refer to **Packet Tracer Activity** for this chapter

In this activity, the replacement of a switch with a router breaks one large *broadcast* domain into two more manageable ones.

5.2.3 Why Separate Hosts Into Networks? - Security

Refer to **Figure** in online course

The IP-based network that has become the Internet originally had a small number of trusted users in U.S. government agencies and the research organizations that they sponsored. In this small community, security was not a significant issue.

The situation has changed as individuals, businesses, and organizations have developed their own IP networks that link to the Internet. The devices, services, communications, and data are the property of those network owners. Network devices from other companies and organizations do not need to connect to their network.

Dividing networks based on ownership means that access to and from resources outside each network can be prohibited, allowed, or monitored.

Roll over the Access Granted and Access Denied buttons on the figure to see different levels of security.

Internetwork access within a company or organization can be similarly secured. For example, a college network can be divided into administrative, research, and student subnetworks. Dividing a network based on user access is a means to secure communications and data from unauthorized access by users both within the organization and outside it.

Security between networks is implemented in an intermediary device (a router or firewall appliance) at the perimeter of the network. The firewall function performed by this device permits only known, trusted data to access the network.

Links:

IP network security

http://www.cisco.com/en/US/docs/internetworking/case/studies/cs003.html

5.2.4 Why Separate Hosts Into Networks? - Address Management

Refer to **Figure** in online course

The Internet consists of millions of hosts, each of which is identified by its unique Network layer address. To expect each host to know the address of every other host would impose a processing burden on these network devices that would severely degrade their performance.

Dividing large networks so that hosts who need to communicate are grouped together reduces the unnecessary overhead of all hosts needing to know all addresses.

For all other destinations, the hosts only need to know the address of an intermediary device, to which they send packets for all other destinations addresses. This intermediary device is called a *gateway*. The gateway is a router on a network that serves as an exit from that network.

5.2.5 How Do We Separate Hosts Into Networks? - Hierarchical Addressing

Refer to **Figure** in online course

To be able to divide networks, we need hierarchical addressing. A hierarchical address uniquely identifies each host. It also has levels that assist in forwarding packets across internetworks, which enables a network to be divided based on those levels.

To support data communications between networks over internetworks, Network layer addressing schemes are hierarchical.

As shown in the figure, postal addresses are prime examples of hierarchical addresses.

Consider the case of sending a letter from Japan to an employee working at Cisco Systems, Inc.

The letter would be addressed:

Employee Name

Cisco Systems, Inc.

170 West Tasman Drive

San Jose, CA 95134

USA

When a letter is posted in the country of origin, the postal authority would only look at the destination country and note that the letter was destined for the U.S. No other address details need to be processed at this level.

Upon arrival in the U.S., the post office first looks at the state, California. The city, street, and company name would not be examined if the letter still needed to be forwarded to the correct state. Once in California, the letter would be directed to San Jose. There the local *mail carrier* would take the letter to West Tasman Drive, and then refer to the street address and deliver it to 170. When the letter is actually on Cisco premises, the employee name would be used to forward it to its ultimate destination.

Referring only to the relevant address level (country, state, city, street, number, and employee) at each stage when directing the letter onto the next hop makes this process very efficient. There is no need for each forwarding stage to know the exact location of the destination; the letter was directed in the general direction until the employee's name was finally used at the destination.

Hierarchical Network layer addresses work in much the same way. Layer 3 addresses supply the network portion of the address. Routers forward packets between networks by referring only to the part of the Network layer address that is required to direct the packet toward the destination network. By the time the packet arrives at the destination host network, the whole destination address of the host will have been used to deliver the packet.

If a large network needs to be divided into smaller networks, additional layers of addressing can be created. Using a hierarchical addressing scheme means that the higher levels of the address (similar to the country in the postal address) can be retained, with the middle level denoting the network addresses (state or city) and the lower level the individual hosts.

5.2.6 Dividing the Networks - Networks from Networks

Refer to
Figure
in online course

If a large network has to be divided, additional layers of addressing can be created. Using hierarchical addressing means that the higher levels of the address are retained; with a subnetwork level and then the host level.

The logical 32-bit IPv4 address is hierarchical and is made up of two parts. The first part identifies the network and the second part identifies a host on that network. Both parts are required for a complete IP address.

For convenience IPv4 addresses are divided in four groups of eight bits (octets). Each octet is converted to its decimal value and the complete address written as the four decimal values separated by a dot (period).

For example - 192.168.18.57

In this example, as the figure shows, the first three octets, (192.168.18), can identify the network portion of the address, and the last octet, (57) identifies the host.

This is hierarchical addressing because the network portion indicates the network on which each unique host address is located. Routers only need to know how to reach each network, rather than needing to know the location of each individual host.

With IPv4 hierarchical addressing, the network portion of the address for all hosts in a network is the same. To divide a network, the network portion of the address is extended to use bits from the host portion of the address. These borrowed host bits are then used as network bits to represent the different subnetworks within the range of the original network.

Given that an IPv4 address is 32 bits, when host bits are used to divide a network the more subnetworks created results in fewer hosts for each subnetwork. Regardless of the number of subnetworks created however, all 32 bits are required to identify an individual host.

The number of bits of an address used as the network portion is called the *prefix length*. For example if a network uses 24 bits to express the network portion of an address the prefix is said to be /24. In the devices in an IPv4 network, a separate 32-bit number called a subnet mask indicates the prefix.

Note: Chapter 6 in this course will cover IPv4 network addressing and subnetworking in detail.

Extending the prefix length or subnet mask enables the creation of these subnetworks. In this way network administrators have the flexibility to divide networks to meet different needs, such as location, managing network performance, and security, while ensuring each host has a unique address.

For the purposes of explanation, however in this chapter the first 24 bits of an IPv4 address will be used as the network portion.

Links:

Internet Assigned Numbers Authority

http://www.iana.org/

5.3 Routing - How Our Data Packets are Handled

5.3.1 Device Parameters - Supporting Communication Outside Our Network

Refer to
Figure
in online course

Within a network or a subnetwork, hosts communicate with each other without the need for any Network layer intermediary device. When a host needs to communicate with another network, an intermediary device, or router, acts as a gateway to the other network.

As a part of its configuration, a host has a default gateway address defined. As shown in the figure, this gateway address is the address of a router interface that is connected to the same network as the host.

Keep in mind that it is not feasible for a particular host to know the address of every device on the Internet with which it may have to communicate. To communicate with a device on another network, a host uses the address of this gateway, or default gateway, to forward a packet outside the local network.

The router also needs a route that defines where to forward the packet next. This is called the next-hop address. If a route is available to the router, the router will forward the packet to the next-hop router that offers a path to the destination network.

Links:

RFC 823

http://www.ietf.org/rfc/rfc0823.txt

5.3.2 IP Packets - Carrying Data End to End

Refer to
Figure
in online course

As you know, the role of the Network layer is to transfer data from the host that originates the data to the host that uses it. During encapsulation at the source host, an IP packet is constructed at Layer 3 to transport the Layer 4 PDU. If the destination host is in the same network as the source host, the packet is delivered between the two hosts on the local media without the need for a router.

However, if the destination host and source host are not in the same network, the packet may be carrying a Transport layer PDU across many networks and through many routers. As it does, the information contained within is not altered by any routers when forwarding decisions are made.

At each hop, the forwarding decisions are based on the information in the IP packet header. The packet with its Network Layer encapsulation also is basically intact throughout the complete process, from the source host to the destination host.

If communication is between hosts in different networks, the local network delivers the packet from the source to its gateway router. The router examines the network portion of the packet destination address and forwards the packet to the appropriate interface. If the destination network is *directly connected* to this router, the packet is forwarded directly to that host. If the destination network is not directly connected, the packet is forwarded on to a second router that is the next-hop router.

The packet forwarding then becomes the responsibility of this second router. Many routers or hops along the way may process the packet before reaching the destination.

Click the steps on the figure to follow the path of the IP packet.

Links:

RFC 791 http://www.ietf.org/rfc/rfc0791.txt

RFC 823 http://www.ietf.org/rfc/rfc0823.txt

5.3.3 A Gateway - The Way Out of Our Network

Refer to **Figure** in online course

The gateway, also known as the default gateway, is needed to send a packet out of the local network. If the network portion of the destination address of the packet is different from the network of the originating host, the packet has to be routed outside the original network. To do this, the packet is sent to the gateway. This gateway is a router interface connected to the local network. The gateway interface has a Network layer address that matches the network address of the hosts. The hosts are configured to recognize that address as the gateway.

Default Gateway

The default gateway is configured on a host. On a Windows computer, the Internet Protocol (TCP/IP) Properties tools are used to enter the default gateway IPv4 address. Both the host IPv4 address and the gateway address must have the same network (and subnet, if used) portion of their respective addresses.

Click on the graphic to display the Windows Properties.

Host gateway configuration http://www.microsoft.com/technet/community/columns/cableguy/cg0903.mspx

Refer to **Figure** in online course

Confirming the Gateway and Route

As shown in the figure, the IP address of the default gateway of a host can be viewed by issuing the `ipconfig` or `route print` commands at the command line of a Windows computer. The `route` command is also used in a *Linux* or UNIX host.

Refer to **Figure** in online course

No packet can be forwarded without a route. Whether the packet is originating in a host or being forwarded by an intermediary device, the device must have a route to identify where to forward the packet.

A host must either forward a packet to the host on the local network or to the gateway, as appropriate. To forward the packets, the host must have routes that represent these destinations.

A router makes a forwarding decision for each packet that arrives at the gateway interface. This forwarding process is referred to as routing. To forward a packet to a destination network, the router requires a route to that network. If a route to a destination network does not exist, the packet cannot be forwarded.

The destination network may be a number of routers or hops away from the gateway. The route to that network would only indicate the next-hop router to which the packet is to be forwarded, not the final router. The routing process uses a route to map the destination network address to the next hop and then forwards the packet to this next-hop address.

Links:

RFC 823 http://www.ietf.org/rfc/rfc0823.txt

5.3.4 A Route - The Path to a Network

Refer to
Figure
in online course

A route for packets for remote destinations is added using the default gateway address as the next hop. Although it is not usually done, a host can also have routes manually added through configurations.

Like end devices, routers also add routes for the connected networks to their *routing table*. When a router interface is configured with an IP address and subnet mask, the interface becomes part of that network. The routing table now includes that network as a directly connected network. All other routes, however, must be configured or acquired via a routing protocol. To forward a packet the router must know where to send it. This information is available as routes in a routing table.

The routing table stores information about connected and remote networks. Connected networks are directly attached to one of the router interfaces. These interfaces are the gateways for the hosts on different local networks. Remote networks are networks that are not directly connected to the router. Routes to these networks can be manually configured on the router by the network administrator or learned automatically using dynamic *routing protocols*.

Routes in a routing table have three main features:

- Destination network

- Next-hop

- Metric

The router matches the destination address in the packet header with the destination network of a route in the routing table and forwards the packet to the next-hop router specified by that route. If there are two or more possible routes to the same destination, the metric is used to decide which route appears on the routing table.

As shown in the figure, the routing table in a Cisco router can be examined with the `show ip route` command.

Note: The routing process and the role of metrics are the subject of a later course and will be covered in detail there.

As you know, packets cannot be forwarded by the router without a route. If a route representing the destination network is not on the routing table, the packet will be dropped (that is, not forwarded). The matching route could be either a connected route or a route to a remote network. The router may also use a *default route* to forward the packet. The default route is used when the destination network is not represented by any other route in the routing table.

Refer to
Figure
in online course

Host Routing Table

A host creates the routes used to forward the packets it originates. These routes are derived from the connected network and the configuration of the default gateway.

Hosts automatically add all connected networks to the routes. These routes for the local networks allow packets to be delivered to hosts that are connected to these networks.

Hosts also require a local routing table to ensure that Network layer packets are directed to the correct destination network. Unlike the routing table in a router, which contains both local and remote routes, the local table of the host typically contains its direct connection or connections to the network and its own default route to the gateway. Configuring the default gateway address on the host creates the local default route.

As shown in the figure, the routing table of a computer host can be examined at the command line by issuing the `netstat -r`, `route`, or `route PRINT` commands.

In some circumstances, you may want to indicate more specific routes from a host. You can use the following options for the route command to modify the routing table contents:

```
route ADD
  route DELETE
route CHANGE
```

Links:

RFC 823 http://www.ietf.org/rfc/rfc0823.txt

5.3.5 The Destination Network

Refer to
Figure
in online course

Routing Table Entries

The destination network shown in a routing table entry, called a route, represents a range of host addresses and sometimes a range of network and host addresses.

The hierarchical nature of Layer 3 addressing means that one route entry could refer to a large general network and another entry could refer to a subnet of that same network. When forwarding a packet, the router will select the most specific route.

Returning to the earlier postal addressing example, consider sending the same letter from Japan to 170 West Tasman Drive San Jose, California USA. Which address would you use: "USA" or "San Jose California USA" or "West Tasman Drive San Jose, California USA" or "170 West Tasman Drive San Jose, California USA"?

The fourth and most specific address would be used. However, for another letter where the street number was unknown, the third option would provide the best address match.

In the same way, a packet destined to the subnet of a larger network would be routed using the route to the subnet. However, a packet addressed to a different subnet within the same larger network would be routed using the more general entry.

As shown in the figure, if a packet arrives at a router with the destination address of 10.1.1.55, the router forwards the packet to a next-hop router associated with a route to network 10.1.1.0. If a route to 10.1.1.0 is not listed on the routing, but a route to 10.1.0.0 is available, the packet is forwarded to the next-hop router for that network.

Therefore, the precedence of route selection for the packet going to 10.1.1.55 would be:

Step 1. 10.1.1.0

Step 2. 10.1.0.0

Step 3. 10.0.0.0

Step 4. 0.0.0.0 (Default route if configured)

Step 5. Dropped

Refer to
Figure
in online course

Default Route

A router can be configured to have a default route. A default route is a route that will match all destination networks. In IPv4 networks, the address 0.0.0.0 is used for this purpose. The default route is used to forward packets for which there is no entry in the routing table for the destination network. Packets with a destination network address that does not match a more specific route in the routing table are forwarded to the next-hop router associated with the default route.

Links:

RFC 823 http://www.ietf.org/rfc/rfc0823.txt

5.3.6 The Next Hop - Where the Packet Goes Next

Refer to
Figure
in online course

A next-hop is the address of the device that will process the packet next. For a host on a network, the address of the default gateway (router interface) is the next-hop for all packets destined for another network.

In the routing table of a router, each route lists a next hop for each destination address that is encompassed by the route. As each packet arrives at a router, the destination network address is examined and compared to the routes in the routing table. When a matching route is determined, the next hop address for that route is used to forward of the packet toward its destination. The router then forwards the packet out the interface to which the next-hop router is connected. The next-hop router is the gateway to networks beyond that intermediate destination.

Networks directly connected to a router have no next-hop address because there is no intermediate Layer 3 device between the router and that network. The router can forward packets directly out the interface onto that network to the destination host.

Some routes can have multiple next-hops. This indicates that there are multiple paths to the same destination network. These are parallel routes that the router can use to forward packets.

Links:

RFC 823 http://www.ietf.org/rfc/rfc0823.txt

5.3.7 Packet Forwarding - Moving the Packet Toward its Destination

Refer to
Figure
in online course

Routing is done **packet-by-packet and hop-by-hop**. Each packet is treated independently in each router along the path. At each hop, the router examines the destination IP address for each packet and then checks the routing table for forwarding information.

The router will do one of three things with the packet:

- Forward it to the next-hop router
- Forward it to the destination host
- Drop it

Packet Examination

As an intermediary device, a router processes the packet at the Network layer. However, packets that arrive at a router's interfaces are encapsulated as a Data Link layer (Layer 2) PDU. As show in the figure, the router first discards the Layer 2 encapsulation so that the packet can be examined.

Next Hop Selection

In the router, the destination address in a packet header is examined. If a matching route in the routing table shows that the destination network is directly connected to the router, the packet is forwarded to the interface to which that network is connected. In this case, there is no next-hop. To be placed onto the connected network, the packet has to be first re-encapsulated by the Layer 2 protocol and then forwarded out the interface.

If the route matching the destination network of the packet is a remote network, the packet is forwarded to the indicated interface, encapsulated by the Layer 2 protocol, and sent to the next-hop address.

Refer to
Figure
in online course

Using the Default Route

As shown in the figure, if the routing table does not contain a more specific route entry for an arriving packet, the packet is forwarded to the interface indicated by a default route, if one exists. At this interface, the packet is encapsulated by the Layer 2 protocol and sent to the next-hop router. The default route is also known as the *Gateway of Last Resort*.

This process may occur a number of times until the packet reaches its destination network. The router at each hop knows only the address of the next-hop; it does not know the details of the pathway to the remote destination host. Furthermore, not all packets going to the same destination will be forwarded to the same next-hop at each router. Routers along the way may learn new routes while the communication is taking place and forward later packets to different next-hops.

Default routes are important because the gateway router is not likely to have a route to every possible network on the Internet. If the packet is forwarded using a default route, it should eventually arrive at a router that has a specific route to the destination network. This router may be the router to which this network is attached. In this case, this router will forward the packet over the local network to the destination host.

As a packet passes through the hops in the internetwork, all routers require a route to forward a packet. If, at any router, no route for the destination network is found in the routing table and there is no default route, that packet is dropped.

IP has no provision to return a packet to the previous router if a particular router has nowhere to send the packet. Such a function would detract from the protocol's efficiency and low overhead. Other protocols are used to report such errors.

Links:

RFC 823 http://www.ietf.org/rfc/rfc0823.txt

In this activity, the rules (algorithms) that routers use to make decisions on how to process packets, depending on the state of their routing tables when the packet arrives, are examined.

5.4 Routing Processes: How Routes are Learned

5.4.1 Routing Protocols - Sharing the Routes

Routing requires that every hop, or router, along the path to a packet's destination have a route to forward the packet. Otherwise, the packet is dropped at that hop. Each router in a path does not need a route to all networks. It only needs to know the next hop on the path to the packet's destination network.

The routing table contains the information that a router uses in its packet forwarding decisions. For the routing decisions, the routing table needs to represent the most accurate state of network pathways that the router can access. Out-of-date routing information means that packets may not be forwarded to the most appropriate next-hop, causing delays or packet loss.

This route information can be manually configured on the router or learned dynamically from other routers in the same internetwork. After the interfaces of a router are configured and operational, the network associated with each interface is installed in the routing table as a directly connected route.

Refer to **Figure** in online course

5.4.2 Static Routing

Routes to remote networks with the associated next hops can be manually configured on the router. This is known as *static routing*. A default route can also be statically configured.

If the router is connected to a number of other routers, knowledge of the internetworking structure is required. To ensure that the packets are routed to use the best possible next hops, each known destination network needs to either have a route or a default route configured. Because packets are forwarded at every hop, every router must be configured with static routes to next hops that reflect its location in the internetwork.

Further, if the internetwork structure changes or if new networks become available, these changes have to be manually updated on every router. If updating is not done in a timely fashion, the routing information may be incomplete or inaccurate, resulting in packet delays and possible packet loss.

5.4.3 Dynamic Routing

Although it is essential for all routers in an internetwork to have up-to-date extensive route knowledge, maintaining the routing table by manual static configuration is not always feasible. Therefore, dynamic routing protocols are used. Routing protocols are the set of rules by which routers dynamically share their routing information. As routers become aware of changes to the networks for which they act as the gateway, or changes to links between routers, this information is passed on to other routers. When a router receives information about new or changed routes, it updates its own routing table and, in turn, passes the information to other routers. In this way, all routers have accurate routing tables that are updated dynamically and can learn about routes to remote networks that are many hops way. An example of router sharing routes is shown in the figure.

Refer to **Figure** in online course

Common routing protocols are:

- Routing Information Protocol (RIP)

- Enhanced Interior Gateway Routing Protocol (EIGRP)

- Open Shortest Path First (OSPF)

Although routing protocols provide routers with up-to-date routing tables, there are costs. First, the exchange of route information adds overhead that consumes network bandwidth. This overhead can be an issue, particularly for low bandwidth links between routers. Second, the route information that a router receives is processed extensively by protocols such as EIGRP and OSPF to make routing table entries. This means that routers employing these protocols must have sufficient processing capacity to both implement the protocol's algorithms and to perform timely packet routing and forwarding.

Static routing does not produce any network overhead and places entries directly into the routing table; no processing is required by the router. The cost for static routing is administrative - the manual configuration and maintenance of the routing table to ensure efficient and effective routing.

In many internetworks, a combination of static, dynamic, and default routes are used to provide the necessary routes. The configuration of routing protocols on routers is an integral component of the CCNA and will be covered extensively by a later course.

Links:

RFC 823 http://www.ietf.org/rfc/rfc0823.txt

Routing basics http://www.cisco.com/en/US/docs/internetworking/technology/handbook/Routing-Basics.html

Refer to **Packet Tracer Activity** for this chapter

In this activity, you will examine a simple visualization of a dynamic routing protocol in "action."

5.5 Labs

5.5.1 Lab - Examining a Device's Gateway

Refer to
Lab Activity
for this chapter

In this lab you will:

- Examine the purpose of a gateway address.
- Configure network parameters on a Windows computer.
- Troubleshoot a hidden gateway address problem.

Refer to **Packet Tracer Activity**
for this chapter

This Packet Tracer activity will examine the role of the gateway in providing access to remote networks.

5.5.2 Lab - Examining a Route

Refer to
Lab Activity
for this chapter

In this lab you will:

- Use the `route` command to modify a Windows computer route table.
- Use a Windows Telnet client to connect to a Cisco router.
- Examine router routes using basic Cisco IOS commands.

Refer to **Packet Tracer Activity**
for this chapter

In this lab you will use Packet Tracer to examine router routing tables using basic Cisco IOS commands.

Summary

Refer to
Figure
in online course

The most significant Network layer (OSI Layer 3) protocol is the Internet Protocol (IP). IP version 4 (IPv4) is the Network layer protocol that will be used as an example throughout this course.

Layer 3 IP routing does not guarantee reliable delivery or establish a connection before data is transmitted. This connectionless and unreliable communication is fast and flexible, but upper layers must provide mechanisms to guarantee delivery of data if it is needed.

The role of the Network layer is to carry data from one host to another regardless of the type of data. The data is encapsulated in a packet. The packet header has fields that include the destination address of the packet.

Hierarchical Network layer addressing, with network and host portions, facilitates the division of networks in to subnets and enables the network address to be used for forwarding packets toward the destination instead of using each individual host address.

If the destination address is not on the same network as the source host, the packet is passed to the default gateway for forwarding to the destination network. The gateway is an interface of a router that examines the destination address. If the destination network has an entry in its routing table, the router forwards the packet either to a connected network or to the next-hop gateway. If no routing entry exists, the router may forward the packet on to a default route, or drop the packet.

Routing table entries can be configured manually on each router to provide static routing or the routers may communicate route information dynamically between each other using a routing protocol.

Refer to
Figure
in online course

Refer to **Packet
Tracer Activity**
for this chapter

In this activity, you will use a GUI to perform simple router configuration so that IP packets can be routed. This is a key step in building a more complete model of the Exploration lab topology.

Packet Tracer Skills Integration Instructions (PDF)

Reflection Questions

Refer to
Figure
in online course

Discuss how lost data can be re-sent when the Network Layer uses unreliable and connectionless means of packet forwarding.

Discuss the network circumstances in which it would be more advantageous to use static routing instead of dynamic routing protocols.

Links

Introduction to internetworking

http://www.cisco.com/en/US/docs/internetworking/technology/handbook/Intro-to-Internet.html

Go to
the online course
to take the quiz.

Quiz

Take the chapter quiz to test your knowledge.

Your Chapter Notes

CHAPTER 6

Addressing the Network - IPv4

Chapter Introduction

Addressing is a key function of Network layer protocols that enables data communication between hosts on the same network or on different networks. Internet Protocol version 4 (IPv4) provides hierarchical addressing for packets that carry our data.

Designing, implementing and managing an effective IPv4 addressing plan ensures that our networks can operate effectively and efficiently.

This chapter examines in detail the structure of IPv4 addresses and their application to the construction and testing of IP networks and subnetworks.

In this chapter, you will learn to:

- Explain the structure IP addressing and demonstrate the ability to convert between 8-bit binary and decimal numbers.

- Given an IPv4 address, classify by type and describe how it is used in the network.

- Explain how addresses are assigned to networks by ISPs and within networks by administrators.

- Determine the network portion of the host address and explain the role of the subnet mask in dividing networks.

- Given IPv4 addressing information and design criteria, calculate the appropriate addressing components.

- Use common testing utilities to verify and test network connectivity and operational status of the IP protocol stack on a host.

6.1 IPv4 Addresses

6.1.1 The Anatomy of an IPv4 Address

Each device on a network must be uniquely defined. At the Network layer, the packets of the communication need to be identified with the source and destination addresses of the two end systems. With IPv4, this means that each packet has a 32-bit source address and a 32-bit destination address in the Layer 3 header.

These addresses are used in the data network as binary patterns. Inside the devices, *digital logic* is applied for their interpretation. For us in the human network, a string of 32 bits is difficult to interpret and even more difficult to remember. Therefore, we represent IPv4 addresses using *dotted decimal* format.

Dotted Decimal

Refer to
Figure
in online course

Refer to
Figure
in online course

Binary patterns representing IPv4 addresses are expressed as dotted decimals by separating each byte of the binary pattern, called an *octet*, with a dot. It is called an octet because each decimal number represents one byte or 8 bits.

For example, the address:

10101100000100000000010000010100

is expressed in dotted decimal as:

172.16.4.20

Keep in mind that devices use binary logic. The dotted decimal format is used to make it easier for people to use and remember addresses.

Network and Host Portions

For each IPv4 address, some portion of the high-order bits represents the network address. At Layer 3, we define a *network* as a group of hosts that have identical bit patterns in the network address portion of their addresses.

Although all 32 bits define the IPv4 host address, we have a variable number of bits that are called the host portion of the address. The number of bits used in this host portion determines the number of hosts that we can have within the network.

Click the labels in the figure to see the different parts of the address.

For example, if we need to have at least 200 hosts in a particular network, we would need to use enough bits in the host portion to be able to represent at least 200 different bit patterns.

To assign a unique address to 200 hosts, we would use the entire last octet. With 8 bits, a total of 256 different bit patterns can be achieved. This would mean that the bits for the upper three octets would represent the network portion.

Note: Calculating the number of hosts and determining which portion of the 32 bits refers to the network will be covered later in this chapter.

6.1.2 Knowing the Numbers - Binary to Decimal Conversion

Refer to
Figure
in online course

To understand the operation of a device in a network, we need to look at addresses and other data the way the device does - in binary notation. This means that we need to have some skill in binary to decimal conversion.

Data represented in binary may represent many different forms of data to the human network. In this discussion, we refer to binary as it relates to IPv4 addressing. This means that we look at each byte (octet) as a decimal number in the range of 0 to 255.

Positional Notation

Learning to convert binary to decimal requires an understanding of the mathematical basis of a numbering system called *positional notation. Positional notation means that a digit represents different values depending on the position it occupies. More specifically, the value that a digit represents is that value multiplied by the power of the base, or radix*, represented by the position the digit occupies. Some examples will help to clarify how this system works.

For the decimal number 245, the value that the 2 represents is $2*10^2$ (2 times 10 to the power of 2). The 2 is in what we commonly refer to as the "100s" position. Positional notation refers to this position as the base^2 position because the base, or radix, is 10 and the power is 2.

Using positional notation in the base 10 number system, 245 represents:

245 = (2 * 10^2) + (4 * 10^1) + (5 * 10^0)

or

245 = (2 * 100) + (4 * 10) + (5 * 1)

Binary Numbering System

In the binary numbering system, the radix is **2**. Therefore, each position represents increasing powers of 2. In 8-bit binary numbers, the positions represent these quantities:

2^7 2^6 2^5 2^4 2^3 2^2 2^1 2^0

128 64 32 16 8 4 2 1

The base 2 numbering system only has two digits: **0** and **1**.

When we interpret a byte as a decimal number, we have the quantity that position represents if the digit is a 1 and we do not have that quantity if the digit is a **0**, as shown in the figure.

1 1 1 1 1 1 1 1

128 64 32 16 8 4 2 1

A **1** in each position means that we add the value for that position to the total. This is the addition when there is a 1 in each position of an octet. The total is 255.

128 + 64 + 32 + 16 + 8 + 4 + 2 + 1 = 255

A **0** in each position indicates that the value for that position is not added to the total. A **0** in every position yields a total of 0.

0 0 0 0 0 0 0 0

128 64 32 16 8 4 2 1

0 + 0 + 0 + 0 + 0 + 0 + 0 + 0 = 0

Notice in the figure that a different combination of ones and zeros will yield a different decimal value.

See the figure for the steps to convert a binary address to a decimal address.

Refer to
Figure
in online course

In the example, the binary number:

10101100000100000000010000010100

Is converted to:

172.16.4.20

Keep these steps in mind:

- Divide the 32 bits into 4 octets.
- Convert each octet to decimal.
- Add a "dot" between each decimal.

6.1.3 Practicing Binary to Decimal Conversions

Refer to
Figure
in online course

The activity in the figure allows you to practice 8-bit binary conversion as much as necessary. We recommend that you work with this tool until you are able to do the conversion without error.

6.1.4 Knowing the Numbers - Decimal to Binary Conversions

Refer to
Figure
in online course

Not only do we need to be able to convert binary to decimal, we also need to be able to convert decimal to binary. We often need to examine an individual octet of an address that is given in dotted decimal notation. Such is the case when the network bits and host bits divide an octet.

As an example, if a host with the 172.16.4.20 were using 28 bits for the network address, we would need to examine the binary in the last octet to discover that this host is on the network 172.16.4.16. This process of extracting the network address from a host address will be explained later.

Address Values are Between 0 and 255

Because our representation of addresses is limited to decimal values for a single octet, we will only examine the process of converting 8-bit binary to the decimal values of 0 to 255.

To begin the conversion process, we start by determining if the decimal number is equal to or greater than our largest decimal value represented by the *most-significant bit*. In the highest position, we determine if the value is equal to or greater than 128. If the value is smaller than 128, we place a 0 in the 128-bit position and move to the 64-bit position.

If the value in the 128-bit position is larger than or equal to 128, we place a 1 in the 128 position and subtract 128 from the number being converted. We then compare the remainder of this operation to the next smaller value, 64. We continue this process for all the remaining bit positions.

Refer to
Figure
in online course

See the figure for an example of these steps. We convert **172** to **10101100**.

Follow the conversion steps to see how an IP address is converted to binary.

Refer to
Figure
in online course

Conversion Summary

The figure summarizes the entire conversion of **172.16.4.20** from dotted decimal notation to binary notation.

6.1.5 Practicing Decimal to Binary Conversion

Refer to
Figure
in online course

The activity in the figure allows you to practice decimal conversion to 8-bit binary as much as necessary. We recommend that you work with this tool until you are able to do the conversion without error.

6.2 Addresses for Different Purposes

6.2.1 Types of Addresses in an IPv4 Network

Refer to
Figure
in online course

Within the address range of each IPv4 network, we have three types of addresses:

Network address - The address by which we refer to the network

Broadcast address - A special address used to send data to all hosts in the network

Host addresses - The addresses assigned to the end devices in the network

Network Address

The network address is a standard way to refer to a network. For example, we could refer to the network shown in the figure as "the 10.0.0.0 network." This is a much more convenient and descriptive way to refer to the network than using a term like "the first network." All hosts in the 10.0.0.0 network will have the same network bits.

Within the IPv4 address range of a network, the lowest address is reserved for the network address. This address has a **0** for each host bit in the host portion of the address.

Roll over the NETWORK ADDRESS tab in the figure.

Broadcast Address

The IPv4 *broadcast address* is a special address for each network that allows communication to all the hosts in that network. To send data to all hosts in a network, a host can send a single packet that is addressed to the broadcast address of the network.

The broadcast address uses the highest address in the network range. This is the address in which the bits in the host portion are all 1s. For the network 10.0.0.0 with 24 network bits, the broadcast address would be 10.0.0.255. This address is also referred to as the *directed broadcast*.

Roll over the BROADCAST ADDRESS tab in the figure.

Host Addresses

As described previously, every end device requires a unique address to deliver a packet to that host. In IPv4 addresses, we assign the values between the network address and the broadcast address to the devices in that network.

Roll over the HOST ADDRESS tab in the figure.

Refer to **Figure** in online course

Network Prefixes

An important question is: How do we know how many bits represent the network portion and how many bits represent the host portion? When we express an IPv4 network address, we add a prefix length to the network address. **The prefix length is the number of bits in the address that gives us the network portion.** For example, in 172.16.4.0 /24, the **/24** is the prefix length - it tells us that the first 24 bits are the network address. This leaves the remaining 8 bits, the last octet, as the host portion. Later in this chapter, we will learn more about another entity that is used to specify the network portion of an IPv4 address to the network devices. It is called the subnet mask. The subnet mask consists of 32 bits, just as the address does, and uses 1s and 0s to indicate which bits of the address are network bits and which bits are host bits.

Networks are not always assigned a /24 prefix. Depending on the number of hosts on the network, the prefix assigned may be different. Having a different prefix number changes the host range and broadcast address for each network.

Roll over the addresses in the figure to view the results of using different prefixes on an address.

Notice that the network address could remain the same, but the host range and the broadcast address are different for the different prefix lengths. In this figure you can also see that the number of hosts that can be addressed on the network changes as well.

6.2.2 Calculating Network, Hosts and Broadcast Addresses

Refer to **Figure** in online course

At this point, you may be wondering: How do we calculate these addresses? This calculation process requires us to look at these addresses in binary.

In the example network divisions, we need to look at the octet of the address where the prefix divides the network portion from the host portion. In all of these examples, it is the last octet. While this is common, the prefix can also divide any of the octets.

To get started understanding this process of determining the address assignments, let's break some examples down into binary.

See the figure for an example of the address assignment for the 172.16.20.0 /25 network.

In the first box, we see the representation of the network address. With a 25 bit prefix, the last 7 bits are host bits. To represent the network address, all of these host bits are '0'. This makes the last octet of the address 0. This makes the network address 172.16.20.0 /25.

In the second box, we see the calculation of the lowest host address. This is always one greater than the network address. In this case, the last of the seven host bits becomes a '1'. With the lowest bit of host address set to a 1, the lowest host address is 172.16.20.1.

The third box shows the calculation of the broadcast address of the network. Therefore, all seven host bits used in this network are all '1s'. From the calculation, we get 127 in the last octet. This gives us a broadcast address of 172.16.20.127.

The fourth box presents the calculation of the highest host address. The highest host address for a network is always one less than the broadcast. This means the lowest host bit is a '0' and all other host bits as '1s'. As seen, this makes the highest host address in this network 172.16.20.126.

Although for this example we expanded all of the octets, we only need to examine the content of the divided octet.

Refer to **Figure** in online course

Flash Practice Activity

In the activity in the figure, you will calculate the network address, host addresses, and broadcast address for given networks. Practice as much as necessary. We recommend that you work with this tool until you are able to do the conversion without error.

6.2.3 Unicast, Broadcast, Multicast - Types of Communication

Refer to **Figure** in online course

In an IPv4 network, the hosts can communicate one of three different ways:

Unicast - the process of sending a packet from one host to an individual host

Broadcast - the process of sending a packet from one host to all hosts in the network

Multicast - the process of sending a packet from one host to a selected group of hosts

These three types of communication are used for different purposes in the data networks. In all three cases, the IPv4 address of the originating host is placed in the packet header as the source address.

Unicast Traffic

Unicast communication is used for the normal host-to-host communication in both a client/server and a peer-to-peer network. Unicast packets use the host address of the destination device as the destination address and can be routed through an internetwork. Broadcast and multicast, however, use special addresses as the destination address. Using these special addresses, broadcasts are generally restricted to the local network. The *scope* of multicast traffic also may be limited to the local network or routed through an internetwork.

Play the animation to see an example of unicast transmission.

In an IPv4 network, the unicast address applied to an end device is referred to as the host address. For unicast communication, the host addresses assigned to the two end devices are used as the source and destination IPv4 addresses. During the encapsulation process, the source host places its IPv4 address in the unicast packet header as the source host address and the IPv4 address of the destination host in the packet header as the destination address. The communication using a unicast packet can be forwarded through an internetwork using the same addresses.

Note: In this course, all communications between devices is unicast communication unless otherwise noted.

Refer to
Figure
in online course

Broadcast Transmission

Because broadcast traffic is used to send packets to all hosts in the network, a packet uses a special broadcast address. When a host receives a packet with the broadcast address as the destination, it processes the packet as it would a packet to its unicast address.

Broadcast transmission is used for the location of special services/devices for which the address is not known or when a host needs to provide information to all the hosts on the network.

Some examples for using broadcast transmission are:

- Mapping upper layer addresses to lower layer addresses
- Requesting an address
- Exchanging routing information by routing protocols

When a host needs information, the host sends a request, called a query, to the broadcast address. All hosts in the network receive and process this query. One or more of the hosts with the requested information will respond, typically using unicast.

Similarly, when a host needs to send information to the hosts on a network, it creates and sends a broadcast packet with the information.

Unlike unicast, where the packets can be routed throughout the internetwork, broadcast packets are usually restricted to the local network. This restriction is dependent on the configuration of the router that borders the network and the type of broadcast. There are two types of broadcasts: directed broadcast and *limited broadcast*.

Directed Broadcast

A directed broadcast is sent to all hosts on a specific network. This type of broadcast is useful for sending a broadcast to all hosts on a non-local network. For example, for a host outside of the network to communicate with the hosts within the 172.16.4.0 /24 network, the destination address of the packet would be 172.16.4.255. This is shown in the figure. Although routers do not forward directed broadcasts by default, they may be configured to do so.

Limited Broadcast

The limited broadcast is used for communication that is limited to the hosts on the local network. These packets use a destination IPv4 address 255.255.255.255. Routers do not forward this broadcast. Packets addressed to the limited broadcast address will only appear on the local network. For this reason, an IPv4 network is also referred to as a broadcast domain. Routers form the boundary for a broadcast domain.

As an example, a host within the 172.16.4.0 /24 network would broadcast to all the hosts in its network using a packet with a destination address of 255.255.255.255.

Play the animation to see an example of broadcast transmission.

As you learned earlier, when a packet is broadcast, it uses resources on the network and also forces every host on the network that receives it to process the packet. Therefore, broadcast traffic should be limited so that it does not adversely affect performance of the network or devices. Because routers separate broadcast domains, subdividing networks with excessive broadcast traffic can improve network performance.

Refer to
Figure
in online course

Multicast Transmission

Multicast transmission is designed to conserve the bandwidth of the IPv4 network. It reduces traffic by allowing a host to send a single packet to a selected set of hosts. To reach multiple destination hosts using unicast communication, a source host would need to send an individual packet addressed to each host. With multicast, the source host can send a single packet that can reach thousands of destination hosts.

Some examples of multicast transmission are:

- Video and audio distribution
- Routing information exchange by routing protocols
- Distribution of software
- News feeds

Multicast Clients

Hosts that wish to receive particular multicast data are called multicast clients. The multicast clients use services initiated by a client program to subscribe to the *multicast group*.

Each multicast group is represented by a single IPv4 multicast destination address. When an IPv4 host subscribes to a multicast group, the host processes packets addressed to this multicast address as well as packets addressed to its uniquely allocated unicast address. As we will see, IPv4 has set aside a special block of addresses from 224.0.0.0 to 239.255.255.255 for multicast groups addressing.

The animation demonstrates clients accepting multicast packets.

Refer to **Packet
Tracer Activity**
for this chapter

In this activity, you will be able to visualize unicasts, broadcasts, and multicasts by using Packet Tracer in simulation mode.

Broadcast:

   http://www.ietf.org/rfc/rfc0919.txt?number=919

Multicast:

   http://www.cisco.com/en/US/tech/tk828/technologies_white_paper09186a0080092942.shtml

   http://www.cisco.com/en/US/docs/internetworking/technology/handbook/IP-Multi.html

6.2.4 Reserved IPv4 Address Ranges

Refer to
Figure
in online course

Expressed in dotted decimal format, the IPv4 address range is 0.0.0.0 to 255.255.255.255. As you have already seen, not all of these addresses can be used as host addresses for unicast communication.

Experimental Addresses

One major block of addresses reserved for special purposes is the IPv4 experimental address range 240.0.0.0 to 255.255.255.254. Currently, these addresses are listed as *reserved for future use* (RFC 3330). This suggests that they could be converted to usable addresses. Currently, they cannot be used in IPv4 networks. However, these addresses could be used for research or experimentation.

Multicast Addresses

As previously shown, another major block of addresses reserved for special purposes is the IPv4 multicast address range 224.0.0.0 to 239.255.255.255. Additionally, the multicast address range is subdivided into different types of addresses: *reserved link local addresses* and *globally scoped addresses*. One additional type of multicast address is the *administratively scoped addresses*, also called limited scope addresses.

The IPv4 multicast addresses 224.0.0.0 to 224.0.0.255 are reserved link local addresses. These addresses are to be used for multicast groups on a local network. Packets to these destinations are always transmitted with a time-to-live (TTL) value of 1. Therefore, a router connected to the local network should never forward them. A typical use of reserved *link-local addresses* is in routing protocols using multicast transmission to exchange routing information.

The globally scoped addresses are 224.0.1.0 to 238.255.255.255. They may be used to multicast data across the Internet. For example, 224.0.1.1 has been reserved for *Network Time Protocol (NTP)* to synchronize the time-of-day clocks of network devices.

Host Addresses

After accounting for the ranges reserved for experimental addresses and multicast addresses, this leaves an address range of 0.0.0.0 to 223.255.255.255 that could be used for IPv4 hosts. However, within this range are many addresses that are already reserved for special purposes. Although we have previously covered some of these addresses, the major reserved addresses are discussed in the next section.

6.2.5 Public and Private Addresses

Refer to
Figure
in online course

Although most IPv4 host addresses are *public addresses* designated for use in networks that are accessible on the Internet, there are blocks of addresses that are used in networks that require limited or no Internet access. These addresses are called *private addresses*.

Private Addresses

The private address blocks are:

- 10.0.0.0 to 10.255.255.255 (10.0.0.0 /8)

- 172.16.0.0 to 172.31.255.255 (172.16.0.0 /12)

- 192.168.0.0 to 192.168.255.255 (192.168.0.0 /16)

Private space address blocks, as shown in the figure, are set aside for use in private networks. The use of these addresses need not be unique among outside networks. **Hosts that do not require access to the Internet at large may make unrestricted use of private addresses.** However, the internal networks still must design network address schemes to ensure that the hosts in the private networks use IP addresses that are unique within their networking environment.

Many hosts in different networks may use the same private space addresses. Packets using these addresses as the source or destination should not appear on the public Internet. The router or firewall device at the perimeter of these private networks must block or translate these addresses. Even if these packets were to make their way to the Internet, the routers would not have routes to forward them to the appropriate private network.

Network Address Translation (NAT)

With services to translate private addresses to public addresses, hosts on a privately addressed network can have access to resources across the Internet. These services, called Network Address Translation (NAT), can be implemented on a device at the edge of the private network.

NAT allows the hosts in the network to "borrow" a public address for communicating to outside networks. While there are some limitations and performance issues with NAT, clients for most applications can access services over the Internet without noticeable problems.

Note: NAT will be covered in detail in a subsequent course.

Public Addresses

The vast majority of the addresses in the IPv4 unicast host range are public addresses. These addresses are designed to be used in the hosts that are publicly accessible from the Internet. Even within these address blocks, there are many addresses that are designated for other special purposes.

Refer to Figure in online course

Refer to Figure in online course

6.2.6 Special IPv4 Addresses

There are certain addresses that cannot be assigned to hosts for various reasons. There are also special addresses that can be assigned to hosts but with restrictions on how those hosts can interact within the network.

Network and Broadcast Addresses

As explained earlier, within each network the first and last addresses cannot be assigned to hosts. These are the network address and the broadcast address, respectively.

Default Route

Also presented earlier, we represent the IPv4 default route as 0.0.0.0. The default route is used as a "catch all" route when a more specific route is not available. The use of this address also reserves all addresses in the 0.0.0.0 - 0.255.255.255 (0.0.0.0 /8) address block.

Loopback

One such reserved address is the IPv4 loopback address 127.0.0.1. **The loopback is a special address that hosts use to direct traffic to themselves.** The loopback address creates a shortcut method for TCP/IP applications and services that run on the same device to communicate with one another. By using the loopback address instead of the assigned IPv4 host address, two services on the same host can bypass the lower layers of the TCP/IP stack. You can also ping the loopback address to test the configuration of TCP/IP on the local host.

Although only the single 127.0.0.1 address is used, addresses 127.0.0.0 to 127.255.255.255 are reserved. Any address within this block will *loop back* within the local host. No address within this block should ever appear on any network.

Link-Local Addresses

IPv4 addresses in the address block 169.254.0.0 to 169.254.255.255 (169.254.0.0 /16) are designated as link-local addresses. **These addresses can be automatically assigned to the local host by the operating system in environments where no IP configuration is available.** These might be used in a small peer-to-peer network or for a host that could not automatically obtain an address from a Dynamic Host Configuration Protocol (DHCP) server.

Communication using IPv4 link-local addresses is only suitable for communication with other devices connected to the same network, as shown in the figure. A host *must not* send a packet with an IPv4 link-local destination address to any router for forwarding and should set the IPv4 TTL for these packets to 1.

Link-local addresses do not provide services outside of the local network. However, many client/server and peer-to-peer applications will work properly with IPv4 link-local addresses.

TEST-NET Addresses

The address block 192.0.2.0 to 192.0.2.255 (192.0.2.0 /24) is set aside for teaching and learning purposes. These addresses can be used in documentation and network examples. **Unlike the experimental addresses, network devices *will* accept these addresses in their configurations.** You may often find these addresses used with the domain names example.com or example.net in RFCs, vendor, and protocol documentation. Addresses within this block should not appear on the Internet.

Links:

Local-Link addresses http://www.ietf.org/rfc/rfc3927.txt?number=3927

Special-Use IPv4 Addresses http://www.ietf.org/rfc/rfc3330.txt?number=3330

Multicast allocation: http://www.iana.org/assignments/multicast-addresses

6.2.7 Legacy IPv4 Addressing

Refer to
Figure
in online course

Historic Network Classes

Historically, RFC1700 grouped the unicast ranges into specific sizes called class A, class B, and class C addresses. It also defined class D (multicast) and class E (experimental) addresses, as previously presented.

The unicast address classes A, B, and C defined specifically-sized networks as well as specific address blocks for these networks, as shown in the figure. A company or organization was assigned an entire class A, class B, or class C address block. This use of address space is referred to as *classful addressing*.

Class A Blocks

A class A address block was designed to support extremely large networks with more than 16 million host addresses. Class A IPv4 addresses used a fixed /8 prefix with the first octet to indicate the network address. The remaining three octets were used for host addresses.

To reserve address space for the remaining address classes, all class A addresses required that the most significant bit of the high-order octet be a zero. This meant that there were only 128 possible class A networks, 0.0.0.0 /8 to 127.0.0.0 /8, before taking out the reserved address blocks. Even though the class A addresses reserved one-half of the address space, because of their limit of 128 networks, they could only be allocated to approximately 120 companies or organizations.

Class B Blocks

Class B address space was designed to support the needs of moderate to large size networks with more than 65,000 hosts. A class B IP address used the two high-order octets to indicate the network address. The other two octets specified host addresses. As with class A, address space for the remaining address classes needed to be reserved.

For class B addresses, the most significant two bits of the high-order octet were **10**. This restricted the address block for class B to 128.0.0.0 /16 to 191.255.0.0 /16. Class B had slightly more efficient allocation of addresses than class A because it equally divided 25% of the total IPv4 address space among approximately 16,000 networks.

Class C Blocks

The class C address space was the most commonly available of the historic address classes. This address space was intended to provide addresses for small networks with a maximum of 254 hosts.

Class C address blocks used a /24 prefix. This meant that a class C network used only the last octet as host addresses with the three high-order octets used to indicate the network address.

Class C address blocks set aside address space for class D (multicast) and class E (experimental) by using a fixed value of **110** for the three most significant bits of the high-order octet. This restricted the address block for class C to 192.0.0.0 /16 to 223.255.255.0 /16. Although it occupied only 12.5% of the total IPv4 address space, it could provide addresses to 2 million networks.

Limits to the Class-based System

Not all organizations' requirements fit well into one of these three classes. **Classful allocation of address space often wasted many addresses, which exhausted the availability of IPv4 addresses.** For example, a company that had a network with 260 hosts would need to be given a class B address with more than 65,000 addresses.

Even though this classful system was all but abandoned in the late 1990s, you will see remnants of it in networks today. For example, when you assign an IPv4 address to a computer, the operating system examines the address being assigned to determine if this address is a class A, class B, or class C. The operating system then assumes the prefix used by that class and makes the appropriate subnet mask assignment.

Another example is the assumption of the mask by some routing protocols. When some routing protocols receive an advertised route, it may assume the prefix length based on the class of the address.

Classless Addressing

The system that we currently use is referred to as *classless addressing. With the classless system, address blocks appropriate to the number of hosts are assigned to companies or organizations without regard to the unicast class.*

6.3 Assigning Addresses

6.3.1 Planning to Address the Network

Refer to **Figure** in online course

The allocation of Network layer address space within the corporate network needs to be well designed. Network administrators should not randomly select the addresses used in their networks. Nor should address assignment within the network be random.

The allocation of these addresses inside the networks should be planned and documented for the purpose of:

- Preventing duplication of addresses

- Providing and controlling access

- Monitoring security and performance

Preventing Duplication of Addresses

As you already know, each host in an internetwork must have a unique address. Without the proper planning and documentation of these network allocations, we could easily assign an address to more than one host.

Providing and Controlling Access

Some hosts provide resources to the internal network as well as to the external network. One example of these devices is servers. Access to these resources can be controlled by the Layer 3 address. If the addresses for these resources are not planned and documented, the security and accessibility of the devices are not easily controlled. For example, if a server has a random address assigned, blocking access to its address is difficult and clients may not be able to locate this resource.

Monitoring Security and Performance

Similarly, we need to monitor the security and performance of the network hosts and the network as a whole. As part of the monitoring process, we examine network traffic looking for addresses that are generating or receiving excessive packets. If we have proper planning and documentation of the network addressing, we can identify the device on the network that has a problematic address.

Assigning Addresses within a Network

As you have already learned, hosts are associated with an IPv4 network by a common network portion of the address. Within a network, there are different types of hosts.

Some examples of different types of hosts are:

- End devices for users
- Servers and peripherals
- Hosts that are accessible from the Internet
- Intermediary devices

Each of these different device types should be allocated to a logical block of addresses *within* the address range of the network.

Roll over the tabs to see different classifications of assigning addresses.

Refer to
Figure
in online course

An important part of planning an IPv4 addressing scheme is deciding when private addresses are to be used and where they are to be applied.

Considerations include:

- Will there be more devices connected to the network than public addresses allocated by the network's ISP?
- Will the devices need to be accessed from outside the local network?
- If devices that may be assigned private addresses require access to the Internet, is the network capable of providing a Network Address Translation (NAT) service?

Roll over the tabs in the figure to see private and public address assignments.

If there are more devices than available public addresses, only those devices that will directly access the Internet - such as web servers - require a public address. A NAT service would allow those devices with private addresses to effectively share the remaining public addresses.

6.3.2 Static or Dynamic Addressing for End User Devices

Refer to
Figure
in online course

Addresses for User Devices

In most data networks, the largest population of hosts includes the end devices such as PCs, IP phones, printers, and PDAs. Because this population represents the largest number of devices within a network, the largest number of addresses should be allocated to these hosts.

IP addresses can be assigned either statically or dynamically.

Static Assignment of Addresses

With a static assignment, the network administrator must manually configure the network information for a host, as shown in the figure. At a minimum, this includes entering the host IP address, subnet mask, and default gateway.

Static addresses have some advantages over dynamic addresses. For instance, they are useful for printers, servers, and other networking devices that need to be accessible to clients on the network. If hosts normally access a server at a particular IP address, it would cause problems if that address changed. Additionally, static assignment of addressing information can provide increased control of network resources. However, it can be time-consuming to enter the information on each host.

When using static IP addressing, it is necessary to maintain an accurate list of the IP address assigned to each device. These are permanent addresses and are not normally reused.

Dynamic Assignment of Addresses

Refer to
Figure
in online course

Because of the challenges associated with static address management, end user devices often have addresses dynamically assigned, using Dynamic Host Configuration Protocol (DHCP), as shown in the figure.

DHCP enables the automatic assignment of addressing information such as IP address, subnet mask, default gateway, and other configuration information. The configuration of the DHCP server requires that a block of addresses, called an *address pool, be defined to be assigned to the DHCP clients on a network. Addresses assigned to this pool should be planned so that they exclude any addresses used for the other types of devices.*

DHCP is generally the preferred method of assigning IP addresses to hosts on large networks because it reduces the burden on network support staff and virtually eliminates entry errors.

Another benefit of DHCP is that an address is not permanently assigned to a host but is only "leased" for a period of time. If the host is powered down or taken off the network, the address is returned to the pool for reuse. This feature is especially helpful for mobile users that come and go on a network.

6.3.3 Assigning Addresses to Other Devices

Refer to
Figure
in online course

Addresses for Servers and Peripherals

Any network resource such as a server or a printer should have a static IPv4 address, as shown in the figure. The client hosts access these resources using the IPv4 addresses of these devices. Therefore, predictable addresses for each of these servers and peripherals are necessary.

Servers and peripherals are a concentration point for network traffic. There are many packets sent to and from the IPv4 addresses of these devices. When monitoring network traffic with a tool like Wireshark, a network administrator should be able to rapidly identify these devices. Using a consistent numbering system for these devices makes the identification easier.

Addresses for Hosts that are Accessible from Internet

In most internetworks, only a few devices are accessible by hosts outside of the corporation. For the most part, these devices are usually servers of some type. As with all devices in a network that provide network resources, the IPv4 addresses for these devices should be static.

In the case of servers accessible by the Internet, each of these must have a public space address associated with it. Additionally, variations in the address of one of these devices will make this device inaccessible from the Internet. In many cases, these devices are on a network that is numbered using private addresses. This means that the router or firewall at the perimeter of the network must be configured to translate the internal address of the server into a public address. Because of this additional configuration in the perimeter intermediary device, it is even more important that these devices have a predictable address.

Addresses for Intermediary Devices

Intermediary devices are also a concentration point for network traffic. **Almost all traffic within or between networks passes through some form of intermediary device.** Therefore, these network devices provide an opportune location for network management, monitoring, and security.

Most intermediary devices are assigned Layer 3 addresses. Either for the device management or for their operation. Devices such as hubs, switches, and wireless access points do not require IPv4 addresses to operate as intermediary devices. However, if we need to access these devices as hosts to configure, monitor, or troubleshoot network operation, they need to have addresses assigned.

Because we need to know how to communicate with intermediary devices, they should have predictable addresses. Therefore, their addresses are typically assigned manually. Additionally, the addresses of these devices should be in a different range within the network block than user device addresses.

Routers and Firewalls

Unlike the other intermediary devices mentioned, routers and firewall devices have an IPv4 address assigned to each interface. Each interface is in a different network and serves as the gateway for the hosts in that network. Typically, the router interface uses either the lowest or highest address in the network. This assignment should be uniform across all networks in the corporation so that network personnel will always know the gateway of the network no matter which network they are working on.

Router and firewall interfaces are the concentration point for traffic entering and leaving the network. Because the hosts in each network use a router or firewall device interface as the gateway out of the network, many packets flow through these interfaces. Therefore, these devices can play a major role in network security by filtering packets based on source and/or destination IPv4 addresses. Grouping the different types of devices into logical addressing groups makes the assignment and operation of this packet filtering more efficient.

6.3.4 Who Assigns the Different Addresses?

Refer to **Figure** in online course

A company or organization that wishes to have network hosts accessible from the Internet must have a block of public addresses assigned. The use of these public addresses is regulated and the company or organization must have a block of addresses allocated to it. This is true for IPv4, IPv6, and multicast addresses.

Internet Assigned Numbers Authority (IANA) (http://www.iana.net) is the master holder of the IP addresses. The IP multicast addresses are obtained directly from IANA. Until the mid-1990s, all IPv4 address space was managed directly by the IANA. At that time, the remaining IPv4 address space was allocated to various other registries to manage for particular purposes or for regional areas. These registration companies are called Regional Internet Registries (RIRs), as shown in the figure. When a RIR requires more IP addresses for allocation or assignment within its region, the IANA allocates IPv6 addresses to the RIRs according to their established needs.

The major registries are:

- AfriNIC (African Network Information Centre) - Africa Region http://www.afrinic.net

- APNIC (Asia Pacific Network Information Centre) - Asia/Pacific Region http://www.apnic.net

- ARIN (American Registry for Internet Numbers) - North America Region http://www.arin.net

- LACNIC (Regional Latin-American and Caribbean IP Address Registry) - Latin America and some Caribbean Islands http://www.lacnic.net

- RIPE NCC (Reseaux IP Europeans) - Europe, the Middle East, and Central Asia http://www.ripe.net

Links:

IPv4 address registries allocations:

> http://www.ietf.org/rfc/rfc1466.txt?number=1466

> http://www.ietf.org/rfc/rfc2050.txt?number=2050

IPV4 Addresses allocation: http://www.iana.org/ipaddress/ip-addresses.htm

IP Addressing lookup: http://www.arin.net/whois/

6.3.5 ISPs

Refer to **Figure** in online course

The Role of the ISP

Most companies or organizations obtain their IPv4 address blocks from an ISP. An ISP will generally supply a small number of usable IPv4 addresses (6 or 14) to their customers as a part of their services. Larger blocks of addresses can be obtained based on justification of needs and for additional service costs.

In a sense, the ISP loans or rents these addresses to the organization. If we choose to move our Internet connectivity to another ISP, the new ISP will provide us with addresses from the address blocks that have been provided to them, and our previous ISP returns the blocks loaned to us to their allocation to be loaned to another customer.

ISP Services

To get access to the services of the Internet, we have to connect our data network to the Internet using an *Internet Service Provider (ISP)*.

ISPs have their own set of internal data networks to manage Internet connectivity and to provide related services. Among the other services that an ISP generally provides to its customers are DNS services, e-mail services, and a website. Depending on the level of service required and available, customers use different tiers of an ISP.

ISP Tiers

ISPs are designated by a hierarchy based on their level of connectivity to the *Internet backbone*. Each lower tier obtains connectivity to the backbone via a connection to a higher tier ISP, as shown in the figure.

Tier 1

At the top of the ISP hierarchy are Tier 1 ISPs. These ISPs are large national or international ISPs that are directly connected to the Internet backbone. The customers of Tier 1 ISPs are either lower-tiered ISPs or large companies and organizations. Because they are at the top of Internet connectivity, they engineer highly reliable connections and services. Among the technologies used to support this reliability are multiple connections to the Internet backbone.

The primary advantages for customers of Tier 1 ISPs are reliability and speed. Because these customers are only one connection away from the Internet, there are fewer opportunities for failures or traffic bottlenecks. The drawback for Tier 1 ISP customers is its high cost.

Tier 2

Tier 2 ISPs acquire their Internet service from Tier 1 ISPs. **Tier 2 ISPs generally focus on business customers.** Tier 2 ISPs usually offer more services than the other two tiers of ISPs. These tier

2 ISPs tend to have the IT resources to operate their own services such as DNS, e-mail servers, and web servers. Other services that Tier 2 ISPs may offer include website development and maintenance, e-commerce/e-business, and VoIP.

The primary disadvantage of Tier 2 ISPs, as compared to Tier 1 ISPs, is slower Internet access. Because Tier 2 ISPs are at least one more connection away from the Internet backbone, they also tend to have lower reliability than Tier 1 ISPs.

Tier 3

Tier 3 ISPs purchase their Internet service from Tier 2 ISPs. **The focus of these ISPs is the retail and home markets in a specific locale.** Tier 3 customers typically do not need many of the services required by Tier 2 customers. Their primary need is connectivity and support.

These customers often have little or no computer or network expertise. Tier 3 ISPs often bundle Internet connectivity as a part of network and computer service contracts for their customers. While they may have reduced bandwidth and less reliability than Tier 1 and Tier 2 providers, they are often good choices for small to medium size companies.

6.3.6 Overview of IPv6

Refer to **Figure** in online course

In the early 1990s, the Internet Engineering Task Force (IETF) grew concerned about the exhaustion of the IPv4 network addresses and began to look for a replacement for this protocol. This activity led to the development of what is now known as IPv6.

Creating expanded addressing capabilities was the initial motivation for developing this new protocol. Other issues were also considered during the development of IPv6, such as:

- Improved packet handling
- Increased scalability and longevity
- QoS mechanisms
- Integrated security

To provide these features, IPv6 offers:

- 128-bit hierarchical addressing - to expand addressing capabilities
- Header format simplification - to improve packet handling
- Improved support for extensions and options - for increased scalability/longevity and improved packet handling
- Flow labeling capability - as QoS mechanisms
- Authentication and privacy capabilities - to integrate security

IPv6 is not merely a new Layer 3 protocol - it is a new protocol suite. New protocols at various layers of the stack have been developed to support this new protocol. There is a new messaging protocol (ICMPv6) and new routing protocols. Because of the increased size of the IPv6 header, it also impacts the underlying network infrastructure.

Transition to IPv6

As you can see from this brief introduction, IPv6 has been designed with scalability to allow for years of internetwork growth. However, IPv6 is being implemented slowly and in select networks. Because of better tools, technologies, and address management in the last few years, IPv4 is still very widely used, and likely to remain so for some time into the future. However, IPv6 may eventually replace IPv4 as the dominant Internet protocol.

Links:

IPv6: http://www.ietf.org/rfc/rfc2460.txt?number=2460

IPv6 addressing: http://www.ietf.org/rfc/rfc3513.txt?number=3513

IPv6 security: http://www.ietf.org/rfc/rfc2401.txt?number=2401

IPv6 security: http://www.ietf.org/rfc/rfc3168.txt?number=3168

IPv6 security: http://www.ietf.org/rfc/rfc4302.txt?number=4302

ICMPv6: http://www.ietf.org/rfc/rfc4443.txt?number=4443

6.4 Is It On My Network?

6.4.1 The Subnet Mask - Defining the Network and Host Portions

Refer to
Figure
in online course

As we learned earlier, an IPv4 address has a network portion and a host portion. We referred to the prefix length as the number of bits in the address giving us the network portion. The prefix is a way to define the network portion that is human readable. The data network must also have this network portion of the addresses defined.

To define the network and host portions of an address, the devices use a separate 32-bit pattern called a subnet mask, as shown in the figure. We express the subnet mask in the same dotted decimal format as the IPv4 address. The subnet mask is created by placing a binary **1** in each bit position that represents the network portion and placing a binary **0** in each bit position that represents the host portion.

The prefix and the subnet mask are different ways of representing the same thing - the network portion of an address.

As shown in the figure, a **/24** prefix is expressed as a subnet mask as **255.255.255.0** (**11111111.11111111.11111111.00000000**). The remaining bits (low order) of the subnet mask are zeroes, indicating the host address within the network.

The subnet mask is configured on a host in conjunction with the IPv4 address to define the network portion of that address.

For example, let's look at the host 172.16.20.35/27:

address

172.16.20.35

10101100.00010000.00010100.00100011

subnet mask

255.255.255.224

11111111.11111111.11111111.11100000

network address

172.16.20.32

10101100.00010000.00010100.00100000

Because the high order bits of the subnet masks are contiguous **1**s, there are only a limited number of subnet values within an octet. You will recall that we only need to expand an octet if the network and host division falls within that octet. Therefore, there are a limited number 8 bit patterns used in address masks.

These patterns are:

00000000 = 0

10000000 = 128

11000000 = 192

11100000 = 224

11110000 = 240

11111000 = 248

11111100 = 252

11111110 = 254

11111111 = 255

If the subnet mask for an octet is represented by **255**, then all the equivalent bits in that octet of the address are network bits. Similarly, if the subnet mask for an octet is represented by **0**, then all the equivalent bits in that octet of the address are host bits. In each of these cases, it is not necessary to expand this octet to binary to determine the network and host portions.

6.4.2 ANDing - What Is In Our Network?

Refer to **Figure** in online course

Inside data network devices, digital logic is applied for their interpretation of the addresses. When an IPv4 packet is created or forwarded, the destination network address must be extracted from the destination address. This is done by a logic called *AND*.

The IPv4 host address is logically ANDed with its subnet mask to determine the network address to which the host is associated. When this ANDing between the address and the subnet mask is performed, the result yields the network address.

The AND Operation

ANDing is one of three basic binary operations used in digital logic. The other two are OR and NOT. While all three are used in data networks, AND is used in determining the network address. Therefore, our discussion here will be limited to logical AND. Logical AND is the comparison of two bits that yields the following results:

1 AND 1 = 1

1 AND 0 = 0

0 AND 1 = 0

0 AND 0 = 0

The result from anything ANDed with a **1** yields a result that is the original bit. That is, **0 AND 1** is **0** and **1 AND 1** is **1**. Consequently, anything ANDed with a **0** yields a **0**. These properties of ANDing are used with the subnet mask to "mask" the host bits of an IPv4 address. Each bit of the address is ANDed with the corresponding bit of the subnet mask.

Because all the bits of the subnet mask that represent host bits are 0s, the host portion of the resulting network address becomes all 0s. Recall that an IPv4 address with all 0s in the host portion represents the network address.

Likewise, all the bits of the subnet mask that indicate network portion are 1s. When each of these 1s is ANDed with the corresponding bit of the address, the resulting bits are identical to the original address bits.

Roll over the tabs in the figure to see the AND operation.

Reasons to Use AND

This ANDing between the host address and subnet mask is performed by devices in a data network for various reasons.

Routers use ANDing to determine an acceptable route for an incoming packet. The router checks the destination address and attempts to associate this address with a next hop. As a packet arrives at a router, the router performs ANDing on the IP destination address in the incoming packet and with the subnet mask of potential routes. This yields a network address that is compared to the route from the routing table whose subnet mask was used.

An originating host must determine if a packet should be sent directly to a host in the local network or be directed to the gateway. To make this determination, a host must first know its own network address.

A host extracts its network address by ANDing its address with its subnet mask. A logical AND is also performed by an originating host between the destination address of the packet and the subnet mask of the this host. This yields the network address of the destination. If this network address matches the network address of the local host, the packet is sent directly to the destination host. If the two network addresses do not match, the packet is sent to the gateway.

The Importance of AND

If the routers and end devices calculate these processes without our intervention, why do we need to learn how to AND? The more we understand and are able to predict about the operation of a network, the more equipped we are to design and/or administer one.

In network verification/troubleshooting, we often need to determine what IPv4 network a host is on or if two hosts are on the same IP network. We need to make this determination from the perspective of the network devices. Due to improper configuration, a host may see itself on a network that was not the intended one. This can create an operation that seems erratic unless diagnosed by examining the ANDing processes used by the host.

Also, a router may have many different routes that can satisfy the forwarding of packet to a given destination. The selection of the route used for any given packet is a complex operation. For example, the prefix forming these routes is not directly associated with the networks assigned to the host. This means that a route in the routing table may represent many networks. If there were issues with routing packets, you would need to determine how the router would make the routing decision.

Although there are subnet calculators available, it is helpful for a network administrator to know how to manually calculate subnets.

Note: No calculators of any kind are permitted during certification exams.

6.4.3 The ANDing Process

Refer to **Figure** in online course

The AND operation is applied to every bit in the binary address.

Play the animation in the figure to follow the AND steps for one example.

6.5 Calculating Addresses

6.5.1 Basic subnetting

Refer to **Figure** in online course

Subnetting allows for creating multiple logical networks from a single address block. Since we use a router to connect these networks together, each interface on a router must have a unique network ID. Every *node* on that link is on the same network.

We create the subnets by using one or more of the host bits as network bits. This is done by extending the mask to borrow some of the bits from the host portion of the address to create additional network bits. The more host bits used, the more subnets that can be defined. For each bit borrowed, we double the number of subnetworks available. For example, if we borrow 1 bit, we can define 2 subnets. If we borrow 2 bits, we can have 4 subnets. However, with each bit we borrow, fewer host addresses are available per subnet.

RouterA in the figure has two interfaces to interconnect two networks. Given an address block of 192.168.1.0 /24, we will create two subnets. We borrow one bit from the host portion by using a subnet mask of 255.255.255.128, instead of the original 255.255.255.0 mask. The most significant bit in the last octet is used to distinguish between the two subnets. For one of the subnets, this bit is a "0" and for the other subnet this bit is a "1".

Formula for calculating subnets

Use this formula to calculate the number of subnets:

2^n where n = the number of bits borrowed

In this example, the calculation looks like this:

$2^1 = 2$ subnets

The number of hosts

To calculate the number of hosts per network, we use the formula of $2^n - 2$ where n = the number of bits left for hosts.

Applying this formula, ($2^7 - 2 = 126$) shows that each of these subnets can have 126 hosts.

For each subnet, examine the last octet in binary. The values in these octets for the two networks are:

Subnet 1:

00000000 = 0

Subnet 2:

10000000 = 128

See the figure for the addressing scheme for these networks.

Refer to **Figure** in online course

Example with 3 subnets

Next, consider an internetwork that requires three subnets. See the figure.

Again we start with the same 192.168.1.0 /24 address block. Borrowing a single bit would only provide two subnets. To provide more networks, we change the subnet mask to 255.255.255.192 and borrow two bits. This will provide four subnets.

Calculate the subnet with this formula:

2^2 = 4 subnets

The number of hosts

To calculate the number of hosts, begin by examining the last octet. Notice these subnets.

Subnet 0: 0 =

00000000

Subnet 1: 64 =

01000000

Subnet 2: 128 =

10000000

Subnet 3: 192 =

11000000

Apply the host calculation formula.

$2^6 - 2$ = 62 hosts per subnet

See the figure for the addressing scheme for these networks.

Refer to
Figure
in online course

Example with 6 subnets

Consider this example with five LANs and a WAN for a total of 6 networks. See the figure.

To accommodate 6 networks, subnet 192.168.1.0 /24 into address blocks using the formula:

2^3 = 8

To get at least 6 subnets, borrow three host bits. A subnet mask of 255.255.255.224 provides the three additional network bits.

The number of hosts

To calculate the number of hosts, begin by examining the last octet. Notice these subnets.

0 =

00000000

32 =

00100000

64 =

01000000

96 =

01100000

128 =

10000000

160 =

10100000

192 =

11000000

224 =

11100000

Apply the host calculation formula:

2^5 - 2 = 30 hosts per subnet.

See the figure for the addressing scheme for these networks.

6.5.2 Subnetting - Dividing Networks into Right Sizes

Refer to **Figure** in online course

Every network within the internetwork of a corporation or organization is designed to accommodate a finite number of hosts.

Some networks, such as point-to-point WAN links, only require a maximum of two hosts. Other networks, such as a user LAN in a large building or department, may need to accommodate hundreds of hosts. Network administrators need to devise the internetwork addressing scheme to accommodate the maximum number of hosts for each network. The number of hosts in each division should allow for growth in the number of hosts.

Determine the Total Number of Hosts

First, consider the total number of hosts required by the entire corporate internetwork. We must use a block of addresses that is large enough to accommodate all devices in all the corporate networks. This includes end user devices, servers, intermediate devices, and router interfaces.

See Step 1 of the figure.

Consider the example of a corporate internetwork that needs to accommodate 800 hosts in its four locations.

Determine the Number and Size of the Networks

Next, consider the number of networks and the size of each required based on common groupings of hosts.

See Step 2 of the figure.

We subnet our network to overcome issues with location, size, and control. In designing the addressing, we consider the factors for grouping the hosts that we discussed previously:

- Grouping based on common geographic location

- Grouping hosts used for specific purposes

- Grouping based on ownership

Each WAN link is a network. We create subnets for the WAN that interconnect different geographic locations. When connecting the different locations, we use a router to account for the hardware differences between the LANs and the WAN.

Although hosts in a common geographic location typically comprise a single block of addresses, we may need to subnet this block to form additional networks at each location. We need to create subnetworks at the different locations that have hosts for common user needs. We may also have other groups of users that require many network resources, or we may have many users that require their own subnetwork. Additionally, we may have subnetworks for special hosts such as servers. Each of these factors needs to be considered in the network count.

We also have to consider any special security or administrative ownership needs that require additional networks.

One useful tool in this address planning process is a network diagram. A diagram allows us to see the networks and make a more accurate count.

To accommodate 800 hosts in the company's four locations, we use binary arithmetic to allocate a /22 block ($2^{10}-2=1022$).

Allocating Addresses

Now that we have a count of the networks and the number of hosts for each network, we need to start allocating addresses from our overall block of addresses.

See Step 3 of the figure.

This process begins by allocating network addresses for locations of special networks. We start with the locations that require the most hosts and work down to the point-to-point links. This process ensures that large enough blocks of addresses are made available to accommodate the hosts and networks for these locations.

When making the divisions and assignment of available subnets, make sure that there are adequately-sized address blocks available for the larger demands. **Also, plan carefully to ensure that the address blocks assigned to the subnet do not overlap.**

Refer to
Figure
in online course

Another helpful tool in this planning process is a spreadsheet. We can place the addresses in columns to visualize the allocation of the addresses.

See Step 1 of the figure.

In our example, we now allocate blocks of addresses to the four locations as well as the WAN links.

With the major blocks allocated, next we subnet any of the locations that require dividing. In our example, we divide the corporate HQ into two networks.

See Step 2 of the figure.

This further division of the addresses is often called *subnetting the subnets*. As with any subnetting, we need to carefully plan the address allocation so that we have available blocks of addresses.

The creation of new, smaller networks from a given address block is done by extending the length of the prefix; that is, adding **1**s to the subnet mask. Doing this allocates more bits to the network portion of the address to provide more patterns for the new subnet. For each bit we borrow, we double the number of networks we have. For example, if we use 1 bit, we have the potential to divide that block into two smaller networks. With a single bit pattern, we can produce two unique bit patterns, 1 and 0. If we borrow 2 bits, we can provide for 4 unique patterns to represent networks 00, 01, 10, and 11. 3 bits would allow 8 blocks, and so on.

The total Number of Usable Hosts

Recall from the previous section that as we divide the address range into subnets, we lose two host addresses for each new network. These are the network address and broadcast address.

The formula for calculating the number of hosts in a network is:

Usable hosts = 2^n - 2

Where *n* is the number of bits remaining to be used for hosts.

Links:

Subnet calculator: http://vlsm-calc.net

6.5.3 Subnetting - Subnetting a Subnet

Refer to
Figure
in online course

Subnetting a subnet, or using Variable Length Subnet Mask (VLSM) was designed to maximize addressing efficiency. When identifying the total number of hosts using traditional subnetting, we allocate the same number of addresses for each subnet. If all the subnets have the same requirements for the number hosts, these fixed size address blocks would be efficient. However, most often that is not the case.

For example, the topology in Figure 1 shows a subnet requirement of seven subnets, one for each of the four LANs and one for each of the three WANs. With the given address of 192.168.20.0, we need to borrow 3 bits from the host bits in the last octet to meet our subnet requirement of seven subnets.

These bits are borrowed bits by changing the corresponding subnet mask bits to "1s" to indicate that these bits are now being used as network bits. The last octet of the mask is then represented in binary by 11100000, which is 224. The new mask of 255.255.255.224 is represented with the /27 notation to represent a total of 27 bits for the mask.

In binary this subnet mask is represented as: **11111111.11111111.11111111.11100000**

After borrowing three of the host bits to use as network bits, this leaves five host bits. These five bits will allow up to 30 hosts per subnet.

Although we have accomplished the task of dividing the network into an adequate number of networks, it was done with a significant waste of unused addresses. For example, only two addresses are needed in each subnet for the WAN links. There are 28 unused addresses in each of the three WAN subnets that have been locked into these address blocks. Further, this limits future growth by reducing the total number of subnets available. This inefficient use of addresses is characteristic of classful addressing.

Applying a standard subnetting scheme to scenario is not very efficient and is wasteful. In fact, this example is a good model for showing how subnetting a subnet can be used to maximize address utilization.

Getting More Subnet for Less Hosts

Recall in previous examples we began with the original subnets and gained additional, smaller, subnets to use for the WAN links. By creating smaller subnets, each subnet is able to support 2 hosts, leaving the original subnets free to be allotted to other devices and preventing many addresses from being wasted.

To create these smaller subnets for the WAN links, begin with 192.168.20.192. We can divide this subnet into many smaller subnets. To provide address blocks for the WANS with two addresses each, we will borrow three additional host bits to be used as network bits.

```
Address: 192.168.20.192
```
In Binary:

```
11000000.10101000.00010100.11000000
 Mask: 255.255.255.252  30 Bits in binary:
11111111.11111111.11111111.11111100
```

The topology in the figure 2 shows an addressing plan that breaks up the 192.168.20.192 /27 subnets into smaller subnets to provide addresses for the WANs. Doing this reduces the number addresses per subnet to a size appropriate for the WANs. With this addressing, we have subnets 4, 5, and 7 available for future networks, as well as several other subnets available for WANs.

Refer to
Figure
in online course

In Figure 1, we will look at addressing from another view. We will consider subnetting based on the number of hosts, including router interfaces and WAN connections. This scenario has the following requirements:

- AtlantaHQ 58 host addresses

- PerthHQ 26 host addresses

- SydneyHQ 10 host addresses

- CorpusHQ 10 host addresses

- WAN links 2 host addresses (each)

It is clear from these requirements that using a standard subnetting scheme would, indeed, be wasteful. In this internetwork, standard subnetting would lock each subnet into blocks of 62 hosts, which would mean a significant waste of potential addresses. This waste is especially evident in figure 2 where we see that the PerthHQ LAN supports 26 users and the SydneyHQ and CorpusHQ LANs routers support only 10 users each.

Therefore, with the given address block of 192.168.15.0 /24, we will begin designing an addressing scheme to meet the requirements and save potential addresses.

Getting More

When creating an appropriate addressing scheme, always begin with the largest requirement. In this case, the AtlantaHQ, with 58 users, has the largest requirement. Starting with 192.168.15.0, we will need 6 host bits to accommodate the requirement of 58 hosts, this allows 2 additional bits for the network portion. The prefix for this network would be /26 and a subnet mask of 255.255.255.192.

Let's begin by subnetting the original address block of 192.168.15.0 /24. Using the Usable hosts = $2^n - 2$ formula, we calculate that 6 host bits allow 62 hosts in the subnet. The 62 hosts would meet the required 58 hosts of the AtlantaHQ company router.

```
Address: 192.168.15.0
```
In Binary:
```
11000000.10101000.00001111.00000000
 Mask: 255.255.255.192
26 Bits in binary: 11111111.11111111.11111111.11000000
```

The next page shows the process of identifying the next sequence of steps.

Refer to
Figure
in online course

The steps for implementing this subnetting scheme are described here.

Assigning the AtlantaHQ LAN

See Steps 1 and 2 in the figure.

The **first step** shows a network-planning chart. The **second step** in the figure shows the entry for the AtlantaHQ. This entry is the results of calculating a subnet from the original 192.168.15.0 /24 block to accommodate the largest LAN, the AtlantaHQ LAN with 58 hosts. Doing this required borrowing an additional 2 host bits, to use a /26 bit mask.

By comparison, the following scheme shows how 192.168.15.0 would be subnetted using fixed block addressing to provide large enough address blocks:

Subnet 0: 192.168.15.0 /26 host address range 1 to 62

Subnet 1: 192.168.15.64 /26 host address range 65 to 126

Subnet 2: 192.168.15.128 /26 host address range 129 to 190

Subnet 3: 192.168.15.192 /26 host address range 193 to 254

The fixed blocks would allow only four subnets and therefore not allow enough address blocks for the majority of the subnets in this internetwork. Instead of continuing to use the next available subnet, we need to ensure we make the size of each subnet consistent with the host requirements. Using an addressing scheme directly correlated to the host requirements requires the use of a different method of subnetting.

Assigning the PerthHQ LAN

See Step 3 in the figure.

In the **third step**, we look at the requirements for the next largest subnet. This is the PerthHQ LAN, requiring 26 host addresses including the router interface. We should begin with next available address of 192.168.15.64 to create an address block for this subnet. By borrowing one more bit, we are able to meet the needs of PerthHQ while limiting the wasted addresses. The borrowed bit gives us a /27 mask with the following address range:

192.168.15.64 /27 host address range 65 to 94

This block of address provides 30 addresses, which meets the requirement of 28 hosts and allows room for growth for this subnet.

Assigning the SydneyHQ LAN and CorpusHQ LAN

See Steps 4 and 5 in the figure.

The **fourth** and **fifth** steps provide the addressing for the next largest subnets: SydneyHQ and CorpusHQ LANs. In these two steps, each LAN has the same need for 10 host addresses. This subnetting requires us to borrow another bit, to extend the mask to /28. Starting with address 192.168.15.96, we get the following address blocks:

Subnet 0: 192.168.15.96 /28 host address range 97 to 110

Subnet 1: 192.168.15.112 /28 host address range 113 to 126

These blocks provide 14 addresses for the hosts and router interfaces on each LAN.

Assigning the WANs

See Steps 6, 7, and 8 in the figure.

The **last three steps** show subnetting for the WAN links. With these point-to-point WAN links only two addresses are required. To meet the requirement, we borrow 2 more bits to use a /30 mask. Using the next available addresses, we get the following address blocks:

Subnet 0: 192.168.15.128 /30 host address range 129 to 130

Subnet 1: 192.168.15.132 /30 host address range 133 to 134

Subnet 2: 192.168.15.136 /30 host address range 137 to 138

Refer to
Figure
in online course

The results shown in our addressing scheme using VLSM displays a wide array of correctly-allocated address blocks. As best practice, we began by documenting our requirements from the largest to the smallest. By starting with the largest requirement, we were able to determine that a fixed block addressing scheme would not allow for efficient use of the IPv4 addresses and, as shown in this example, would not provide enough addresses.

From the allocated address block, we borrowed bits to create the address ranges that would fit our topology. Figure 1 shows the assigned ranges. Figure 2 shows the topology with the addressing information.

Using VLSM to allocate the addresses made it possible to apply the subnetting guidelines for grouping hosts based on:

- Grouping based on common geographic location

- Grouping hosts used for specific purposes

- Grouping based on ownership

In our example, we based the grouping on the number of hosts in a common geographic location.

Refer to
Figure
in online course

VLSM Chart

Address planning can also be accomplished using a variety of tools. One method is to use a VLSM chart to identify which blocks of addresses are available for use and which ones are already assigned. This method helps to prevent assigning addresses that have already been allocated. Using the network from our example, we can walk through the address planning using the VLSM chart, to see its use.

The first graphic shows the top portion of the chart. A complete chart for your use is available using the link below.

VLSM_Subnetting_Chart.pdf

This chart can be used to do address planning for networks with prefixes in the /25 - /30 range. These are the most commonly used network ranges for subnetting.

As before, we start with the subnet that has the largest number of hosts. In this case, it is AtlantaHQ with 58 hosts.

Choosing a block for the AtlantaHQ LAN

Following the chart header from left to right, we find the header that indicates a block size of sufficient size for the 58 hosts. This is the /26 column. In this column, we see that there are four blocks of this size:

.0 /26 host address range 1 to 62

.64 /26 host address range 65 to 126

.128 /26 host address range 129 to 190

.192 /26 host address range 193 to 254

Because no addresses have been allocated, we can choose any one of these blocks. Although there might be reasons for using a different block, we commonly use the first available block, the .0 /26. This allocation is shown in Figure 2.

Once we assign the address block, these addresses are considered used. Be sure to mark this block as well as any larger blocks that contain these addresses. By marking these, we can see which address cannot be used and which are still available. Looking at Figure 3, when we allocate the .0 /26 block to the AtlantaHQ, we mark all the blocks that contain these addresses.

Choosing a block for the PerthHQ LAN

Next, we need an address block for the PerthHQ LAN of 26 hosts. Moving across the chart header, we find the column that has the subnets of sufficient size for this LAN. Then we move down the chart to the first available block. In Figure 3, the section of the chart available for PerthHQ is highlighted. The borrowed bit makes the block of addresses available for this LAN. Although we could have chosen any of the available blocks, typically we proceed to the first available block that satisfies the need.

The address range for this block is:

.64 /27 host address range 65 to 94

Choosing blocks for the SydneyHQ LAN and the CorpusHQ LAN

As shown in Figure 4, we continue to mark the address blocks to prevent overlapping of address assignment. To meet the needs of the SydneyHQ LAN and CorpusHQ LAN, we again locate the next available blocks. This time we move to the /28 column and move down to the .96 and .112 blocks. Notice that the section of the chart available for SydneyHQ and CorpusHQ is highlighted.

These blocks are:

.96 /28 host address range 97 to 110

.112 /28 host address range 113 to 126

Choosing blocks for the WANs

The last addressing requirement is for the WAN connections between the networks. Looking at Figure 5, we move to the far right column for /30 prefix. We then move down and highlight three available blocks. These blocks will provide the 2 addresses per WAN.

These three blocks are:

.128 /30 host address range 129 to 130

.132 /30 host address range 133 to 134

.136 /30 host address range 137 to 138

Looking at Figure 6, the addresses assigned to the WAN are marked to indicate that the blocks containing these can no longer be assigned. Notice with the assignment of these WAN ranges that we have marked several larger blocks that cannot be assigned. These are:

.128 /25

.128 /26

.128 /27

.128 /28

.128 /29

.136 /29

Because these addresses are part of these larger blocks, the assignment of these blocks would overlap the use of these addresses.

As we have seen, the usage of VLSM enables us to maximize addressing while minimizing waste. The chart method shown is just one additional tool that network administrators and network technicians can use to create an addressing scheme that is less wasteful than the fixed size block approach.

6.5.4 Determining the Network Address

Refer to **Figure** in online course

The activity in the figure provides practice in determining the network addresses. You will be presented with random masks and host addresses. For each pair of masks and host addresses, you will be required to enter the correct network address. You will then be shown if your answer is correct.

6.5.5 Calculating the Number of Hosts

Refer to
Figure
in online course

The activity in the figure provides practice in determining the maximum number of hosts for a network. You will be presented with random masks and host addresses. For each pair of masks and host addresses, you will be required to enter the maximum number of hosts for the network described. You will then be shown if your answer is correct.

6.5.6 Determining Valid Addresses for Hosts

Refer to
Figure
in online course

The activity in the figure provides practice in determining the hosts, network, and broadcast addresses for a network. You will be presented with random masks and host addresses. For each pair of masks and host addresses, you will be required to enter the hosts, network, and broadcast addresses. You will then be shown if your answer is correct.

6.5.7 Assigning Addresses

Refer to **Packet
Tracer Activity**
for this chapter

In this activity, you will be given a pool of addresses and masks to assign a host with an address, a subnet mask, and a gateway to allow it to communicate in a network.

6.5.8 Addressing in a Tiered Internetwork

Refer to **Packet
Tracer Activity**
for this chapter

In this activity, you will be given a topology and a list of possible IP addresses. You will assign the interfaces of a router with the appropriate IP address and subnet mask that would satisfy the host requirements of each network while leaving the minimum number of unused IP addresses possible.

6.6 Testing the Network Layer

6.6.1 Ping 127.0.0.1 - Testing the Local Stack

Refer to
Figure
in online course

Ping is a utility for testing IP connectivity between hosts. Ping sends out requests for responses from a specified host address. Ping uses a Layer 3 protocol that is a part on the TCP/IP suite called Internet Control Message Protocol (ICMP). Ping uses an ICMP Echo Request datagram.

If the host at the specified address receives the Echo request, it responds with an ICMP Echo Reply datagram. For each packet sent, ping measures the time required for the reply.

As each response is received, ping provides a display of the time between the ping being sent and the response received. This is a measure of the network performance. Ping has a timeout value for the response. If a response is not received within that timeout, ping gives up and provides a message indicating that a response was not received.

After all the requests are sent, the ping utility provides an output with the summary of the responses. This output includes the success rate and average round-trip time to the destination.

Pinging the Local Loopback

There are some special testing and verification cases for which we can use ping. One case is for testing the internal configuration of IP on the local host. To perform this test, we ping the special reserve address of local loopback (127.0.0.1), as shown in the figure.

A response from 127.0.0.1 indicates that IP is properly installed on the host. This response comes from the Network layer. This response is *not*, however, an indication that the addresses, masks, or gateways are properly configured. Nor does it indicate anything about the status of the lower layer of the network stack. This simply tests IP down through the Network layer of the IP protocol. If we get an error message, it is an indication that TCP/IP is not operational on the host.

6.6.2 Ping Gateway - Testing Connectivity to the Local LAN

Refer to **Figure** in online course

You can also use ping to test the host ability to communicate on the local network. This is generally done by pinging the IP address of the gateway of the host, as shown in the figure. A ping to the gateway indicates that the host and the router's interface serving as that gateway are both operational on the local network.

For this test, the gateway address is most often used, because the router is normally always operational. If the gateway address does not respond, you can try the IP address of another host that you are confident is operational in the local network.

If either the gateway or another host responds, then the local hosts can successfully communicate over the local network. If the gateway does not respond but another host does, this could indicate a problem with the router's interface serving as the gateway.

One possibility is that we have the wrong address for the gateway. Another possibility is that the router interface may be fully operational but have security applied to it that prevents it from processing or responding to ping requests. It is also possible that other hosts may have the same security restriction applied.

6.6.3 Ping Remote Host - Testing Connectivity to Remote LAN

Refer to **Figure** in online course

You can also use ping to test the ability of the local IP host to communicate across an internetwork. The local host can ping an operational host of a remote network, as shown in the figure.

If this ping is successful, you will have verified the operation of a large piece of the internetwork. It means that we have verified our host's communication on the local network, the operation of the router serving as our gateway, and all other routers that might be in the path between our network and the network of the remote host.

Additionally, you have verified the same functionality of the remote host. If, for any reason, the remote host could not use its local network to communicate outside its network, then it would not have responded.

Remember, many network administrators limit or prohibit the entry of ICMP datagrams into the corporate network. Therefore, the lack of a ping response could be due to security restrictions and not because of non-operational elements of the networks.

Refer to **Packet Tracer Activity** for this chapter

In this activity, you will examine the behavior of `ping` in several common network situations.

6.6.4 Traceroute (tracert) - Testing the Path

Refer to **Figure** in online course

Ping is used to indicate the connectivity between two hosts. Traceroute (`tracert`) is a utility that allows us to observe the path between these hosts. The trace generates a list of hops that were successfully reached along the path.

This list can provide us with important verification and troubleshooting information. If the data reaches the destination, then the trace lists the interface on every router in the path.

If the data fails at some hop along the way, we have the address of the last router that responded to the trace. This is an indication of where the problem or security restrictions are.

Round Trip Time (RTT)

Using traceroute provides round trip time (RTT) for each hop along the path and indicates if a hop fails to respond. The round trip time (RTT) is the time a packet takes to reach the remote host and for the response from the host to return. An asterisk (*) is used to indicate a lost packet.

This information can be used to locate a problematic router in the path. If we get high response times or data losses from a particular hop, this is an indication that the resources of the router or its connections may be stressed.

Time to Live (TTL)

Traceroute makes use of a function of the Time to Live (TTL) field in the Layer 3 header and ICMP Time Exceeded Message. The TTL field is used to limit the number of hops that a packet can cross. When a packet enters a router, the TTL field is decremented by 1. When the TTL reaches zero, a router will not forward the packet and the packet is dropped.

In addition to dropping the packet, the router normally sends an ICMP Time Exceeded message addressed to the originating host. This ICMP message will contain the IP address of the router that responded.

Play the animation in the figure to see how Traceroute takes advantage of TTL.

The first sequence of messages sent from `traceroute` will have a TTL field of one. This causes the TTL to time out the packet at the first router. This router then responds with an ICMP Message. Traceroute now has the address of the first hop.

Traceroute then progressively increments the TTL field (2, 3, 4...) for each sequence of messages. This provides the trace with the address of each hop as the packets timeout further down the path. The TTL field continues to be increased until the destination is reached or it is incremented to a predefined maximum.

Once the final destination is reached, the host responds with either an ICMP Port Unreachable message or an ICMP Echo Reply message instead of the ICMP Time Exceeded message.

Refer to **Packet Tracer Activity** for this chapter

In this activity, you will first investigate how traceroute (`tracert`) is actually built out of a series of ICMP echo requests. Then you will experiment with a routing loop, where a packet would circulate forever if not for its time to live field.

6.6.5 ICMPv4 - The Protocol Supporting Testing and Messaging

Refer to **Figure** in online course

Although IPv4 is not a reliable protocol, it does provide for messages to be sent in the event of certain errors. These messages are sent using services of the Internet Control Messaging Protocol (ICMPv4). The purpose of these messages is to provide feedback about issues related to the processing of IP packets under certain conditions, not to make IP reliable. ICMP messages are not required and are often not allowed for security reasons.

ICMP is the messaging protocol for the TCP/IP suite. ICMP provides control and error messages and is used by the ping and traceroute utilities. Although ICMP uses the basic support of IP as if it were a higher-level protocol ICMP, it is actually a separate Layer 3 of the TCP/IP suite.

The types of ICMP messages - and the reasons why they are sent - are extensive. We will discuss some of the more common messages.

ICMP messages that may be sent include:

- Host confirmation

- Unreachable Destination or Service

- Time exceeded

- Route redirection

- Source quench

Host Confirmation

An ICMP Echo Message can be used to determine if a host is operational. The local host sends an ICMP Echo Request to a host. The host receiving the echo message replies with the ICMP Echo Reply, as shown in the figure. This use of the ICMP Echo messages is the basis of the ping utility.

Unreachable Destination or Service

The ICMP Destination Unreachable can used to notify a host that the destination or service is unreachable. When a host or gateway receives a packet that it cannot deliver, it may send an ICMP Destination Unreachable packet to the host originating the packet. The Destination Unreachable packet will contain codes that indicate why the packet could not be delivered.

Among the Destination Unreachable codes are:

0 = net unreachable

1 = host unreachable

2 = protocol unreachable

3 = port unreachable

Codes for *net unreachable* and *host unreachable* are responses from a router when it cannot forward a packet. If a router receives a packet for which it does not have a route, it may respond with an ICMP Destination Unreachable with a code = 0, indicating net unreachable. If a router receives a packet for which it has an attached route but is unable to deliver the packet to the host on the attached network, the router may respond with an ICMP Destination Unreachable with a code = 1, indicating that the network is known but the host is unreachable.

The codes 2 and 3 (*protocol unreachable* and *port unreachable*) are used by an end host to indicate that the TCP segment or UDP datagram contained in a packet could not be delivered to the upper layer service.

When the end host receives a packet with a Layer 4 PDU that is to be delivered to an unavailable service, the host may respond to the source host with an ICMP Destination Unreachable with a code = 2 or code = 3, indicating that the service is not available. The service may not be available because no daemon is running providing the service or because security on the host is not allowing access to the service.

Time Exceeded

An ICMP Time Exceeded message is used by a router to indicate that a packet cannot be forwarded because the TTL field of the packet has expired. If a router receives a packet and decrements the TTL field in the packet to zero, it discards the packet. The router may also send an ICMP Time Exceeded message to the source host to inform the host of the reason the packet was dropped.

Route Redirection

A router may use the ICMP Redirect Message to notify the hosts on a network that a better route is available for a particular destination. This message may only be used when the source host is on the same physical network as both gateways. If a router receives a packet for which it has a route and for which the next hop is attached to the same interface as the packet arrived, the router may send an ICMP Redirect Message to the source host. This message will inform the source host of the next hop contained in a route in the routing table.

Source Quench

The ICMP Source Quench message can be used to tell the source to temporarily stop sending packets. If a router does not have enough buffer space to receive incoming packets, a router will discard the packets. If the router has to do so, it may also send an ICMP Source Quench message to source hosts for every message that it discards.

A destination host may also send a source quench message if datagrams arrive too fast to be processed.

When a host receives an ICMP Source Quench message, it reports it to the Transport layer. The source host can then use the TCP flow control mechanisms to adjust the transmission.

Links:

RFC 792 http://www.ietf.org/rfc/rfc0792.txt?number=792

RFC 1122 http://www.ietf.org/rfc/rfc1122.txt?number=1122

RFC 2003 http://www.ietf.org/rfc/rfc2003.txt?number=2003

6.7   Labs and Activities

6.7.1   Lab - Ping and Traceroute

Refer to **Lab Activity** for this chapter

This lab demonstrates the `ping` and `tracert` commands from a host. You will observe the steps of the operation of these commands in a network.

Refer to **Packet Tracer Activity** for this chapter

This Packet Tracer activity demonstrates the `ping` and `tracert` commands from a host. You will observe the steps of the operation of these commands in a network.

6.7.2   Lab - Examining ICMP Packet

Refer to **Lab Activity** for this chapter

In this lab, you will use Wireshark to capture ICMP packets to observe the different ICMP codes.

Refer to **Packet Tracer Activity** for this chapter

This Packet Tracer activity will examine ICMP packets issued from hosts on a network.

6.7.3   Activity: IPv4 Address Subnetting Part 1

Refer to **Lab Activity** for this chapter

This lab is designed to teach how to compute major network IP address information from a given IP address.

6.7.4   Activity: IPv4 Address Subnetting Part 2

Refer to **Lab Activity** for this chapter

This lab is designed to teach you how to compute subnet information for a given IP address and subnetwork mask.

6.7.5   Lab: Subnet and Router Configuration

Refer to **Lab Activity** for this chapter

In this lab activity, you will design and apply an IP addressing scheme for a given topology. After cabling the network you will then configure each device using the appropriate basic configuration commands. When the configuration is complete the appropriate IOS commands will be used to verify that the network is working properly.

Refer to **Packet Tracer Activity** for this chapter

In this Packet Tracer activity, you will design and apply an IP addressing scheme for a given topology. After cabling the network you will then configure each device using the appropriate basic configuration commands. When the configuration is complete the appropriate IOS commands will be used to verify that the network is working properly.

Summary and Review

Refer to **Figure** in online course

IPv4 addresses are hierarchical with network, subnetwork, and host portions. An IPv4 address can represent a complete network, a specific host, or the broadcast address of the network.

Different addresses are used for unicast, multicast, and broadcast data communications.

Addressing authorities and ISPs allocate address ranges to users, who in turn can assign these addresses to their network devices statically or dynamically. The allocated address range can be divided into subnetworks by calculating and applying subnet masks.

Careful addressing planning is required to make best use of the available address space. Size, location, use, and access requirements are all considerations in the address planning process.

Once implemented, an IP network needs to be tested to verify its connectivity and operational performance.

Refer to **Figure** in online course

In this activity, you will apply your newly learned skill of subnetting to the ongoing goal of building an increasingly sophisticated model of the Exploration lab topology.

Refer to **Packet Tracer Activity** for this chapter

Packet Tracer Skills Integration Instructions (PDF)

To Learn More

Refer to **Figure** in online course

Reflection Questions

Discuss the requirements of an IPv4 addressing plan for an organization whose operations are spread over a number of locations. The organization has a number of different functional areas at most locations that require servers, printers, and mobile devices in addition to regular desktop PCs and laptops. What other address space issues would have to be considered if the organization required Internet access for its users as well as access to specific servers by its customers?

Discuss and consider how an organization could rearrange its current /20 IPv4 addressing plan if it needed to expand its network to have more, smaller subnetworks, each with a varying number of potential hosts.

Chapter Quiz

Go to the online course to take the quiz.

Take the chapter quiz to test your knowledge.

Your Chapter Notes

CHAPTER 7

Data Link Layer

Chapter Introduction

To support our communication, the OSI model divides the functions of a data network into layers.

To recap:

- The Application layer provides the interface to the user.
- The Transport layer is responsible for dividing and managing communications between the processes running in the two end systems.
- The Network layer protocols organize our communication data so that it can travel across internetworks from the originating host to a destination host.

For Network layer packets to be transported from source host to destination host, they must traverse different physical networks. These physical networks can consist of different types of physical media such as copper wires, microwaves, optical fibers, and satellite links. Network layer packets do not have a way to directly access these different media.

It is the role of the OSI Data Link layer to prepare Network layer packets for transmission and to control access to the physical media.

This chapter introduces the general functions of the Data Link layer and the protocols associated with it.

Learning Objectives

Upon completion of this chapter, you will be able to:

- Explain the role of Data Link layer protocols in data transmission.
- Describe how the Data Link layer prepares data for transmission on network media.
- Describe the different types of media access control methods.
- Identify several common logical network topologies and describe how the logical topology determines the media access control method for that network.
- Explain the purpose of encapsulating packets into frames to facilitate media access.
- Describe the Layer 2 frame structure and identify generic fields.
- Explain the role of key frame header and trailer fields, including addressing, QoS, type of protocol, and Frame Check Sequence.

7.1 Data Link Layer - Accessing the Media

7.1.1 Data Link Layer - Supporting & Connecting to Upper Layer Services

Figure
in online course

Refer to
Figure
in online course

The Data Link layer provides a means for exchanging data over a common local media.

The Data Link layer performs two basic services:

- Allows the upper layers to access the media using techniques such as framing
- Controls how data is placed onto the media and is received from the media using techniques such as media access control and error detection

As with each of the OSI layers, there are terms specific to this layer:

Frame - The Data Link layer PDU

Node - The Layer 2 notation for network devices connected to a common medium

Media/medium (physical)* - The physical means for the transfer of information between two nodes

Network (physical)** - Two or more nodes connected to a common medium

The Data Link layer is responsible for the exchange of frames between nodes over the media of a physical network.

* It is important to understand the meaning of the words medium and media within the context of this chapter. Here, these words refer to the material that actually carries the signals representing the transmitted data. Media is the physical copper cable, optical fiber, or atmosphere through which the signals travel. In this chapter media does not refer to content programming such as audio, animation, television, and video as used when referring to digital content and multimedia.

** A physical network is different from a logical network. Logical networks are defined at the Network layer by the arrangement of the hierarchical addressing scheme. Physical networks represent the interconnection of devices on a common media. Sometimes, a physical network is also referred to as a *network segment*.

Refer to
Figure
in online course

Upper Layer Access to Media

As we have discussed, a network model allows each layer to function with minimal concern for the roles of the other layers. The Data Link layer relieves the upper layers from the responsibility of putting data on the network and receiving data from the network. This layer provides services to support the communication processes for each medium over which data is to be transmitted.

In any given exchange of Network layer packets, there may be numerous Data Link layer and media transitions. At each hop along the path, an intermediary device - usually a router - accepts frames from a medium, decapsulates the frame, and then forwards the packet in a new frame appropriate to the medium of that segment of the physical network.

Imagine a data conversation between two distant hosts, such as a PC in Paris with an Internet server in Japan. Although the two hosts may be communicating with their *peer* Network layer protocols (IP for example), it is likely that numerous Data Link layer protocols are being used to transport the IP packets over various types of LANs and WANs. This packet exchange between two hosts requires a diversity of protocols that must exist at the Data Link layer. Each transition at a router could require a different Data Link layer protocol for transport on a new medium.

Notice in the figure that each link between devices uses a different medium. Between the PC and the router may be an Ethernet link. The routers are connected through a satellite link, and the laptop is connected through a wireless link to the last router. In this example, as an IP packet travels from the PC to the laptop, it will be encapsulated into Ethernet frame, decapsulated, processed, and then encapsulated into a new data link frame to cross the satellite link. For the final link, the packet will use a wireless data link frame from the router to the laptop.

The Data Link layer effectively insulates the communication processes at the higher layers from the media transitions that may occur end-to-end. A packet is received from and directed to an upper layer protocol, in this case IPv4 or IPv6, that does not need to be aware of which media the communication will use.

Without the Data Link layer, a Network layer protocol, such as IP, would have to make provisions for connecting to every type of media that could exist along a delivery path. Moreover, IP would have to adapt every time a new network technology or medium was developed. This process would hamper protocol and network media innovation and development. This is a key reason for using a layered approach to networking.

The range of Data Link layer services has to include all of the currently used types of media and the methods for accessing them. Because of the number of communication services provided by the Data Link layer, it is difficult to generalize their role and provide examples of a generic set of services. For that reason, please note that any given protocol may or may not support all these Data Link layer services.

Internetworking Basics - http://www.cisco.com/en/US/docs/internetworking/technology/handbook/Intro-to-Internet.html

MTU - http://www.tcpipguide.com/free/t_IPDatagramSizeMaximumTransmissionUnitMTUFragmentat.htm

7.1.2 Data Link Layer - Controlling Transfer across Local Media

Refer to
Figure
in online course

Layer 2 protocols specify the encapsulation of a packet into a frame and the techniques for getting the encapsulated packet on and off each medium. The technique used for getting the frame on and off media is called the media access control method. For the data to be transferred across a number of different media, different media access control methods may be required during the course of a single communication.

Each network environment that packets encounter as they travel from a local host to a remote host can have different characteristics. For example, one network environment may consist of many hosts contending to access the network medium on an ad hoc basis. Another environment may consist of a direct connection between only two devices over which data flows sequentially as bits in an orderly way.

The media access control methods described by the Data Link layer protocols define the processes by which network devices can access the network media and transmit frames in diverse network environments.

A node that is an end device uses an adapter to make the connection to the network. For example, to connect to a LAN, the device would use the appropriate Network Interface Card (NIC) to connect to the LAN media. The adapter manages the framing and media access control.

At intermediary devices such as a router, where the media type could change for each connected network, different physical interfaces on the router are used to encapsulate the packet into the appropriate frame, and a suitable media access control method is used to access each link. The router in the figure has an Ethernet interface to connect to the LAN and a serial interface to connect to the WAN. As the router processes frames, it will use Data Link layer services to receive the frame from one medium, decapsulate it to the Layer 3 PDU, re-encapsulate the PDU into a new frame, and place the frame on the medium of the next link of the network.

7.1.3 Data Link Layer - Creating a Frame

Refer to
Figure
in online course

The description of a frame is a key element of each Data Link layer protocol. Data Link layer protocols require control information to enable the protocols to function. Control information may tell:

- Which nodes are in communication with each other

- When communication between individual nodes begins and when it ends

- Which errors occurred while the nodes communicated

- Which nodes will communicate next

The Data Link layer prepares a packet for transport across the local media by encapsulating it with a header and a trailer to create a frame.

Unlike the other PDUs that have been discussed in this course, the Data Link layer frame includes:

- Data - The packet from the Network layer

- Header - Contains control information, such as addressing, and is located at the beginning of the PDU

- Trailer - Contains control information added to the end of the PDU

These frame elements will be discussed in more detail later in this chapter.

Formatting Data for Transmission

Refer to
Figure
in online course

When data travels on the media, it is converted into a stream of bits, or 1s and 0s. If a node is receiving long streams of bits, how does it determine where a frame starts and stops or which bits represent the address?

Framing breaks the stream into decipherable groupings, with control information inserted in the header and trailer as values in different fields. This format gives the physical signals a structure that can be received by nodes and decoded into packets at the destination.

Typical field types include:

- Start and stop indicator fields - The beginning and end limits of the frame

- Naming or addressing fields

- Type field - The type of PDU contained in the frame

- Control - Flow control services

- A data field -The frame payload (Network layer packet)

Fields at the end of the frame form the trailer. These fields are used for error detection and mark the end of the frame.

Not all protocols include all of these fields. The standards for a specific Data Link protocol define the actual frame format. Examples of frame formats will be discussed at the end of this chapter.

7.1.4 Data Link Layer - Connecting Upper Layer Services to the Media

Refer to
Figure
in online course

The Data Link layer exists as a connecting layer between the software processes of the layers above it and the Physical layer below it. As such, it prepares the Network layer packets for transmission across some form of media, be it copper, fiber, or the atmosphere.

In many cases, the Data Link layer is embodied as a physical entity, such as an Ethernet *network interface card* (NIC), which inserts into the system bus of a computer and makes the connection between running software processes on the computer and physical media. The NIC is not solely a physical entity, however. Software associated with the NIC enables the NIC to perform its intermediary functions of preparing data for transmission and encoding the data as signals to be sent on the associated media.

Refer to **Figure** in online course

Data Link Sublayers

To support a wide variety of network functions, the Data Link layer is often divided into two sublayers: an upper sublayer and a lower sublayer.

- The upper sublayer defines the software processes that provide services to the Network layer protocols.

- The lower sublayer defines the media access processes performed by the hardware.

Separating the Data Link layer into sublayers allows for one type of frame defined by the upper layer to access different types of media defined by the lower layer. Such is the case in many LAN technologies, including Ethernet.

The two common LAN sublayers are:

Logical Link Control

Logical Link Control (LLC) places information in the frame that identifies which Network layer protocol is being used for the frame. This information allows multiple Layer 3 protocols, such as IP and IPX, to utilize the same network interface and media.

Media Access Control

Media Access Control (MAC) provides Data Link layer addressing and delimiting of data according to the physical signaling requirements of the medium and the type of Data Link layer protocol in use.

7.1.5 Data Link Layer - Standards

Refer to **Figure** in online course

Unlike the protocols of the upper layers of the TCP/IP suite, Data Link layer protocols are generally not defined by Request for Comments (RFCs). Although the Internet Engineering Task Force (IETF) maintains the functional protocols and services for the TCP/IP protocol suite in the upper layers, the IETF does not define the functions and operation of that model's Network access layer. The TCP/IP Network Access layer is the equivalent of the OSI Data Link and Physical layers. These two layer will be discussed in separate chapters for closer examination..

The functional protocols and services at the Data Link layer are described by engineering organizations (such as IEEE, ANSI, and ITU) and communications companies. Engineering organizations set public and open standards and protocols. Communications companies may set and use proprietary protocols to take advantage of new advances in technology or market opportunities.

Data Link layer services and specifications are defined by multiple standards based on a variety of technologies and media to which the protocols are applied. Some of these standards integrate both Layer 2 and Layer 1 services.

Engineering organizations that define open standards and protocols that apply to the Data Link layer include:

- International Organization for Standardization (ISO)

- Institute of Electrical and Electronics Engineers (IEEE)

- *American National Standards Institute (ANSI)*

- *International Telecommunication Union (ITU)*

Unlike the upper layer protocols, which are implemented mostly in software such as the host operating system or specific applications, Data Link layer processes occur both in software and hardware. The protocols at this layer are implemented within the electronics of the network adapters with which the device connects to the physical network.

For example, a device implementing the Data Link layer on a computer would be the network interface card (NIC). For a laptop, a wireless PCMCIA adapter is commonly used. Each of these adapters is the hardware that complies with the Layer 2 standards and protocols.

http://www.iso.org

http://www.ieee.org

http://www.ansi.org

http://www.itu.int

7.2 Media Access Control Techniques

7.2.1 Placing Data on the Media

Refer to
Figure
in online course

Regulating the placement of data frames onto the media is known as media access control.
Among the different implementations of the Data Link layer protocols, there are different methods of controlling access to the media. These media access control techniques define if and how the nodes share the media.

Media access control is the equivalent of traffic rules that regulate the entrance of motor vehicles onto a roadway. The absence of any media access control would be the equivalent of vehicles ignoring all other traffic and entering the road without regard to the other vehicles.

However, not all roads and entrances are the same. Traffic can enter the road by merging, by waiting for its turn at a stop sign, or by obeying signal lights. A driver follows a different set of rules for each type of entrance.

In the same way, there are different ways to regulate the placing of frames onto the media. The protocols at the Data Link layer define the rules for access to different media. Some media access control methods use highly-controlled processes to ensure that frames are safely placed on the media. These methods are defined by sophisticated protocols, which require mechanisms that introduce overhead onto the network.

The method of media access control used depends on:

- Media sharing - If and how the nodes share the media

- Topology - How the connection between the nodes appears to the Data Link layer

7.2.2 Media Access Control for Shared Media

Refer to
Figure
in online course

Some network topologies share a common medium with multiple nodes. At any one time, there may be a number of devices attempting to send and receive data using the network media. There are rules that govern how these devices share the media.

There are two basic media access control methods for shared media:

- Controlled - Each node has its own time to use the medium

■ Contention-based - All nodes compete for the use of the medium

Click the tabs in the figure to see the differences in the two methods.

Controlled Access for Shared Media

When using the controlled access method, network devices take turns, in sequence, to access the medium. This method is also known as scheduled access or *deterministic*. If a device does not need to access the medium, the opportunity to use the medium passes to the next device in line. When one device places a frame on the media, no other device can do so until the frame has arrived at the destination and has been processed by the destination.

Although controlled access is well-ordered and provides predictable *throughput*, deterministic methods can be inefficient because a device has to wait for its turn before it can use the medium.

Contention-based Access for Shared Media

Also referred to as non-deterministic, contention-based methods allow any device to try to access the medium whenever it has data to send. To prevent complete chaos on the media, these methods use a *Carrier Sense Multiple Access (CSMA)* process to first detect if the media is carrying a signal. If a *carrier* signal on the media from another node is detected, it means that another device is transmitting. When the device attempting to transmit sees that the media is busy, it will wait and try again after a short time period. If no carrier signal is detected, the device transmits its data. Ethernet and wireless networks use contention-based media access control.

It is possible that the CSMA process will fail and two devices will transmit at the same time. This is called a *data collision*. If this occurs, the data sent by both devices will be corrupted and will need to be resent.

Contention-based media access control methods do not have the overhead of controlled access methods. A mechanism for tracking whose turn it is to access the media is not required. However, the contention-based systems do not scale well under heavy media use. As use and the number of nodes increases, the probability of successful media access without a collision decreases. Additionally, The recovery mechanisms required to correct errors due to these collisions further diminishes the throughput.

CSMA is usually implemented in conjunction with a method for resolving the media contention. The two commonly used methods are:

CSMA/Collision Detection

In CSMA/Collision Detection (*CSMA/CD*), the device monitors the media for the presence of a data signal. If a data signal is absent, indicating that the media is free, the device transmits the data. If signals are then detected that show another device was transmitting at the same time, all devices stop sending and try again later. Traditional forms of Ethernet use this method.

CSMA/Collision Avoidance

In CSMA/Collision Avoidance (*CSMA/CA*), the device examines the media for the presence of a data signal. If the media is free, the device sends a notification across the media of its intent to use it. The device then sends the data. This method is used by 802.11 wireless networking technologies.

Note: CSMA/CD will be covered in more detail in Chapter 9.

7.2.3 Media Access Control for Non-Shared Media

Refer to **Figure** in online course

Media access control protocols for non-shared media require little or no control before placing frames onto the media. These protocols have simpler rules and procedures for media access control. Such is the case for point-to-point topologies.

In point-to-point topologies, the media interconnects just two nodes. In this arrangement, the nodes do not have to share the media with other hosts or determine if a frame is destined for that node. Therefore, Data Link layer protocols have little to do for controlling non-shared media access.

Full Duplex and Half Duplex

In point-to-point connections, the Data Link layer has to consider whether the communication is *half-duplex* or *full-duplex*.

Click the tabs in the figure to see the differences in the two methods.

Half-duplex communication means that the devices can both transmit and receive on the media but cannot do so simultaneously. Ethernet has established arbitration rules for resolving conflicts arising from instances when more than one station attempts to transmit at the same time.

In full-duplex communication, both devices can transmit and receive on the media at the same time. The Data Link layer assumes that the media is available for transmission for both nodes at any time. Therefore, there is no media arbitration necessary in the Data Link layer.

The details of a specific media access control technique can only be examined by studying a specific protocol. Within this course, we will study traditional Ethernet, which uses CSMA/CD. Other techniques will be covered in later courses.

7.2.4 Logical Topology vs Physical Topology

Refer to
Figure
in online course

The topology of a network is the arrangement or relationship of the network devices and the interconnections between them. Network topologies can be viewed at the physical level and the logical level.

The *physical topology is an arrangement of the nodes and the physical connections between them. The representation of how the media is used to interconnect the devices is the physical topology. These will be covered in later chapters of this course.*

A *logical topology* is the way a network transfers frames from one node to the next. This arrangement consists of virtual connections between the nodes of a network independent of their physical layout. These logical signal paths are defined by Data Link layer protocols. The Data Link layer "sees" the logical topology of a network when controlling data access to the media. It is the logical topology that influences the type of network framing and media access control used.

The physical or cabled topology of a network will most likely not be the same as the logical topology.

Logical topology of a network is closely related to the mechanism used to manage network access. Access methods provide the procedures to manage network access so that all stations have access. When several entities share the same media, some mechanism must be in place to control access. Access methods are applied to networks to regulate this media access. Access methods will be discussed in more detail later.

Logical and physical topologies typically used in networks are:

- Point-to-Point

- Multi-Access

- Ring

The logical implementations of these topologies and their associated media access control methods are considered in the following sections.

7.2.5 Point-to-Point Topology

Refer to **Figure** in online course

A point-to-point topology connects two nodes directly together, as shown in the figure. In data networks with point-to-point topologies, the media access control protocol can be very simple. All frames on the media can only travel to or from the two nodes. The frames are placed on the media by the node at one end and taken off the media by the node at the other end of the point-to-point circuit.

In point-to-point networks, if data can only flow in one direction at a time, it is operating as a half-duplex link. If data can successfully flow across the link from each node simultaneously, it is a full-duplex link.

Data Link layer protocols could provide more sophisticated media access control processes for logical point-to-point topologies, but this would only add unnecessary protocol overhead.

Logical Point-to-Point Networks

Refer to **Figure** in online course

The end nodes communicating in a point-to-point network can be physically connected via a number of intermediate devices. However the use of physical devices in the network does not affect the logical topology. As shown in the figure, the source and destination node may be indirectly connected to each other over some geographical distance. In some cases, the logical connection between nodes forms what is called a *virtual circuit*. *A virtual circuit is a logical connection created within a network between two network devices. The two nodes on either end of the virtual circuit exchange the frames with each other. This occurs even if the frames are directed through intermediary devices. Virtual circuits are important logical communication constructs used by some Layer 2 technologies.*

The media access method used by the Data Link protocol is determined by the *logical* point-to-point topology, not the *physical* topology. This means that the logical point-to-point connection between two nodes may not necessarily be between two physical nodes at each end of a single physical link.

7.2.6 Multi-Access Topology

Refer to **Figure** in online course

A logical multi-access topology enables a number of nodes to communicate by using the same shared media. Data from only one node can be placed on the medium at any one time. Every node sees all the frames that are on the medium, but only the node to which the frame is addressed processes the contents of the frame.

Having many nodes share access to the medium requires a Data Link media access control method to regulate the transmission of data and thereby reduce collisions between different signals.

The media access control methods used by logical multi-access topologies are typically CSMA/CD or CSMA/CA. However, *token passing* methods can also be used.

A number of media access control techniques are available for this type of logical topology. The Data Link layer protocol specifies the media access control method that will provide the appropriate balance between frame control, frame protection, and network overhead.

Play the animation to see how nodes access the media in a multi-access topology.

7.2.7 Ring Topology

Refer to
Figure
in online course

In a logical ring topology, each node in turn receives a frame. If the frame is not addressed to the node, the node passes the frame to the next node. This allows a ring to use a controlled media access control technique called *token passing*.

Nodes in a logical ring topology remove the frame from the ring, examine the address, and send it on if it is not addressed for that node. In a ring, all nodes around the ring- between the source and destination node examine the frame.

There are multiple media access control techniques that could be used with a logical ring, depending on the level of control required. For example, only one frame at a time is usually carried by the media. If there is no data being transmitted, a signal (known as a token) may be placed on the media and a node can only place a data frame on the media when it has the token.

Remember that the Data Link layer "sees" a logical ring topology. The actual physical cabling topology could be another topology.

Play the animation to see how nodes access the media in a logical ring topology.

7.3 Media Access Control Addressing and Framing Data

7.3.1 Data Link Layer Protocols - The Frame

Refer to
Figure
in online course

Remember that although there are many different Data Link layer protocols that describe Data Link layer frames, each frame type has three basic parts:

- Header
- Data
- Trailer

All Data Link layer protocols encapsulate the Layer 3 PDU within the data field of the frame. However, the structure of the frame and the fields contained in the header and trailer vary according to the protocol.

The Data Link layer protocol describes the features required for the transport of packets across different media. These features of the protocol are integrated into the encapsulation of the frame. When the frame arrives at its destination and the Data Link protocol takes the frame off the media, the framing information is read and discarded.

There is no one frame structure that meets the needs of all data transportation across all types of media. As shown in the figure, depending on the environment, the amount of control information needed in the frame varies to match the media access control requirements of the media and logical topology.

7.3.2 Framing - Role of the Header

Refer to
Figure
in online course

As shown in the figure, the frame header contains the control information specified by the Data Link layer protocol for the specific logical topology and media used.

Frame control information is unique to each type of protocol. It is used by the Layer 2 protocol to provide features demanded by the communication environment.

Typical frame header fields include:

- Start Frame field - Indicates the beginning of the frame

- Source and Destination address fields - Indicates the source and destination nodes on the media

- Priority/Quality of Service field - Indicates a particular type of communication service for processing

- Type field - Indicates the upper layer service contained in the frame

- Logical connection control field - Used to establish a logical connection between nodes

- Physical link control field - Used to establish the media link

- Flow control field - Used to start and stop traffic over the media

- Congestion control field - Indicates congestion in the media

The field names above are nonspecific fields listed as examples. Different Data Link layer protocols may use different fields from those mentioned. Because the purposes and functions of Data Link layer protocols are related to the specific topologies and media, each protocol has to be examined to gain a detailed understanding of its frame structure. As protocols are discussed in this course, more information about the frame structure will be explained.

7.3.3 Addressing - Where the Frame Goes

Refer to **Figure** in online course

The data Link layer provides addressing that is used in transporting the frame across the shared local media. Device addresses at this layer are referred to as physical addresses. Data Link layer addressing is contained within the frame header and specifies the frame destination node on the local network. The frame header may also contain the source address of the frame.

Unlike Layer 3 logical addresses that are hierarchical, physical addresses do not indicate on what network the device is located. If the device is moved to another network or subnet, it will still function with the same Layer 2 physical address.

Because the frame is only used to transport data between nodes across the local media, the Data Link layer address is only used for local delivery. Addresses at this layer have no meaning beyond the local network. Compare this to Layer 3, where addresses in the packet header are carried from source host to destination host regardless of the number of network hops along the route.

If the packet in the frame must pass onto another network segment, the intermediate device - a router - will decapsulate the original frame, create a new frame for the packet, and send it onto the new segment. The new frame will use source and destination addressing as necessary to transport the packet across the new media.

Addressing Requirements

The need for Data Link layer addressing at this layer depends on the logical topology.

Point-to-point topologies, with just two interconnected nodes, do not require addressing. Once on the medium, the frame has only one place it can go.

Because ring and multi-access topologies can connect many nodes on a common medium, addressing is required for these typologies. When a frame reaches each node in the topology, the node examines the destination address in the header to determine if it is the destination of the frame.

7.3.4 Framing - Role of the Trailer

Refer to
Figure
in online course

Data Link layer protocols add a trailer to the end of each frame. The trailer is used to determine if the frame arrived without error. This process is called *error detection*. Note that this is different from *error correction*. Error detection is accomplished by placing a logical or mathematical summary of the bits that comprise the frame in the trailer.

Frame Check Sequence

The Frame Check Sequence (FCS) field is used to determine if errors occurred in the transmission and reception of the frame. Error detection is added at the Data Link layer because this is where data is transferred across the media. The media is a potentially unsafe environment for data. The signals on the media could be subject to interference, distortion, or loss that would substantially change the bit values that those signals represent. The error detection mechanism provided by the use of the FCS field discovers most errors caused on the media.

To ensure that the content of the received frame at the destination matches that of the frame that left the source node, a transmitting node creates a logical summary of the contents of the frame. This is known as the *cyclic redundancy check (CRC)* value. This value is placed in the Frame Check Sequence (FCS) field of the frame to represent the contents of the frame.

When the frame arrives at the destination node, the receiving node calculates its own logical summary, or CRC, of the frame. The receiving node compares the two CRC values. If the two values are the same, the frame is considered to have arrived as transmitted. If the CRC value in the FCS differs from the CRC calculated at the receiving node, the frame is discarded.

There is always the small possibility that a frame with a good CRC result is actually corrupt. Errors in bits may cancel each other out when the CRC is calculated. Upper layer protocols would then be required to detect and correct this data loss.

The protocol used in the Data Link layer, will determine if error correction will take place. The FCS is used to detect the error, but not every protocol will support correcting the error.

7.3.5 Data Link Layer Protocols - The Frame

Refer to
Figure
in online course

In a TCP/IP network, all OSI Layer 2 protocols work with the Internet Protocol at OSI Layer 3. However, the actual Layer 2 protocol used depends on the logical topology of the network and the implementation of the Physical layer. Given the wide range of physical media used across the range of topologies in networking, there are a correspondingly high number of Layer 2 protocols in use.

Protocols that will be covered in CCNA courses include:

- Ethernet

- Point-to-Point Protocol (PPP)

- High-Level Data Link Control (HDLC)

- Frame Relay

- Asynchronous Transfer Mode (ATM)

Each protocol performs media access control for specified Layer 2 logical topologies. This means that a number of different network devices can act as nodes that operate at the Data Link layer when implementing these protocols. These devices include the network adapter or network interface cards (NICs) on computers as well as the interfaces on routers and Layer 2 switches.

The Layer 2 protocol used for a particular network topology is determined by the technology used to implement that topology. The technology is, in turn, determined by the size of the network - in terms of the number of hosts and the geographic scope - and the services to be provided over the network.

LAN Technology

A Local Area Network typically uses a high bandwidth technology that is capable of supporting large numbers of hosts. A LAN's relatively small geographic area (a single building or a multi-building campus) and its high density of users make this technology cost effective.

WAN Technology

However, using a high bandwidth technology is usually not cost-effective for Wide Area Networks that cover large geographic areas (cities or multiple cities, for example). The cost of the long distance physical links and the technology used to carry the signals over those distances typically results in lower bandwidth capacity.

Difference in bandwidth normally results in the use of different protocols for LANs and WANs.

Refer to **Figure** in online course

Ethernet Protocol for LANs

Ethernet is a family of networking technologies that are defined in the IEEE 802.2 and 802.3 standards. Ethernet standards define both the Layer 2 protocols and the Layer 1 technologies. Ethernet is the most widely used LAN technology and supports data bandwidths of 10, 100, 1000, or 10,000 Mbps.

The basic frame format and the IEEE sublayers of OSI Layers 1 and 2 remain consistent across all forms of Ethernet. However, the methods for detecting and placing data on the media vary with different implementations.

Ethernet provides unacknowledged connectionless service over a shared media using CSMA/CD as the media access methods. Shared media requires that the Ethernet frame header use a Data Link layer address to identify the source and destination nodes. As with most LAN protocols, this address is referred to as the MAC address of the node. An Ethernet MAC address is 48 bits and is generally represented in hexadecimal format.

The Ethernet frame has many fields, as shown in the figure. At the Data Link layer, the frame structure is nearly identical for all speeds of Ethernet. However, at the Physical layer, different versions of Ethernet place the bits onto the media differently.

Ethernet II is the Ethernet frame format used in TCP/IP networks.

Ethernet is such an important part of data networking, we have devoted a chapter to it. We also use it in examples throughout this series of courses.

Refer to **Figure** in online course

Point-to-Point Protocol for WANs

Point-to-Point Protocol (PPP) is a protocol used to deliver frames between two nodes. Unlike many Data Link layer protocols that are defined by electrical engineering organizations, the PPP standard is defined by RFCs. PPP was developed as a WAN protocol and remains the protocol of choice to implement many serial WANs. PPP can be used on various physical media, including twisted pair, fiber optic lines, and satellite transmission, as well as for virtual connections.

PPP uses a layered architecture. To accommodate the different types of media, PPP establishes logical connections, called sessions, between two nodes. The PPP session hides the underlying physical media from the upper PPP protocol. These sessions also provide PPP with a method for encapsulating multiple protocols over a point-to-point link. Each protocol encapsulated over the link establishes its own PPP session.

PPP also allows the two nodes to negotiate options within the PPP session. This includes authentication, compression, and multilink (the use of multiple physical connections).

See the figure for the basic fields in a PPP frame.

PPP protocol: http://www.ietf.org/rfc/rfc1661.txt?number=1661

PPP Vendor Extensions: http://www.ietf.org/rfc/rfc2153.txt?number=2153

Refer to
Figure
in online course

Wireless Protocol for LANs

802.11 is an extension of the IEEE 802 standards. It uses the same 802.2 LLC and 48-bit addressing scheme as other 802 LANs, However there are many differences at the MAC sublayer and Physical layer. In a wireless environment, the environment requires special considerations. There is no definable physical connectivity; therefore, external factors may interfere with data transfer and it is difficult to control access. To meet these challenges, wireless standards have additional controls.

The Standard IEEE 802.11, commonly referred to as *Wi-Fi*, is a contention-based system using a Carrier Sense Multiple Access/Collision Avoidance (CSMA/CA) media access process. CSMA/CA specifies a random *backoff* procedure for all nodes that are waiting to transmit. The most likely opportunity for medium contention is just after the medium becomes available. Making the nodes back off for a random period greatly reduces the likelihood of a collision.

802.11 networks also use Data Link acknowledgements to confirm that a frame is received successfully. If the sending station does not detect the acknowledgement frame, either because the original data frame or the acknowledgment was not received intact, the frame is retransmitted. This explicit acknowledgement overcomes interference and other radio-related problems.

Other services supported by 802.11 are authentication, association (connectivity to a wireless device), and privacy (encryption).

An 802.11 frame is shown in the figure. It contains these fields:

Protocol Version field - Version of 802.11 frame in use

Type and Subtype fields - Identifies one of three functions and sub functions of the frame: control, data, and management

To DS field - Set to 1 in data frames destined for the distribution system (devices in the wireless structure)

From DS field - Set to 1 in data frames exiting the distribution system

More Fragments field - Set to 1 for frames that have another fragment

Retry field - Set to 1 if the frame is a retransmission of an earlier frame

Power Management field - Set to 1 to indicate that a node will be in power-save mode

More Data field - Set to 1 to indicate to a node in power-save mode that more frames are buffered for that node

Wired Equivalent Privacy (WEP) field - Set to 1 if the frame contains WEP encrypted information for security

Order field - Set to 1 in a data type frame that uses Strictly Ordered service class (does not need reordering)

Duration/ID field - Depending on the type of frame, represents either the time, in microseconds, required to transmit the frame or an association identity (AID) for the station that transmitted the frame

Destination Address (DA) field - MAC address of the final destination node in the network

Source Address (SA) field - MAC address of the node the initiated the frame

Receiver Address (RA) field - MAC address that identifies the wireless device that is the immediate recipient of the frame

Transmitter Address (TA) field - MAC address that identifies the wireless device that transmitted the frame

Sequence Number field - Indicates the sequence number assigned to the frame; retransmitted frames are identified by duplicate sequence numbers

Fragment Number field - Indicates the number for each fragment of a frame

Frame Body field - Contains the information being transported; for data frames, typically an IP packet

FCS field - Contains a 32-bit cyclic redundancy check (CRC) of the frame

7.4 Putting it All Together

7.4.1 Follow Data Through an Internetwork

Refer to **Figure** in online course

The figure on the next page presents a simple data transfer between two hosts across an internetwork. We highlight the function of each layer during the communication. For this example we will depict an HTTP request between a client and a server.

To focus on the data transfer process, we are omitting many elements that may occur in a real transaction. In each step we are only bringing attention to the major elements. Many parts of the headers are ignored, for example.

We are assuming that all routing tables are converged and *ARP* tables are complete. Additionally, we are assuming that a TCP session is already established between the client and server. We will also assume that the DNS lookup for the WWW server is already cached at the client.

In the WAN connection between the two routers, we are assuming that PPP has already established a physical circuit and has established a PPP session.

On the next page, you can step through this communication. We encourage you to read each explanation carefully and study the operation of the layers for each device.

Refer to **Figure** in online course

Interactive

In this activity, you can examine in further detail the step-by-step animation on the previous page.

Refer to **Packet Tracer Activity** for this chapter

7.5 Labs and Activities

7.5.1 Investigating Layer 2 Frame Headers

Refer to **Packet Tracer Activity** for this chapter

In this activity, you can explore some of the most common Layer 2 encapsulations.

7.5.2 Lab - Frame Examination

Refer to **Lab Activity** for this chapter

In this lab, you will use Wireshark to capture and analyze Ethernet II frame header fields.

Summary and Review

Refer to **Figure** in online course

The OSI Data Link layer prepares Network layer packets for placement onto the physical media that transports data.

The wide range of data communications media requires a correspondingly wide range of Data Link protocols to control data access to these media.

Media access can be orderly and controlled or it can be contention-based. The logical topology and physical medium help determine the media access method.

The Data Link layer prepares the data for placement on the media by encapsulating the Layer 3 packet into a frame.

A frame has header and trailer fields that include Data Link source and destination addresses, QoS, type of protocol, and Frame Check Sequence values.

Refer to **Figure** in online course

Refer to **Packet Tracer Activity** for this chapter

In this activity, you will continue to build a more complex model of the Exploration lab network.

To Learn More

Refer to **Figure** in online course

Reflection Questions

How did the widespread adoption of the OSI model change the development of network technologies? How does today's data communications environment differ from that of twenty years ago because of the adoption of the model?

Discuss and compare Carrier Sense Multi-Access Data Link media access protocol features and operation with those of deterministic media access protocols.

Discuss and consider the issues that the developers of a new physical data communications medium have to resolve to ensure interoperability with the existing upper layer TCP/IP protocols.

Go to the online course to take the quiz.

Chapter Quiz

Take the chapter quiz to test your knowledge.

Your Chapter Notes

CHAPTER 8

OSI Physical Layer

Chapter Introduction

Refer to
Figure
in online course

Upper OSI layer protocols prepare data from the human network for transmission to its destination. The Physical layer controls how data is transmitted on the communication media.

The role of the OSI Physical layer is to encode the binary digits that represent Data Link layer frames into signals and to transmit and receive these signals across the physical media - copper wires, optical fiber, and wireless - that connect network devices.

This chapter introduces the general functions of the Physical layer as well as the standards and protocols that manage the transmission of data across local media.

In this chapter, you will learn to:

- Explain the role of Physical layer protocols and services in supporting communication across data networks.

- Describe the purpose of Physical layer signaling and encoding as they are used in networks.

- Describe the role of signals used to represent bits as a frame is transported across the local media.

- Identify the basic characteristics of copper, fiber, and wireless network media.

- Describe common uses of copper, fiber, and wireless network media.

8.1 The Physical Layer - Communication Signals

8.1.1 Physical Layer - Purpose

Refer to
Figure
in online course

The OSI Physical layer provides the means to transport across the network media the bits that make up a Data Link layer frame. This layer accepts a complete frame from the Data Link layer and encodes it as a series of signals that are transmitted onto the local media. The encoded bits that comprise a frame are received by either an end device or an intermediate device.

The delivery of frames across the local media requires the following Physical layer elements:

- The physical media and associated connectors

- A representation of bits on the media

- Encoding of data and control information

- Transmitter and receiver circuitry on the network devices

At this stage of the communication process, the user data has been segmented by the Transport layer, placed into packets by the Network layer, and further encapsulated as frames by the Data Link layer. **The purpose of the Physical layer is to create the electrical, optical, or microwave signal that represents the bits in each frame.** These signals are then sent on the media one at a time.

It is also the job of the Physical layer to retrieve these individual signals from the media, restore them to their bit representations, and pass the bits up to the Data Link layer as a complete frame.

8.1.2 Physical Layer - Operation

Refer to
Figure
in online course

The media does not carry the frame as a single entity. The media carries signals, one at a time, to represent the bits that make up the frame.

There are three basic forms of network media on which data is represented:

- Copper cable

- Fiber

- Wireless

The representation of the bits - that is, the type of signal - depends on the type of media. For copper cable media, the signals are patterns of electrical pulses. For fiber, the signals are patterns of light. For wireless media, the signals are patterns of radio transmissions.

Identifying a Frame

When the Physical layer encodes the bits into the signals for a particular medium, it must also distinguish where one frame ends and the next frame begins. Otherwise, the devices on the media would not recognize when a frame has been fully received. In that case, the destination device would only receive a string of signals and would not be able to properly reconstruct the frame. As described in the previous chapter, indicating the beginning of frame is often a function of the Data Link layer. However, in many technologies, the Physical layer may add its own signals to indicate the beginning and end of the frame.

To enable a receiving device to clearly recognize a frame boundary, the transmitting device adds signals to designate the start and end of a frame. These signals represent particular bit patterns that are only used to denote the start or end of a frame.

The process of encoding a frame of data from the logical bits into the physical signals on the media, and the characteristics of particular physical media, are covered in detail in the following sections of this chapter.

8.1.3 Physical Layer - Standards

Refer to
Figure
in online course

The Physical layer consists of hardware, developed by engineers, in the form of electronic circuitry, media, and connectors. Therefore, it is appropriate that the standards governing this hardware are defined by the relevant electrical and communications engineering organizations.

By comparison, the protocols and operations of the upper OSI layers are performed by software and are designed by software engineers and computer scientists. As we saw in a previous chapter, the services and protocols in the TCP/IP suite are defined by the Internet Engineering Task Force (IETF) in RFCs.

Similar to technologies associated with the Data Link layer, the Physical layer technologies are defined by organizations such as:

- The International Organization for Standardization (ISO)

- The Institute of Electrical and Electronics Engineers (IEEE)

- The American National Standards Institute (ANSI)

- The International Telecommunication Union (ITU)

- The Electronics Industry Alliance/Telecommunications Industry Association (*EIA/TIA*)

- National telecommunications authorities such as the *Federal Communication Commission (FCC)* in the USA.

Physical Layer Technologies and Hardware

Refer to **Figure** in online course

The technologies defined by these organizations include four areas of the Physical layer standards:

- Physical and electrical properties of the media

- Mechanical properties (materials, dimensions, *pinouts*) of the connectors

- Bit representation by the signals (encoding)

- Definition of control information signals

Click Signals, Connectors, and Cables in the figure to see the hardware.

Hardware components such as network adapters (NICs), interfaces and connectors, cable materials, and cable designs are all specified in standards associated with the Physical layer.

8.1.4 Physical layer Fundamental Principles

Refer to **Figure** in online course

The three fundamental functions of the Physical layer are:

- The physical components

- Data encoding

- Signaling

The physical elements are the electronic hardware devices, media and connectors that transmit and carry the signals to represent the bits.

Encoding

Encoding is a method of converting a stream of data bits into a predefined code. Codes are groupings of bits used to provide a predictable pattern that can be recognized by both the sender and the received. Using predictable patterns helps to distinguish data bits from control bits and provide better media error detection.

In addition to creating codes for data, encoding methods at the Physical layer may also provide codes for control purposes such as identifying the beginning and end of a frame. The transmitting host will transmit the specific pattern of bits or a code to identify the beginning and end of the frame.

Signaling

The Physical layer must generate the electrical, optical, or wireless signals that represent the "1" and "0" on the media. The method of representing the bits is called the signaling method. The Physical layer standards must define what type of signal represents a "1" and a "0". This can be as simple as a change in the level of an electrical signal or optical pulse or a more complex signaling method.

In the next sections, you will examine different methods of signaling and encoding.

8.2 Physical Signaling and Encoding: Representing Bits

8.2.1 Signaling Bits for the Media

Refer to
Figure
in online course

Eventually, all communication from the human network becomes binary digits, which are transported individually across the physical media.

Although all the bits that make up a frame are presented to the Physical layer as a unit, the transmission of the frame across the media occurs as a stream of bits sent one at a time. The Physical layer represents each of the bits in the frame as a signal. Each signal placed onto the media has a specific amount of time to occupy the media. This is referred to as its *bit time. Signals are processed by the receiving device and returned to its representation as bits.*

At the Physical layer of the receiving node, the signals are converted back into bits. The bits are then examined for the start of frame and end of frame bit patterns to determine that a complete frame has been received. The Physical layer then delivers all the bits of a frame to the Data Link layer.

Successful delivery of the bits requires some method of synchronization between transmitter and receiver. The signals representing the bits must be examined at specific times during the bit time to properly determine if the signal represents a "**1**" or a "**0**". The synchronization is accomplished by the use of a clock. In LANs, each end of the transmission maintains its own clock. Many signaling methods use predictable transitions in the signal to provide synchronization between the clocks of the transmitting and the receiving devices.

Signaling Methods

Bits are represented on the medium by changing one or more of the following characteristics of a signal:

- Amplitude

- Frequency

- Phase

The nature of the actual signals representing the bits on the media will depend on the signaling method in use. Some methods may use one attribute of signal to represent a single **0** and use another attribute of signal to represent a single **1**.

As an example, with Non-Return to Zero (NRZ), a **0** may be represented by one voltage level on the media during the bit time and a **1** might be represented by a different voltage on the media during the bit time.

There are also methods of signaling that use transitions, or the absence of transitions, to indicate a logic level. For example, Manchester Encoding indicates a **0** by a high to low voltage transition in the middle of the bit time. For a **1** there is a low to high voltage transition in the middle of the bit time.

The signaling method used must be compatible with a standard so that the receiver can detect the signals and decode them. The standard contains an agreement between the transmitter and the receiver on how to represent 1s and 0s. If there is no signaling agreement - that is, if different standards are used at each end of the transmission - communication across the physical medium will fail.

Signaling methods to represent bits on the media can be complex. We will look at two of the simpler techniques to illustrate the concept.

Refer to
Figure
in online course

NRZ Signaling

As a first example, we will examine a simple signaling method, Non Return to Zero (NRZ). In NRZ, the bit stream is transmitted as a series of voltage values, as shown in the figure.

A low voltage value represents a logical **0** and a high voltage value represents a logical **1**. The voltage range depends on the particular Physical layer standard in use.

This simple method of signaling is only suited for slow speed data links. NRZ signaling uses bandwidth inefficiently and is susceptible to electromagnetic interference. Additionally, the boundaries between individual bits can be lost when long strings of 1s or 0s are transmitted consecutively. In that case, no voltage transitions are detectable on the media. Therefore, the receiving nodes do not have a transition to use in resynchronizing bit times with the transmitting node.

Manchester Encoding

Refer to **Figure** in online course

Instead of representing bits as pulses of simple voltage values, in the Manchester Encoding scheme, bit values are represented as voltage transitions.

For example, a transition from a low voltage to a high voltage represents a bit value of 1. A transition from a high voltage to a low voltage represents a bit value of 0.

As shown in the figure, one voltage transition must occur in the middle of each bit time. This transition can be used to ensure that the bit times in the receiving nodes are synchronized with the transmitting node.

The transition in the middle of the bit time will be either the up or down direction for each unit of time in which a bit is transmitted. For consecutive bit values, a transition on the bit boundary "sets up" the appropriate mid-bit time transition that represents the bit value.

Although Manchester Encoding is not efficient enough to be used at higher signaling speeds, it is the signaling method employed by 10BaseT Ethernet (Ethernet running at 10 Megabits per second).

8.2.2 Encoding - Grouping Bits

Refer to **Figure** in online course

In the prior section, we describe the signaling process as how bits are represented on physical media. In this section, we use of the word encoding to represent the symbolic grouping of bits prior to being presented to the media. By using an encoding step before the signals are placed on the media, we improve the efficiency at higher speed data transmission.

As we use higher speeds on the media, we have the possibility that data will be corrupted. By using the coding groups, we can detect errors more efficiently. Additionally, as the demand for data speeds increase, we seek ways to represent more data across the media, by transmitting fewer bits. Coding groups provide a method of making this data representation.

The Physical layer of a network device needs to be able to detect legitimate data signals and ignore random non-data signals that may also be on the physical medium. The stream of signals being transmitted needs to start in such a way that the receiver recognizes the beginning and end of the frame.

Signal Patterns

One way to provide frame detection is to begin each frame with a pattern of signals representing bits that the Physical layer recognizes as denoting the start of a frame. Another pattern of bits will signal the end of the frame. Signal bits not framed in this manner are ignored by the Physical layer standard being used.

Valid data bits need to be grouped into a frame; otherwise, data bits will be received without any context to give them meaning to the upper layers of the networking model. This framing method can be provided by the Data Link layer, the Physical layer, or by both.

The figure depicts some of the purposes of signaling patterns. Signal patterns can indicate: start of frame, end of frame, and frame contents. These signal patterns can be decoded into bits. The bits are interpreted as codes. The codes indicate where the frames start and stop.

Refer to **Figure** in online course

Code Groups

Encoding techniques use bit patterns called symbols. The Physical layer may use a set of encoded symbols - called *code groups* - to represent encoded data or control information. **A code group is a consecutive sequence of code bits that are interpreted and mapped as data bit patterns**. For example, code bits 10101 could represent the data bits 0011.

As shown in the figure, code groups are often used as an intermediary encoding technique for higher speed LAN technologies. This step occurs at the Physical layer prior to the generation of signals of voltages, light pulses, or radio frequencies. By transmitting symbols, the error detection capabilities and timing synchronization between transmitting and receiving devices are enhanced. These are important considerations in supporting high speed transmission over the media.

Although using code groups introduces overhead in the form of extra bits to transmit, they improve the robustness of a communications link. This is particularly true for higher speed data transmission.

Advantages using code groups include:

- Reducing bit level error

- Limiting the effective energy transmitted into the media

- Helping to distinguish data bits from control bits

- Better media error detection

Reducing Bit Level Errors

To properly detect an individual bit as a **0** or as a **1**, the receiver must know how and when to sample the signal on the media. This requires that the timing between the receiver and transmitter be synchronized. In many Physical layer technologies, transitions on the media are used for this synchronization. If the bit patterns being transmitted on the media do not create frequent transitions, this synchronization may be lost and individual bit error can occur. Code groups are designed so that the symbols force an ample number of bit transitions to occur on the media to synchronize this timing. They do this by using symbols to ensure that not too many **1**s or **0**s are used in a row.

Limiting Energy Transmitted

In many code groups, the symbols ensure that the number of **1**s and **0**s in a string of symbols are evenly balanced. The process of balancing the number of 1s and 0s transmitted is called DC balancing. This prevents excessive amounts of energy from being injected into the media during transmission, thereby reducing the interference radiated from the media. In many media signaling methods, a logic level, for example a **1**, is represented by the presence of energy being sent into the media while the opposite logic level, a **0**, is represented as the absence of this energy. Transmitting a long series of 1s could overheat the transmitting laser and the photo diodes in the receiver, potentially causing higher error rates.

Distinguish Data from Control

The code groups have three types of symbols:

- Data symbols - Symbols that represent the data of the frame as it is passed down to the Physical layer.

- Control symbols - Special codes injected by the Physical layer used to control transmission. These include end-of-frame and idle media symbols.

- Invalid symbols - Symbols that have patterns not allowed on the media. The receipt of an invalid symbol indicates a frame error.

The symbols encoded onto the media are all unique. The symbols representing the data being sent through the network have different bit patterns than the symbols used for control. These differences allow the Physical layer in the receiving node to immediately distinguish data from control information.

Better Media Error Detection

In addition to the data symbols and control symbols, code groups contain invalid symbols. These are the symbols that could create long series of 1s or 0s on the media; therefore, they are not used by the transmitting node. If a receiving node receives one of these patterns, the Physical layer can determine that there has been an error in data reception.

Refer to **Figure** in online course

4B/5B

An example, we will examine a simple code group called 4B/5B. Code groups that are currently used in modern networks are generally more complex.

In this technique, 4 bits of data are turned into 5-bit code symbols for transmission over the media system. In 4B/5B, each byte to be transmitted is broken into four-bit pieces or *nibbles and encoded as five-bit values known as symbols. These symbols represent the data to be transmitted as well as a set of codes that help control transmission on the media. Among the codes are symbols that indicate the beginning and end of the frame transmission. Although this process adds overhead to the bit transmissions, it also adds features that aid in the transmission of data at higher speeds.*

4B/5B ensures that there is at least one level change per code to provide synchronization. Most of the codes used in 4B/5B balance the number of 1s and 0s used in each symbol.

As shown in the figure, 16 of the possible 32 combinations of code groups are allocated for data bits, and the remaining code groups are used for control symbols and invalid symbols. Six of the symbols are used for special functions identifying the transition from idle to frame data and end of stream delimiter. The remaining 10 symbols indicate invalid codes.

8.2.3 Data Carrying Capacity

Refer to **Figure** in online course

Different physical media support the transfer of bits at different speeds. Data transfer can be measured in three ways:

- Bandwidth
- Throughput
- Goodput

Bandwidth

The capacity of a medium to carry data is described as the raw data **bandwidth** of the media. **Digital bandwidth measures the amount of information that can flow from one place to another in a given amount of time.** Bandwidth is typically measured in kilobits per second (kbps) or megabits per second (Mbps).

The practical bandwidth of a network is determined by a combination of factors: the properties of the physical media and the technologies chosen for signaling and detecting network signals.

Physical media properties, current technologies, and the laws of physics all play a role in determining available bandwidth.

Refer to **Figure** in online course

The figure shows the commonly used units of bandwidth.

Throughput

Throughput is the measure of the transfer of bits across the media over a given period of time. Due to a number of factors, throughput usually does not match the specified bandwidth in Physical layer implementations such as Ethernet.

Many factors influence throughput. Among these factors are the amount of traffic, the type of traffic, and the number of network devices encountered on the network being measured. In a multi-access topology such as Ethernet, nodes are competing for media access and its use. Therefore, the throughput of each node is degraded as usage of the media increases.

In an internetwork or network with multiple segments, throughput cannot be faster than the slowest link of the path from source to destination. Even if all or most of the segments have high bandwidth, it will only take one segment in the path with low throughput to create a bottleneck to the throughput of the entire network.

Goodput

A third measurement has been created to measure the transfer of usable data. That measure is known as *goodput*. Goodput is the measure of usable data transferred over a given period of time, and is therefore the measure that is of most interest to network users.

As shown in the figure, goodput measures the effective transfer of user data between Application layer entities, such as between a source web server process and a destination web browser device.

Unlike throughput, which measures the transfer of bits and not the transfer of usable data, goodput accounts for bits devoted to protocol overhead. Goodput is throughput minus traffic overhead for establishing sessions, acknowledgements, and encapsulation.

As an example, consider two hosts on a LAN transferring a file. The bandwidth of the LAN is 100 Mbps. Due to the sharing and media overhead the throughput between the computers is only 60 Mbps. With the overhead of the encapsulation process of the TCP/IP stack, the actual rate of the data received by the destination computer, goodput, is only 40Mbps.

8.3 Physical Media - Connecting Communication

8.3.1 Types of Physical Media

Refer to
Figure
in online course

The Physical layer is concerned with network media and signaling. This layer produces the representation and groupings of bits as voltages, radio frequencies, or light pulses. Various standards organizations have contributed to the definition of the physical, electrical, and mechanical properties of the media available for different data communications. These specifications guarantee that cables and connectors will function as anticipated with different Data Link layer implementations.

As an example, standards for copper media are defined for the:

- Type of copper cabling used

- Bandwidth of the communication

- Type of connectors used

- Pinout and color codes of connections to the media

- Maximum distance of the media

The figure shows some of the characteristics of networking media.

This section will also describe some of the important characteristics of commonly used copper, optical, and wireless media.

8.3.2 Copper Media

Refer to
Figure
in online course

The most commonly used media for data communications is cabling that uses copper wires to signal data and control bits between network devices. Cabling used for data communications usually consists of a series of individual copper wires that form circuits dedicated to specific signaling purposes.

Other types of copper cabling, known as coaxial cable, have a single conductor that runs through the center of the cable that is encased by, but insulated from, the other shield. The copper media type chosen is specified by the Physical layer standard required to link the Data Link layers of two or more network devices.

These cables can be used to connect nodes on a LAN to intermediate devices, such as routers and switches. Cables are also used to connect WAN devices to a data services provider such as a telephone company. Each type of connection and the accompanying devices have cabling requirements stipulated by Physical layer standards.

Networking media generally make use of modular jacks and plugs, which provide easy connection and disconnection. Also, a single type of physical connector may be used for multiple types of connections. For example, the RJ-45 connector is used widely in LANs with one type of media and in some WANs with another media type.

The figure shows some commonly used copper media and connectors.

Refer to
Figure
in online course

External Signal Interference

Data is transmitted on copper cables as electrical pulses. A detector in the network interface of a destination device must receive a signal that can be successfully decoded to match the signal sent.

The timing and voltage values of these signals are susceptible to interference or "noise" from outside the communications system. These unwanted signals can distort and corrupt the data signals being carried by copper media. Radio waves and electromagnetic devices such as fluorescent lights, electric motors, and other devices are potential sources of noise.

Cable types with shielding or twisting of the pairs of wires are designed to minimize signal degradation due to electronic noise.

The susceptibility of copper cables to electronic noise can also be limited by:

- Selecting the cable type or category most suited to protect the data signals in a given networking environment

- Designing a cable infrastructure to avoid known and potential sources of interference in the building structure

- Using cabling techniques that include the proper handling and termination of the cables

The figure shows some sources of interference.

8.3.3 Unshielded Twisted Pair (UTP) Cable

Refer to
Figure
in online course

Unshielded twisted-pair (UTP) cabling, as it is used in Ethernet LANs, consists of four pairs of color-coded wires that have been twisted together and then encased in a flexible plastic sheath. As seen in the figure, the color codes identify the individual pairs and wires in the pairs and aid in cable termination.

The twisting has the effect of canceling unwanted signals. When two wires in an electrical circuit are placed close together, external electromagnetic fields create the same interference in each wire. The pairs are twisted to keep the wires in as close proximity as is physically possible. When this common interference is present on the wires in a twisted pair, the receiver processes it in equal yet opposite ways. As a result, the signals caused by electromagnetic interference from external sources are effectively cancelled.

This cancellation effect also helps avoid interference from internal sources called *crosstalk*. *Crosstalk is the interference caused by the magnetic field around the adjacent pairs of wires in the cable. When electrical current flows through a wire, it creates a circular magnetic field around the wire. With the current flowing in opposite directions in the two wires in a pair, the magnetic fields - as equal but opposite forces - have a cancellation effect on each other. Additionally, the different pairs of wires that are twisted in the cable use a different number of twists per meter to help protect the cable from crosstalk between pairs.*

UTP Cabling Standards

The UTP cabling commonly found in workplaces, schools, and homes conforms to the standards established jointly by the Telecommunications Industry Association (TIA) and the Electronics Industries Alliance (EIA). TIA/EIA-568A stipulates the commercial cabling standards for LAN installations and is the standard most commonly used in LAN cabling environments. Some of the elements defined are:

- Cable types
- Cable lengths
- Connectors
- Cable termination
- Methods of testing cable

The electrical characteristics of copper cabling are defined by the Institute of Electrical and Electronics Engineers (IEEE). IEEE rates UTP cabling according to its performance. Cables are placed into categories according to their ability to carry higher bandwidth rates. For example, Category 5 (Cat5) cable is used commonly in 100BASE-TX FastEthernet installations. Other categories include Enhanced Category 5 (Cat5e) cable and Category 6 (Cat6).

Cables in higher categories are designed and constructed to support higher data rates. As new gigabit speed Ethernet technologies are being developed and adopted, Cat5e is now the minimally acceptable cable type, with Cat6 being the recommended type for new building installations.

Some people connect to data network using existing telephone systems. Often the cabling in these systems are some form of UTP that are lower grade than the current Cat5+ standards.

Installing less expensive but lower rated cabling is potentially wasteful and shortsighted. If the decision is later made to adopt a faster LAN technology, total replacement of the installed cable infrastructure may be required.

Refer to
Figure
in online course

UTP Cable Types

UTP cabling, terminated with RJ-45 connectors, is a common copper-based medium for interconnecting network devices, such as computers, with intermediate devices, such as routers and network switches.

Different situations may require UTP cables to be wired according to different wiring conventions. This means that the individual wires in the cable have to be connected in different orders to different sets of pins in the RJ-45 connectors. The following are main cable types that are obtained by using specific wiring conventions:

- Ethernet Straight-through

- Ethernet Crossover

- Rollover

The figure shows the typical application of these cables as well as a comparison of these three cable types.

Using a crossover or straight-through cable incorrectly between devices may not damage the devices, but connectivity and communication between the devices will not take place. This is a common error in the lab and checking that the device connections are correct should be the first troubleshooting action if connectivity is not achieved.

8.3.4 Other Copper Cable

Refer to
Figure
in online course

Two other types of copper cable are used:

Step 1. Coaxial

Step 2. Shielded Twisted-Pair (STP)

Coaxial Cable

Coaxial cable consists of a copper conductor surrounded by a layer of flexible insulation, as shown in the figure.

Over this insulating material is a woven copper braid, or metallic foil, that acts as the second wire in the circuit and as a shield for the inner conductor. This second layer, or shield, also reduces the amount of outside electromagnetic interference. Covering the shield is the cable jacket.

All the elements of the coaxial cable encircle the center conductor. Because they all share the same axis, this construction is called coaxial, or coax for short.

Uses of Coaxial Cable

The coaxial cable design has been adapted for different purposes. Coax is an important type of cable that is used in wireless and cable access technologies. Coax cables are used to attach antennas to wireless devices. The coaxial cable carries radio frequency (RF) energy between the antennas and the radio equipment.

Coax is also the most widely used media for transporting high radio frequency signals over wire, especially cable television signals. Traditional cable television, exclusively transmitting in one direction, was composed completely of coax cable.

Cable service providers are currently converting their one-way systems to two-way systems to provide Internet connectivity to their customers. To provide these services, portions of the coaxial cable and supporting amplification elements are replaced with multi-fiber-optic cable. However, the final connection to the customer's location and the wiring inside the customer's premises is still coax cable. This combined use of fiber and coax is referred to as *hybrid fiber coax (HFC)*.

In the past, coaxial cable was used in Ethernet installations. Today UTP offers lower costs and higher bandwidth than coaxial and has replaced it as the standard for all Ethernet installations.

There are different types of connectors used with coax cable. The figure shows some of these connector types.

Refer to
Figure
in online course

Shielded Twisted-Pair (STP) Cable

Another type of cabling used in networking is shielded twisted-pair (STP). As shown in the figure, STP uses four pairs of wires that are wrapped in an overall metallic braid or foil.

STP cable shields the entire bundle of wires within the cable as well as the individual wire pairs. STP provides better noise protection than UTP cabling, however at a significantly higher price.

For many years, STP was the cabling structure specified for use in Token Ring network installations. With the use of Token Ring declining, the demand for shielded twisted-pair cabling has also waned. The new 10 GB standard for Ethernet has a provision for the use of STP cabling. This may provide a renewed interest in shielded twisted-pair cabling.

8.3.5 Copper Media Safety

Refer to
Figure
in online course

Electrical Hazards

A potential problem with copper media is that the copper wires could conduct electricity in undesirable ways. This could subject personnel and equipment to a range of electrical hazards.

A defective network device could conduct currents to the chassis of other network devices. Additionally, network cabling could present undesirable voltage levels when used to connect devices that have power sources with different ground potentials. Such situations are possible when copper cabling is used to connect networks in different buildings or on different floors of buildings that use different power facilities. Finally, copper cabling may conduct voltages caused by lightning strikes to network devices.

The result of undesirable voltages and currents can include damage to network devices and connected computers, or injury to personnel. It is important that copper cabling be installed appropriately, and according to the relevant specifications and building codes, in order to avoid potentially dangerous and damaging situations.

Fire Hazards

Cable insulation and sheaths may be flammable or produce toxic fumes when heated or burned. Building authorities or organizations may stipulate related safety standards for cabling and hardware installations.

8.3.6 Fiber Media

Refer to
Figure
in online course

Fiber-optic cabling uses either glass or plastic fibers to guide light impulses from source to destination. The bits are encoded on the fiber as light impulses. Optical fiber cabling is capable of very large raw data bandwidth rates. Most current transmission standards have yet to approach the potential bandwidth of this media.

Fiber Compared to Copper Cabling

Given that the fibers used in fiber-optic media are not electrical conductors, the media is immune to electromagnetic interference and will not conduct unwanted electrical currents due to grounding issues. Because optical fibers are thin and have relatively low signal loss, they can be operated at much greater lengths than copper media, without the need for signal regeneration. Some optical fiber Physical layer specifications allow lengths that can reach multiple kilometers.

Optical fiber media implementation issues include:

- More expensive (usually) than copper media over the same distance (but for a higher capacity)

- Different skills and equipment required to terminate and splice the cable infrastructure

- More careful handling than copper media

At present, in most enterprise environments, optical fiber is primarily used as backbone cabling for high-traffic point-to-point connections between data distribution facilities and for the interconnection of buildings in multi-building campuses. Because optical fiber does not conduct electricity and has low signal loss, it is well suited for these uses.

Refer to **Figure** in online course

Cable Construction

Optical fiber cables consist of a PVC jacket and a series of strengthening materials that surround the optical fiber and its cladding. The cladding surrounds the actual glass or plastic fiber and is designed to prevent light loss from the fiber. Because light can only travel in one direction over optical fiber, two fibers are required to support full duplex operation. Fiber-optic patch cables bundle together two optical fiber cables and terminate them with a pair of standard single fiber connectors. Some fiber connectors accept both the transmitting and receiving fibers in a single connector.

Refer to **Figure** in online course

Generating and Detecting the Optical Signal

Either lasers or light emitting diodes (LEDs) generate the light pulses that are used to represent the transmitted data as bits on the media. Electronic semi-conductor devices called photodiodes detect the light pulses and convert them to voltages that can then be reconstructed into data frames.

Note: The laser light transmitted over fiber-optic cabling can damage the human eye. Care must be taken to avoid looking into the end of an active optical fiber.

Single-mode and Multimode Fiber

Fiber optic cables can be broadly classified into two types: single-mode and multimode.

Single-mode optical fiber carries a single ray of light, usually emitted from a laser. Because the laser light is uni-directional and travels down the center of the fiber, this type of fiber can transmit optical pulses for very long distances.

Multimode fiber typically uses LED emitters that do not create a single coherent light wave. Instead, light from an LED enters the multimode fiber at different angles. Because light entering the fiber at different angles takes different amounts of time to travel down the fiber, long fiber runs may result in the pulses becoming blurred on reception at the receiving end. This effect, known as *modal dispersion, limits the length of multimode fiber segments.*

Multimode fiber, and the LED light source used with it, are cheaper than single-mode fiber and its laser-based emitter technology.

8.3.7 Wireless Media

Refer to **Figure** in online course

Wireless media carry electromagnetic signals at radio and microwave frequencies that represent the binary digits of data communications. As a networking medium, wireless is not restricted to conductors or pathways, as are copper and fiber media.

Wireless data communication technologies work well in open environments. However, certain construction materials used in buildings and structures, and the local terrain, will limit the effective coverage. In addition, wireless is susceptible to interference and can be disrupted by such common devices as household cordless phones, some types of fluorescent lights, microwave ovens, and other wireless communications.

Further, because wireless communication coverage requires no access to a physical strand of media, devices and users who are not authorized for access to the network can gain access to the transmission. Therefore, network security is a major component of wireless network administration.

Refer to **Figure** in online course

Types of Wireless Networks

The IEEE and telecommunications industry standards for wireless data communications cover both the Data Link and Physical layers. Four common data communications standards that apply to wireless media are:

- Standard IEEE **802.11** - Commonly referred to as Wi-Fi, is a Wireless LAN (WLAN) technology that uses a contention or non-deterministic system with a Carrier Sense Multiple Access/Collision Avoidance (CSMA/CA) media access process.

- Standard IEEE **802.15** - Wireless Personal Area Network (WPAN) standard, commonly known as "Bluetooth", uses a device pairing process to communicate over distances from 1 to 100 meters.

- Standard IEEE **802.16** - Commonly known as Worldwide Interoperability for Microwave Access (WiMAX), uses a point-to-multipoint topology to provide wireless broadband access.

- Global System for Mobile Communications (GSM) - Includes Physical layer specifications that enable the implementation of the Layer 2 General Packet Radio Service (GPRS) protocol to provide data transfer over mobile cellular telephony networks.

Other wireless technologies such as satellite communications provide data network connectivity for locations without another means of connection. Protocols including GPRS enable data to be transferred between earth stations and satellite links.

In each of the above examples, Physical layer specifications are applied to areas that include: data to radio signal encoding, frequency and power of transmission, signal reception and *decoding* requirements, and antenna design and construction.

The Wireless LAN

A common wireless data implementation is enabling devices to wirelessly connect via a LAN. In general, a wireless LAN requires the following network devices:

- Wireless Access Point (AP) - Concentrates the wireless signals from users and connects, usually through a copper cable, to the existing copper-based network infrastructure such as Ethernet.

- Wireless NIC adapters - Provides wireless communication capability to each network host.

As the technology has developed, a number of WLAN Ethernet-based standards have emerged. Care needs to be taken in purchasing wireless devices to ensure compatibility and interoperability.

Standards include:

IEEE 802.11a - Operates in the 5 GHz frequency band and offers speeds of up to 54 Mbps. Because this standard operates at higher frequencies, it has a smaller coverage area and is less effective at penetrating building structures. Devices operating under this standard are not interoperable with the 802.11b and 802.11g standards described below.

IEEE 802.11b - Operates in the 2.4 GHz frequency band and offers speeds of up to 11 Mbps. Devices implementing this standard have a longer range and are better able to penetrate building structures than devices based on 802.11a.

IEEE 802.11g - Operates in the 2.4 GHz frequency band and offers speeds of up to 54 Mbps. Devices implementing this standard therefore operate at the same radio frequency and range as 802.11b but with the bandwidth of 802.11a.

IEEE 802.11n - The IEEE 802.11n standard is currently in draft form. The proposed standard defines frequency of 2.4 Ghz or 5 GHz. The typical expected data rates are 100 Mbps to 210 Mbps with a distance range of up to 70 meters.

Refer to **Figure** in online course

The benefits of wireless data communications technologies are evident, especially the savings on costly premises wiring and the convenience of host mobility. However, network administrators need to develop and apply stringent security policies and processes to protect wireless LANs from unauthorized access and damage.

These wireless standards and Wireless LAN implementations will be covered in more detail in the LAN Switching and Wireless course.

Refer to **Packet Tracer Activity** for this chapter

In this activity, you can explore a wireless router connected to an ISP in a setup typical of a home or small business. You are encouraged to build your own models as well, possibly incorporating such wireless devices.

8.3.8 Media Connectors

Common Copper Media Connectors

Refer to **Figure** in online course

Different Physical layer standards specify the use of different connectors. These standards specify the mechanical dimensions of the connectors and the acceptable electrical properties of each type for the different implementations in which they are employed.

Although some connectors may look the same, they may be wired differently according to the Physical layer specification for which they were designed. The ISO 8877 specified RJ-45 connector is used for a range of Physical layer specifications, one of which is Ethernet. Another specification, EIA-TIA 568, describes the wire color codes to pin assignments (pinouts) for *Ethernet straight-through* and crossover cables.

Although many types of copper cables can be purchased pre-made, in some situations, especially in LAN installations, the termination of copper media may be performed onsite. These terminations include crimped connections to terminate Cat5 media with RJ-45 plugs to make patch cables, and the use of punched down connections on 110 patch panels and RJ-45 jacks. The figure shows some of the Ethernet wiring components.

Correct Connector Termination

Refer to **Figure** in online course

Each time copper cabling is terminated, there is the possibility of signal loss and the introduction of noise to the communication circuit. Ethernet workplace cabling specifications stipulate the cabling necessary to connect a computer to an active network intermediary device. When terminated improperly, each cable is a potential source of Physical layer performance degradation. **It is essential that all copper media terminations be of high quality to ensure optimum performance with current and future network technologies.**

In some cases, for example in some WAN technologies, if an improperly wired RJ-45-terminated cable is used, damaging voltage levels may be applied between interconnected devices. This type of damage will generally occur when a cable is wired for one Physical layer technology and is used with a different technology.

Common Optical Fiber Connectors

Refer to **Figure** in online course

Fiber-optic connectors come in a variety of types. The figure shows some of the most common:

Straight-Tip (ST) (trademarked by AT&T) - a very common bayonet style connector widely used with multimode fiber.

Subscriber Connector (SC) - a connector that uses a push-pull mechanism to ensure positive insertion. This connector type is widely used with single-mode fiber.

Lucent Connector (LC) - A small connector becoming popular for use with single-mode fiber and also supports multi-mode fiber.

Terminating and splicing fiber-optic cabling requires special training and equipment. Incorrect termination of fiber optic media will result in diminished signaling distances or complete transmission failure.

Three common types of fiber-optic termination and splicing errors are:

- Misalignment - the fiber-optic media are not precisely aligned to one another when joined.

- End gap - the media do not completely touch at the splice or connection.

- End finish - the media ends are not well polished or dirt is present at the termination.

It is recommended that an Optical Time Domain Reflectometer (OTDR) be used to test each fiber-optic cable segment. This device injects a test pulse of light into the cable and measures back scatter and reflection of light detected as a function of time. The OTDR will calculate the approximate distance at which these faults are detected along the length of the cable.

A field test can be performed by shining a bright flashlight into one end of the fiber while observing the other end of the fiber. If light is visible, then the fiber is capable of passing light. Although this does not ensure the performance of the fiber, it is a quick and inexpensive way to find a broken fiber.

8.4 Lab - Media Connectors

8.4.1 Media Connectors Lab Activity

Refer to
Lab Activity
for this chapter

Effective network troubleshooting requires the ability to both visually distinguish between straight-through and crossover UTP cables and to test for correct and faulty cable terminations.

This lab provides the opportunity to practice physically examining and testing UTP cables.

Summary and Review

Refer to
Figure
in online course

Layer 1 of the OSI model is responsible for the physical interconnection of devices. Standards at this layer define the characteristics of the electrical, optical, and radio frequency representation of the bits that comprise Data Link layer frames to be transmitted. Bit values can be represented as electronic pulses, pulses of light, or changes in radio waves. Physical layer protocols encode the bits for transmission and decode them at the destination.

Standards at this layer are also responsible for describing the physical, electrical, and mechanical characteristics of the physical media and connectors that interconnect network devices.

Various media and Physical layer protocols have different data-carrying capacities. Raw data bandwidth is the theoretical upper limit of a bit transmission. Throughput and goodput are different measures of observed data transfer over a specific period of time.

Refer to
Figure
in online course

In this activity, you will examine how Packet Tracer provides a representation of the physical location and appearance of the virtual networking devices you have been creating in logical topology mode.

Refer to **Packet Tracer Activity** for this chapter

Packet Tracer Skills Integration Instructions (PDF)

To Learn More

Refer to
Figure
in online course

Reflection Questions

Discuss how copper media, optical fiber, and wireless media could be used to provide network access at your academy. Review what networking media are used now and what could be used in the future.

Discuss the factors that might limit the widespread adoption of wireless networks despite the obvious benefits of this technology. How might these limitations be overcome?

Go to
the online course
to take the quiz.

Chapter Quiz

Take the chapter quiz to test your knowledge.

Your Chapter Notes

CHAPTER 9

Ethernet

Chapter Introduction

Refer to
Figure
in online course

Up to this point in the course, each chapter focused on the different functions of each layer of the OSI and TCP/IP protocol models as well as how protocols are used to support network communication. Several key protocols - TCP, UDP, and IP - are continually referenced in these discussions because they provide the foundation for how the smallest of networks to the largest, the Internet, work today. These protocols comprise the TCP/IP protocol stack and since the Internet was built using these protocols, Ethernet is now the predominant LAN technology in the world.

Internet Engineering Task Force (IETF) maintains the functional protocols and services for the TCP/IP protocol suite in the upper layers. However, the functional protocols and services at the OSI Data Link layer and Physical layer are described by various engineering organizations (IEEE, ANSI, ITU) or by private companies (proprietary protocols). Since Ethernet is comprised of standards at these lower layers, generalizing, it may best be understood in reference to the OSI model. The OSI model separates the Data Link layer functionalities of addressing, framing and accessing the media from the Physical layer standards of the media. Ethernet standards define both the Layer 2 protocols and the Layer 1 technologies. Although Ethernet specifications support different media, bandwidths, and other Layer 1 and 2 variations, the basic frame format and address scheme is the same for all varieties of Ethernet.

This chapter examines the characteristics and operation of Ethernet as it has evolved from a shared media, contention-based data communications technology to today's high bandwidth, full-duplex technology.

Learning Objectives

Upon completion of this chapter, you will be able to:

- Describe the evolution of Ethernet

- Explain the fields of the Ethernet Frame

- Describe the function and characteristics of the media access control method used by Ethernet protocol

- Describe the Physical and Data Link layer features of Ethernet

- Compare and contrast Ethernet hubs and switches

- Explain the *Address Resolution Protocol (ARP)*

9.1 Overview of Ethernet

9.1.1 Ethernet - Standards and Implementation

Refer to
Figure
in online course

IEEE Standards

The first LAN in the world was the original version of Ethernet. Robert Metcalfe and his coworkers at Xerox designed it more than thirty years ago. The first Ethernet standard was published in 1980 by a consortium of Digital Equipment Corporation, Intel, and Xerox (DIX). Metcalfe wanted Ethernet to be a shared standard from which everyone could benefit, and therefore it was released as an open standard. The first products that were developed from the Ethernet standard were sold in the early 1980s.

In 1985, the Institute of Electrical and Electronics Engineers (IEEE) standards committee for Local and Metropolitan Networks published standards for LANs. These standards start with the number 802. The standard for Ethernet is 802.3. The IEEE wanted to make sure that its standards were compatible with those of the International Standards Organization (ISO) and OSI model. To ensure compatibility, the IEEE 802.3 standards had to address the needs of Layer 1 and the lower portion of Layer 2 of the OSI model. As a result, some small modifications to the original Ethernet standard were made in 802.3.

Ethernet operates in the lower two layers of the OSI model: the Data Link layer and the Physical layer.

9.1.2 Ethernet - Layer 1 and Layer 2

Refer to
Figure
in online course

Ethernet operates across two layers of the OSI model. The model provides a reference to which Ethernet can be related but it is actually implemented in the lower half of the Data Link layer, which is known as the Media Access Control (MAC) sublayer, and the Physical layer only.

Ethernet at Layer 1 involves signals, bit streams that travel on the media, physical components that put signals on media, and various topologies. Ethernet Layer 1 performs a key role in the communication that takes place between devices, but each of its functions has limitations.

As the figure shows, Ethernet at Layer 2 addresses these limitations. The Data Link sublayers contribute significantly to technological compatibility and computer communications. The MAC sublayer is concerned with the physical components that will be used to communicate the information and prepares the data for transmission over the media..

The Logical Link Control (LLC) sublayer remains relatively independent of the physical equipment that will be used for the communication process.

9.1.3 Logical Link Control - Connecting to the Upper Layers

Refer to
Figure
in online course

Ethernet separates the functions of the Data Link layer into two distinct sublayers: the Logical Link Control (LLC) sublayer and the Media Access Control (MAC) sublayer. The functions described in the OSI model for the Data Link layer are assigned to the LLC and MAC sublayers. The use of these sublayers contributes significantly to compatibility between diverse end devices.

For Ethernet, the IEEE 802.2 standard describes the LLC sublayer functions, and the 802.3 standard describes the MAC sublayer and the Physical layer functions. Logical Link Control handles the communication between the upper layers and the networking software, and the lower layers, typically the hardware. The LLC sublayer takes the network protocol data, which is typically an IPv4 packet, and adds control information to help deliver the packet to the destination node. Layer 2 communicates with the upper layers through LLC.

LLC is implemented in software, and its implementation is independent of the physical equipment. In a computer, the LLC can be considered the driver software for the Network Interface Card (NIC). The NIC driver is a program that interacts directly with the hardware on the NIC to pass the data between the media and the Media Access Control sublayer.

http://standards.ieee.org/getieee802/download/802.2-1998.pdf

http://standards.ieee.org/regauth/llc/llctutorial.html

http://www.wildpackets.com/support/compendium/reference/sap_numbers

9.1.4 MAC - Getting Data to the Media

Refer to **Figure** in online course

Media Access Control (MAC) is the lower Ethernet sublayer of the Data Link layer. Media Access Control is implemented by hardware, typically in the computer Network Interface Card (NIC).

The Ethernet MAC sublayer has two primary responsibilities:

- Data Encapsulation
- Media Access Control

Data Encapsulation

Data encapsulation provides three primary functions:

- Frame delimiting
- Addressing
- Error detection

The data encapsulation process includes frame assembly before transmission and frame parsing upon reception of a frame. In forming the frame, the MAC layer adds a header and trailer to the Layer 3 PDU. The use of frames aids in the transmission of bits as they are placed on the media and in the grouping of bits at the receiving node.

The framing process provides important delimiters that are used to identify a group of bits that make up a frame. This process provides synchronization between the transmitting and receiving nodes.

The encapsulation process also provides for Data Link layer addressing. Each Ethernet header added in the frame contains the physical address (MAC address) that enables a frame to be delivered to a destination node.

An additional function of data encapsulation is error detection. Each Ethernet frame contains a trailer with a cyclic redundancy check (CRC) of the frame contents. After reception of a frame, the receiving node creates a CRC to compare to the one in the frame. If these two CRC calculations match, the frame can be trusted to have been received without error.

Media Access Control

The MAC sublayer controls the placement of frames on the media and the removal of frames from the media. As its name implies, it manages the media access control. This includes the initiation of frame transmission and recovery from transmission failure due to collisions.

Logical Topology

The underlying logical topology of Ethernet is a multi-access bus. This means that all the nodes (devices) in that network segment share the medium. This further means that all the nodes in that segment receive all the frames transmitted by any node on that segment.

Because all the nodes receive all the frames, each node needs to determine if a frame is to be accepted and processed by that node. This requires examining the addressing in the frame provided by the MAC address.

Ethernet provides a method for determining how the nodes share access to the media. The media access control method for classic Ethernet is Carrier Sense Multiple Access with *Collision* Detection (CSMA/CD). This method is described later in the chapter.

http://standards.ieee.org/regauth/groupmac/tutorial.html

9.1.5 Physical Implementations of Ethernet

Refer to **Figure** in online course

Most of the traffic on the Internet originates and ends with Ethernet connections. Since its inception in the 1970s, Ethernet has evolved to meet the increased demand for high-speed LANs. When optical fiber media was introduced, Ethernet adapted to this new technology to take advantage of the superior bandwidth and low error rate that fiber offers. Today, the same protocol that transported data at 3 Mbps can carry data at 10 *Gbps*.

The success of Ethernet is due to the following factors:

- Simplicity and ease of maintenance

- Ability to incorporate new technologies

- Reliability

- Low cost of installation and upgrade

The introduction of Gigabit Ethernet has extended the original LAN technology to distances that make Ethernet a *Metropolitan Area Network (MAN)* and WAN standard.

As a technology associated with the Physical layer, Ethernet specifies and implements encoding and decoding schemes that enable frame bits to be carried as signals across the media. Ethernet devices make use of a broad range of cable and connector specifications.

In today's networks, Ethernet uses UTP copper cables and optical fiber to interconnect network devices via intermediary devices such as hubs and switches. With all of the various media types that Ethernet supports, the Ethernet frame structure remains consistent across all of its physical implementations. It is for this reason that it can evolve to meet today's networking requirements.

9.2 Ethernet - Communication through the LAN

9.2.1 Historic Ethernet

Refer to **Figure** in online course

The foundation for Ethernet technology was first established in 1970 with a program called Alohanet. Alohanet was a digital radio network designed to transmit information over a shared radio frequency between the Hawaiian Islands.

Alohanet required all stations to follow a protocol in which an unacknowledged transmission required re-transmitting after a short period of waiting. The techniques for using a shared medium in this way were later applied to wired technology in the form of Ethernet.

Ethernet was designed to accommodate multiple computers that were Interconnected on a shared bus topology.

The first version of Ethernet incorporated a media access method known as Carrier Sense Multiple Access with Collision Detection (CSMA/CD). CSMA/CD managed the problems that result when multiple devices attempt to communicate over a shared physical medium.

Refer to **Figure** in online course

Early Ethernet Media

The first versions of Ethernet used coaxial cable to connect computers in a bus topology. Each computer was directly connected to the backbone. These early versions of Ethernet were known as Thicknet, (10BASE5) and Thinnet (10BASE2).

10BASE5, or Thicknet, used a thick coaxial that allowed for cabling distances of up to 500 meters before the signal required a repeater. 10BASE2, or Thinnet, used a thin coaxial cable that was smaller in diameter and more flexible than Thicknet and allowed for cabling distances of 185 meters.

The ability to migrate the original implementation of Ethernet to current and future Ethernet implementations is based on the practically unchanged structure of the Layer 2 frame. Physical media, media access, and media control have all evolved and continue to do so. But the Ethernet frame header and trailer have essentially remained constant.

The early implementations of Ethernet were deployed in a low-bandwidth LAN environment where access to the shared media was managed by CSMA, and later CSMA/CD. In additional to being a logical bus topology at the Data Link layer, Ethernet also used a physical bus topology. This topology became more problematic as LANs grew larger and LAN services made increasing demands on the infrastructure.

The original thick coaxial and thin coaxial physical media were replaced by early categories of UTP cables. Compared to the coaxial cables, the UTP cables were easier to work with, lightweight, and less expensive.

The physical topology was also changed to a star topology using hubs. Hubs concentrate connections. In other words, they take a group of nodes and allow the network to see them as a single unit. When a frame arrives at one port, it is copied to the other ports so that all the segments on the LAN receive the frame. Using the hub in this bus topology increased network reliability by allowing any single cable to fail without disrupting the entire network. However, repeating the frame to all other ports did not solve the issue of collisions. Later in this chapter, you will see how issues with collisions in Ethernet networks are managed with the introduction of switches into the network.

Note: A logical multi-access topology is also referred to as a logical bus topology.

9.2.2 Ethernet Collision Management

Refer to **Figure** in online course

Legacy Ethernet

In 10BASE-T networks, typically the central point of the network segment was a hub. This created a shared media. Because the media is shared, only one station could successfully transmit at a time. This type of connection is described as a *half-duplex* communication.

As more devices were added to an Ethernet network, the amount of frame collisions increased significantly. During periods of low communications activity, the few collisions that occur are managed by CSMA/CD, with little or no impact on performance. As the number of devices and subsequent data traffic increase, however, the rise in collisions can have a significant impact on the user's experience.

A good analogy is when we leave for work or school early in the morning, the roads are relatively clear and not congested. Later when more cars are on the roads, there can be collisions and traffic slows down.

Current Ethernet

A significant development that enhanced LAN performance was the introduction of switches to replace hubs in Ethernet-based networks. This development closely corresponded with the development of 100BASE-TX Ethernet. Switches can control the flow of data by isolating each port and sending a frame only to its proper destination (if the destination is known), rather than send every frame to every device.

The switch reduces the number of devices receiving each frame, which in turn reduces or minimizes the possibility of collisions. This, and the later introduction of *full-duplex* communications (having a connection that can carry both transmitted and received signals at the same time), has enabled the development of 1Gbps Ethernet and beyond.

9.2.3 Moving to 1Gbps and Beyond

Refer to **Figure** in online course

The applications that cross network links on a daily basis tax even the most robust networks. For example, the increasing use of Voice over IP (VoIP) and multimedia services requires connections that are faster than 100 Mbps Ethernet.

Gigabit Ethernet is used to describe Ethernet implementations that provide bandwidth of 1000 Mbps (1 Gbps) or greater. This capacity has been built on the full-duplex capability and the UTP and fiber-optic media technologies of earlier Ethernet.

The increase in network performance is significant when potential throughput increases from 100 Mbps to 1 Gbps and above.

Upgrading to 1 Gbps Ethernet does not always mean that the existing network infrastructure of cables and switches has to be completely replaced. Some of the equipment and cabling in modern, well-designed and installed networks may be capable of working at the higher speeds with only minimal upgrading. This capability has the benefit of reducing the total cost of ownership of the network.

Refer to **Figure** in online course

Ethernet Beyond the LAN

The increased cabling distances enabled by the use of fiber-optic cable in Ethernet-based networks has resulted in a blurring of the distinction between LANs and WANs. Ethernet was initially limited to LAN cable systems within single buildings, and then extended to between buildings. It can now be applied across a city in what is known as a Metropolitan Area Network (MAN).

9.3 The Ethernet Frame

9.3.1 The Frame - Encapsulating the Packet

Refer to **Figure** in online course

The Ethernet frame structure adds headers and trailers around the Layer 3 PDU to encapsulate the message being sent.

Both the Ethernet header and trailer have several sections of information that are used by the Ethernet protocol. Each section of the frame is called a field. There are two styles of Ethernet framing: the DIX Ethernet standard which is now Ethernet II and the IEEE 802.3 standard which has been updated several times to include new technologies.

The differences between framing styles are minimal. The most significant difference between the two standards are the addition of a Start Frame Delimiter (SFD) and the change of the Type field to a Length field in the 802.3, as shown in the figure.

Ethernet Frame Size

Both the Ethernet II and IEEE 802.3 standards define the minimum frame size as 64 bytes and the maximum as 1518 bytes. This includes all bytes from the Destination MAC Address field through the Frame Check Sequence (FCS) field. The Preamble and Start Frame Delimiter fields are not included when describing the size of a frame. The IEEE 802.3ac standard, released in 1998, ex-

Refer to
Figure
in online course

tended the maximum allowable frame size to 1522 bytes. The frame size was increased to accommodate a technology called *Virtual Local Area Network (VLAN)*. VLANs are created within a switched network and will be presented in a later course.

If the size of a transmitted frame is less than the minimum or greater than the maximum, the receiving device drops the frame. Dropped frames are likely to be the result of collisions or other unwanted signals and are therefore considered invalid.

Roll over each field name to see its description.

Preamble and Start Frame Delimiter Fields

The Preamble (7 bytes) and Start Frame Delimiter (SFD) (1 byte) fields are used for synchronization between the sending and receiving devices. These first eight bytes of the frame are used to get the attention of the receiving nodes. Essentially, the first few bytes tell the receivers to get ready to receive a new frame.

Destination MAC Address Field

The Destination MAC Address field (6 bytes) is the identifier for the intended recipient. As you will recall, this address is used by Layer 2 to assist devices in determining if a frame is addressed to them. The address in the frame is compared to the MAC address in the device. If there is a match, the device accepts the frame.

Source MAC Address Field

The Source MAC Address field (6 bytes) identifies the frame's originating NIC or interface. Switches also use this address to add to their lookup tables. The role of switches will be discussed later in the chapter.

Length/Type Field

For any IEEE 802.3 standard earlier than 1997 the Length field defines the exact length of the frame's data field. This is used later as part of the FCS to ensure that the message was received properly. If the purpose of the field is to designate a type as in Ethernet II, the Type field describes which protocol is implemented.

These two uses of the field were officially combined in 1997 in the IEEE 802.3x standard because both uses were common. The Ethernet II Type field is incorporated into the current 802.3 frame definition. When a node receives a frame, it must examine the Length field to determine which higher-layer protocol is present. If the two-octet value is equal to or greater than 0x0600 hexadecimal or 1536 decimal, then the contents of the Data Field are decoded according to the EtherType protocol indicated. Whereas if the value is equal to or less than 0x05DC hexadecimal or 1500 decimal then the Length field is being used to indicate the use of the IEEE 802.3 frame format. This is how Ethernet II and 802.3 frames are differentiated.

Data and Pad Fields

The Data and Pad fields (46 - 1500 bytes) contains the encapsulated data from a higher layer, which is a generic Layer 3 PDU, or more commonly, an IPv4 packet. All frames must be at least 64 bytes long. If a small packet is encapsulated, the Pad is used to increase the size of the frame to this minimum size.

Links

IEEE mantains a list of EtherType public assignment.

Refer to
Figure
in online course

http://standards.ieee.org/regauth/ethertype/eth.txt

Frame Check Sequence Field

The Frame Check Sequence (FCS) field (4 bytes) is used to detect errors in a frame. It uses a cyclic redundancy check (CRC). The sending device includes the results of a CRC in the FCS field of the frame.

The receiving device receives the frame and generates a CRC to look for errors. If the calculations match, no error occurred. Calculations that do not match are an indication that the data has changed; therefore, the frame is dropped. A change in the data could be the result of a disruption of the electrical signals that represent the bits.

9.3.2 The Ethernet MAC Address

Refer to
Figure
in online course

Initially, Ethernet was implemented as part of a bus topology. Every network device was connected to the same, shared media. In low traffic or small networks, this was an acceptable deployment. The main problem to solve was how to identify each device. The signal could be sent to every device, but how would each device identify if it were the intended receiver of the message?

A unique identifier called a Media Access Control (MAC) address was created to assist in determining the source and destination address within an Ethernet network. Regardless of which variety of Ethernet was used, the naming convention provided a method for device identification at a lower level of the OSI model.

As you will recall, MAC addressing is added as part of a Layer 2 PDU. An Ethernet MAC address is a 48-bit binary value expressed as 12 hexadecimal digits.

Refer to
Figure
in online course

MAC Address Structure

The MAC address value is a direct result of IEEE-enforced rules for vendors to ensure globally unique addresses for each Ethernet device. The rules established by IEEE require any vendor that sells Ethernet devices to register with IEEE. The IEEE assigns the vendor a 3-byte code, called the Organizationally Unique Identifier (OUI).

IEEE requires a vendor to follow two simple rules:

- All MAC addresses assigned to a NIC or other Ethernet device must use that vendor's assigned OUI as the first 3 bytes.

- All MAC addresses with the same OUI must be assigned a unique value (vendor code or serial number) in the last 3 bytes.

The MAC address is often referred to as a *burned-in address* (BIA) because it is burned into ROM (Read-Only Memory) on the NIC. This means that the address is encoded into the ROM chip permanently - it cannot be changed by software.

However, when the computer starts up, the NIC copies the address into *RAM*. When examining frames, it is the address in RAM that is used as the source address to compare with the destination address. The MAC address is used by the NIC to determine if a message should be passed to the upper layers for processing.

Network Devices

When the source device is forwarding the message to an Ethernet network, the header information within the destination MAC address is attached. The source device sends the data through the network. Each NIC in the network views the information to see if the MAC address matches its physical address. If there is no match, the device discards the frame. When the frame reaches the destination where the MAC of the NIC matches the destination MAC of the frame, the NIC passes the frame up the OSI layers, where the *decapsulation* process take place.

All devices connected to an Ethernet LAN have MAC-addressed interfaces. Different hardware and software manufacturers might represent the MAC address in different hexadecimal formats. The address formats might be similar to 00-05-9A-3C-78-00, 00:05:9A:3C:78:00, or 0005.9A3C.7800. MAC addresses are assigned to workstations, servers, printers, switches, and routers - any device that must originate and/or receive data on the network.

9.3.3 Hexadecimal Numbering and Addressing

Refer to **Figure** in online course

Hexadecimal Numbering

Hexadecimal ("Hex") is a convenient way to represent binary values. Just as decimal is a base ten numbering system and binary is base two, hexadecimal is a base sixteen system.

The base 16 numbering system uses the numbers 0 to 9 and the letters A to F. The figure shows the equivalent decimal, binary, and hexadecimal values for binary 0000 to 1111. It is easier for us to express a value as a single hexadecimal digit than as four bits.

Understanding Bytes

Given that 8 bits (a byte) is a common binary grouping, binary 00000000 to 11111111 can be represented in hexadecimal as the range 00 to FF. Leading zeroes are always displayed to complete the 8-bit representation. For example, the binary value 0000 1010 is shown in hexadecimal as 0A.

Representing Hexadecimal Values

Note: It is important to distinguish hexadecimal values from decimal values regarding the characters 0 to 9, as shown in the figure.

Hexadecimal is usually represented in text by the value preceded by 0x (for example 0x73) or a subscript 16. Less commonly, it may be followed by an H, for example 73H. However, because subscript text is not recognized in command line or programming environments, the technical representation of hexadecimal is preceded with "0x" (zero X). Therefore, the examples above would be shown as 0x0A and 0x73 respectively.

Hexadecimal is used to represent Ethernet MAC addresses and IP Version 6 addresses. You have seen hexadecimal used in the Packets Byte pane of Wireshark where it is used to represent the binary values within frames and packets.

Hexadecimal Conversions

Number conversions between decimal and hexadecimal values are straightforward, but quickly dividing or multiplying by 16 is not always convenient. If such conversions are required, it is usually easier to convert the decimal or hexadecimal value to binary, and then to convert the binary value to either decimal or hexadecimal as appropriate.

With practice, it is possible to recognize the binary bit patterns that match the decimal and hexadecimal values. The figure shows these patterns for selected 8-bit values.

Refer to **Figure** in online course

Viewing the MAC

A tool to examine the MAC address of our computer is the ipconfig /all or ifconfig. In the graphic, notice the MAC address of this computer. If you have access, you may wish to try this on your own computer.

You may want to research the OUI of the MAC address to determine the manufacturer of your NIC.

9.3.4 Another Layer of Addressing

Refer to
Figure
in online course

Data Link Layer

OSI Data Link layer (Layer 2) physical addressing, implemented as an Ethernet MAC address, is used to transport the frame across the local media. Although providing unique host addresses, physical addresses are non-hierarchical. They are associated with a particular device regardless of its location or to which network it is connected.

These Layer 2 addresses have no meaning outside the local network media. A packet may have to traverse a number of different Data Link technologies in local and wide area networks before it reaches its destination. A source device therefore has no knowledge of the technology used in intermediate and destination networks or of their Layer 2 addressing and frame structures.

Network Layer

Network layer (Layer 3) addresses, such as IPv4 addresses, provide the ubiquitous, logical addressing that is understood at both source and destination. To arrive at its eventual destination, a packet carries the destination Layer 3 address from its source. However, as it is framed by the different Data Link layer protocols along the way, the Layer 2 address it receives each time applies only to that local portion of the journey and its media.

In short:

- The Network layer address enables the packet to be forwarded toward its destination.

- The Data Link layer address enables the packet to be carried by the local media across each segment.

9.3.5 Ethernet Unicast, Multicast & Broadcast

Refer to
Figure
in online course

In Ethernet, different MAC addresses are used for Layer 2 **unicast**, **multicast**, and **broadcast** communications.

Unicast

A unicast MAC address is the unique address used when a frame is sent from a single transmitting device to single destination device.

In the example shown in the figure, a host with IP address 192.168.1.5 (source) requests a web page from the server at IP address 192.168.1.200. For a unicast packet to be sent and received, a destination IP address must be in the IP packet header. A corresponding destination MAC address must also be present in the Ethernet frame header. The IP address and MAC address combine to deliver data to one specific destination host.

Refer to
Figure
in online course

Broadcast

With a broadcast, the packet contains a destination IP address that has all ones (1s) in the host portion. This numbering in the address means that all hosts on that local network (broadcast domain) will receive and process the packet. Many network protocols, such as Dynamic Host Configuration Protocol (DHCP) and Address Resolution Protocol (ARP), use broadcasts. How ARP uses broadcasts to map Layer 2 to Layer 3 addresses is discussed later in this chapter.

As shown in the figure, a broadcast IP address for a network needs a corresponding broadcast MAC address in the Ethernet frame. On Ethernet networks, the broadcast MAC address is 48 ones displayed as Hexadecimal FF-FF-FF-FF-FF-FF.

Refer to
Figure
in online course

Multicast

Recall that multicast addresses allow a source device to send a packet to a group of devices. Devices that belong to a multicast group are assigned a multicast group IP address. The range of multicast addresses is from 224.0.0.0 to 239.255.255.255. Because multicast addresses represent a group of addresses (sometimes called a host group), they can only be used as the destination of a packet. The source will always have a unicast address.

Examples of where multicast addresses would be used are in remote gaming, where many players are connected remotely but playing the same game, and distance learning through video conferencing, where many students are connected to the same class.

As with the unicast and broadcast addresses, the multicast IP address requires a corresponding multicast MAC address to actually deliver frames on a local network. The multicast MAC address is a special value that begins with 01-00-5E in hexadecimal. The value ends by converting the lower 23 bits of the IP multicast group address into the remaining 6 hexadecimal characters of the Ethernet address. The remaining bit in the MAC address is always a "0".

An example, as shown in the graphic, is hexadecimal 01-00-5E-00-00-01. Each hexadecimal character is 4 binary bits.

http://www.iana.org/assignments/ethernet-numbers

http://www.cisco.com/en/US/docs/app_ntwk_services/waas/acns/v51/configuration/central/guide/51ipmul.html

http://www.cisco.com/en/US/docs/internetworking/technology/handbook/IP-Multi.html

9.4 Ethernet Media Access Control

9.4.1 Media Access Control in Ethernet

Refer to **Figure** in online course

In a shared media environment, all devices have guaranteed access to the medium, but they have no prioritized claim on it. If more than one device transmits simultaneously, the physical signals collide and the network must recover in order for communication to continue.

Collisions are the cost that Ethernet pays to get the low overhead associated with each transmission.

Ethernet uses Carrier Sense Multiple Access with Collision Detection (CSMA/CD) to detect and handle collisions and manage the resumption of communications.

Because all computers using Ethernet send their messages on the same media, a distributed coordination scheme (CSMA) is used to detect the electrical activity on the cable. A device can then determine when it can transmit. When a device detects that no other computer is sending a frame, or carrier signal, the device will transmit, if it has something to send.

9.4.2 CSMA/CD - The Process

Refer to **Figure** in online course

Carrier Sense

In the CSMA/CD access method, all network devices that have messages to send must listen before transmitting.

If a device detects a signal from another device, it will wait for a specified amount of time before attempting to transmit.

When there is no traffic detected, a device will transmit its message. While this transmission is occurring, the device continues to listen for traffic or collisions on the LAN. After the message is sent, the device returns to its default listening mode.

Multi-access

If the distance between devices is such that the *latency* of one device's signals means that signals are not detected by a second device, the second device may start to transmit, too. The media now has two devices transmitting their signals at the same time. Their messages will propagate across the media until they encounter each other. At that point, the signals mix and the message is destroyed. Although the messages are corrupted, the jumble of remaining signals continues to propagate across the media.

Collision Detection

When a device is in listening mode, it can detect when a collision occurs on the shared media. The detection of a collision is made possible because all devices can detect an increase in the amplitude of the signal above the normal level.

Once a collision occurs, the other devices in listening mode - as well as all the transmitting devices - will detect the increase in the signal amplitude. Once detected, every device transmitting will continue to transmit to ensure that all devices on the network detect the collision.

Jam Signal and Random Backoff

Once the collision is detected by the transmitting devices, they send out a jamming signal. This jamming signal is used to notify the other devices of a collision, so that they will invoke a *backoff algorithm*. This backoff algorithm causes all devices to stop transmitting for a random amount of time, which allows the collision signals to subside.

After the delay has expired on a device, the device goes back into the "listening before transmit" mode. A random backoff period ensures that the devices that were involved in the collision do not try to send their traffic again at the same time, which would cause the whole process to repeat. But, this also means that a third device may transmit before either of the two involved in the original collision have a chance to re-transmit.

Hubs and Collision Domains

Refer to **Figure** in online course

Given that collisions will occur occasionally in any shared media topology - even when employing CSMA/CD - we need to look at the conditions that can result in an increase in collisions. Because of the rapid growth of the Internet:

- More devices are being connected to the network.

- Devices access the network media more frequently.

- Distances between devices are increasing.

Recall that hubs were created as intermediary network devices that enable more nodes to connect to the shared media. Also known as multi-port repeaters, hubs retransmit received data signals to all connected devices, except the one from which it received the signals. Hubs do not perform network functions such as directing data based on addresses.

Hubs and repeaters are intermediary devices that extend the distance that Ethernet cables can reach. Because hubs operate at the Physical layer, dealing only with the signals on the media, collisions can occur between the devices they connect and within the hubs themselves.

Further, using hubs to provide network access to more users reduces the performance for each user because the fixed capacity of the media has to be shared between more and more devices.

The connected devices that access a common media via a hub or series of directly connected hubs make up what is known as a *collision domain*. *A collision domain is also referred to as a* network segment. *Hubs and repeaters therefore have the effect of increasing the size of the collision domain.*

As shown in the figure, the interconnection of hubs form a physical topology called an extended star. The extended star can create a greatly expanded collision domain.

An increased number of collisions reduces the network's efficiency and effectiveness until the collisions become a nuisance to the user.

Although CSMA/CD is a frame collision management system, it was designed to manage collisions for only limited numbers of devices and on networks with light network usage. Therefore, other mechanisms are required when large numbers of users require access and when more active network access is needed.

We will see that using switches in place of hubs can begin to alleviate this problem.

http://standards.ieee.org/getieee802/802.3.html

Refer to **Packet Tracer Activity** for this chapter

In this Packet Tracer Activity, you will build large collision domains to view the effects of collisions on data transmission and network operation.

9.4.3 Ethernet Timing

Refer to **Figure** in online course

Faster Physical layer implementations of Ethernet introduce complexities to the management of collisions.

Latency

As discussed, each device that wants to transmit must first "listen" to the media to check for traffic. If no traffic exists, the station will begin to transmit immediately. The electrical signal that is transmitted takes a certain amount of time (latency) to propagate (travel) down the cable. Each hub or repeater in the signal's path adds latency as it forwards the bits from one port to the next.

This accumulated delay increases the likelihood that collisions will occur because a listening node may transition into transmitting signals while the hub or repeater is processing the message. Because the signal had not reached this node while it was listening, it thought that the media was available. This condition often results in collisions.

Refer to **Figure** in online course

Timing and Synchronization

In half-duplex mode, if a collision has not occurred, the sending device will transmit 64 bits of timing synchronization information, which is known as the Preamble.

The sending device will then transmit the complete frame.

Ethernet with throughput speeds of 10 Mbps and slower are *asynchronous*. An asynchronous communication in this context means that each receiving device will use the 8 bytes of timing information to synchronize the receive circuit to the incoming data and then discard the 8 bytes.

Ethernet implementations with throughput of 100 Mbps and higher are *synchronous*. Synchronous communication in this context means that the timing information is not required. However, for compatibility reasons, the Preamble and Start Frame Delimiter (SFD) fields are still present.

Refer to **Figure** in online course

Bit Time

For each different media speed, a period of time is required for a bit to be placed and sensed on the media. This period of time is referred to as the bit time. On 10-Mbps Ethernet, one bit at the MAC layer requires 100 nanoseconds (nS) to transmit. At 100 Mbps, that same bit requires 10 nS to transmit. And at 1000 Mbps, it only takes 1 nS to transmit a bit. As a rough estimate, 20.3 centimeters (8 inches) per nanosecond is often used for calculating the propagation delay on a UTP cable. The result is that for 100 meters of UTP cable, it takes just under 5 bit times for a 10BASE-T signal to travel the length the cable.

For CSMA/CD Ethernet to operate, the sending device must become aware of a collision before it has completed transmission of a minimum-sized frame. At 100 Mbps, the device timing is barely able to accommodate 100 meter cables. At 1000 Mbps, special adjustments are required because nearly an entire minimum-sized frame would be transmitted before the first bit reached the end of the first 100 meters of UTP cable. For this reason, half-duplex mode is not permitted in 10-Gigabit Ethernet.

These timing considerations have to be applied to the *interframe spacing* and *backoff times* (both of which are discussed in the next section) to ensure that when a device transmits its next frame, the risk of a collision is minimized.

Slot Time

In half-duplex Ethernet, where data can only travel in one direction at once, *slot time becomes an important parameter in determining how many devices can share a network. For all speeds of Ethernet transmission at or below 1000 Mbps, the standard describes how an individual transmission may be no smaller than the slot time.*

Determining slot time is a trade-off between the need to reduce the impact of collision recovery (backoff and retransmission times) and the need for network distances to be large enough to accommodate reasonable network sizes. The compromise was to choose a maximum network diameter (about 2500 meters) and then to set the minimum frame length long enough to ensure detection of all worst-case collisions.

Slot time for 10- and 100-Mbps Ethernet is 512 bit times, or 64 octets. Slot time for 1000-Mbps Ethernet is 4096 bit times, or 512 octets.

The slot time ensures that if a collision is going to occur, it will be detected within the first 512 bits (4096 for Gigabit Ethernet) of the frame transmission. This simplifies the handling of frame retransmissions following a collision.

Slot time is an important parameter for the following reasons:

- The 512-bit slot time establishes the minimum size of an Ethernet frame as 64 bytes. Any frame less than 64 bytes in length is considered a *"collision fragment"* or *"runt frame"* and is automatically discarded by receiving stations.

- The slot time establishes a limit on the maximum size of a network's segments. If the network grows too big, late collisions can occur. Late collisions are considered a failure in the network because the collision is detected too late by a device during the frame transmission to be automatically handled by CSMA/CD.

Slot time is calculated assuming maximum cable lengths on the largest legal network architecture. All hardware propagation delay times are at the legal maximum and the 32-bit jam signal is used when collisions are detected.

The actual calculated slot time is just longer than the theoretical amount of time required to travel between the furthest points of the collision domain, collide with another transmission at the last possible instant, and then have the collision fragments return to the sending station and be detected. See the figure.

For the system to work properly, the first device must learn about the collision before it finishes sending the smallest legal frame size.

To allow 1000 Mbps Ethernet to operate in half-duplex mode, the extension field was added to the frame when sending small frames purely to keep the transmitter busy long enough for a collision fragment to return. This field is present only on 1000-Mbps, half-duplex links and allows minimum-sized frames to be long enough to meet slot time requirements. Extension bits are discarded by the receiving device.

9.4.4 Interframe Spacing and Backoff

Interframe Spacing

The Ethernet standards require a minimum spacing between two non-colliding frames. This gives the media time to stabilize after the transmission of the previous frame and time for the devices to process the frame. Referred to as the *interframe spacing*, this time is measured from the last bit of the FCS field of one frame to the first bit of the Preamble of the next frame.

After a frame has been sent, all devices on a 10 Mbps Ethernet network are required to wait a minimum of 96 bit times (9.6 microseconds) before any device can transmit its next frame. On faster versions of Ethernet, the spacing remains the same - 96 bit times - but the interframe spacing time period grows correspondingly shorter.

Synchronization delays between devices may result in the loss of some of frame preamble bits. This in turn may cause minor reduction of the interframe spacing when hubs and repeaters regenerate the full 64 bits of timing information (the Preamble and SFD) at the start of every frame forwarded. On higher speed Ethernet some time sensitive devices could potentially fail to recognize individual frames resulting in communication failure.

Jam Signal

As you will recall, Ethernet allows all devices to compete for transmitting time. In the event that two devices transmit simultaneously, the network CSMA/CD attempts to resolve the issue. But remember, when a larger number of devices are added to the network, it is possible for the collisions to become increasingly difficult to resolve.

As soon as a collision is detected, the sending devices transmit a 32-bit "jam" signal that will enforce the collision. This ensures all devices in the LAN to detect the collision.

It is important that the jam signal not be detected as a valid frame; otherwise the collision would not be identified. The most commonly observed data pattern for a jam signal is simply a repeating 1, 0, 1, 0 pattern, the same as the Preamble.

The corrupted, partially transmitted messages are often referred to as collision fragments or runts. Normal collisions are less than 64 octets in length and therefore fail both the minimum length and the FCS tests, making them easy to identify.

Backoff Timing

After a collision occurs and all devices allow the cable to become idle (each waits the full interframe spacing), the devices whose transmissions collided must wait an additional - and potentially progressively longer - period of time before attempting to retransmit the collided frame. The waiting period is intentionally designed to be random so that two stations do not delay for the same amount of time before retransmitting, which would result in more collisions. This is accomplished in part by expanding the interval from which the random retransmission time is selected on each retransmission attempt. The waiting period is measured in increments of the parameter slot time.

If media congestion results in the MAC layer unable to send the frame after 16 attempts, it gives up and generates an error to the Network layer. Such an occurrence is rare in a properly operating network and would happen only under extremely heavy network loads or when a physical problem exists on the network.

The methods described in this section allowed Ethernet to provide greater service in a shared media topology based on the use of hubs. In the coming switching section, we will see how, with the use of switches, the need for CSMA/CD starts to diminish or, in some cases, is removed altogether.

9.5 Ethernet Physical Layer

9.5.1 Overview of Ethernet Physical Layer

Refer to
Figure
in online course

The differences between standard Ethernet, Fast Ethernet, Gigabit Ethernet, and 10 Gigabit Ethernet occur at the Physical layer, often referred to as the *Ethernet PHY*.

Ethernet is covered by the IEEE 802.3 standards. Four data rates are currently defined for operation over optical fiber and twisted-pair cables:

- 10 Mbps - 10Base-T Ethernet

- 100 Mbps - Fast Ethernet

- 1000 Mbps - Gigabit Ethernet

- 10 Gbps - 10 Gigabit Ethernet

While there are many different implementations of Ethernet at these various data rates, only the more common ones will be presented here. The figure shows some of the Ethernet PHY characteristics.

The portion of Ethernet that operates on the Physical layer will be discussed in this section, beginning with 10Base-T and continuing to 10 Gbps varieties.

9.5.2 10 and 100 Mbps Ethernet

Refer to
Figure
in online course

The principal 10 Mbps implementations of Ethernet include:

- 10BASE5 using Thicknet coaxial cable

- 10BASE2 using Thinnet coaxial cable

- 10BASE-T using Cat3/Cat5 unshielded twisted-pair cable

The early implementations of Ethernet, 10BASE5, and 10BASE2 used coaxial cable in a physical bus. These implementations are no longer used and are not supported by the newer 802.3 standards.

10 Mbps Ethernet - 10BASE-T

10BASE-T uses Manchester-encoding over two unshielded twisted-pair cables. The early implementations of 10BASE-T used Cat3 cabling. However, Cat5 or later cabling is typically used today.

10 Mbps Ethernet is considered to be classic Ethernet and uses a physical star topology. Ethernet 10BASE-T links could be up to 100 meters in length before requiring a hub or repeater.

10BASE-T uses two pairs of a four-pair cable and is terminated at each end with an 8-pin RJ-45 connector. The pair connected to pins 1 and 2 are used for transmitting and the pair connected to pins 3 and 6 are used for receiving. The figure shows the RJ45 pinout used with 10BASE-T Ethernet.

10BASE-T is generally not chosen for new LAN installations. However, there are still many 10BASE-T Ethernet networks in existence today. The replacement of hubs with switches in

Refer to
Figure
in online course

10BASE-T networks has greatly increased the throughput available to these networks and has given Legacy Ethernet greater longevity. The 10BASE-T links connected to a switch can support either half-duplex or full-duplex operation.

100 Mbps - Fast Ethernet

In the mid to late 1990s, several new 802.3 standards were established to describe methods for transmitting data over Ethernet media at 100 Mbps. These standards used different encoding requirements for achieving these higher data rates.

100 Mbps Ethernet, also known as Fast Ethernet, can be implemented using twisted-pair copper wire or fiber media. The most popular implementations of 100 Mbps Ethernet are:

- 100BASE-TX using Cat5 or later UTP

- 100BASE-FX using fiber-optic cable

Because the higher frequency signals used in Fast Ethernet are more susceptible to noise, two separate encoding steps are used by 100-Mbps Ethernet to enhance signal integrity.

100BASE-TX

100BASE-TX was designed to support transmission over either two pairs of Category 5 UTP copper wire or two strands of optical fiber. The 100BASE-TX implementation uses the same two pairs and pinouts of UTP as 10BASE-T. However, 100BASE-TX requires Category 5 or later UTP. The 4B/5B encoding is used for 100BASE-TX Ethernet.

As with 10BASE-TX, 100Base-TX is connected as a physical star. The figure shows an example of a physical star topology. However, unlike 10BASE-T, 100BASE-TX networks typically use a switch at the center of the star instead of a hub. At about the same time that 100BASE-TX technologies became mainstream, LAN switches were also being widely deployed. These concurrent developments led to their natural combination in the design of 100BASE-TX networks.

100BASE-FX

The 100BASE-FX standard uses the same signaling procedure as 100BASE-TX, but over optical fiber media rather than UTP copper. Although the encoding, decoding, and clock recovery procedures are the same for both media, the signal transmission is different - electrical pulses in copper and light pulses in optical fiber. 100BASE-FX uses Low Cost Fiber Interface Connectors (commonly called the duplex SC connector).

Fiber implementations are point-to-point connections, that is, they are used to interconnect two devices. These connections may be between two computers, between a computer and a switch, or between two switches.

9.5.3 1000 Mbps Ethernet

Refer to
Figure
in online course

1000 Mbps - Gigabit Ethernet

The development of Gigabit Ethernet standards resulted in specifications for UTP copper, single-mode fiber, and multimode fiber. On Gigabit Ethernet networks, bits occur in a fraction of the time that they take on 100 Mbps networks and 10 Mbps networks. With signals occurring in less time, the bits become more susceptible to noise, and therefore timing is critical. The question of performance is based on how fast the network adapter or interface can change voltage levels and how well that voltage change can be detected reliably 100 meters away, at the receiving NIC or interface.

At these higher speeds, encoding and decoding data is more complex. Gigabit Ethernet uses two separate encoding steps. Data transmission is more efficient when codes are used to represent the binary bit stream. Encoding the data enables synchronization, efficient usage of bandwidth, and improved signal-to-noise ratio characteristics.

1000BASE-T Ethernet

1000BASE-T Ethernet provides full-duplex transmission using all four pairs in Category 5 or later UTP cable. Gigabit Ethernet over copper wire enables an increase from 100 Mbps per wire pair to 125 Mbps per wire pair, or 500 Mbps for the four pairs. Each wire pair signals in full duplex, doubling the 500 Mbps to 1000 Mbps.

1000BASE-T uses 4D-PAM5 line encoding to obtain 1 Gbps data throughput. This encoding scheme enables the transmission signals over four wire pairs simultaneously. It translates an 8-bit byte of data into a simultaneous transmission of four code symbols (4D), which are sent over the media, one on each pair, as 5-level Pulse Amplitude Modulated (PAM5) signals. This means that every symbol corresponds to two bits of data. Because the information travels simultaneously across the four paths, the circuitry has to divide frames at the transmitter and reassemble them at the receiver. The figure shows a representation of the circuitry used by 1000BASE-T Ethernet.

1000BASE-T allows the transmission and reception of data in both directions - on the same wire and at the same time. This traffic flow creates permanent collisions on the wire pairs. These collisions result in complex voltage patterns. The hybrid circuits detecting the signals use sophisticated techniques such as echo cancellation, Layer 1 Forward Error Correction (FEC), and prudent selection of voltage levels. Using these techniques, the system achieves the 1-Gigabit throughput.

To help with synchronization, the Physical layer encapsulates each frame with start-of-stream and end-of-stream delimiters. Loop timing is maintained by continuous streams of IDLE symbols sent on each wire pair during the interframe spacing.

Unlike most digital signals where there are usually a couple of discrete voltage levels, 1000BASE-T uses many voltage levels. In idle periods, nine voltage levels are found on the cable. During data transmission periods, up to 17 voltage levels are found on the cable. With this large number of states, combined with the effects of noise, the signal on the wire looks more analog than digital. Like analog, the system is more susceptible to noise due to cable and termination problems.

1000BASE-SX and 1000BASE-LX Ethernet Using Fiber-Optics

The fiber versions of Gigabit Ethernet - 1000BASE-SX and 1000BASE-LX - offer the following advantages over UTP: noise immunity, small physical size, and increased unrepeated distances and bandwidth.

All 1000BASE-SX and 1000BASE-LX versions support full-duplex binary transmission at 1250 Mbps over two strands of optical fiber. The transmission coding is based on the 8B/10B encoding scheme. Because of the overhead of this encoding, the data transfer rate is still 1000 Mbps.

Each data frame is encapsulated at the Physical layer before transmission, and link synchronization is maintained by sending a continuous stream of IDLE code groups during the interframe spacing.

The principal differences among the 1000BASE-SX and 1000BASE-LX fiber versions are the link media, connectors, and wavelength of the optical signal. These differences are shown in the figure.

9.5.4 Ethernet - Future Options

The IEEE 802.3ae standard was adapted to include 10 Gbps, full-duplex transmission over fiber-optic cable. The 802.3ae standard and the 802.3 standards for the original Ethernet are very similar. 10-Gigabit Ethernet (10GbE) is evolving for use not only in LANs, but also for use in WANs and MANs.

Because the frame format and other Ethernet Layer 2 specifications are compatible with previous standards, 10GbE can provide increased bandwidth to individual networks that is interoperable with the existing network infrastructure.

10Gbps can be compared to other varieties of Ethernet in these ways:

- Frame format is the same, allowing interoperability between all varieties of legacy, fast, gigabit, and 10 gigabit Ethernet, with no reframing or protocol conversions necessary.

- Bit time is now 0.1 ns. All other time variables scale accordingly.

- Because only full-duplex fiber connections are used, there is no media contention and CSMA/CD is not necessary.

- The IEEE 802.3 sublayers within OSI Layers 1 and 2 are mostly preserved, with a few additions to accommodate 40 km fiber links and interoperability with other fiber technologies.

With 10Gbps Ethernet, flexible, efficient, reliable, relatively low cost end-to-end Ethernet networks become possible.

Future Ethernet Speeds

Although 1-Gigabit Ethernet is now widely available and 10-Gigabit products are becoming more available, the IEEE and the 10-Gigabit Ethernet Alliance are working on 40-, 100-, or even 160-Gbps standards. The technologies that are adopted will depend on a number of factors, including the rate of maturation of the technologies and standards, the rate of adoption in the market, and the cost of emerging products.

9.6 Hubs and Switches

9.6.1 Legacy Ethernet - Using Hubs

Refer to
Figure
in online course

In previous sections, we have seen how classic Ethernet uses shared media and contention-based media access control. Classic Ethernet uses hubs to interconnect nodes on the LAN segment. Hubs do not perform any type of traffic filtering. Instead, the hub forwards all the bits to every device connected to the hub. This forces all the devices in the LAN to share the bandwidth of the media.

Additionally, this classic Ethernet implementation often results in high levels of collisions on the LAN. Because of these performance issues, this type of Ethernet LAN has limited use in today's networks. Ethernet implementations using hubs are now typically used only in small LANs or in LANs with low bandwidth requirements.

Sharing media among devices creates significant issues as the network grows. The figure illustrates some of the issues presented here.

Scalability

In a hub network, there is a limit to the amount of bandwidth that devices can share. With each device added to the shared media, the average bandwidth available to each device decreases. With each increase in the number of devices on the media, performance is degraded.

Latency

Network latency is the amount of time it takes a signal to reach all destinations on the media. Each node in a hub-based network has to wait for an opportunity to transmit in order to avoid collisions. Latency can increase significantly as the distance between nodes is extended. Latency is also affected by a delay of the signal across the media as well as the delay added by the processing of the signals through hubs and repeaters. **Increasing the length of media or the number of hubs and repeaters connected to a segment results in increased latency.** With greater latency, it is more likely that nodes will not receive initial signals, thereby increasing the collisions present in the network.

Network Failure

Because classic Ethernet shares the media, any device in the network could potentially cause problems for other devices. If any device connected to the hub generates detrimental traffic, the communication for all devices on the media could be impeded. This harmful traffic could be due to incorrect speed or full-duplex settings on a NIC.

Collisions

According to CSMA/CD, a node should not send a packet unless the network is clear of traffic. If two nodes send packets at the same time, a collision occurs and the packets are lost. Then both nodes send a jam signal, wait for a random amount of time, and retransmit their packets. Any part of the network where packets from two or more nodes can interfere with each other is considered a collision domain. A network with a larger number of nodes on the same segment has a larger collision domain and typically has more traffic. As the amount of traffic in the network increases, the likelihood of collisions increases.

Switches provide an alternative to the contention-based environment of classic Ethernet.

9.6.2 Ethernet - Using Switches

Refer to
Figure
in online course

In the last few years, switches have quickly become a fundamental part of most networks. **Switches allow the segmentation of the LAN into separate collision domains.** Each port of the switch represents a separate collision domain and provides the full media bandwidth to the node or nodes connected on that port. With fewer nodes in each collision domain, there is an increase in the average bandwidth available to each node, and collisions are reduced.

A LAN may have a centralized switch connecting to hubs that still provide the connectivity to nodes. Or, a LAN may have all nodes connected directly to a switch. Theses topologies are shown in the figure.

In a LAN where a hub is connected to a switch port, there is still shared bandwidth, which may result in collisions within the shared environment of the hub. However, the switch will isolate the segment and limit collisions to traffic between the hub's ports.

Refer to
Figure
in online course

Nodes are Connected Directly

In a LAN where all nodes are connected directly to the switch, the throughput of the network increases dramatically. The three primary reasons for this increase are:

- Dedicated bandwidth to each port
- Collision-free environment
- Full-duplex operation

These physical star topologies are essentially point to point links.

Click the performance factors in the figure.

Dedicated Bandwidth

Each node has the full media bandwidth available in the connection between the node and the switch. Because a hub replicates the signals it receives and sends them to all other ports, classic

Ethernet hubs form a logical bus. This means that all the nodes have to share the same bandwidth of this bus. With switches, each device effectively has a dedicated point-to-point connection between the device and the switch, without media contention.

As an example, compare two 100 Mbps LANs, each with 10 nodes. In network segment A, the 10 nodes are connected to a hub. Each node shares the available 100 Mbps bandwidth. This provides an average of 10 Mbps to each node. In network segment B, the 10 nodes are connected to a switch. In this segment, all 10 nodes have the full 100 Mbps bandwidth available to them.

Even in this small network example, the increase in bandwidth is significant. As the number of nodes increases, the discrepancy between the available bandwidth in the two implementations increases significantly.

Collision-Free Environment

A dedicated point-to-point connection to a switch also removes any media contention between devices, allowing a node to operate with few or no collisions. In a moderately-sized classic Ethernet network using hubs, approximately 40% to 50% of the bandwidth is consumed by collision recovery. In a switched Ethernet network - where there are virtually no collisions - the overhead devoted to collision recovery is virtually eliminated. This provides the switched network with significantly better throughput rates.

Full-Duplex Operation

Switching also allows a network to operate as a full-duplex Ethernet environment. Before switching existed, Ethernet was half-duplex only. This meant that at any given time, a node could either transmit or receive. With full-duplex enabled in a switched Ethernet network, the devices connected directly to the switch ports can transmit and receive simultaneously, at the full media bandwidth.

The connection between the device and the switch is collision-free. This arrangement effectively doubles the transmission rate when compared to half-duplex. For example, if the speed of the network is 100 Mbps, each node can transmit a frame at 100 Mbps and, at the same time, receive a frame at 100 Mbps.

Using Switches Instead of Hubs

Most modern Ethernet use switches to the end devices and operate full duplex. Because switches provide so much greater throughput than hubs and increase performance so dramatically, it is fair to ask: why not use switches in every Ethernet LAN? There are three reasons why hubs are still being used:

- Availability - LAN switches were not developed until the early 1990s and were not readily available until the mid 1990s. Early Ethernet networks used UTP hubs and many of them remain in operation to this day.

- Economics - Initially, switches were rather expensive. As the price of switches has dropped, the use of hubs has decreased and cost is becoming less of a factor in deployment decisions.

- Requirements - The early LAN networks were simple networks designed to exchange files and share printers. For many locations, the early networks have evolved into the converged networks of today, resulting in a substantial need for increased bandwidth available to individual users. In some circumstances, however, a shared media hub will still suffice and these products remain on the market.

The next section explores the basic operation of switches and how a switch achieves the enhanced performance upon which our networks now depend. A later course will present more details and additional technologies related to switching.

Refer to **Packet Tracer Activity** for this chapter

In this activity, we provide a model for comparing the collisions found in hub-based networks with the collision-free behavior of switches.

Refer to **Figure** in online course

9.6.3 Switches - Selective Forwarding

Ethernet switches selectively forward individual frames from a receiving port to the port where the destination node is connected. This *selective forwarding* process can be thought of as establishing a momentary point-to-point connection between the transmitting and receiving nodes. The connection is made only long enough to forward a single frame. During this instant, the two nodes have a full bandwidth connection between them and represent a logical point-to-point connection.

To be technically accurate, this temporary connection is not made between the two nodes simultaneously. In essence, this makes the connection between hosts a point-to-point connection. In fact, any node operating in full-duplex mode can transmit anytime it has a frame, without regard to the availability of the receiving node. This is because a LAN switch will buffer an incoming frame and then forward it to the proper port when that port is idle. This process is referred to as *store and forward*.

With store and forward switching, the switch receives the entire frame, checks the FSC for errors, and forwards the frame to the appropriate port for the destination node. Because the nodes do not have to wait for the media to be idle, the nodes can send and receive at full media speed without losses due to collisions or the overhead associated with managing collisions.

Forwarding is Based on the Destination MAC

The switch maintains a table, called a *MAC table*. that matches a destination MAC address with the port used to connect to a node. For each incoming frame, the destination MAC address in the frame header is compared to the list of addresses in the MAC table. If a match is found, the port number in the table that is paired with the MAC address is used as the exit port for the frame.

The MAC table can be referred to by many different names. It is often called the *switch table*. Because switching was derived from an older technology called *transparent bridging*, the table is sometimes called the *bridge* table. For this reason, many processes performed by LAN switches can contain *bridge* or *bridging* in their names.

A bridge is a device used more commonly in the early days of LAN to connect - or bridge - two physical network segments. Switches can be used to perform this operation as well as allowing end device connectivity to the LAN. Many other technologies have been developed around LAN switching. Many of these technologies will be presented in a later course. One place where bridges are prevalent is in Wireless networks. We use Wireless Bridges to interconnect two wireless network segments. Therefore, you may find both terms - *switching* and *bridging* - in use by the networking industry.

Refer to **Figure** in online course

Switch Operation

To accomplish their purpose, Ethernet LAN switches use five basic operations:

- Learning
- Aging
- Flooding
- Selective Forwarding
- Filtering

Learning

The MAC table must be populated with MAC addresses and their corresponding ports. The Learning process allows these mappings to be dynamically acquired during normal operation.

As each frame enters the switch, the switch examines the source MAC address. Using a lookup procedure, the switch determines if the table already contains an entry for that MAC address. If no entry exists, the switch creates a new entry in the MAC table using the source MAC address and pairs the address with the port on which the entry arrived. The switch now can use this mapping to forward frames to this node.

Aging

The entries in the MAC table acquired by the Learning process are time stamped. This timestamp is used as a means for removing old entries in the MAC table. After an entry in the MAC table is made, a procedure begins a countdown, using the timestamp as the beginning value. After the value reaches 0, the entry in the table will be refreshed when the switch next receives a frame from that node on the same port.

Flooding

If the switch does not know to which port to send a frame because the destination MAC address is not in the MAC table, the switch sends the frame to all ports except the port on which the frame arrived. The process of sending a frame to all segments is known as *flooding. The switch does not forward the frame to the port on which it arrived because any destination on that segment will have already received the frame. Flooding is also used for frames sent to the broadcast MAC address.*

Selective Forwarding

Selective forwarding is the process of examining a frame's destination MAC address and forwarding it out the appropriate port. This is the central function of the switch. When a frame from a node arrives at the switch for which the switch has already learned the MAC address, this address is matched to an entry in the MAC table and the frame is forwarded to the corresponding port. Instead of flooding the frame to all ports, the switch sends the frame to the destination node via its nominated port. This action is called *forwarding*.

Filtering

In some cases, a frame is not forwarded. This process is called frame *filtering*. One use of filtering has already been described: a switch does not forward a frame to the same port on which it arrived. A switch will also drop a corrupt frame. If a frame fails a CRC check, the frame is dropped. An additional reason for filtering a frame is security. A switch has security settings for blocking frames to and/or from selective MAC addresses or specific ports.

9.6.4 Ethernet - Comparing Hubs and Switches

Refer to **Figure** in online course

In this interactive activity, you are given the destination and source MAC addresses of a frame, a switching table, and the source node of a frame.

Using this information, you are to determine how the switch processes the frame by indicating to which ports the frame will be forwarded and how the switch will handle the frame.

Then check your answers.

You have the opportunity to use practice problems provided by the activity or you can try entering your own examples.

Refer to **Packet Tracer Activity** for this chapter

In this activity, you will have the opportunity to visualize and experiment with the behavior of switches in a network.

9.7 Address Resolution Protocol (ARP)

9.7.1 The ARP Process - Mapping IP to MAC Addresses

Refer to
Figure
in online course

The ARP protocol provides two basic functions:

- Resolving IPv4 addresses to MAC addresses

- Maintaining a cache of mappings

Resolving IPv4 Addresses to MAC Addresses

For a frame to be placed on the LAN media, it must have a destination MAC address. When a packet is sent to the Data Link layer to be encapsulated into a frame, the node refers to a table in its memory to find the Data Link layer address that is mapped to the destination IPv4 address. This table is called the *ARP table or the ARP cache. The ARP table is stored in the RAM of the device.*

Each entry, or row, of the ARP table has a pair of values: an IP Address and a MAC address. We call the relationship between the two values a map - it simply means that you can locate an IP address in the table and discover the corresponding MAC address. The ARP table caches the mapping for the devices on the local LAN.

To begin the process, a transmitting node attempts to locate in the ARP table the MAC address mapped to an IPv4 destination. If this map is cached in the table, the node uses the MAC address as the destination MAC in the frame that encapsulates the IPv4 packet. The frame is then encoded onto the networking media.

Maintaining the ARP Table

The ARP table is maintained dynamically. There are two ways that a device can gather MAC addresses. One way is to monitor the traffic that occurs on the local network segment. As a node receives frames from the media, it can record the source IP and MAC address as a mapping in the ARP table. As frames are transmitted on the network, the device populates the ARP table with address pairs.

Another way a device can get an address pair is to broadcast an ARP request. ARP sends a Layer 2 broadcast to all devices on the Ethernet LAN. The frame contains an ARP request packet with the IP address of the destination host. The node receiving the frame that identifies the IP address as its own responds by sending an ARP reply packet back to the sender as a unicast frame. This response is then used to make a new entry in the ARP table.

These dynamic entries in the ARP table are timestamped in much the same way that MAC table entries are timestamped in switches. If a device does not receive a frame from a particular device by the time the timestamp expires, the entry for this device is removed from the ARP table.

Additionally, static map entries can be entered in an ARP table, but this is rarely done. Static ARP table entries do not expire over time and must be manually removed.

Creating the Frame

What does a node do when it needs to create a frame and the ARP cache does not contain a map of an IP address to a destination MAC address? When ARP receives a request to map an IPv4 address to a MAC address, it looks for the cached map in its ARP table. If an entry is not found, the encapsulation of the IPv4 packet fails and the Layer 2 processes notify ARP that it needs a map.

The ARP processes then send out an ARP request packet to discover the MAC address of the destination device on the local network. If a device receiving the request has the destination IP address, it responds with an ARP reply. A map is created in the ARP table. Packets for that IPv4 address can now be encapsulated in frames.

If no device responds to the ARP request, the packet is dropped because a frame cannot be created. This encapsulation failure is reported to the upper layers of the device. If the device is an intermediary device, like a router, the upper layers may choose to respond to the source host with an error in an ICMPv4 packet.

Click the step numbers in the figure to see the process used to get the MAC address of node on the local physical network.

In the lab, you will use Wireshark to observe ARP requests and responses across a network.

9.7.2 The ARP Process - Destinations outside the Local Network

Refer to **Figure** in online course

All frames must be delivered to a node on the local network segment. If the destination IPv4 host is on the local network, the frame will use the MAC address of this device as the destination MAC address.

If the destination IPv4 host is not on the local network, the source node needs to deliver the frame to the router interface that is the gateway or next hop used to reach that destination. The source node will use the MAC address of the gateway as the destination address for frames containing an IPv4 packet addressed to hosts on other networks.

The gateway address of the router interface is stored in the IPv4 configuration of the hosts. When a host creates a packet for a destination, it compares the destination IP address and its own IP address to determine if the two IP addresses are located on the same Layer 3 network. If the receiving host is not on the same network, the source uses the ARP process to determine a MAC address for the router interface serving as the gateway.

In the event that the gateway entry is not in the table, the normal ARP process will send an ARP request to retrieve the MAC address associated with the IP address of the router interface.

Click the step numbers in the figure to see the process used to get the MAC address of the gateway.

Refer to **Figure** in online course

Proxy ARP

There are circumstances under which a host might send an ARP request seeking to map an IPv4 address outside of the range of the local network. In these cases, the device sends ARP requests for IPv4 addresses not on the local network instead of requesting the MAC address associated with the IPv4 address of the gateway. To provide a MAC address for these hosts, a router interface may use a proxy ARP to respond on behalf of these remote hosts. This means that the ARP cache of the requesting device will contain the MAC address of the gateway mapped to any IP addresses not on the local network. Using proxy ARP, a router interface acts as if it is the host with the IPv4 address requested by the ARP request. By "faking" its identity, the router accepts responsibility for routing packets to the "real" destination.

One such use of this process is when an older implementation of IPv4 cannot determine whether the destination host is on the same logical network as the source. In these implementations, ARP always sends ARP requests for the destination IPv4 address. If proxy ARP is disabled on the router interface, these hosts cannot communicate out of the local network.

Another case where a proxy ARP is used is when a host believes that it is directly connected to the same logical network as the destination host. This generally occurs when a host is configured with an improper mask.

As shown in the figure, Host A has been improperly configured with a /16 subnet mask. This host believes that it is directly connected to all of the 172.16.0.0 /16 network instead of to the 172.16.10.0 /24 subnet.

When attempts are made to communicate with any IPv4 host in the range of 172.16.0.1 to 172.16.255.254, Host A will send an ARP request for that IPv4 address. The router can use a proxy ARP to respond to requests for the IPv4 address of Host C (172.16.20.100) and Host D (172.16.20.200). Host A will subsequently have entries for these addresses mapped to the MAC address of the e0 interface of the router (00-00-0c-94-36-ab).

Yet another use for a proxy ARP is when a host is not configured with a default gateway. Proxy ARP can help devices on a network reach remote subnets without the need to configure routing or a default gateway.

By default, Cisco routers have proxy ARP enabled on LAN interfaces.

http://www.cisco.com/en/US/tech/tk648/tk361/technologies_tech_note09186a0080094adb.shtml

9.7.3 The ARP Process - Removing Address Mappings

Refer to
Figure
in online course

For each device, an ARP cache timer removes ARP entries that have not been used for a specified period of time. The times differ depending on the device and its operating system. For example, some Windows operating systems store ARP cache entries for 2 minutes. If the entry is used again during that time, the ARP timer for that entry is extended to 10 minutes.

Commands may also be used to manually remove all or some of the entries in the ARP table. After an entry has been removed, the process for sending an ARP request and receiving an ARP reply must occur again to enter the map in the ARP table.

In the lab for this section, you will use the **arp** command to view and to clear the contents of a computer's ARP cache. Note that this command, despite its name, does not invoke the execution of the Address Resolution Protocol in any way. It is merely used to display, add, or remove the entries of the ARP table. ARP service is integrated within the IPv4 protocol and implemented by the device. Its operation is transparent to both upper layer applications and users.

9.7.4 ARP Broadcasts - Issues

Refer to
Figure
in online course

Overhead on the Media

As a broadcast frame, an ARP request is received and processed by every device on the local network. On a typical business network, these broadcasts would probably have minimal impact on network performance. However, if a large number of devices were to be powered up and all start accessing network services at the same time, there could be some reduction in performance for a short period of time. For example, if all students in a lab logged into classroom computers and attempted to access the Internet at the same time, there could be delays.

However, after the devices send out the initial ARP broadcasts and have learned the necessary MAC addresses, any impact on the network will be minimized.

Security

In some cases, the use of ARP can lead to a potential security risk. ARP spoofing, or *ARP poisoning*, is a technique used by an attacker to inject the wrong MAC address association into a network by issuing fake ARP requests. An attacker forges the MAC address of a device and then frames can be sent to the wrong destination.

Manually configuring static ARP associations is one way to prevent ARP spoofing. Authorized MAC addresses can be configured on some network devices to restrict network access to only those devices listed.

9.8 Chapter Labs

9.8.1 Lab - Address Resolution Protocol (ARP)

Refer to **Lab Activity** for this chapter

Refer to **Packet Tracer Activity** for this chapter

This lab introduces the Windows **arp** utility command to examine and change ARP cache entries on a host computer. Then Wireshark is used to capture and analyze ARP exchanges between network devices.

In this activity, you will use Packet Tracer to examine and change ARP cache entries on a host computer.

9.8.2 Lab - Cisco Switch MAC Table Examination

Refer to **Lab Activity** for this chapter

Refer to **Packet Tracer Activity** for this chapter

In this lab, you will connect to a switch via a Telnet session, log in, and use the required operating system commands to examine the stored MAC addresses and their association to switch ports.

In this activity, you will use Packet tracer to examine the stored MAC addresses and their association to switch ports.

9.8.3 Lab - Intermediary Device as an End Device

Refer to **Lab Activity** for this chapter

Refer to **Packet Tracer Activity** for this chapter

This lab uses Wireshark to capture and analyze frames to determine which network nodes originated the frames. A Telnet session between a host computer and switch is then captured and analyzed for frame content.

In this activity, you will use Packet Tracer to analyze frames originating from a switch.

Summary and Review

Ethernet is an effective and widely used TCP/IP Network Access protocol. Its common frame structure has been implemented across a range of media technologies, both copper and fiber, making the most common LAN protocol in use today.

Refer to
Figure
in online course

As an implementation of the IEEE 802.2/3 standards, the Ethernet frame provides MAC addressing and error checking. Being a shared media technology, early Ethernet had to apply a CSMA/CD mechanism to manage the use of the media by multiple devices. Replacing hubs with switches in the local network has reduced the probability of frame collisions in half-duplex links. Current and future versions, however, inherently operate as full-duplex communications links and do not need to manage media contention to the same detail.

The Layer 2 addressing provided by Ethernet supports unicast, multicast, and broadcast communications. Ethernet uses the Address Resolution Protocol to determine the MAC addresses of destinations and map them against known Network layer addresses.

In this activity, you will continue to build a more complex model of the Exploration lab network.

Packet Tracer Skills Integration Instructions (PDF)

Refer to
Figure
in online course

To Learn More

Refer to **Packet Tracer Activity** for this chapter

Reflection Questions

Discuss the move of Ethernet from a LAN technology to also becoming a Metropolitan and Wide Area technology. What has made this possible?

Refer to
Figure
in online course

Initially used only for data communications networks, Ethernet is now also being applied in real-time industrial control networking. Discuss the physical and operational challenges that Ethernet has to overcome to be fully applied in this area.

Go to
the online course
to take the quiz.

Chapter Quiz

Take the chapter quiz to test your knowledge.

Your Chapter Notes

CHAPTER 10

Planning and Cabling Networks

Chapter Introduction

Refer to
Figure
in online course

Before using an IP phone, accessing instant messaging, or conducting any number of other interactions over a data network, we must connect end devices and intermediary devices via cable or wireless connections to form a functioning network. It is this network that will support our communication in the human network.

Up to this point in the course, we have considered the services that a data network can provide to the human network, examined the features of each layer of the OSI model and the operations of TCP/IP protocols, and looked in detail at Ethernet, a universal LAN technology. The next step is to learn how to assemble these elements together in a functioning network.

In this chapter, we will examine various media and the distinct roles they play with the devices that they connect. You will identify the cables needed to make successful LAN and WAN connections and learn how to use device management connections.

The selection of devices and the design of a network addressing scheme will be presented and then applied in the networking labs.

Learning Objectives

Upon completion of this chapter, you will be able to:

- Identify the basic network media required to make a LAN connection.

- Identify the types of connections for intermediate and end device connections in a LAN.

- Identify the pinout configurations for straight-through and crossover cables.

- Identify the different cabling types, standards, and ports used for WAN connections.

- Define the role of device management connections when using Cisco equipment.

- Design an addressing scheme for an internetwork and assign ranges for hosts, network devices, and the router interface.

- Compare and contrast the importance of network designs.

10.1 LANs - Making the Physical Connection

10.1.1 Choosing the Appropriate LAN Device

Refer to
Figure
in online course

For this course, the choice of which router to deploy is determined by the Ethernet interfaces that match the technology of the switches at the center of the LAN. It is important to note that routers offer many services and features to the LAN. These services and features are covered in the more advanced courses.

Each LAN will have a router as its gateway connecting the LAN to other networks. Inside the LAN will be one or more hubs or switches to connect the end devices to the LAN.

Internetwork Devices

Routers are the primary devices used to interconnect networks. Each port on a router connects to a different network and routes packets between the networks. Routers have the ability to break up broadcast domains and collision domains.

Routers are also used to interconnect networks that use different technologies. They can have both LAN and WAN interfaces.

The router's LAN interfaces allow routers to connect to the LAN media. This is usually UTP cabling, but modules can be added for using *fiber-optics*. Depending on the series or model of router, there can be multiple interface types for connection of LAN and WAN cabling.

Intranetwork Devices

Refer to
Figure
in online course

To create a LAN, we need to select the appropriate devices to connect the end device to the network. The two most common devices used are hubs and switches.

Hub

A hub receives a signal, regenerates it, and sends the signal over all ports. The use of hubs creates a logical bus. This means that the LAN uses multiaccess media. The ports use a shared bandwidth approach and often have reduced performance in the LAN due to collisions and recovery. Although multiple hubs can be interconnected, they remain a single collision domain.

Hubs are less expensive than switches. A hub is typically chosen as an intermediary device within a very small LAN, in a LAN that requires low throughput requirements, or when finances are limited.

Switch

A switch receives a frame and regenerates each bit of the frame on to the appropriate destination port. This device is used to segment a network into multiple collision domains. Unlike the hub, a switch reduces the collisions on a LAN. Each port on the switch creates a separate collision domain. This creates a point-to-point logical topology to the device on each port. Additionally, a switch provides dedicated bandwidth on each port, which can increase LAN performance. A LAN switch can also be used to interconnect network segments of different speeds.

In general, switches are chosen for connecting devices to a LAN. Although a switch is more expensive than a hub, its enhanced performance and reliability make it cost effective.

There is a range of switches available with a variety of features that enable the interconnection of multiple computers in a typical enterprise LAN setting.

10.1.2 Device Selection Factors

Refer to
Figure
in online course

To meet user requirements, a LAN needs to be planned and designed. Planning ensures that all requirements, cost factors and deployment options are given due consideration.

When selecting a device for a particular LAN, there are a number of factors that need to be considered. These factors include, but are not limited to:

- Cost

- Speed and Types of Ports/Interfaces

- Expandability

Refer to
Figure
in online course

- Manageability

- Additional Features and Services

Factors to Consider in Choosing a Switch

Although there are many factors that must be considered when selecting a switch, the next topic will explore two: cost and interface characteristics.

Cost

The cost of a switch is determined by its capacity and features. The switch capacity includes the number and types of ports available and the switching speed. Other factors that impact the cost are its network management capabilities, embedded security technologies, and optional advanced switching technologies.

Using a simple "cost per port" calculation, it may appear initially that the best option is to deploy one large switch at a central location. However, this apparent cost savings may be offset by the expense from the longer cable lengths required to connect every device on the LAN to one switch. This option should be compared with the cost of deploying a number of smaller switches connected by a few long cables to a central switch.

Another cost consideration is how much to invest in redundancy. The operation of the entire physical network is affected if there are problems with a single central switch.

Redundancy can be provided in a number of ways. We can provide a secondary central switch to operate concurrently with the primary central switch. We can also provide additional cabling to provide multiple interconnections between the switches. The goal of redundant systems is to allow the physical network to continue its operation even if one device fails.

Refer to
Figure
in online course

Speed and Types of Ports/Interfaces

The need for speed is ever-present in a LAN environment. Newer computers with built-in 10/100/1000 Mbps NICs are available. Choosing Layer 2 devices that can accommodate increased speeds allows the network to evolve without replacing the central devices.

When selecting a switch, choosing the number and type of ports is a critical decision. Ask yourself these questions: Would you purchase a switch with:

- Just enough ports for today's needs?

- A mixture of UTP speeds?

- Both UTP and fiber ports?

Consider carefully how many UTP ports will be needed and how many fiber ports will be needed. Likewise, consider how many ports will need 1 Gbps capability and how many ports only require 10/100 Mbps bandwidths. Also, consider how soon more ports will be needed.

Refer to
Figure
in online course

Factors to Consider in Choosing a Router

When selecting a router, we need to match the characteristics of the router to its purpose. Similar to the switch, cost and interface types and speeds must be considered as well. Additional factors for choosing a router include:

- Expandability

- Media

- Operating System Features

Expandability

Networking devices, such as routers and switches, come in both fixed and modular physical configurations. Fixed configurations have a specific number and type of ports or interfaces. Modular devices have expansion slots that provide the flexibility to add new modules as requirements evolve. Most modular devices come with a basic number of fixed ports as well as expansion slots. Since routers can be used for connecting different numbers and types of networks, care must be taken to select the appropriate modules and interfaces for the specific media.

Operating System Features

Depending on the version of the operating system, the router can support certain features and services such as:

- Security

- Quality of Service (QoS)

- Voice over IP (VoIP)

- Routing multiple Layer 3 protocols

- Special services such as Network Address Translation (NAT) and Dynamic Host Configuration Protocol (DHCP)

For the selection of devices, the budget is an important consideration. Routers can be expensive based on interfaces and features needed. Additional modules, such as fiber-optics, can increase the costs. The media used to connect to the router should be supported without needing to purchase additional modules. This can keep costs to a minimum.

10.2 Device Interconnections

10.2.1 LAN and WAN - Getting Connected

Refer to
Figure
in online course

When planning the installation of LAN cabling, there are four physical areas to consider:

- Work area

- Telecommunications room, also known as the distribution facility

- Backbone cabling, also known as vertical cabling

- Distribution cabling, also known as horizontal cabling

Total Cable Length

For UTP installations, the ANSI/TIA/EIA-568-B standard specifies that the total combined length of cable spanning three of the areas listed above, excluding the backbone cable, is limited to a maximum distance of 100 meters per channel. This standard also specifies maximum backbone distances, ranging from 90m for UTP to 3000m for single mode fiber cable, based on application and media type.

Work Areas

The work areas are the locations devoted to the end devices used by individual users. Each work area has a minimum of two jacks that can be used to connect an individual device to the network. We use patch cables to connect individual devices to these wall jacks. Allowed patch cable length depends on the horizontal cable and telecommunication room cable lengths. Recall that the maximum length for these three area can not exceed 100m. The EIA/TIA standard specifies that the

UTP patch cords used to connect devices to the wall jacks must meet or exceed the performance requirements in ANSI/TIA/EIA-568-B.

Straight-through cable is the most common patch cable used in the work area. This type of cable is used to connect end devices, such as computers, to a network. When a hub or switch is placed in the work area, a crossover cable is typically used to connect the device to the wall jack.

Telecommunications Room

The telecommunications room is where connections to intermediary devices take place. These rooms contain the intermediary devices - hubs, switches, routers, and data service units (DSUs) - that tie the network together. These devices provide the transitions between the backbone cabling and the horizontal cabling.

Inside the telecommunications room, patch cords make connections between the patch panels, where the horizontal cables terminate, and the intermediary devices. Patch cables also interconnect these intermediary devices.

The Electronics Industry Alliance/Telecommunications Industry Association (EIA/TIA) standards specify two different types of UTP patch cables. One type is a patch cord, with a length of up to 5 meters, which is used to interconnect equipment and patch panels in the telecommunications room. Another type of patch cable can be up to 5 meters in length and is used to connect devices to a termination point on the wall.

These rooms often serve dual purposes. In many organizations, the telecommunications room also contains the servers used by the network.

Horizontal Cabling

Horizontal cabling refers to the cables connecting the telecommunication rooms with the work areas. The maximum length for a cable from a termination point in the telecommunication room to the termination at the work area outlet must not exceed 90 meters. This 90 meter maximum horizontal cabling distance is referred to as the *permanent link* because it is installed in the building structure. The horizontal media runs from a patch panel in the telecommunications room to a wall jack in each work area. Connections to the devices are made with patch cables.

Backbone Cabling

Backbone cabling refers to the cabling used to connect the telecommunication rooms to the equipment rooms, where the servers are often located. Backbone cabling also interconnects multiple telecommunications rooms throughout the facility. These cables are sometimes routed outside the building to the WAN connection or ISP.

Backbones, or vertical cabling, are used for aggregated traffic, such as traffic to and from the Internet and access to corporate resources at a remote location. A large portion of the traffic from the various work areas will use the backbone cabling to access resources outside the area or facility. Therefore, backbones typically require high bandwidth media such as fiber-optic cabling.

Refer to
Figure
in online course

Types of Media

Choosing the cables necessary to make a successful LAN or WAN connection requires consideration of the different media types. As you recall, there are many different Physical layer implementations that support multiple media types:

- UTP (Category 5, 5e, 6, and 7)
- Fiber-optics
- Wireless

Each media type has its advantages and disadvantages. Some of the factors to consider are:

- Cable length - Does the cable need to span across a room or from building to building?

- Cost - Does the budget allow for using a more expensive media type?

- Bandwidth - Does the technology used with the media provide adequate bandwidth?

- Ease of installation - Does the implementation team have the ability to install the cable or is a vendor required?

- Susceptible to EMI/RFI - Is the local environment going to interfere with the signal?

Refer to
Figure
in online course

Cable Length

The total length of cable required to connect a device includes all cables from the end devices in the work area to the intermediary device in the telecommunication room (usually a switch). This includes cable from the devices to the wall plug, the cable through the building from wall plug to the cross-connecting point, or patch panel, and cable from patch panel to the switch. If the switch is located in a telecommunication rooms on different floors in a building or in different buildings, the cable between these points must be included in the total length.

Attenuation is reduction of the strength of a signal as it moves down a media. The longer the media, the more *attenuation* will affect the signal. At some point, the signal will not be detectable. **Cabling distance is a significant factor in data signal performance. Signal attenuation and exposure to possible interference increase with cable length.**

For example, when using UTP cabling for Ethernet, the horizontal (or fixed) cabling length needs to stay within the recommended maximum distance of 90 meters to avoid attenuation of the signal. Fiber-optic cables may provide a greater cabling distance-up to 500 meters to a few kilometers depending on the technology. However, fiber-optic cable can also suffer from attenuation when these limits are reached.

Cost

The cost associated with LAN cabling can vary from media type to media type, and the staff might not realize the impact on the budget. In a perfect setting, the budget would allow for fiber-optic cabling to every device in the LAN. Although fiber provides greater bandwidth than UTP, the material and installation costs are significantly higher. In practice, this level of performance is not usually required and is not a reasonable expectation in most environments. Network designers must match the performance needs of the users with the cost of the equipment and cabling to achieve the best cost/performance ratio.

Bandwidth

The devices in a network have different bandwidth requirements. When selecting the media for individual connections, carefully consider the bandwidth requirements.

For example, a server generally has a need for more bandwidth than a computer dedicated to a single user. For a server connection, consider media that will provide high bandwidth, and can grow to meet increased bandwidth requirements and newer technologies. A fiber cable may be a logical choice for a server connection.

Currently, the technology used in fiber-optic media offers the greatest bandwidth available among the choices for LAN media. Given the seemingly unlimited bandwidth available in fiber cables, much greater speeds for LANs are expected. Wireless is also supporting huge increases in bandwidth, but it has limitations in distance and power consumption.

Refer to
Figure
in online course

Ease of Installation

The ease of cable installation varies according to cable types and building architecture. Access to floor or roof spaces, and the physical size and properties of the cable influence how easily a cable can be installed in various buildings. Cables in buildings are typically installed in raceways.

As shown in the figure, a raceway is an enclosure or tube that encloses and protects the cable. A raceway also keeps cabling neat and easy to thread.

UTP cable is relatively lightweight and flexible and has a small diameter, which allows it to fit into small spaces. The connectors, RJ-45 plugs, are relatively easy to install and are a standard for all Ethernet devices.

Many fiber-optic cables contain a thin glass fiber. This creates issues for the bend radius of the cable. Crimps or sharp bends can break the fiber. The termination of the cable connectors (ST, SC, MT-RJ) are significantly more difficult to install and require special equipment.

Wireless networks require cabling, at some point, to connect devices, such as access points, to the wired LAN. Because there are fewer cables required in a wireless network, wireless is often easier to install than UTP or fiber cable. However, a wireless LAN requires more careful planning and testing. Also, there are many external factors, such as other radio frequency devices and building construction, that can effect its operation.

Electromagnetic Interference/Radio Frequency Interference

Electromagnetic Interference (*EMI*) and Radio Frequency Interference (*RFI*) must be taken into consideration when choosing a media type for a LAN. EMI/RFI in an industrial environment can significantly impact data communications if the wrong cable is used.

Interference can be produced by electrical machines, lightning, and other communications devices, including computers and radio equipment.

As an example, consider an installation where devices in two separate buildings are interconnected. The media used to interconnect these buildings will be exposed to the possibility of lightning strikes. Additionally, there maybe a great distance between these two buildings. For this installation, fiber cable is the best choice.

Wireless is the medium most susceptible to RFI. Before using wireless technology, potential sources of interference must be identified and, if possible, minimized.

10.2.2 Making LAN Connections

Refer to **Figure** in online course

UTP cabling connections are specified by the Electronics Industry Alliance/Telecommunications Industry Association (EIA/TIA).

The RJ-45 connector is the male component crimped on the end of the cable. When viewed from the front, the pins are numbered from 8 to 1. When viewed from above with the opening gate facing you, the pins are numbered 1 through 8, from left to right. This orientation is important to remember when identifying a cable.

Refer to **Figure** in online course

Types of Interfaces

In an Ethernet LAN, devices use one of two types of UTP interfaces - *MDI* or *MDIX.*

The MDI (media-dependent interface) uses the normal Ethernet pinout. Pins 1 and 2 are used for transmitting and pins 3 and 6 are used for receiving. Devices such as computers, servers, or routers will have MDI connections.

The devices that provide LAN connectivity - usually hubs or switches - typically use MDIX (media-dependent interface, crossover) connections. The MDIX connection swaps the transmit pairs internally. This swapping allows the end devices to be connected to the hub or switch using a straight-through cable.

Typically, when connecting different types of devices, use a straight-through cable. And when connecting the same type of device, use a crossover cable.

Straight-through UTP Cables

A straight-through cable has connectors on each end that are terminated the same in accordance with either the T568A or T568B standards.

Identifying the cable standard used allows you to determine if you have the right cable for the job. More importantly, it is a common practice to use the same color codes throughout the LAN for consistency in documentation.

Use straight-through cables for the following connections:

- Switch to a router Ethernet port

- Computer to switch

- Computer to hub

Refer to
Figure
in online course

Crossover UTP Cables

For two devices to communicate through a cable that is directly connected between the two, the transmit terminal of one device needs to be connected to the receive terminal of the other device.

The cable must be terminated so the transmit pin, Tx, taking the signal from device A at one end, is wired to the receive pin, Rx, on device B. Similarly, device B's Tx pin must be connected to device A's Rx pin. If the Tx pin on a device is numbered 1, and the Rx pin is numbered 2, the cable connects pin 1 at one end with pin 2 at the other end. These "crossed over" pin connections give this type of cable its name, crossover.

To achieve this type of connection with a UTP cable, one end must be terminated as EIA/TIA T568A pinout, and the other end terminated with T568B pinout.

To summarize, crossover cables directly connect the following devices on a LAN:

- Switch to switch

- Switch to hub

- Hub to hub

- Router to router Ethernet port connection

- Computer to computer

- Computer to a router Ethernet port

Refer to
Figure
in online course

On the figure, identify the cable type used based on the devices being connected.

As a reminder, the common uses are listed again:

Use straight-through cables for connecting:

- Switch to router

- Computer to switch

- Computer to hub

Use crossover cables for connecting:

- Switch to switch

- Switch to hub

- Hub to hub

- Router to router

- Computer to computer

- Computer to router

MDI/MDIX Selection

Many devices allow the UTP Ethernet port to be set to MDI or MDIX. This can be done in one of three ways, depending on the features of the device:

Step 1. On some devices, ports may have a mechanism that electrically swaps the transmit and receive pairs. The port can be changed from MDI to MDIX by engaging the mechanism.

Step 2. As part of the configuration, some devices allow for selecting whether a port functions as MDI or as MDIX.

Step 3. Many newer devices have an automatic crossover feature. This feature allows the device to detect the required cable type and configures the interfaces accordingly. On some devices, this auto-detection is performed by default. Other devices require an interface configuration command for enabling MDIX auto-detection.

10.2.3 Making WAN Connections

Refer to **Figure** in online course

By definition, WAN links can span extremely long distances. These distances can range across the globe as they provide the communication links that we use to manage e-mail accounts, view web pages, or conduct a teleconference session with a client.

Wide area connections between networks take a number of forms, including:

- Telephone line RJ11 connectors for dialup or Digital Subscriber Line (DSL) connections

- 60 pin Serial connections

In the course labs, you may be using Cisco routers with one of two types of physical serial cables. Both cables use a large Winchester 15 Pin connector on the network end. This end of the cable is used as a V.35 connection to a Physical layer device such as a *CSU/DSU*.

The first cable type has a male DB-60 connector on the Cisco end and a male *Winchester connector* on the network end. The second type is a more compact version of this cable and has a Smart Serial connector on the Cisco device end. It is necessary to be able to identify the two different types in order to connect successfully to the router.

Data Communications Equipment and Data Terminal Equipment

Refer to **Figure** in online course

The following terms describe the types of devices that maintain the link between a sending and a receiving device:

- *Data Communications Equipment (DCE)* **- A device that supplies the clocking services to another device. Typically, this device is at the WAN access provider end of the link.**

■ *Data Terminal Equipment (DTE)* **- A device that receives clocking services from another device and adjusts accordingly. Typically, this device is at the WAN customer or user end of the link.**

If a serial connection is made directly to a service provider or to a device that provides signal clocking such as a channel service unit/data service unit (CSU/DSU), the router is considered to be data terminal equipment (DTE) and will use a DTE serial cable.

Be aware that there will be occasions, especially in our labs, when the local router is required to provide the clock rate and will therefore use a data communications equipment (DCE) cable.

DCEs and DTEs are used in WAN connections. The communication via a WAN connection is maintained by providing a clock rate that is acceptable to both the sending and the receiving device. In most cases, the telco or ISP provides the clocking service that synchronizes the transmitted signal.

For example, if a device connected via a WAN link is sending its signal at 1.544 Mbps, each receiving device must use a clock, sending out a sample signal every 1/1,544,000th of a second. The timing in this case is extremely short. The devices must be able to synchronize to the signal that is sent and received very quickly.

By assigning a clock rate to the router, the timing is set. This allows a router to adjust the speed of its communication operations, thereby synchronizing with the devices connected to it.

Refer to
Figure
in online course

In the Lab

When making WAN connections between two routers in a lab environment, connect two routers with a serial cable to simulate a point-to-point WAN link. In this case, decide which router is going to be the one in control of clocking. Routers are DTE devices by default, but they can be configured to act as DCE devices.

The V35 compliant cables are available in DTE and DCE versions. To create a point-to-point serial connection between two routers, join together a DTE and DCE cable. Each cable comes with a connector that mates with its complementary type. These connectors are configured so that you cannot join two DCE or two DTE cables together by mistake.

Refer to **Packet
Tracer Activity**
for this chapter

In this activity, you will practice skills important in networking lab work by making interconnections in Packet Tracer.

10.3 Developing an Addressing Scheme

10.3.1 How Many Hosts in the Network?

Refer to
Figure
in online course

To develop an addressing scheme for a network, start with determining the total number of hosts. Consider every device that will require an IP address, now and in the future.

The end devices requiring an IP address include:

■ User computers

■ Administrator computers

■ Servers

■ Other end devices such as printers, IP phones, and IP cameras

Network devices requiring an IP address include:

■ Router LAN interfaces

- Router WAN (serial) interfaces

Network devices requiring an IP address for management include:

- Switches

- Wireless Access Points

There may be other devices on a network requiring an IP address. Add them to this list and estimate how many addresses will be needed to account for growth in the network as more devices are added.

Once the total number of hosts - current and future - has been determined, consider the range of addresses available and where they fit within the given network address.

Next, determine if all hosts will be part of the same network, or whether the network as a whole will be divided into separate subnets.

Recall that the number of hosts on one network or subnet is calculated using the formula 2 to the nth power minus 2 ($2^n - 2$), where n is the number of bits available as host bits. Recall also that we subtract two addresses - the network address and the network broadcast address - cannot be assigned to hosts.

10.3.2 How Many Networks?

Refer to
Figure
in online course

There are many reasons to divide a network into subnets:

- *Manage Broadcast Traffic* - Broadcasts can be controlled because one large broadcast domain is divided into a number of smaller domains. Not every host in the system receives every broadcast.

- *Different Network Requirements* - If different groups of users require specific network or computing facilities, it is easier to manage these requirements if those users who share requirements are all together on one subnet.

- *Security* - Different levels of network security can be implemented based on network addresses. This enables the management of access to different network and data services.

Counting the Subnets

Each subnet, as a physical network segment, requires a router interface as the gateway for that subnet.

In addition, each connection between routers is a separate subnet.

Click Play in the figure to see each of the five separate subnets in a sample network.

The number of subnets on one network is also calculated using the formula 2^n, where n is the number of bits "borrowed" from the given IP network address available to create subnets.

Subnet Masks

Having determined the required number of hosts and subnets, the next step is to apply one subnet mask for the entire network and then calculate the following values:

- A unique subnet and subnet mask for each physical segment

- A range of usable host addresses for each subnet

Refer to
Lab Activity
for this chapter

In this lab, you will determine the number of networks in a given topology and design an appropriate addressing scheme . After assigning subnets to the networks, you will examine the usage of the available address space.

10.3.3 Designing the Address Standard for our Internetwork

Refer to
Figure
in online course

To assist troubleshooting and expedite adding new hosts to the network, use addresses that fit a common pattern across all subnets. Each of these different device types should be allocated to a logical block of addresses within the address range of the network.

Some of the different categories for hosts are:

- General users
- Special users
- Network resources
- Router LAN interfaces
- Router WAN links
- Management access

For example, when allocating an IP address to a router interface that is the gateway for a LAN, it is common practice to use the first (lowest) or last (highest) address within the subnet range. This consistent approach aids in configuration and troubleshooting.

Similarly, when assigning addresses to devices that manage other devices, using a consistent pattern within a subnet makes these addresses easily recognizable. For example, in the figure, addresses with 64 - 127 in the octets always represent the general users. A network administrator monitoring or adding security can do so for all addresses ending in these values.

Roll over the device groupings in the figure for an example of how to allocate addresses based on device categories.

In addition, remember to document your IP addressing scheme on paper. This will be an important aid in troubleshooting and evolving the network.

10.4 Calculating the Subnets

10.4.1 Calculating Addresses: Case 1

Refer to
Figure
in online course

In this section, we will use a sample topology to practice allocating addresses to hosts.

The figure shows the network topology for this example. By starting with a given IP address and prefix (subnet mask) assigned by the network administrator, we can begin creating our network documentation.

The number and grouping of hosts are:

Student LAN

Student Computers: 460

Router (LAN Gateway): 1

Switches (management): 20

Total for student subnetwork: 481

Instructor LAN

Instructor Computers: 64

Router (LAN Gateway): 1

Switches (management): 4

Total for instructor subnetwork: 69

Administrator LAN

Administrator Computers: 20

Server: 1

Router (LAN Gateway): 1

Switch (management): 1

Total for administration subnetwork: 23

WAN

Router - Router WAN: 2

Total for WAN: 2

Allocation Methods

There are two methods available for allocating addresses to an internetwork. We can use *Variable Length Subnet Masking (VLSM)*, where we assign the prefix and host bits to each network based on the number of hosts in that network. Or, we can use a non-VLSM approach, where all subnets use the same prefix length and the same number of host bits.

For our network example, we will demonstrate both approaches.

Refer to **Figure** in online course

Calculating and Assigning Addresses-without VLSM

When using the non-VLSM method of assigning addresses, all subnets have the same number of addresses assigned to them. In order to provide each network with an adequate number of addresses, we base the number of addresses for all networks on the addressing requirements for the largest network.

In Case 1, the Student LAN is the largest network, requiring 481 addresses.

We will use this formula to calculate the number of hosts:

Usable hosts = $2^n - 2$

We use 9 as the value for n because 9 is the first power of 2 that is over 481.

Borrowing 9 bits for the host portion yields this calculation:

$2^9 = 512$

$512 - 2 = 510$ usable host addresses

This meets the current requirement for at least 481 addresses, with a small allowance for growth. This also leaves 23 network bits (32 total bits - 9 host bits).

Because there are four networks in our internetwork, we will need four blocks of 512 addresses each, for a total of 2048 addresses. We will use the address block 172.16.0.0 /23. This provides addresses in the range from 172.16.0.0 to 172.16.7.255.

Let's examine the address calculations for the networks:

Address: 172.16.0.0

In binary:

10101100.00010000.00000000.00000000

Mask: 255.255.254.0

23 bits in binary:

11111111.11111111.11111110.00000000

This mask will provide the four address ranges shown in the figure.

Student LAN

For the Student network block, the values would be:

172.16.0.1 to 172.16.1.254 with a broadcast address of 172.16.1.255.

Instructor LAN

The Instructor network requires a total of 69 addresses. The remaining addresses in this block of 512 addresses will go unused. The values for the Instructor network are:

172.16.2.1 to 172.16.3.254 with a broadcast address of 172.16.3.255.

Administrator LAN

Assigning the 172.16.4.0 /23. block to the Administrator LAN, assigns an address range of:

172.16.4.1 to 172.16.5.254 with a broadcast address of 172.16.5.255.

Only 23 of the 512 addresses will actually be used in the Instructor LAN.

WAN

In the WAN, we have a point-to-point connection between the two routers. This network only requires two IPv4 addresses for the routers on this serial link. As shown in the figure, assigning this address block to the WAN link wastes 508 addresses.

We can use VLSM in this internetwork to save addressing space, but using VLSM requires more planning. The next section demonstrates the planning associated with the use of VLSM.

Refer to
Figure
in online course

Calculating and Assigning Addresses - with VLSM

For the VLSM assignment, we can allocate a much smaller block of addresses to each network, as appropriate.

The address block 172.16.0.0/22 (subnet mask 255.255.252.0) has been assigned to this internetwork as a whole. Ten bits will be used to define host addresses and sub networks. This yields a total of 1024 IPv4 local addresses in the range of 172.16.0.0 to 172.16.3.255.

Student LAN

The largest subnetwork is the Student LAN which requires 481 addresses.

Using the formula **usable hosts = 2^n - 2**, borrowing 9 bits for the host portion gives 512 - 2 = 510 usable host addresses. This meets the current requirement, with a small allowance for growth.

Using 9 bits for hosts leaves 1 bit that can be used locally to define the subnet address. Using the lowest available address gives us a subnet address of 172.16.0.0 /23.

The Student subnet mask calculation is:

Address: 172.16.0.0

In binary:

10101100.00010000.00000000.00000000

Mask: 255.255.254.0

23 bits in binary:

11111111.11111111.11111110.00000000

In the Student network, the IPv4 host range would be:

172.16.0.1 through 172.16.1.254 with a broadcast address of 172.16.1.255.

Because the Student LAN has been assigned these addresses, they are not available for assignment to the remaining subnets: Instructor LAN, Administrator LAN, and the WAN. The addresses still to be assigned are in the range 172.16.2.0 to 172.16.3.255.

Instructor LAN

The next largest network is the Instructor LAN. This network requires at least 69 addresses. Using 6 in the power of 2 formula, $2^6 - 2$, only provides 62 usable addresses. We must use an address block using 7 host bits. The calculation $2^7 - 2$ will yield a block of 126 addresses. This leaves 25 bits to assign to network address. The next available block of this size is the 172.16.2.0 /25 network.

Address: 172.16.2.0

In binary:

10101100.00010000.00000010.00000000

Mask: 255.255.255.128

25 bits in binary:

11111111.11111111.11111111.10000000

This provides an IPv4 host range of:

172.16.2.1 to 172.16.2.126 with a broadcast address of 172.16.2.127.

From our original address block of 172.16.0.0 /22, we allocated addresses 172.16.0.0 to 172.16.2.127. The remaining addresses to be allocated are 172.16.2.128 to 172.16.3.255.

Administrator LAN

For the Administrator LAN, we need to accommodate 23 hosts. This will require the use of 5 host bits using the calculation: $2^5 - 2$.

The next available block of addresses that can accommodate these hosts is the 172.16.2.128 /27 block.

Address: 172.16.2.128

In binary:

10101100.00010000.00000010.10000000

Mask: 255.255.255.224

26 bits in binary:

11111111.11111111.11111111.11100000

This provides an IPv4 host range of:

172.16.2.129 to 172.16.2.158 with a broadcast address of 172.16.2.159.

This yields 30 unique IPv4 addresses for the Administrator LAN.

WAN

The last segment is the WAN connection, requiring 2 host addresses. Only 2 host bits will accommodate the WAN links. 2^2 - 2 = 2.

This leaves 8 bits to define the local subnet address. The next available address block is 172.16.2.160 /30.

Address: 172.16.2.160

In binary:

10101100.00010000.0000001**0.10100**000

Mask: 255.255.255.252

30 bits in binary:

11111111.11111111.111111**11.111111**00

This provides an IPv4 host range of:

172.16.2.161 to 172.16.2.162 with a broadcast address of 172.16.2.163.

This completes the allocation of addresses using VLSM for Case 1. If an adjustment is necessary to accommodate future growth, addresses in the range of 172.16.2.164 to 172.16.3.255 are still available.

10.4.2 Calculating Addresses: Case 2

Refer to **Figure** in online course

In Case 2, the challenge is to subnet this internetwork while limiting the number of wasted hosts and subnets.

The figure shows 5 different subnets, each with different host requirements. The given IP address is 192.168.1.0/24.

The host requirements are:

- NetworkA - 14 hosts
- NetworkB - 28 hosts
- NetworkC - 2 hosts
- NetworkD - 7 hosts
- NetworkE - 28 hosts

As we did with Case 1, we begin the process by subnetting for the largest host requirement first. In this case, the largest requirements are for NetworkB and NetworkE, each with 28 hosts.

We apply the formula: usable hosts = 2^n - 2. For networks B and E, 5 bits are borrowed from the host portion and the calculation is 2^5 = 32 - 2. Only 30 usable host addresses are available due to the 2 reserved addresses. Borrowing 5 bits meets the requirement but gives little room for growth.

So you may consider borrowing 3 bits for subnets leaving 5 bits for the hosts. This allows 8 subnets with 30 hosts each.

We allocate addresses for networks B and E first:

Network B will use Subnet 0: 192.168.1.0/27

host address range 1 to 30

Network E will use Subnet 1: 192.168.1.32/27

host address range 33 to 62

The next largest host requirement is NetworkA, followed by NetworkD.

Borrowing another bit and subnetting the network address 192.168.1.64 yields a host range of:

Network A will use Subnet 0: 192.168.1.64/28

host address range 65 to 78

Network D will use Subnet 1: 192.168.1.80/28

host address range 81 to 94

This allocation supports 14 hosts on each subnet and satisfies the requirement.

Network C has only two hosts. Two bits are borrowed to meet this requirement.

Starting from 192.168.1.96 and borrowing 2 more bits results in subnet 192.168.1.96/30.

Network C will use Subnet 1: 192.168.1.96/30

host address range 97 to 98

In Case 2, we have met all requirements without wasting many potential subnets and available addresses.

In this case, bits were borrowed from addresses that had already been subnetted. As you will recall from a previous section, this method is known as Variable Length Subnet Masking, or VLSM.

10.5 Device Interconnections

10.5.1 Device Interfaces

Refer to **Figure** in online course

It is important to understand that Cisco devices, routers, and switches have several types of interfaces associated with them. You have worked with these interfaces in the labs. These interfaces, also commonly called ports, are where cables are connected to the device. See the figure for some example interfaces.

LAN Interfaces - Ethernet

The Ethernet interface is used for connecting cables that terminate with LAN devices such as computers and switches. This interface can also be used to connect routers to each other. This use will be covered in more detail in future courses.

Several conventions for naming Ethernet interfaces are popular, including AUI (older Cisco devices using a transceiver), Ethernet, FastEthernet and Fa 0/0. The name used depends on the type and model of the device.

WAN Interfaces - Serial

Serial WAN interfaces are used for connecting WAN devices to the CSU/DSU. A CSU/DSU is a device used to make the physical connection between data networks and WAN provider's circuits.

Serial interfaces between routers will also be used in our labs as part of various courses. For lab purposes, we will make a back-to-back connection between two routers using serial cables, and set a clock rate on one of the interfaces.

You may also need to configure other Data Link and Physical layer parameters on a router. To establish communication with a router via a console on a remote WAN, a WAN interface is assigned a Layer 3 address (IPv4 address).

Console Interface

The console interface is the primary interface for initial configuration of a Cisco router or switch. It is also an important means of troubleshooting. It is important to note that with physical access to the router's console interface, an unauthorized person can interrupt or compromise network traffic. **Physical security of network devices is extremely important**.

Auxiliary (AUX) Interface

This interface is used for remote management of the router. Typically, a modem is connected to the AUX interface for dial-in access. From a security standpoint, enabling the option to connect remotely to a network device carries with it the responsibility of maintaining vigilant device management.

10.5.2 Making the Device Management Connection

Refer to
Figure
in online course

Typically, networking devices do not have their own displays, keyboards, or input devices such as trackballs and mice. Accessing a network device for configuration, verification, or troubleshooting is made via a connection between the device and a computer. To enable this connection, the computer runs a program called a terminal emulator.

A terminal emulator is a software program that allows one computer to access the functions on another device. It allows a person to use the display and keyboard on one computer to operate another device, as if the keyboard and display were directly connected to the other device. The cable connection between the computer running the terminal emulation program and the device is often made via the serial interface.

To connect to a router or switch for device management using terminal emulation, follow these steps:

Step 1:

Connect a computer to the *console port* using the console cable supplied by Cisco. The console cable, supplied with each router and switch, has a DB-9 connector on one end and an RJ-45 connector on the other end. (Older Cisco devices came supplied with an RJ-45 to DB-9 adapter. This adapter is used with a *rollover cable* that has an RJ-45 connector at each end.)

The connection to the console is made by plugging the DB-9 connector into an available EIA/TIA 232 serial port on the computer. It is important to remember that if there is more than one serial port, note which port number is being used for the console connection. Once the serial connection to the computer is made, connect the RJ-45 end of the cable directly into the console interface on the router.

Many newer computers do not have an EIA/TIA 232 serial interface. If your computer has only a USB interface, use a USB-to-serial conversion cable to access the console port. Connect the conversion cable to a USB port on the computer and then connect the console cable or RJ-45 to DB-9 adapter to this cable.

Step 2:

With the devices directly connected via cable, configure a terminal emulator with the proper settings. The exact instructions for configuring a terminal emulator will depend on the particular emulator. For the purpose of this course, we will usually use HyperTerminal because most varieties of

Windows have it. This program can be found under **All Programs** > **Accessories** > **Communications**. Select **HyperTerminal**.

Open HyperTerminal, confirm the chosen serial port number, and then configure the port with these settings:

- Bits per second: 9600 bps
- Data bits: 8
- Parity: None
- Stop bits: 1
- Flow control: None

Step 3:

Log in to the router using the terminal emulator software. If all settings and cable connections are done properly, you can access the router by pressing the **Enter** key on the keyboard.

During the lab, you will have the opportunity to use several types of terminal emulators. Each one may be slightly different in appearance, but their uses are the same.

10.6   Chapter Labs

10.6.1   Lab - Creating a Small Lab Topology

Refer to **Lab Activity** for this chapter

In this lab, you will create a small network that requires connecting network devices, configuring host computers for basic network connectivity, and verifying that connectivity.

Refer to **Packet Tracer Activity** for this chapter

In this activity you will create a small network that requires connecting network devices and configuring host computers for basic network connectivity. SubnetA and SubnetB are subnets that are currently needed. SubnetC and SubnetD are anticipated subnets, not yet connected to the network.

10.6.2   Lab - Establishing a Console Session with HyperTerminal

Refer to **Lab Activity** for this chapter

Cisco routers and switches are configured using the device Internetworking Operation System (IOS). The command-line interface (CLI) of the IOS is accessed via a terminal that can be emulated on Windows computers.

This lab introduces two Windows-based terminal emulation programs, HyperTerminal and TeraTerm. These programs can be used to connect a computer's serial (COM) port to the console port of the Cisco device running IOS.

Refer to **Packet Tracer Activity** for this chapter

Upon completion of this activity, you will be able to connect a router and computer using a console cable. You will also configure HyperTerminal to establish a console session with a Cisco IOS router and switch.

10.6.3   Lab - Establishing a Console Session with Minicom

Refer to **Lab Activity** for this chapter

This lab introduces the Linux-based terminal emulation program, Minicom, which can be used to connect a computer's serial port to the console port of Cisco device running IOS.

Summary and Review

Refer to
Figure
in online course

This chapter discussed the planning and design processes that contribute to the installation of a successful, operating network.

The various LAN and WAN media types and their associated cables and connectors were considered so that the most appropriate interconnection decisions can be made.

Determining the number of hosts and subnets in a network required now - and simultaneously planning for future growth - ensures that data communications are available at the best combination of cost and performance.

Similarly, a planned and consistently implemented addressing scheme is an important factor in ensuring that networks work well with provisions to scale as needed. Such addressing schemes also facilitate easy configuration and troubleshooting.

Terminal access to routers and switches is a means to configure addresses and network features on these devices.

Refer to
Figure
in online course

In this activity, you will devise a subnet scheme, create and interconnect networking devices in a model lab network, apply your IP addressing scheme to the network you created, and test your network.

Refer to **Packet Tracer Activity** for this chapter

Packet Tracer Skills Integration Instructions (PDF)

Refer to
Figure
in online course

To Learn More

Structured Cabling Supplement

Structured cabling skills are crucial for any networking professional. Structured cabling creates a physical topology where telecommunications cabling is organized into hierarchical termination and interconnection structures according to standards. The word *telecommunications* is used to express the necessity of dealing with electrical power wires, telephone wires, and cable television coaxial cable in addition to copper and optical networking media.

Structured cabling is an OSI Layer 1 issue. Without Layer 1 connectivity, the Layer 2 switching and Layer 3 routing process that makes data transfer across large networks possible cannot occur. Especially for people new to the networking workforce, many of the day-to-day jobs deal with structured cabling.

Many different standards are used to define the rules of structured cabling. These standards vary around the world. Three standards of central importance in structured cabling are ANSI TIA/EIA-568-B, ISO/IEC 11801, and IEEE 802.x.

This supplement provides the opportunity to complete a structured cabling case study. This can be done on paper only, or part of a hands-on structured cabling installation project.

Chapter Quiz

Go to
the online course
to take the quiz.

Take the chapter quiz to test your knowledge.

Your Chapter Notes

CHAPTER 11

Configuring and Testing Your Network

Chapter Introduction

Refer to
Figure
in online course

In this chapter, we will examine the process for connecting and configuring computers, switches, and routers into an Ethernet LAN.

We will introduce the basic configuration procedures for Cisco network devices. These procedures require the use of the Cisco *Internetwork Operating System (IOS)* and the related configuration files for intermediary devices.

An understanding of the configuration process using the IOS is essential for network administrators and network technicians. The labs will familiarize you with common practices used to configure and monitor Cisco devices.

Learning Objectives

Upon completion of this chapter, you will be able to:

- Define the role of the Internetwork Operating System (IOS).
- Define the purpose of a configuration file.
- Identify several classes of devices that have the IOS embedded.
- Identify the factors contributing to the set of IOS commands available to a device.
- Identify the IOS modes of operation.
- Identify the basic IOS commands.
- Compare and contrast the basic **show** commands.

11.1 Configuring Cisco devices - IOS basics

11.1.1 Cisco IOS

Refer to
Figure
in online course

Similar to a personal computer, a router or switch cannot function without an operating system. Without an operating system, the hardware does not have any capabilities. The Cisco Internetwork Operating System (IOS) is the system software in Cisco devices. It is the core technology that extends across most of the Cisco product line. The Cisco IOS is used for most Cisco devices regardless of the size and type of the device. It is used for routers, LAN switches, small Wireless Access Points, large routers with dozens of interfaces, and many other devices.

The Cisco IOS provides devices with the following network services:

- Basic routing and switching functions
- Reliable and secure access to networked resources
- Network scalability

The IOS operational details vary on different internetworking devices, depending on the device's purpose and feature set.

The services provided by the Cisco IOS are generally accessed using a command line interface (CLI). The features accessible via the CLI vary based on the version of the IOS and the type of device.

The IOS file itself is several megabytes in size and is stored in a semi-permanent memory area called flash. Flash memory provides non-volatile storage. This means that the contents of the memory are not lost when the device loses power. Even though the contents are not lost they can be changed or overwritten if needed.

Using flash memory allows the IOS to be upgraded to newer versions or to have new features added. In many router architectures, the IOS is copied into RAM when the device is powered on and the IOS runs from RAM when the device is operating. This function increases the performance of the device.

Refer to
Figure
in online course

Access Methods

There are several ways to access the CLI environment. The most usual methods are:

- Console

- Telnet or SSH

- AUX port

Console

The CLI can be accessed through a console session, also known as the CTY line. A console uses a low speed serial connection to directly connect a computer or terminal to the console port on the router or switch.

The console port is a management port that provides out-of-band access to a router. The console port is accessible even if no networking services have been configured on the device. **The console port is often used to access a device when the networking services have not been started or have failed.**

Examples of console use are:

- The initial configuration of the network device

- Disaster recovery procedures and troubleshooting where remote access is not possible

- Password recovery procedures

When a router is first placed into service, networking parameters have not been configured. Therefore, the router cannot communicate via a network. To prepare for the initial startup and configuration, a computer running terminal emulation software is connected to the console port of the device. Configuration commands for setting up the router can be entered on the connected computer.

During operation, if a router cannot be accessed remotely, a connection to the console can enable a computer to determine the status of the device. By default, the console conveys the device startup, debugging, and error messages.

For many IOS devices, console access does not require any form of security, by default. However, the console should be configured with passwords to prevent unauthorized device access. In the event that a password is lost, there is a special set of procedures for bypassing the password and accessing the device. **The device should be located in a locked room or equipment rack to prevent physical access.**

Telnet and SSH

A method for remotely accessing a CLI session is to telnet to the router. Unlike the console connection, Telnet sessions require active networking services on the device. The network device must have at least one active interface configured with a Layer 3 address, such as an IPv4 address. Cisco IOS devices include a Telnet server process that launches when the device is started. The IOS also contains a Telnet client.

A host with a Telnet client can access the vty sessions running on the Cisco device. For security reasons, the IOS requires that the Telnet session use a password, as a minimum authentication method. The methods for establishing logins and passwords will be discussed in a later section.

The Secure Shell (SSH) protocol is a more secure method for remote device access. This protocol provides the structure for a remote login similar to Telnet, except that it utilizes more secure network services.

SSH provides stronger password authentication than Telnet and uses encryption when transporting session data. The SSH session encrypts all communications between the client and the IOS device. This keeps the user ID, password, and the details of the management session private. **As a best practice, always use SSH in place of Telnet whenever possible.**

Most newer versions of the IOS contain an SSH server. In some devices, this service is enabled by default. Other devices require the SSH server to be enabled.

IOS devices also include an SSH client that can be used to establish SSH sessions with other devices. Similarly, you can use a remote computer with an SSH client to start a secure CLI session. SSH client software is not provided by default on all computer operating systems. You may need to acquire, install, and configure SSH client software for your computer.

AUX

Another way to establish a CLI session remotely is via a telephone dialup connection using a modem connected to the router's AUX port. Similar to the console connection, this method does not require any networking services to be configured or available on the device.

The AUX port can also be used locally, like the console port, with a direct connection to a computer running a terminal emulation program. The console port is required for the configuration of the router, but not all routers have an auxiliary port. The console port is also preferred over the auxiliary port for troubleshooting because it displays router startup, debugging, and error messages by default.

Generally, the only time the AUX port is used locally instead of the console port is when there are problems using the console port, such as when certain console parameters are unknown.

11.1.2 Configuration Files

Refer to **Figure** in online course

Network devices depend on two types of software for their operation: operating system and configuration. Like the operating system in any computer, the operating system facilitates the basic operation of the device's hardware components.

Configuration files contain the Cisco IOS software commands used to customize the functionality of a Cisco device. Commands are parsed (translated and executed) by the Cisco IOS software when the system is booted (from the startup-config file) or when commands are entered in the CLI while in configuration mode.

A network administrator creates a configuration that defines the desired functionality of a Cisco device. The configuration file is typically a few hundred to a few thousand bytes in size.

Types of Configuration Files

A Cisco network device contains two configuration files:

- The running configuration file - used during the current operation of the device

- The startup configuration file - used as the backup configuration and is loaded when the device is started

A configuration file may also be stored remotely on a server as a backup.

Startup Configuration File

The startup configuration file (startup-config) is used during system startup to configure the device. The **startup configuration file** or **startup-config** file is stored in non-volatile RAM (*NVRAM*). Since NVRAM is non-volatile, when the Cisco device is turned off, the file remains intact. The startup-config files are loaded into RAM each time the router is started or reloaded. Once the configuration file is loaded into RAM, it is considered the **running configuration** or **running-config**.

Running Configuration

Once in RAM, this configuration is used to operate the network device.

The running configuration is modified when the network administrator performs device configuration. **Changes to the running configuration will immediately affect the operation of the Cisco device.** After making any changes, the administrator has the option of saving those changes back to the startup-config file so that they will be used the next time the device restarts.

Because the running configuration file is in RAM, it is lost if the power to the device is turned off or if the device is restarted. Changes made to the running-config file will also be lost if they are not saved to the startup-config file before the device is powered down.

11.1.3 Cisco IOS Modes

Refer to
Figure
in online course

The Cisco IOS is designed as a modal operating system. The term *modal* describes a system where there are different modes of operation, each having its own domain of operation. The CLI uses a hierarchical structure for the modes.

In order from top to bottom, the major modes are:

- User executive mode

- Privileged executive mode

- Global configuration mode

- Other specific configuration modes

Each mode is used to accomplish particular tasks and has a specific set of commands that are available when in that mode. For example, to configure a router interface, the user must enter interface configuration mode. All configurations that are entered in interface configuration mode apply only to that interface.

Some commands are available to all users; others can be executed only after entering the mode in which that command is available. Each mode is distinguished with a distinctive prompt, and only commands that are appropriate for that mode are allowed.

The hierarchical modal structure can be configured to provide security. Different authentication can be required for each hierarchal mode. This controls the level of access that network personnel can be granted.

The figure shows the IOS modal structure with typical prompts and features.

Refer to
Figure
in online course

Command Prompts

When using the CLI, the mode is identified by the command-line prompt that is unique to that mode. The prompt is composed of the words and symbols on the line to the left of the entry area. The word *prompt* is used because the system is prompting you to make an entry.

By default, every prompt begins with the device name. Following the name, the remainder of the prompt indicates the mode. For example, the default prompt for the *global configuration mode* on a router would be:

```
Router(config)#
```

As commands are used and modes are changed, the prompt changes to reflect the current context, as shown in the figure.

Refer to
Figure
in online course

Primary Modes

The two primary modes of operation are:

- User EXEC

- Privileged EXEC

As a security feature, the Cisco IOS software separates the EXEC sessions into two access modes. These two primary access modes are used within the Cisco CLI hierarchical structure.

Each mode has similar commands. However, the privileged EXEC mode has a higher level of authority in what it allows to be executed.

User Executive Mode

The *user executive mode*, or user EXEC for short, has limited capabilities but is useful for some basic operations. The user EXEC mode is at the top of the modal hierarchical structure. This mode is the first entrance into the CLI of an IOS router.

The user EXEC mode allows only a limited number of basic monitoring commands. This is often referred to as view-only mode. The user EXEC level does not allow the execution of any commands that might change the configuration of the device.

By default, there is no authentication required to access the user EXEC mode from the console. It is a good practice to ensure that authentication is configured during the initial configuration.

The user EXEC mode is identified by the CLI prompt that ends with the > symbol. This is an example that shows the > symbol in the prompt:

```
Switch>
```

Privileged EXEC Mode

The execution of configuration and management commands requires that the network administrator use the privileged EXEC mode, or a specific mode further down the hierarchy.

The privileged EXEC mode can be identified by the prompt ending with the **#** symbol.

```
Switch#
```

By default, privileged EXEC does not require authentication. It is a good practice to ensure that authentication is configured.

Global configuration mode and all other more specific configuration modes can only be reached from the privileged EXEC mode. In a later section of this chapter, we will examine device configuration and some of the configuration modes.

Refer to
Figure
in online course

Moving between the User EXEC and Privileged EXEC Modes

The **enable** and **disable** commands are used to change the CLI between the user EXEC mode and the privileged EXEC mode, respectively.

In order to access the privileged EXEC mode, use the **enable** command. The privileged EXEC mode is sometimes called the *enable mode.*

The syntax for entering the **enable** command is:

`Router>enable`

This command is executed without the need for an argument or keyword. Once <Enter> is pressed, the router prompt changes to:

`Router#`

The # at the end of the prompt indicates that the router is now in privileged EXEC mode.

If password authentication has been configured for the privileged EXEC mode, the IOS prompts for the password.

For example:

```
Router>enable
 Password:
Router#
```

The **disable** command is used to return from the privileged EXEC to the user EXEC mode.

For example:

```
Router#disable
Router>
```

11.1.4 Basic IOS Command Structure

Refer to
Figure
in online course

Each IOS command has specific format or syntax and is executed at the appropriate prompt. The general syntax for a command is the **command** followed by any appropriate keywords and arguments. Some commands include a subset of keywords and arguments that provide additional functionality. The figure shows these parts of a command.

The command is the initial word or words entered in the command line. The commands are not case-sensitive. Following the command are one or more keywords and arguments.

The keywords describe specific parameters to the command interpreter. For example, the **show** command is used to display information about the device. This command has various keywords that can be used to define what particular output should be displayed. For example:

`Switch#show running-config`

The command **show** is followed by the keyword **running-config**. The keyword specifies that the running configuration is to be displayed as the output.

A command might require one or more arguments. Unlike a keyword, an argument is generally not a predefined word. An argument is a value or variable defined by the user. As an example, when applying a description to an interface with the **description** command, enter a line such as this:

`Switch(config-if)#description MainHQ Office Switch`

The command is: **description**. The argument is: *MainHQ Office Switch*. The user defines the argument. For this command, the argument can be any text string of up to 80 characters.

After entering each complete command, including any keywords and arguments, press the <Enter> key to submit the command to the command interpreter.

Refer to
Figure
in online course

IOS Conventions

The figure and the following examples demonstrate some conventions for documenting IOS commands.

For the **ping** command:

Format:

Router>ping *IP address*
Example with values:

Router>**ping 10.10.10.5**
The command is **ping** and the argument is the *IP address*.

Similarly, the syntax for entering the **traceroute** command is:

Format:

Switch>**traceroute** *IP address*
Example with values:

Switch>**traceroute** *192.168.254.254*
The command is **traceroute** and the argument is the *IP address*.

Commands are used to execute an action, and the keywords are used to identify where or how to execute the command.

For another example, return to examining the **description** command.

Format:

Router(config-if)#**description** *string*
Example with values:

Switch(config-if)#**description** *Interface to Building a LAN*
The command is **description**, and the argument applied to the interface is the text string, *Interface to Building a LAN*. Once the command is executed, that description will be applied to the particular interface.

11.1.5 Using CLI Help

Refer to
Figure
in online course

The IOS has several forms of help available:

- Context-sensitive help
- Command Syntax Check
- Hot Keys and Shortcuts

Context-Sensitive Help

The context-sensitive help provides a list of commands and the arguments associated with those commands within the context of the current mode. To access context-sensitive help, enter a question mark, ?, at any prompt. There is an immediate response without the need to use the <Enter> key.

One use of context-sensitive help is to get a list of available commands. This can be used when you are unsure of the name for a command or you want to see if the IOS supports a particular command in a particular mode.

For example, to list the commands available at the user EXEC level, type a question mark **?** at the Router> prompt.

Another use of context-sensitive help is to display a list of commands or keywords that start with a specific character or characters. After entering a character sequence, if a question mark is immediately entered-without a space-the IOS will display a list of commands or keywords for this context that start with the characters that were entered.

For example, enter **sh?** to get a list of commands that begin with the character sequence **sh**.

A final type of context-sensitive help is used to determine which options, keywords, or arguments are matched with a specific command. When entering a command, enter a space followed by a ? to determine what can or should be entered next.

As shown in the figure, after entering the command **clock set 19:50:00**, we can enter the **?** to determine the options or keywords that fit with this command.

Refer to
Figure
in online course

Command Syntax Check

When a command is submitted by pressing the <Enter> key, the command line interpreter parses the command from left to right to determine what action is being requested. The IOS generally only provides negative feedback. If the interpreter understands the command, the requested action is executed and the CLI returns to the appropriate prompt. However, if the interpreter cannot understand the command being entered, it will provide feedback describing what is wrong with the command.

There are three different types of error messages:

- Ambiguous command

- Incomplete command

- Incorrect command

Refer to
Figure
in online course

See the figure for the types of errors and the remedies.

Hot Keys and Shortcuts

Refer to
Figure
in online course

The IOS CLI provides hot keys and shortcuts that make configuring, monitoring, and troubleshooting easier.

The figure shows most of the shortcuts. The following are worthy of special note:

- *Tab* - Completes the remainder of the command or keyword

- *Ctrl-R* - Redisplays a line

- *Ctrl-Z* - Exits configuration mode and returns to the EXEC

- *Down Arrow* - Allows user to scroll forward through former commands

- *Up Arrow* - Allows user to scroll backward through former commands

- *Ctrl-Shift-6* - Allows the user to interrupt an IOS process such as **ping** or **traceroute**

- *Ctrl-C* - Aborts the current command and exits the configuration mode

Examining these in more detail:

Tab - Tab complete is used to complete the remainder of abbreviated commands and parameters if the abbreviation contains enough letters to be different from any other currently available commands or parameters. When enough of the command or keyword has been entered to appear unique, press the **Tab** key and the CLI will display the rest of the command or keyword.

This is a good technique to use when you are learning because it allows you to see the full word used for the command or keyword.

Ctrl-R - Redisplay line will refresh the line just typed. Use **Ctrl-R** to redisplay the line. For example, you may find that the IOS is returning a message to the CLI just as you are typing a line. You can use **Ctrl-R** to refresh the line and avoid having to retype it.

In this example, a message regarding a failed interface is returned in the middle of a command.

```
Switch#show mac-
  16w4d: %LINK-5-CHANGED: Interface FastEthernet0/10, changed state to down
  16w4d: %LINEPROTO-5-UPDOWN: Line protocol on Interface FastEthernet0/10, changed
  state to down
```

To redisplay to line that you were typing use Ctrl-R:

```
Switch#show mac
```

Ctrl-Z - Exit configuration mode. To leave a configuration mode and return to privileged EXEC mode, use **Ctrl-Z**. Because the IOS has a hierarchal mode structure, you may find yourself several levels down. Rather than exit each mode individually, use **Ctrl-Z** to return directly to the privileged EXEC prompt at the top level.

Up and Down arrows - Using previous commands. The Cisco IOS software buffers several past commands and characters so that entries can be recalled. The buffer is useful for reentering commands without retyping.

Key sequences are available to scroll through these buffered commands. Use the **up arrow** key (**Ctrl P**) to display the previously entered commands. Each time this key is pressed, the next successively older command will be displayed. Use the **down arrow** key (**Ctrl N**) to scroll forward through the history to display the more recent commands.

Ctrl-Shift-6 - Using the escape sequence. When an IOS process is initiated from the CLI, such as a ping or traceroute, the command runs until it is complete or is interrupted. While the process is running, the CLI is unresponsive. To interrupt the output and interact with the CLI, press **Ctrl-Shift-6**.

Ctrl-C - This interrupts the entry of a command and exits the configuration mode. This is useful when entering a command you may decide that you wish to cancel the command and exits the configuration mode.

Abbreviated commands or keywords. Commands and keywords can be abbreviated to the minimum number of characters that identifies a unique selection. For example, the `configure` command can be abbreviated to `conf` because `configure` is the only command that begins with `conf`. An abbreviation of `con` will not work because more than one command begins with `con`.

Keywords can also be abbreviated.

As another example, `show interfaces` can be abbreviated like this:

```
Router#show interfaces
Router#show int
```

You can abbreviate both the command and the keywords, for example:

```
Router#sh int
```

11.1.6 IOS "Examination" Commands

Refer to **Figure** in online course

In order to verify and troubleshoot network operation, we must examine the operation of the devices. The basic examination command is the `show` command.

There are many different variations of this command. As you develop more skill with the IOS, you will learn to use and interpret the output of the `show` commands. Use the `show ?` command to get a list of available commands in a given context, or mode.

The figure indicates how the typical **show** command can provide information about the configuration, operation, and status of parts of a Cisco router.

In this course, we use some of the more basic **show** commands.

Refer to
Figure
in online course

Some of the most commonly used commands are:

show interfaces

Displays statistics for all interfaces on the device. To view the statistics for a specific interface, enter the **show interfaces** command followed by the specific interface slot/port number. For example:

Router#**show interfaces serial 0/1**

show version

Displays information about the currently loaded software version, along with hardware and device information. Some of the information shown from this command are:

- **Software Version** - IOS software version (stored in flash)

- **Bootstrap Version** - Bootstrap version (stored in Boot ROM)

- **System up-time** - Time since last reboot

- **System restart info** - Method of restart (e.g., power cycle, crash)

- **Software image name** - IOS filename stored in flash

- **Router Type and Processor type** - Model number and processor type

- **Memory type and allocation (Shared/Main)** - Main Processor RAM and Shared Packet I/O buffering

- **Software Features** - Supported protocols / feature sets

- **Hardware Interfaces** - Interfaces available on router

- **Configuration Register** - Sets bootup specifications, console speed setting, and related parameters.

The figure shows a sample of typical **show version** output.

- **show arp** - Displays the ARP table of the device.

- **show mac-address-table** - (switch only) Displays the MAC table of a switch.

- **show startup-config** - Displays the saved configuration located in NVRAM.

- **show running-config** - Displays the contents of the currently running configuration file or the configuration for a specific interface, or map class information.

- **show ip interfaces** - Displays IPv4 statistics for all interfaces on a router. To view the statistics for a specific interface, enter the **show ip interfaces** command followed by the specific interface slot/port number. Another important format of this command is **show ip interface brief**. This is useful to get a quick summary of the interfaces and their operational state.

For example:

Router#**show ip interface brief**
 Interface IP-Address OK? Method Status Protocol
 FastEthernet0/0 172.16.255.254 YES manual up up
 FastEthernet0/1 unassigned YES unset down down
 Serial0/0/0 10.10.10.5 YES manual up up

```
Serial0/0/1 unassigned YES unset down down
```

The More Prompt

When a command returns more output than can be displayed on a single screen, the —**More**— prompt appears at the bottom of the screen. When a —**More**— prompt appears, press the **Spacebar** to view the next portion of output. To display only the next line, press the **Enter** key. If any other key is pressed, the output is cancelled and you are returned to the prompt.

Refer to **Packet Tracer Activity** for this chapter

In this activity, you will use Packet Tracer to examine common IOS **show** commands.

11.1.7 IOS Configuration Modes

Refer to **Figure** in online course

Global Configuration Mode

The primary configuration mode is called **global configuration** or **global config**. From global config, CLI configuration changes are made that affect the operation of the device as a whole.

We also use the global config mode as a precursor to accessing specific configuration modes.

The following CLI command is used to take the device from privileged EXEC mode to the global configuration mode and to allow entry of configuration commands from a terminal:

```
Router#configure terminal
```

Once the command is executed, the prompt changes to show that the router is in global configuration mode.

```
Router(config)#
```

Specific Configuration Modes

From the global config mode, there are many different configuration modes that may be entered. Each of these modes allows the configuration of a particular part or function of the IOS device. The list below shows a few of them:

- *Interface mode* - to configure one of the network interfaces (Fa0/0, S0/0/0,..)

- *Line mode* - to configure one of the lines (physical or virtual) (console, AUX, VTY,..)

- *Router mode* - to configure the parameters for one of the routing protocols

The figure shows the prompts for some modes. **Remember, as configuration changes are made within an interface or process, the changes only affect that interface or process.**

To exit a specific configuration mode and return to global configuration mode, enter **exit** at a prompt. To leave configuration mode completely and return to privileged EXEC mode, enter **end** or use the key sequence **Ctrl-Z**.

Once a change has been made from the global mode, it is good practice to save it to the startup configuration file stored in NVRAM. This prevents changes from being lost due to power failure or a deliberate restart. The command to save the running configuration to startup configuration file is:

```
Router#copy running-config startup-config
```

Refer to **Packet Tracer Activity** for this chapter

In this activity, you will use Packet Tracer to practice accessing IOS configuration modes

11.2 Applying a Basic Configuration Using Cisco IOS

11.2.1 Devices Need Names

Refer to
Figure
in online course

The hostname is used in CLI prompts. If the hostname is not explicitly configured, a router uses the factory-assigned default hostname "Router." A switch has a factory-assigned default hostname, "Switch." Imagine if an internetwork had several routers that were all named with the default name "Router." This would create considerable confusion during network configuration and maintenance.

When accessing a remote device using Telnet or SSH, it is important to have confirmation that an attachment has been made to the proper device. If all devices were left with their default names, we could not identify that the proper device is connected.

By choosing and documenting names wisely, it is easier to remember, discuss, and identify network devices. To name devices in a consistent and useful way requires the establishment of a naming convention that spans the company or, at least, the location. **It is a good practice to create the naming convention at the same time as the addressing scheme to allow for continuity within the organization.**

Some guidelines for naming conventions are that names should:

- Start with a letter
- Not contain a space
- End with a letter or digit
- Have characters of only letters, digits, and dashes
- Be 63 characters or fewer

The hostnames used in the device IOS preserve capitalization and lower case characters. Therefore, it allows you to capitalize a name as you ordinarily would. This contrasts with most Internet naming schemes, where uppercase and lowercase characters are treated identically. RFC 1178 provides some of the rules that can be used as a reference for device naming.

As part of the device configuration, a unique hostname should be configured for each device.

Note: Device host names are only used by administrators when they use the CLI to configure and monitor devices. Unless configured to do so, the devices themselves do not use these names when they discover each other and interoperate.

Refer to
Figure
in online course

Applying Names - an Example

Let's use an example of three routers connected together in a network spanning three different cities (Atlanta, Phoenix, and Corpus) as shown in the figure.

To create a naming convention for routers, take into consideration the location and the purpose of the devices. Ask yourself questions such as these: Will these routers be part of an organization's headquarters? Does each router have a different purpose? For example, is the Atlanta router a primary junction point in the network or is it one junction in a chain?

In this example, we will identify each router as a branch headquarters for each city. The names could be AtlantaHQ, PhoenixHQ, and CorpusHQ. Had each router been a junction in a successive chain, the names could be AtlantaJunction1, PhoenixJunction2, and CorpusJunction3.

In the network documentation, we would include these names, and the reasons for choosing them, to ensure continuity in our naming convention as devices are added.

Once the naming convention has been identified, the next step is to apply the names to the router using the CLI. This example will walk us through the naming of the Atlanta router.

Configure IOS Hostname

From the privileged EXEC mode, access the global configuration mode by entering the `configure terminal` command:

Router#`configure terminal`

After the command is executed, the prompt will change to:

Router(config)#

In the global mode, enter the hostname:

Router(config)#`hostname AtlantaHQ`

After the command is executed, the prompt will change to:

AtlantaHQ(config)#

Notice that the hostname appears in the prompt. To exit global mode, use the `exit` command.

Always make sure that your documentation is updated each time a device is added or modified. Identify devices in the documentation by their location, purpose, and address.

Note: To negate the effects of a command, preface the command with the **no** keyword.

For example, to remove the name of a device, use:

AtlantaHQ(config)# `no hostname`
Router(config)#

Notice that the **no** **hostname** command caused the router to revert to the default hostname of "Router."

> Refer to **Packet Tracer Activity** for this chapter

In this activity, you will use Packet Tracer to configure hostnames on routers and switches.

Links

RFC 1178, "Choosing a Name for Your Computer,"

http://www.faqs.org/rfcs/rfc1178.html

11.2.2 Limiting Device Access - Configuring Passwords and Using Banners

> Refer to **Figure** in online course

Physically limiting access to network devices with closets and locked racks is a good practice; however, passwords are the primary defense against unauthorized access to network devices. **Every device should have locally configured passwords to limit access.** In a later course, we will introduce how to strengthen security by requiring a userID along with a password. For now, we will present basic security precautions using only passwords.

As discussed previously, the IOS uses hierarchical modes to help with device security. As part of this security enforcement, the IOS can accept several passwords to allow different access privileges to the device.

The passwords introduced here are:

- *Console password* - limits device access using the console connection

- *Enable password* - limits access to the privileged EXEC mode

- *Enable secret password* - encrypted, limits access to the privileged EXEC mode

- *VTY password* - limits device access using Telnet

As good practice, use different authentication passwords for each of these levels of access. Although logging in with multiple and different passwords is inconvenient, it is a necessary precaution to properly protect the network infrastructure from unauthorized access.

Additionally, use *strong passwords* that are not easily guessed. The use of weak or easily guessed passwords continues to be a security issue in many facets of the business world.

Consider these key points when choosing passwords:

- Use passwords that are more than 8 characters in length.

- Use a combination of upper and lowercase and/or numeric sequences in passwords.

- Avoid using the same password for all devices.

- Avoid using common words such as **password** or **administrator**, because these are easily guessed.

Note: In most of the labs, we will be using simple passwords such as **cisco** or **class**. These passwords are considered weak and easily guessable and should be avoided in a production environment. We only use these passwords for convenience in a classroom setting.

As shown in the figure, when prompted for a password, the device will not echo the password as it is being entered. In other words, the password characters will not appear when you type. This is done for security purposes - many passwords are gathered by prying eyes.

Console Password

The console port of a Cisco IOS device has special privileges. The console port of network devices must be secured, at a bare minimum, by requiring the user to supply a strong password. This reduces the chance of unauthorized personnel physically plugging a cable into the device and gaining device access.

The following commands are used in global configuration mode to set a password for the console line:

```
Switch(config)#line console 0
 Switch(config-line)#password password
Switch(config-line)#login
```

From global configuration mode, the command `line console 0` is used to enter line configuration mode for the console. The zero is used to represent the first (and in most cases only) console interface for a router.

The second command, `password` *password* specifies a password on a line.

The `login` command configures the router to require authentication upon login. When `login` is enabled and a password set, there will be a prompt to enter a password.

Once these three commands are executed, a password prompt will appear each time a user attempts to gain access to the console port.

Refer to
Figure
in online course

Enable and Enable Secret Passwords

To provide additional security, use the `enable password` **command or the** `enable secret` **command. Either of these commands can be used to establish authentication before accessing privileged EXEC (enable) mode.**

Always use the `enable secret` command, *not* the older `enable password` command, if possible. The `enable secret` command provides greater security because the password is encrypted. The `enable password` command can be used only if `enable secret` has not yet been set.

The `enable password` command would be used if the device uses an older copy of the Cisco IOS software that does not recognize the `enable secret` command.

The following commands are used to set the passwords:

```
Router(config)#enable password password
Router(config)#enable secret password
```

Note: If no `enable password` or `enable secret` password is set, the IOS prevents privileged EXEC access from a Telnet session.

Without an `enable password` having been set, a Telnet session would appear this way:

```
Switch>enable
 % No password set
Switch>
```

VTY Password

The **vty** lines allow access to a router via Telnet. By default, many Cisco devices support five VTY lines that are numbered 0 to 4. A password needs to be set for all available **vty** lines. The same password can be set for all connections. However, it is often desirable that a unique password be set for one line to provide a fall-back for administrative entry to the device if the other connections are in use.

The following commands are used to set a password on vty lines:

```
Router(config)#line vty 0 4
  Router(config-line)#password password
Router(config-line)#login
```

By default, the IOS includes the `login` command on the VTY lines. This prevents Telnet access to the device without first requiring authentication. If, by mistake, the `no login` command is set, which removes the requirement for authentication, unauthorized persons could connect to the line using Telnet. This would be a major security risk.

Encrypting Password Display

Another useful command prevents passwords from showing up as plain text when viewing the configuration files. This is the `service password-encryption` command.

This command causes the encryption of passwords to occur when a password is configured. The `service password-encryption` command applies weak encryption to all unencrypted passwords. This encryption does not apply to passwords as they are sent over media only in the configuration. The purpose of this command is to keep unauthorized individuals from viewing passwords in the configuration file.

If you execute the `show running-config` or `show startup-config` command prior to the `service password-encryption` command being executed, the unencrypted passwords are visible in the configuration output. The `service password-encryption` can then be executed and the encryption will be applied to the passwords. Once the encryption has been applied, removing the encryption service does not reverse the encryption.

Refer to **Figure** in online course

Banner Messages

Although requiring passwords is one way to keep unauthorized personnel out of a network, it is vital to provide a method for declaring that only authorized personnel should attempt to gain entry into the device. To do this, add a banner to the device output.

Banners can be an important part of the legal process in the event that someone is prosecuted for breaking into a device. Some legal systems do not allow prosecution, or even the monitoring of users, unless a notification is visible.

The exact content or wording of a banner depends on the local laws and corporate policies. Here are some examples of information to include in a banner:

- "Use of the device is specifically for authorized personnel."

- "Activity may be monitored."

■ "Legal action will be pursued for any unauthorized use."

Because banners can be seen by anyone who attempts to log in, the message must be worded very carefully. Any wording that implies that a login is "welcome" or "invited" is not appropriate. If a person disrupts the network after gaining unauthorized entry, proving liability will be difficult if there is the appearance of an invitation.

The creation of banners is a simple process; however, banners should be used appropriately. When a banner is utilized it should never welcome someone to the router. It should detail that only authorized personnel are allowed to access the device. Further, the banner can include scheduled system shutdowns and other information that affects all network users.

The IOS provides multiple types of banners. One common banner is the message of the day (MOTD). It is often used for legal notification because it is displayed to all connected terminals.

Configure MOTD using the `banner motd` command from global mode.

As shown in the figure, the `banner motd` command requires the use of delimiters to identify the content of the banner message. The `banner motd` command is followed by a space and a delimiting character. Then, one or more lines of text are entered to represent the banner message. A second occurrence of the delimiting character denotes the end of the message. The delimiting character can be any character as long as it does not occur in the message. For this reason, symbols such as the "#" are often used.

To configure a MOTD, from global configuration mode enter the `banner motd` command:

```
Switch(config)#banner motd # message #
```

Once the command is executed, the banner will be displayed on all subsequent attempts to access the device until the banner is removed.

Refer to **Packet Tracer Activity** for this chapter

In this activity, you will use Packet Tracer to practice the IOS commands for setting passwords and banners on switches and routers.

11.2.3 Managing Configuration Files

Refer to **Figure** in online course

As we have discussed, modifying a running configuration affects the operation of the device immediately.

After making changes to a configuration, consider these options for the next step:

■ Make the changed configuration the new startup configuration.

■ Return the device to its original configuration.

■ Remove all configuration from the device.

Make the Changed Configuration the New Startup Configuration

Remember, because the running configuration is stored in RAM, it is temporarily active while the Cisco device is running (powered on). If power to the router is lost or if the router is restarted, all configuration changes will be lost unless they have been saved.

Saving the running configuration to the startup configuration file in NVRAM preserves the changes as the new startup configuration.

Before committing to the changes, use the appropriate `show` commands to verify the device's operation. As shown in the figure, the `show running-config` command can be used to see a running configuration file.

When the changes are verified to be correct, use the `copy running-config startup-config` command at the privileged EXEC mode prompt. The following example shows the command:

`Switch#copy running-config startup-config`

Once executed, the running configuration file replaces the startup configuration file.

Return the Device to Its Original Configuration

If the changes made to the running configuration do not have the desired effect, it may become necessary to restore the device to its previous configuration. Assuming that we have not overwritten the startup configuration with the changes, we can replace the running configuration with the startup configuration. This is best done by restarting the device using the `reload` command at the privileged EXEC mode prompt.

When initiating a reload, the IOS will detect that the running config has changes that were not saved to startup configuration. A prompt will appear to ask whether to save the changes made. To discard the changes, enter **n** or **no**.

An additional prompt will appear to confirm the reload. To confirm, press the **Enter** key. Pressing any other key will abort the process.

For example:

```
Router#reload
 System configuration has been modified. Save? [yes/no]: n
 Proceed with reload? [confirm]
 *Apr 13 01:34:15.758: %SYS-5-RELOAD: Reload requested by console. Reload Reason:
 Reload Command.
 System Bootstrap, Version 12.3(8r)T8, RELEASE SOFTWARE (fc1)
 Technical Support: http://www.cisco.com/techsupport
 Copyright (c) 2004 by cisco Systems, Inc.
 PLD version 0x10
 GIO ASIC version 0x127
 c1841 processor with 131072 Kbytes of main memory
Main memory is configured to 64 bit mode with parity disabled
```

> Refer to
> **Figure**
> in online course

Backing Up Configurations Offline

Configuration files should be stored as backup files in the event of a problem. Configuration files can be stored on a Trivial File Transfer Protocol (TFTP) server, a CD, a USB memory stick, or a floppy disk stored in a safe place. A configuration file should also be included in the network documentation.

Backup Configuration on TFTP Server

As shown in the figure, one option is to save the running configuration or the startup configuration to a TFTP server. Use either the `copy running-config tftp` or `copy startup-config tftp` command and follow these steps:

Step 1. Enter the `copy running-config tftp` command.

Step 2. Enter the IP address of the host where the configuration file will be stored.

Step 3. Enter the name to assign to the configuration file.

Step 4. Press Enter to confirm each choice.

See the figure to view this process.

Removing All Configurations

If undesired changes are saved to the startup configuration, it may be necessary to clear all the configurations. This requires erasing the startup configuration and restarting the device.

The startup configuration is removed by using the **erase startup-config** command.

To erase the startup configuration file use **erase NVRAM:startup-config** or **erase startup-config** at the privileged EXEC mode prompt:

`Router#erase startup-config`

Once the command is issued, the router will prompt you for confirmation:

Erasing the nvram filesystem will remove all configuration files! Continue? [confirm]

Confirm is the default response. To confirm and erase the startup configuration file, press the **Enter** key. Pressing any other key will abort the process.

Caution: Exercise care when using the erase command. This command can be used to erase any file in the device. Improper use of the command can erase the IOS itself or another critical file.

After removing the startup configuration from NVRAM, reload the device to remove the current running configuration file from RAM. The device will then load the default startup configuration that was originally shipped with the device into the running configuration.

Refer to
Figure
in online course

Backup Configurations with Text Capture (HyperTerminal)

Configuration files can be saved/archived to a text document. This sequence of steps ensures that a working copy of the configuration files is available for editing or reuse later.

When using HyperTerminal, follow these steps:

Step 1. On the **Transfer** menu, click **Capture Text**.

Step 2. Choose the location.

Step 3. Click **Start** to begin capturing text.

Step 4. Once capture has been started, execute the **show running-config** or **show startup-config** command at the privileged EXEC prompt. Text displayed in the terminal window will be placed into the chosen file.

Step 5. After the configurations have been displayed, **Stop** the capture.

Step 6. View the output to verify that it was not corrupted.

See the figure for an example.

Refer to
Figure
in online course

Backup Configurations with Text Capture (TeraTerm)

Configuration files can be saved/archived to a text document using TeraTerm.

As shown in the figure, the steps are:

Step 1. On the File menu, click **Log**.

Step 2. Choose the location. TeraTerm will begin capturing text.

Step 3. Once capture has been started, execute the **show running-config** or **show startup-config** command at the privileged EXEC prompt. Text displayed in the terminal window will be placed into the chosen file.

Step 4. When the capture is complete, select **Close** in the TeraTerm: Log window.

Step 5. View the output to verify that it was not corrupted.

Restoring Text Configurations

A configuration file can be copied from storage to a device. When copied into the terminal, the IOS executes each line of the configuration text as a command. This means that the file will require editing to ensure that encrypted passwords are in plain text and that non-command text such as "—More—" and IOS messages are removed. This process is discussed in the lab.

Further, at the CLI, the device must be set at the global configuration mode to receive the commands from the text file being copied.

When using HyperTerminal, the steps are:

Step 1. Locate the file to be copied into the device and open the text document.

Step 2. Copy all of the text.

Step 3. On the Edit menu, click **paste to host**.

When using TeraTerm, the steps are:

Step 1. On the **File** menu, click **Send** file.

Step 2. Locate the file to be copied into the device and click **Open**.

Step 3. TeraTerm will paste the file into the device.

The text in the file will be applied as commands in the CLI and become the running configuration on the device. This is a convenient method for manually configuring a router.

In this activity, you will use Packet Tracer to practice IOS configuration management.

Refer to **Packet Tracer Activity** for this chapter

11.2.4 Configuring Interfaces

Refer to **Figure** in online course

Throughout this chapter, we have discussed commands that are generic to IOS devices. Some configurations are specific to a type of device. One such configuration is the configuration of interfaces on a router.

Most intermediary network devices have an IP address for the purpose of device management. Some devices, such as switches and wireless access points, can operate without having an IP address.

Because the purpose of a router is to interconnect different networks, each interface on a router has its own unique IPv4 address. The address assigned to each interface exists in a separate network devoted to the interconnection of routers.

There are many parameters that can be configured on router interfaces. We will discuss the most basic interface commands, which are summarized in the figure.

Refer to **Figure** in online course

Configuring Router Ethernet Interfaces

Router Ethernet interfaces are used as the gateways for the end devices on the LANs directly connected to the router.

Each Ethernet interface must have an IP address and subnet mask to route IP packets.

To configure an Ethernet interface follow these steps:

Step 1. Enter global configuration mode.

Step 2. Enter interface configuration mode.

Step 3. Specify the interface address and subnet mask.

Step 4. Enable the interface.

As shown in the figure, configure the Ethernet IP address using the following commands:

```
Router(config)#interface FastEthernet 0/0
 Router(config-if)#ip address ip_address netmask
Router(config-if)#no shutdown
```

Enabling the Interface

By default, interfaces are disabled. To enable an interface, enter the `no shutdown` command from the interface configuration mode. If an interface needs to be disabled for maintenance or troubleshooting, use the `shutdown` command.

Configuring Router Serial Interfaces

Serial interfaces are used to connect WANs to routers at a remote site or ISP.

To configure a serial interface follow these steps:

Step 1. Enter global configuration mode.

Step 2. Enter interface mode.

Step 3. Specify the interface address and subnet mask.

Step 4. Set the clock rate if a DCE cable is connected. Skip this step if a DTE cable is connected.

Step 5. Turn on the interface.

Each connected serial interface must have an IP address and subnet mask to route IP packets.

Configure the IP address with the following commands:

```
Router(config)#interface Serial 0/0/0
Router(config-if)#ip address ip_address netmask
```

Serial interfaces require a clock signal to control the timing of the communications. In most environments, a DCE device such as a CSU/DSU will provide the clock. By default, Cisco routers are DTE devices, but they can be configured as DCE devices.

On serial links that are directly interconnected, as in our lab environment, one side must operate as DCE to provide a clocking signal. The clock is enabled and the speed is specified with the `clock rate` command. Some bit rates might not be available on certain serial interfaces. This depends on the capacity of each interface.

In the lab, if a clock rate needs to be set on an interface identified as DCE, use the 56000 clock rate.

As shown in the figure, the commands that are used to set a clock rate and enable a serial interface are:

```
Router(config)#interface Serial 0/0/0
 Router(config-if)#clock rate 56000
Router(config-if)#no shutdown
```

Once configuration changes are made to the router, remember to use the `show` commands to verify the accuracy of the changes, and then save the changed configuration as the startup configuration.

Refer to
Figure
in online course

As the hostname helps to identify the device on a network, an interface description indicates the purpose of the interface. A description of what an interface does or where it is connected should be part of the configuration of each interface. This description can be useful for troubleshooting.

The interface description will appear in the output of these commands: `show startup-config`, `show running-config`, and `show interfaces`.

For example, this description provides valuable information about the purpose of the interface:

This interface is the gateway for the administration LAN.

A description can assist in determining the devices or locations connected to the interface. Here is another example:

Interface F0/0 is connected to the main switch in the administration building.

When support personnel can easily identify the purpose of an interface or connected device, they can more easily understand the scope of a problem, and this can lead to reaching a resolution sooner.

Circuit and contact information can also be embedded in the interface description. The following description for a serial interface provides the information the network administrator may need before deciding to test a WAN circuit. This description indicates where the circuit terminates, the circuit ID, and the phone number of the company supplying the circuit:

FR to GAD1 circuit ID:AA.HCGN.556460 DLCI 511 - support# 555.1212

To create a description, use the command `description`. This example shows the commands used to create a description for a FastEthernet interface:

```
HQ-switch1#configure terminal
 HQ-switch1(config)#interface fa0/1
HQ-switch1(config-if)#description Connects to main switch in Building A
```

Once the description is applied to the interface, use the `show interfaces` command to verify the description is correct.

See the figure for an example.

Refer to
Figure
in online course

Configuring a Switch Interface

A LAN switch is an intermediary device that interconnects segments within a network. Therefore, the physical interfaces on the switch do not have IP addresses. Unlike a router where the physical interfaces are connected to different networks, a physical interface on a switch connects devices within a network.

Switch interfaces are also enabled by default. As shown in the Switch 1 figure, we can assign descriptions but do not have to enable the interface.

In order to be able to manage a switch, we assign addresses to the device. With an IP address assigned to the switch, it acts like a host device. Once the address is assigned, we access the switch with telnet, ssh or web services.

The address for a switch is assigned to a virtual interface represented as a Virtual LAN interface (VLAN). In most cases, this is the interface VLAN 1. In the Switch 2 figure, we assign an IP address to the VLAN 1 interface. Like the physical interfaces of a router, we also must enable this interface with the `no shutdown` command.

Like any other host, the switch needs a gateway address defined to communicate outside of the local network. As shown in the Switch 2 figure, we assign this gateway with the `ip default-gateway` command.

Refer to **Packet
Tracer Activity**
for this chapter

In this activity, you will use Packet Tracer to practice the IOS commands to configure interfaces.

11.3 Verifying Connectivity

11.3.1 Test the Stack

Refer to
Figure
in online course

The Ping Command

Using the `ping` command is an effective way to test connectivity. The test is often referred to as *testing the protocol stack*, because the `ping` command moves from Layer 3 of the OSI model to Layer 2 and then Layer 1. Ping uses the ICMP protocol to check for connectivity.

Using `ping` in a Testing Sequence

In this section, we will use the router IOS `ping` command in a planned sequence of steps to establish valid connections, starting with the individual device and then extending to the LAN and, finally, to remote networks. By using the `ping` command in this ordered sequence, problems can be isolated. The `ping` command will not always pinpoint the nature of the problem, but it can help to identify the source of the problem, an important first step in troubleshooting a network failure.

The `ping` command provides a method for checking the protocol stack and IPv4 address configuration on a host. There are additional tools that can provide more information than `ping`, such as Telnet or Trace, which will be discussed in more detail later.

IOS Ping Indicators

A ping from the IOS will yield to one of several indications for each ICMP echo that was sent. The most common indicators are:

- ! - indicates receipt of an ICMP echo reply
- . - indicates a timed out while waiting for a reply
- U - an ICMP unreachable message was received

The "!" (exclamation mark) indicates that the ping completed successfully and verifies Layer 3 connectivity.

The "." (period) can indicate problems in the communication. It may indicate connectivity problem occurred somewhere along the path. It also may indicate a router along the path did not have a route to the destination and did not send an ICMP destination unreachable message. It also may indicate that ping was blocked by device security.

The "U" indicates that a router along the path did not have a route to the destination address and responded with an ICMP unreachable message.

Testing the Loopback

As a first step in the testing sequence, the `ping` command is used to verify the internal IP configuration on the local host. Recall that this test is accomplished by using the `ping` command on a reserved address called the *loopback* (127.0.0.1). This verifies the proper operation of the protocol stack from the Network layer to the Physical layer - and back - without actually putting a signal on the media.

Ping commands are entered into a command line.

Enter the `ping` loopback command with this syntax:

```
C:\>ping 127.0.0.1
```

The reply from this command would look something like this:

```
Reply from 127.0.0.1: bytes=32 time<1ms TTL=128
 Reply from 127.0.0.1: bytes=32 time<1ms TTL=128
 Reply from 127.0.0.1: bytes=32 time<1ms TTL=128
 Reply from 127.0.0.1: bytes=32 time<1ms TTL=128
 Ping statistics for 127.0.0.1:
 Packets: Sent = 4, Received = 4, Lost = 0 (0% loss),
 Approximate round trip times in milli-seconds:
Minimum = 0ms, Maximum = 0ms, Average = 0ms
```

The result indicates that four test packets were sent - each 32 bytes in size - and were returned from host 127.0.0.1 in a time of less than 1 ms. TTL stands for Time to Live and defines the number of hops that the ping packet has remaining before it will be dropped.

Refer to **Packet Tracer Activity** for this chapter

In this activity, you will use the IOS `ping` command in Packet Tracer to determine if the state of IP connection operational.

11.3.2 Testing the Interface Assignment

Refer to **Figure** in online course

In the same way that you use commands and utilities to verify a host configuration, you need to learn commands to verify the interfaces of intermediary devices. The IOS provides commands to verify the operation of router and switch interfaces.

Verifying the Router Interfaces

One of the most used commands is the `show ip interface brief` command. This provides a more abbreviated output than the `show ip interface` command. This provides a summary of the key information for all the interfaces.

Looking at the Router 1 figure, we can see that this output shows all interfaces attached on the router, the IP address, if any, assigned to each interface, and the operational status of the interface.

Looking at the line for the FastEthernet 0/0 interface, we see that the IP address is 192.168.254.254. Looking at the last two columns, we can see the Layer 1 and Layer 2 status of the interface. The **up** in the Status column shows that this interface is operational at Layer 1. The **up** in the Protocol column indicates that the Layer 2 protocol is operational.

In the same figure, notice that the Serial 0/0/1 interface has not been enabled. This is indicated by **administratively down** in the Status column. This interface can be enabled with the `no shutdown` command.

Testing Router Connectivity

As with an end device, we can verify the Layer 3 connectivity with the `ping` and `traceroute` commands. In the Router 1 figure, you can see sample outputs from a `ping` to a host in the local LAN and a trace to a remote host across the WAN.

Verifying the Switch Interfaces

Examining the Switch 1 figure, you can see the use of the `show ip interface brief` command to verify the condition of the switch interfaces. As you learned earlier, the IP address for the switch is applied to a VLAN interface. In this case, the Vlan1 interface is assigned an IP address 192.168.254.250. We can also see that this interface has been enabled and is operational.

Examining the FastEthernet0/1 interface, you can see that this interface is down. This indicates that no device is connected to the interface or the network interface of the devices that is connected is not operational.

In contrast, the outputs for the FastEthernet0/2 and FastEthernet0/3 interfaces are operational. This is indicated by both the Status and Protocol being shown as **up**.

Testing Switch Connectivity

Like other hosts, the switch can test its Layer 3 connectivity with the `ping` and `traceroute` commands. The Switch1 figure also shows a ping to the local host and a trace to a remote host.

Two important things to keep in mind are that an IP address is not required for a switch to perform its job of frame forwarding and that the switch requires a gateway to communicate outside its local network.

Refer to **Figure** in online course

The next step in the testing sequence is to verify that the NIC address is bound to the IPv4 address and that the NIC is ready to transmit signals across the media.

In this example, also shown in the figure, assume that the IPv4 address assigned to a NIC is **10.0.0.5**.

To verify the IPv4 address, use the following steps:

At the command line, enter the following:

```
C:\>ping 10.0.0.5
 A successful reply would resemble:
 Reply from 10.0.0.5: bytes=32 time<1ms TTL=128
 Reply from 10.0.0.5: bytes=32 time<1ms TTL=128
 Reply from 10.0.0.5: bytes=32 time<1ms TTL=128
 Reply from 10.0.0.5: bytes=32 time<1ms TTL=128
 Ping statistics for 10.0.0.5:
 Packets: Sent = 4, Received = 4, Lost = 0 (0% loss),
 Approximate round trip times in milli-seconds:
Minimum = 0ms, Maximum = 0ms, Average = 0ms
```

This test verifies that the NIC driver and most of the NIC hardware are working properly. It also verifies that the IP address is properly bound to the NIC, without actually putting a signal on the media.

If this test fails, it is likely that there are issues with the NIC hardware and software driver that may require reinstallation of either or both. This procedure is dependent on the type of host and its operating system.

Refer to **Packet Tracer Activity** for this chapter

In this activity, you will use the **ping** command in Packet Tracer to test interface responses.

11.3.3 Testing Local Network

Refer to **Figure** in online course

The next test in the sequence is to test hosts on the local LAN.

Successfully pinging remote hosts verifies that both the local host (the router in this case) and the remote host are configured correctly. This test is conducted by pinging each host one by one on the LAN.

See the figure for an example.

If a host responds with Destination Unreachable, note which address was not successful and continue to ping the other hosts on the LAN.

Another failure message is Request Timed Out. This indicates that no response was made to the ping attempt in the default time period indicating that network latency may be an issue.

Extended Ping

To examine this the IOS offers an "extended" mode of the ping command. This mode is entered by typing **ping** in privileged EXEC mode, at the CLI prompt without a destination IP address. A series of prompts are then presented as shown in this example. Pressing Enter accepts the indicated default values.

```
Router#ping
 Protocol [ip]:
 Target IP address:10.0.0.1
 Repeat count [5]:
 Datagram size [100]:
 Timeout in seconds [2]:5
Extended commands [n]: n
```

Entering a longer timeout period than the default allows for possible latency issues to be detected. If the ping test is successful with a longer value, a connection exists between the hosts, but latency may be an issue on the network.

Note that entering "**y**" to the "Extended commands" prompt provides more options that are useful in troubleshooting - you will explore these options in the Lab and Packet Tracer activities.

Refer to **Packet Tracer Activity** for this chapter

In this activity, you will use the **ping** command in Packet Tracer to determine if a router can actively communicate across the local network.

11.3.4 Testing Gateway and Remote Connectivity

Refer to **Figure** in online course

The next step in the testing sequence is to use the **ping** command to verify that a local host can connect with a gateway address. This is extremely important because the gateway is the host's entry and exit to the wider network. If the **ping** command returns a successful response, connectivity to the gateway is verified.

To begin, choose a station as the source device. In this case, we chose 10.0.0.1, as shown in the figure. Use the **ping** command to reach the gateway address, in this case, 10.0.0.254.

```
c:\>ping 10.0.0.254
```

The gateway IPv4 address should be readily available in the network documentation, but if it is not available, use the **ipconfig** command to discover the gateway IP address.

If the gateway test fails, back up one step in the sequence and test another host in the local LAN to verify that the problem is not the source host. Then verify the gateway address with the network administrator to ensure that the proper address is being tested.

If all devices are configured properly, check the physical cabling to ensure that it is secure and properly connected. Keep an accurate record of what attempts have been made to verify connectivity. This will assist in solving this problem and, perhaps, future problems.

Testing Route Next Hop

In a router, use the IOS to test the next hop of the individual routes. As you learned, each route has the next hop listed in the routing table. To determine the next hop, examine the routing table from the output of the show ip route command. Frames carrying packets that are directed to the destination network listed in the routing table are sent to the device that represents the next hop. If the next hop is not accessible, the packet will be dropped. To test the next hop, determine the appropriate route to the destination and try to ping the appropriate next hop for that route in the routing table. A failed ping indicates that there might be a configuration or hardware problem. However, the ping may also be prohibited by security in the device. If the ping is successful you can move on to testing connectivity to remote hosts.

Refer to **Figure** in online course

Testing Remote Hosts

Once verification of the local LAN and gateway is complete, testing can proceed to remote devices, which is the next step in the testing sequence.

The figure depicts a sample network topology. There are 3 hosts within a LAN, a router (acting as the gateway) that is connected to another router (acting as the gateway for a remote LAN), and 3 remote hosts. The verification tests should begin within the local network and progress outward to the remote devices.

Begin by testing the outside interface of a router that is directly connected to a remote network. In this case, the **ping** command is testing the connection to 192.168.0.253, the outside interface of the local network gateway router.

If the **ping** command is successful, connectivity to the outside interface is verified. Next, ping the outside IP address of the remote router, in this case, 192.168.0.254. If successful, connectivity to the remote router is verified. If there is a failure, try to isolate the problem. Retest until there is a valid connection to a device and double-check all addresses.

The **ping** command will not always help with identifying the underlying cause to a problem, but it can isolate problems and give direction to the troubleshooting process. Document every test, the devices involved, and the results.

Check for Router Remote Connectivity

A router forms a connection between networks by forwarding packets between them. To forward packets between any two networks, the router must be able to communicate with both the source and the destination networks. The router will need routes to both networks in its routing table.

To test the communication to the remote network, you can ping a known host on this remote network. If you cannot successfully ping the host on the remote network from a router, you should first check the routing table for an appropriate route to reach the remote network. It may be that the router uses the default route to reach a destination. If there is no route to reach this network, you will need to identify why the route does not exist. As always, you also must rule out that the ping is not administratively prohibited.

Refer to **Packet Tracer Activity** for this chapter

In this activity you will use the the **ping** command in Packet Tracer to verify that a local host can communicate across the internetwork to a given remote host and identify several conditions that might cause the test to fail.

11.3.5 Tracing and Interpreting Trace Results

Refer to **Figure** in online course

The next step in the testing sequence is to perform a trace.

A trace returns a list of hops as a packet is routed through a network. The form of the command depends on where the command is issued. When performing the trace from a Windows computer, use **tracert**. When performing the trace from a router CLI, use **traceroute**.

Ping and Trace

Ping and trace can be used together to diagnose a problem.

Let's assume that a successful connection has been established between Host 1 and Router A, as shown in the figure.

Next, let's assume that Host 1 pings Host 2 using this command.

```
C:\>ping 10.1.0.2
```
The **ping** command returns this result:

```
Pinging 10.1.0.2 with 32 bytes of data:
 Request timed out.
 Request timed out.
 Request timed out.
 Request timed out.
 Ping statistics for 10.1.0.2:
 Packets: Sent = 4, Received = 0, Lost = 4 (100% loss)
The ping test failed.
```

This is a test of communication beyond the local network to a remote device. Because the local gateway responded but the host beyond did not, the problem appears to be somewhere beyond the local network. A next step is to isolate the problem to a particular network beyond the local network. The **trace** commands can show the path of the last successful communication.

Trace to a Remote Host

Like **ping** commands, **trace** commands are entered in the command line and take an IP address as the argument.

Assuming that the command will be issued from a Windows computer, we use the **tracert** form:

```
C:\>tracert 10.1.0.2
 Tracing route to 10.1.0.2 over a maximum of 30 hops
  1 2 ms 2 ms 2 ms 10.0.0.254
  2 * * * Request timed out.
  3 * * * Request timed out.
 4 ^C
```

The only successful response was from the gateway on Router A. Trace requests to the next hop timed out, meaning that the next hop did not respond. The trace results indicate that the failure is therefore in the internetwork beyond the LAN.

Refer to **Figure** in online course

Testing Sequence - Putting it all Together

As a review, let's walk through the testing sequence in another scenario.

Test 1: Local Loopback - Successful

```
C:\>ping 127.0.0.1
 Pinging 127.0.0.1 with 32 bytes of data:
 Reply from 127.0.0.1: bytes=32 time<1ms TTL=128
 Reply from 127.0.0.1: bytes=32 time<1ms TTL=128
 Reply from 127.0.0.1: bytes=32 time<1ms TTL=128
 Reply from 127.0.0.1: bytes=32 time<1ms TTL=128
 Ping statistics for 127.0.0.1:
 Packets: Sent = 4, Received = 4, Lost = 0 (0% loss),
 Approximate round trip times in milli-seconds:
Minimum = 0ms, Maximum = 0ms, Average = 0ms
```

Host 1has the IP stack properly configured.

Test 2: Local NIC - Successful

```
C:\>ping 192.168.23.3
 Pinging 192.168.23.3 with 32 bytes of data:
 Reply from 192.168.23.3: bytes=32 time<1ms TTL=128
 Reply from 192.168.23.3: bytes=32 time<1ms TTL=128
 Reply from 192.168.23.3: bytes=32 time<1ms TTL=128
 Reply from 192.168.23.3: bytes=32 time<1ms TTL=128
 Ping statistics for 192.168.23.3:
 Packets: Sent = 4, Received = 4, Lost = 0 (0% loss),Approximate round trip times
   in milli-seconds:
Minimum = 0ms, Maximum = 0ms, Average = 0ms
```

The IP address is properly assigned to the NIC and the electronics in the NIC respond to the IP address.

Test 3: Ping Local Gateway - Successful

```
C:\>ping 192.168.23.254
 Pinging 192.168.23.254 with 32 bytes of data:
 Reply from 192.168.23.254: bytes=32 time<1ms TTL=128
 Reply from 192.168.23.254: bytes=32 time<1ms TTL=128
 Reply from 192.168.23.254: bytes=32 time<1ms TTL=128
 Reply from 192.168.23.254: bytes=32 time<1ms TTL=128
 Ping statistics for 192.168.23.254:
 Packets: Sent = 4, Received = 4, Lost = 0 (0% loss),
 Approximate round trip times in milli-seconds:
Minimum = 0ms, Maximum = 0ms, Average = 0ms
```

The default gateway is operational. This also verifies the operation of the local network.

Test 4: Ping Remote Host - Failure

```
C:\>ping 192.168.11.1
 Pinging 192.168.11.1 with 32 bytes of data:
 Request timed out.
 Request timed out.
 Request timed out.
 Request timed out.
 Ping statistics for 192.168.11.1:
Packets: Sent = 4, Received = 0, Lost = 4 (100% loss)
```

This is a test of the communication beyond the local network. Because the gateway responded but the host beyond did not, the problem appears to be somewhere beyond the local network.

Test 5: Traceroute to Remote Host - Failure at First Hop

```
C:\>tracert 192.168.11.1
 Tracing route to 192.168.11.1 over a maximum of 30 hops
 1 * * * Request timed out.
 2 * * * Request timed out.
3 ^C
```

There appear to be conflicting results. The default gateway responds, indicating that there is communication between Host1 and the gateway. On the other hand, the gateway does not appear to be responding to traceroute.

One explanation is that the local host is not configured properly to use 192.168.23.254 as the default gateway. To confirm this, we examine the configuration of Host1.

Test 6: Examine Host Configuration for Proper Local Gateway - Incorrect

```
C:\>ipconfig
 Windows IP Configuration
 Ethernet adapter Local Area Connection:
 IP Address. . . . . . . . . . . . : 192.168.23. 3
 Subnet Mask . . . . . . . . . . : 255.255.255.0
Default Gateway . . . . . . . : 192.168.23.253
```

From the output of the **ipconfig** command, it can be determined that the gateway is not properly configured on the host. This explains the false indication that the problem was in the internetwork beyond the local network. Even though the address 192.168.23.254 responded, this was not the address configured in Host1 as the gateway.

Unable to build a frame, Host1 drops the packet. In this case, there is no response indicated from the trace to the remote host.

In this activity, you will use the various **ping** commands to identify network connectivity problems.

In this activity, you will use the **tracert** and **traceroute** commands to observe a path used across an internetwork.

Refer to **Packet Tracer Activity** for this chapter

Refer to **Packet Tracer Activity** for this chapter

11.4 Monitoring and Documenting of Networks

11.4.1 Basic Network Baselines

Refer to **Figure** in online course

One of the most effective tools for monitoring and troubleshooting network performance is to establish a *network baseline. A baseline is a process for studying the network at regular intervals to ensure that the network is working as designed. It is more than a single report detailing the health of the network at a certain point in time. Creating an effective network performance baseline is accomplished over a period of time. Measuring performance at varying times and loads will assist in creating a better picture of overall network performance.*

The output derived from network commands can contribute data to the network baseline. The figure shows the information to record.

One method for starting a baseline is to copy and paste the results from an executed ping, trace, or other relevant command into a text file. These text files can be time stamped with the date and saved into an archive for later retrieval.

An effective use of the stored information is to compare the results over time. Among items to consider are error messages and the response times from host to host. If there is a considerable increase in response times, there may be a latency issue to address.

The importance of creating documentation cannot be emphasized enough. Verification of host-to-host connectivity, latency issues, and resolutions of identified problems can assist a network administrator in keeping a network running as efficiently as possible.

Corporate networks should have extensive baselines; more extensive than we can describe in this course. Professional-grade software tools are available for storing and maintaining baseline information. In this course, we will cover some basic techniques and discuss the purpose of baselines.

Refer to **Figure** in online course

Host Capture

One common method for capturing baseline information is to copy the output from the command line window and paste it into a text file.

To capture the results of the `ping` command, begin by executing a command in the command line similar to this one. Substitute a valid IP address on your network.

`C:\>ping 10.66.254.159`
The reply will appear below the command.

See the figure for an example.

With the output still in the command window, follow these steps:

Step 1. Right-click the command prompt window, then click **Select All**.

Step 2. Press **Ctrl-C** to copy the output.

Step 3. Open a text editor.

Step 4. Press **Ctrl-V** to paste the text.

Step 5. Save the text file with the date and time as part of the name.

Run the same test over a period of days and save the data each time. An examination of the files will begin to reveal patterns in network performance and provide the baseline for future troubleshooting.

When selecting text from the command window, use the **Select All** command to copy all the text in the window. Use the **Mark** command to select a portion of the text.

See the figure for instructions when using Windows XP Professional.

Refer to **Figure** in online course

IOS Capture

Capturing `ping` command output can also be completed from the IOS prompt. The following steps describe how to capture the output and save to a text file.

When using HyperTerminal for access, the steps are:

Step 1. On the Transfer menu, click **Capture Text**.

Step 2. Choose **Browse** to locate or type the name of the saving the file.

Step 3. Click **Start** to begin capturing text

Step 4. Execute the `ping` command in the user EXEC mode or at the privileged EXEC prompt. The router will place the text displayed on the terminal in the location chosen.

Step 5. View the output to verify that it was not corrupted.

Step 6. On the Transfer menu, click **Capture Text**, and then click **Stop Capture**.

Data generated using either the computer prompt or the router prompt can contribute to the baseline.

Links:

Baseline Best Practices

11.4.2 Capturing and Interpreting Trace Information

Refer to
Figure
in online course

As previously discussed, trace can be used to trace the steps, or hops, between hosts. If the request reaches the intended destination, the output shows every router that the packet traverses. This output can be captured and used in the same way that `ping` output is used.

Sometimes the security settings at the destination network will prevent the trace from reaching the final destination. However, we can still capture a baseline of the hops along the path.

Recall that the form for using trace from a Windows host is tracert.

To trace the route from your computer to cisco.com, enter this command in a command line:
`C:\>tracert www.cisco.com`
See the figure for sample output.

The steps for saving the trace output are identical to the steps for saving ping output: Select the text from the command window and paste it into a text file.

The data from a trace can be added to the data from the `ping` commands to provide a combined picture of network performance. For example, if the speed of a `ping` command decreases over time, compare the trace output for the same time period. Examining the response times on a hop-by-hop comparison may reveal a particular point of longer response time. This delay may be due to congestion at that hop creating a bottleneck in the network.

Another case might show that the hop pathway to the destination may vary over time as the routers select different best paths for the trace packets. These variations may show patterns that could be useful in scheduling large transfers between sites.

Refer to
Figure
in online course

Router Capture

Capturing the traceroute output can also be done from the router prompt. The following steps show how to capture the output and save it to a file.

Recall that the form of trace for the router CLI is **traceroute**.

When using HyperTerminal, the steps used are:

Step 1. On the Transfer menu, click **Capture Text**.

Step 2. Choose a use Browse to locate or type the name of the saving the file.

Step 3. Click **Start** to begin capturing text

Step 4. Execute the `traceroute` command in the user EXEC mode or at the privileged EXEC prompt. The router will place the text displayed on the terminal in the location chosen.

Step 5. View the output to verify that it was not corrupted.

Step 6. On the Transfer menu, click **Capture Text**, and then click **Stop Capture**.

Store the text files generated by these tests in a safe location, along with the rest of the network documentation.

11.4.3 Learning About the Nodes on the Network

Refer to **Figure** in online course

If an appropriate addressing scheme exists, identifying IPv4 addresses for devices in a network should be a simple task. Identifying the physical (MAC) addresses, however, can be a daunting task. You would need access to all of the devices and sufficient time to view the information, one host at a time. Because this is not a practical option in many cases, there is an alternate means of MAC address identification using the **arp** command.

The **arp** command provides for the mapping of physical addresses to known IPv4 addresses. A common method for executing the **arp** command is to execute it from the command prompt. This method involves sending out an ARP request. The device that needs the information sends out a broadcast ARP request to the network, and only the local device that matches the IP address of the request sends back an ARP reply containing its IP-MAC pair.

To execute an **arp** command, at the command prompt of a host, enter:

```
C:\host1>arp -a
```

As shown in the figure the **arp** command lists all devices currently in the ARP cache, which includes the IPv4 address, physical address, and the type of addressing (static/dynamic), for each device.

The cache can be cleared by using the **arp** **-d** command, in the event the network administrator wants to repopulate the cache with updated information.

Note: The ARP cache is only populated with information from devices that have been recently accessed. To ensure that the ARP cache is populated, ping a device so that it will have an entry in the ARP table.

Ping Sweep

Another method for collecting MAC addresses is to employ a *ping sweep* across a range of IP addresses. A ping sweep is a scanning method that can be executed at the command line or by using network administration tools. These tools provide a way to specify a range of hosts to ping with one command.

Using the ping sweep, network data can be generated in two ways. First, many of the ping sweep tools construct a table of responding hosts. These tables often list the hosts by IP address and MAC address. This provides a map of active hosts at the time of the sweep.

As each ping is attempted, an ARP request is made to get the IP address in the ARP cache. This activates each host with recent access and ensures that the ARP table is current. The **arp** command can return the table of MAC addresses, as discussed above, but now there is reasonable confidence that the ARP table is up-to-date.

Refer to **Figure** in online course

Switch Connections

One additional tool that can be helpful is a mapping of how hosts are connected to a switch. This mapping can be obtained by issuing the **show** *mac-address-table* command.

Using a command line from a switch, enter the **show** command with the *mac-address-table* argument:

```
Sw1-2950#show mac-address-table
```

See the figure for sample output.

This table in the figure lists the MAC address of the hosts that are connected to this switch. Like other output in the command window, this information can be copied and pasted into a file. Data can also be pasted into a spreadsheet for easier manipulation later.

An analysis of this table also reveals that the Fa0/23 interface is either a shared segment or is connected to another switch. Several MAC addresses are representing multiple nodes. This is an indication that a port is connected to another intermediary device such as a hub, wireless access point, or another switch.

Additional commands and tools for data gathering presented in later courses.

Refer to
Lab Activity
for this chapter

Documenting Network Performance

Use 100 successive pings to the same remote host. Paste these entries into an Excel spreadsheet and create a chart showing the mean, median, mode, and the number and percentage of dropped packets. **Hint:** Dropped packets have a consistently large value assigned to them.

Conduct this test for 3 samples spread out over a 24-hour period and repeated every day for 5 days at approximately the same time.

To get a better picture of network performance, try increasing the packet size by 100 bytes at a time for 20 pings. Plot the average values for each of the 20 pings to see the effect of the increase in packet size. Also, note any time there is a large change in throughput.

11.5 Lab Activity

11.5.1 Basic Cisco Device Configuration

Refer to
Lab Activity
for this chapter

Refer to **Packet
Tracer Activity**
for this chapter

In this lab, you will configure common settings on a Cisco Router and Cisco Switch.

In this activity, you will use PT to configure common settings on a Cisco router and Cisco switch.

11.5.2 Managing Device Configuration

Refer to
Lab Activity
for this chapter

Refer to **Packet
Tracer Activity**
for this chapter

In this lab, you will configure common settings on a Cisco Router, save the configuration to a TFTP server, and restore the configuration from a TFTP server.

In this activity, you will use PT to configure common settings on a Cisco Router, save the configuration to a TFTP server, and restore the configuration from a TFTP server.

11.5.3 Configure Host Computers for IP Networking

Refer to
Lab Activity
for this chapter

In this lab, you will create a small network that requires connecting network devices and configuring host computers for basic network connectivity. The Appendix is a reference for configuring the logical network.

11.5.4 Network Testing

Refer to
Lab Activity
for this chapter

In this lab, you will create a small network that requires connecting network devices and configuring host computers for basic network connectivity. SubnetA and SubnetB are subnets that are currently needed. SubnetC, SubnetD, SubnetE, and SubnetF are anticipated subnets, not yet connected to the network.

11.5.5 Network Documentation with Utility Commands

Refer to
Lab Activity
for this chapter

Network documentation is a very important tool for the network administration. A well-documented network can save network engineers significant amounts of time in troubleshooting and planning future growth.

In this lab, you will create a small network that requires connecting network devices and configuring host computers for basic network connectivity. SubnetA and SubnetB are subnets that are currently needed. SubnetC is an anticipated subnet, not yet connected to the network.

Refer to
Lab Activity
for this chapter

11.5.6 Case Study

Summary and Review

Refer to
Figure
in online course

This chapter introduced the issues to be considered when connecting and configuring computers, switches, and routers to build an Ethernet-based local area network.

The Cisco Internetwork Operating System (IOS) software and the configuration files for routers and switches were presented. This included accessing and using the IOS CLI modes and configuration processes, and understanding the significance of the prompt and help functions.

Managing IOS configuration files and using a methodical structured approach to testing and documenting network connectivity are key network administrator and network technician skills.

Summary of IOS features and commands:

User EXEC Mode

- **enable** - Enter Privileged EXEC mode

Privileged EXEC Mode

- `copy running-config startup-config` - Copy the active configuration to NVRAM.
- `copy startup-config running-config` - Copy the configuration in NVRAM to RAM.
- `erase startup-configuration` - Erase the configuration located in NVRAM.
- `ping` *ip_address* - Ping to that address.
- `traceroute` *ip_address* - Trace each hop to that address.
- `show interfaces` - Display statistics for all interfaces on a device.
- `show clock` - Show the time set in the router.
- `show version` - Display currently loaded IOS version, hardware, and device information.
- `show arp` - Display the ARP table of the device.
- `show startup-config` - Display the saved configuration located in NVRAM.
- `show running-config` - Display the contents of the currently running configuration file.
- `show ip interface` - Display IP statistics for interface(s) on a router.
- `configure terminal` - Enter terminal configuration mode.

Terminal Configuration Mode

- `hostname` *hostname* - Assign a host name to device.
- `enable password` *password* - Set an unencrypted enable password.
- `enable secret` *password* - Set a strongly encrypted enable password.
- `service password-encryption` - Encrypt display of all passwords except secret.
- `banner motd` *# message #* - Sets a message-of-the-day banner.
- `line console 0` - Enter console line configuration mode.
- `line vty 0 4` - Enter virtual terminal (Telnet) line configuration mode.
- `interface` *Interface_name* - Enter interface configuration mode.

Line Configuration Mode

- **login** - Enable password checking at login.

- **password** *password* - Set line password.

Interface Configuration Mode

- **ip address** *ip_address netmask* - Set interface IP address and subnet mask.

- **description** *description* - Set interface description.

- **clock rate** *value* - Set clock rate for DCE device.

- **no shutdown** - Set interface to up.

- **shutdown** - Administratively set interface to down.

Refer to
Figure
in online course

Refer to **Packet
Tracer Activity**
for this chapter

Refer to
Figure
in online course

This culminating activity will allow you to practice the skills and conceptual understandings you have been developing throughout the entire course.

Packet Tracer Skills Integration Instructions (PDF)

To Learn More

The IOS feature set of Cisco routers and switches varies significantly across the model range of these devices. This chapter has introduced some of the basic IOS commands and features that are common across most devices. Although some of the more advanced features are covered in later Cisco courses, often during the regular day-to-day administration of a network, other information may be required more immediately.

The Cisco Systems website, http://www.cisco.com, is the source of the technical documentation used to install, operate, and troubleshoot Cisco networking devices. A free cisco.com registration provides access to online tools and information. It is recommended that students register on the website to make use of this resource during their study, and to prepare for using it when in the workplace.

Cisco Router and Switch IOS Password Recovery

An example of the technical documentation available from cisco.com is the procedure to use to recover lost or forgotten passwords on a device. This chapter explained the importance of securing access to the IOS with the use of encrypted passwords. However, for a number of reasons, and particularly in a classroom lab environment, a password may be lost or forgotten, thereby preventing access to the device.

A search for password recovery documents for the 1841 router and 2960 switch (the current recommended CCNA Exploration lab devices) on cisco.com returned the following documents that provide the procedures to follow:

```
http://www.cisco.com/warp/public/474/pswdrec_1700.pdf
http://www.cisco.com/warp/public/474/pswdrec_2900xl.pdf
```

If your lab has other models of Cisco routers or switches, equivalent documents can be obtained by conducting a search on Cisco.com.

Go to
the online course
to take the quiz.

Chapter Quiz

Take the chapter quiz to test your knowledge.

Your Chapter Notes

ACK
In TCP ACK is used in the initial 3 way hand-shake to acknowledge the sending station's sequence number and in the actual sending of data the ACK is used to acknowledge sent segments.

acknowledgment
Acknowledgments are sent by receiving stations to sending stations to confirm receipt of data.

address pool
A group of addresses assigned by the IANA or one of its associated organizations.

Address Resolution Protocol (ARP)
Address Resolution Protocol (ARP). The method for finding a host's hardware address when only its network layer address is known. Primarily used to translate IP addresses to Ethernet MAC addresses.

administratively scoped addresses
Administratively scoped addresses are also called limited scope addresses. These addresses are restricted to a local group or organization.

American National Standards Institute (ANSI)
American National Standards Institute. private non-profit organization that oversees the development of voluntary consensus standards for products, services, processes, systems, and personnel in the United States.

AND
A Boolean operation used to combine search terms and find a result. If x = 1 and y =1 then z = 1. If x = 1 and y = 0 then z = 0. If x = 0 and y = 1 then z = 0. If x = 1 and y = 0 then z = 0.

applications
A complete software program designed for end users.

ARP
Address Resolution Protocol. A host wishing to discover another host's MAC address broadcasts an ARP request onto the network. The host on the network that has the IP address in the request then replies with its MAC address.

ARP cache
Storage of ARP entries that show MAC address and the associated IP address.

ARP poisoning
The sending of fake ARP messages to an Ethernet LAN. These frames contain false MAC addresses that "confuse" network devices, such as switches. As a result frames intended for one node can be mistakenly sent to another node. Also known as ARP spoofing.

ARP table
A cache in which a device keeps a table of MAC addresses and their associated layer 3 address.

asynchronous transmission mode
Term describing digital signals that are transmitted without precise clocking. Such signals generally have different frequencies and phase relationships. Asynchronous transmissions usually encapsulate individual characters in control bits (called start and stop bits) that designate the beginning and end of each character.

attenuation
The decrease in signal strength along an electrical or optical cable.

authentication
A process whereupon a person must prove that they are legitimate users of that certain resource.

authoritative
A source of information that is highly reliable and known for its accuracy.

aux port
Auxiliary port of a router. Is used for out of band connectivity with the router. It is usually used to get dial-in access to the router.

backoff
The (usually random) retransmission delay enforced by contentious MAC protocols after a network node with data to transmit determines that the physical medium is already in use.

backoff algorithm
When a collision is detected each sender will delay before retransmitting. Each sender chooses a random delay between 0 and d (d is some standard delay value). If another collision occurs, each computer doubles the range from which the delay is chosen, that means, the random delay will now be between 0 and 2d. If another collision occurs the range will be between 0 and 4d and so on. After each collision the range of the random delay increases.

bandwidth
The amount of data that can be transmitted in a certain amount of time. For digital bandwidth, it is usually expressed in bits per second (bps). For analog bandwidth, it is expressed in cycles per second, or Hertz (Hz).

benchmarks
A standard by which something can be measured or judged. A benchmark is usually used when testing network performance and comparing it to the performance results of the benchmark.

binary
A numbering system characterized by ones and zeros (1 = on, 0 = off).

binary values
A combination of binary digits that represent a certain value.

bit time
The time it takes for one bit to be transmitted from a NIC operating at some predefined standard speed. The time is measured between the time the logical link control layer 2 sub layer receives the instruction from the operating system until the bit actually leaves the NIC.

bits
A bit is a binary digit, taking a value of either 0 or 1. Binary digits are units of information storage and communication in computing.

bridge
A layer 2 device that connects multiple network segments at the data link layer of the OSI model.

bridge table
The table that the bridge creates that associates mac addresses with the outgoing port.

bridging
The process of forwarding frames from one port to another port or from segment to segment.

broadcast
A form of transmission whereupon one device transmits to all devices within the network or on another network.

broadcast address
An address that is meant to represent a transmission from one device to all devices based on the specified broadcast address.

broadcast domain
A logical network composed of all the computers and networking devices that can be reached by sending a frame to the data link layer broadcast address.

burned-in-address
The MAC address of a network interface card. It is called burned-in because the address cannot be changed.

cache
A temporary storage where data that is accessed frequently can be stored. Once the data is stored in the cache, accessing the cached copy instead of accessing the original data, so that the average access time is lower. For example a proxy server that has a cache.

carrier
Electromagnetic wave or alternating current of a single frequency, suitable for modulation by another, data-bearing signal.

Carrier Sense Multiple Access (CSMA)
A protocol in which a node wishing to transmit listens for a carrier wave before trying to send. If a carrier is sensed, the node waits for the transmission in progress to finish before initiating its own transmission.

CCNA
Cisco Certified Network Associate. The associate level certification founded by Cisco Systems.

channel
The medium used to transport information from a sender to a receiver.

checksum
A checksum is a form of redundancy check, a simple way to protect the integrity of data by detecting errors in data that are sent through space (telecommunications) or time (storage). It works by adding up the basic components of a message, typically the asserted bits, and storing the resulting value. Anyone can later perform the same operation on the data, compare the result to the authentic checksum, and (assuming that the sums match) conclude that the message was probably not corrupted

classful addressing
In the early days of IPv4, IP addresses are divided into 5 classes, namely, Class A, Class B, Class C, Class D, and Class E.

classless addressing
Ipv4 addressing scheme that uses a subnet mask that does not follow classful addressing rules. It provides increased flexibility when dividing ranges of IP addresses into separate networks.

client
A client is a computer system that accesses a service on another computer remotely by accessing the network.

client/server model
A network architecture that connects a client to a server whereupon the client accesses services provided by the server.

cloud
The cloud symbol is used to represent network communications without showing specific details of the network architecture. The cloud typically is used to hide the details of Layer 1 and Layer 2.

coaxial
Components that share a common axis. In the case of Coaxial cable there are three different layers of material surrounding the inner conducting material. The outer conductor, the insulator and the protective outer jacket.

code
A set of symbols for communicating information or instructions.

code groups
A code group is a consecutive sequence of code bits that are interpreted and mapped as data bit patterns.

collaboration tool
A collaboration tool is something that helps people work together on a particular file or piece of software. Many people use the term collaboration tool in a software context, for instance, collaboration software such as google docs, Microsoft sharepoint server.

collaborative (information systems)
Information systems that allow the creation of a document or documents that can be edited by more than one person in real-time.

Collision
In Ethernet, the result of two nodes transmitting simultaneously. The frames from each device impact and are damaged when they meet on the physical media.

Collision avoidance (CA)
Used in multiple access topologies such as wireless LAN networks. When a node wants to transmit, it sends a signal called Request-To-Send (RTS) with the length of the data frame to send. If the receiving station wishes to allow the transmission, it replies the sender a signal called Clear-To-Send (CTS) with the length of the frame that is about to receive. If another node hears the RTS will not transmit in order to avoid conflict with the CTS.

collision domain

A network segment where if one particular device sends a frame on a network segment, every other device on that same segment will process that frame. This also means that if two or more devices on that same segment transmit a frame at the same time there will be a collision.

collision fragment

Collision fragments are the product of a collision on a shared medium. The fragments sizes are less than 64 bytes.

Command Line Interface (CLI)

A method for interacting with computers using text as input. CLI can generally be considered as consisting of syntax and semantics. The syntax is the grammar that all commands must follow.

computer virus

A computer virus is a computer program that can copy itself and infect a computer without permission or knowledge of the user.

conduit (cabling)

A tube or duct for enclosing electric wires or cable.

congestion

The state of a network when there is not sufficient bandwidth to support the amount of network traffic.

console password

A password configured on the console line of the router or switch that requires a user to access the console port only after providing a password.

console port

A port in which we can connect a terminal or computer with a terminal emulator to the network device in order to communicate and configure the network device.

control data

Data that guides a process. A flag in a data-link frame is an example of control data.

converge

When different intermediary devices exchange information in order to have a consistent viewpoint of the network. We can also use another form of the root word converge in the phrase "converged network". This kind of network aggregates various forms of traffic such as voice, video and data on the same network infrastructure.

converged network

A network that allows for voice, video and data to use the same IP network.

crosstalk

The effect by which a signal transmitted on one circuit or channel of a wire creates an undesired effect in another circuit or channel.

CSMA/CA

Collision Sense Multiple Access with Collision Avoidance. A "flavor" of CSMA that includes CA (Collision Avoidance).

CSMA/CD

Carrier sense multiple access with collision detection. Media-access mechanism wherein devices ready to transmit data first check the channel for a carrier. If no carrier is sensed for a specific period of time, a device can transmit. If two devices transmit at once, a collision occurs and is detected by all colliding devices. This collision subsequently delays retransmissions from those devices for some random length of time. CSMA/CD access is used by Ethernet and IEEE 802.3.

CSU/DSU

Channel Service Unit/Data Service Unit. A hardware device that converts a digital data frame from a local area network (LAN) into a frame appropriate to a wide-area network (WAN) and vice versa.

cyclic redundancy check (CRC)

Cyclical Redundancy Check is a type of hash function (one way encryption), which is used to produce a small, fixed-size checksum of a block of data, such as a packet or a computer file. A CRC is computed and appended before transmission or storage, and verified afterwards by the recipient to confirm that no changes have happened in transit.

daemon

A computer program that runs in the background and are usually initiated as processes.

data collision

When two stations transmit at the same time on a multiple access topology and the frames of both sending stations collide with each other altering the original frame structure and creating fragments.

Data Communications Equipment (DCE)

Data communications equipment (EIA expansion) or data circuit-terminating equipment (ITU-T expansion). The devices and connections of a communications network that comprise the network end of the user-to-network interface. The DCE provides a physical connection to the network, forwards traffic, and provides a clocking signal used to synchronize data transmission between DCE and DTE devices. Modems and interface cards are examples of DCE. Compare with DTE.

data networks

Digital networks used to send data between computers.

Data Service Units (DSU)

A device used in digital transmission for connecting a CSU (Channel Service Unit) to Data Terminal Equipment such as a router.

Data Terminal Equipment (DTE)

The interface between the router and the DCE (CSU/DSU). Controls data coming inbound (WAN to LAN) or outbound (LAN to WAN).

datagrams

A data packet that traverses an IP based network.

decapsulation

The process of removing encapsulations in a receiving device. As PDUs arrive on each layer of the OSI model by the receiving computer the system discards of the previous layer's PDU in order to analyze its current layer's respective PDU.

decoding

The reverse of encoding. Usually a sending station encodes and the receiving station decodes. There are many different meanings of decoding. Line encoding and decryption are contexts of decoding.

default gateway

A device on a network that serves as an access point to another network. A default gateway is used by a host when an IP packet's destination address belongs to someplace outside the local subnet. A router is a good example of a default gateway.

default route

The route used by a router when no other known route exists for a given packet's destination address.

denial of service

An attempt to make a computer resource unavailable to its intended user. Also called DoS.

destination address

The address to which the data is going.

deterministic

Used in multiple access topologies where there are rules that govern who can transmit. An example of a deterministic network is a Token Ring topology where the station that has the token can transmit. While there is only one station with the token, the other stations wait for possession of the same in order to transmit.

digital logic

Also known as Boolean algebra. These consist of the AND, OR, IF operations.

digital signatures

A type of asymmetric cryptography used to simulate the security properties of a signature in digital form rather than written form.

directed broadcast

A single copy of a directed broadcast is routed to the specified network, where it is broadcast to all terminals on that network.

directly connected

A network that is directly connected to a device's interface. For example, networks that interface with the router are known to be directly connected.

distributed information systems

A method of computer processing in which different parts of a program run simultaneously on two or more computers that are communicating with each other over a network.

DNS resolver

In Unix/Linux computer systems, resolver is a set of software routines used for making, sending and interpreting query and reply messages with Internet domain name servers.

domain name

Names used for the Domain Name System (DNS), for example the special name which follows the @ sign in an email address, or the Top-level domains like .com.

Domain Name System (DNS)

Translates domain names (computer hostnames) to IP addresses.

dotted decimal

The format in which an ip address follows. For example: 10.0.0.1.

download

Transferring data (usually a file) from another computer to the computer you are using.

dynamic and/or private ports

Ports in the 49152-65535 range and are not used by any defined application.

Dynamic Host Configuration Protocol (DHCP)

DHCP (Dynamic Host Configuration Protocol) is the protocol used to request and assign an IP address, default gateway, and DNS server address to a network host.

EIA/TIA

Electronic Industries Alliance and the Telecommunication Industry Association. Responsible for developing standards. Responsible for the cabling standard EIA/TIA 568 a and b.

electronic impulses

A surge of electrical power in one direction.

e-mail

Electronic mail (abbreviated "e-mail" or, often, "email") is a store and forward method of composing, sending, storing, and receiving messages over electronic communication systems.

e-mail client

Program used to download and send email. Email clients use pop3 to receive emails and use SMTP to send emails.

EMI

Interference in a radio receiver or other electrical circuit by electromagnetic radiation emitted from an external source.

enable mode

Term used to represent the privileged exec mode.

enable password

Unencrypted password used from User exec mode to enter Privileged exec mode.

enable secret password

Strong encrypted password that is required when a user wishes to enter priviledged exec mode.

encapsulation

The wrapping of data in a particular protocol header.

encoding

The process of transforming data from one form to another form. Line encoding is the process by which information from a source is converted into symbols to be communicated.

encrypted

The process of obscuring information to make it unreadable without special knowledge, sometimes referred to as scrambling.

encryption

Data which has had a specific algorithm applied so as to alter the appearance of the data making it incomprehensible to those who are not authorized to see the information.

end devices

A device such as a desktop or mobile device that is used by an end user.

end-to-end

End user device to end user device.

error recovery

A procedure that allows a user to recover from errors such as failure of either host system or transfer process.

Ethernet crossover

UTP cabling where the pins order on one end follows the 568a pinning order and the other end of the cable follows the 568b pinning order. Use when connecting two pieces of equipment that have the same pinage on both ports.

Ethernet PHY

Ethernet PHY is the physical interface transceiver meaning that it deals with layer 1 (the physical layer, hence the PHY) of Ethernet.

Ethernet straight-through

UTP cabling where the pins order on one end follows the 568a pinning order and the other end of the cable follows the same 568a pinning order. Used when connecting a computer or a router to a switch.

expansion slot

A slot on a motherboard in which you can insert a kind of card to expand the computer's capabilities. For example an AGP slot is known as na expansion slot.

extranets

Part of a company's Intranet that is extended to users outside the company (e.g.: normally over the Internet).

Federal Communication Commission (FCC)

Federal Communications Commission. Responsible for the regulation of all non-Federal Government use of radio and television, all interstate telecommunications (wire, satellite and cable) as well as all international communications that originate or terminate in the United States.

fiber-optics

Physical medium that uses glass or plastic threads to transmit data. A fiber optic cable consists of a bundle of these threads, each of which is capable of transmitting electric signals into light waves.

filtering

The act of selecting data and discarding it based on certain predefined criteria.

FIN (Finish)

A message used in TCP that is used by a device that wishes to terminate its session with the other device. This is done by inserting the FIN flag in the flag field found in the TCP segment.

firewall

A firewall is a hardware device or a software application designed to protect network devices from outside network users and/or malicious applications and files.

flooding

The sending of frames through all outgoing ports.

flow

Stream of data traveling between two endpoints across a network (for example, from one LAN station to another). Multiple flows can be transmitted on a single circuit.

flow control

Flow control is the management of data flow between devices in a network. It is used to avoid too much data arriving before a device can handle it, causing data overflow.

fragment offset

Field within an IP datagram that provides information about the position of the fragment within the original datagram.

fragmentation

The fragmenting of IP datagrams in order to meet the MTU requirements of a layer 2 protocols.

frame

The layer two PDU which has been encoded by a data link layer protocol for digital transmission. Some different kinds of frames are Ethernet frames and PPP frames.

full-duplex

Communication that allows for receipt and transmission simultaneously. A station can transmit and receive at the same time. There are no collisions with full duplex transmission.

gateway

In the IP community, an older term referring to a routing device. Today, the term router is used to describe nodes that perform this function, and gateway refers to a special-purpose device that performs an application-layer conversion of information from one protocol stack to another. Compare with router.

Gbps

Gigabits (a billion bits) per second.

global configuration mode
From the privileged mode we enter the global configuration mode where we can configure global parameters or enter other configuration submodes such as interface, router, and line configuration submodes.

globally scoped addresses
Unique addresses that are public domain addresses.

goodput
Application level throughput. It is the number of useful bits per unit of time from a certain source address to a certain destination, excluding protocol overhead, and excluding retransmitted data packets.

half-duplex
Communication that only allows for one station to receive while the other station is transmitting.

hardware
Hardware are physical components of a computer, such as the hard drive, memory chip, motherboard, CPU, etc.

hardware interface
A physical connector that joins electrical circuits together. A hardware interface completes the connection of both ends. For instance, a hardware interface is where you connect the cable connector to the piece of equipment.

hashing algorithms
Reproducible method of turning some kind of data into a (relatively) small number that may serve as a digital "fingerprint" of the data. The algorithm "chops and mixes" (i.e., substitutes or transposes) the data to create such fingerprints, called hash values.

header
The informational data at the beginning of a data block that devices use to process the datagram.

hexadecimal
A base 16 numeral system whose characters begin at 0 -9 and A - F (to represent 10 - 15).

Hierarchical
Something that is classified according to various criteria into successive levels or layers. For instance, you can plan your network addressing in hierarchical way in order to provide for efficient routing.

hierarchical addressing
An addressing scheme in which a network is partitioned into sections, with the section identifier forming one part of each destinations address, and the destination identifier forming another.

hop
The passage of a data packet between two network nodes (for example, between two routers).

host
A device that communicates over a network.

host address
An address of a network host. When talking about host addresses, we are usually talking the network layer address.

host-group
A host-group is a group defined by a class D address (multicast, ranging from 224.0.0.0 - 239.255.255.255) whereupon hosts can pertain to multicast groups. Hosts that have the same multicast address are part of the same host-group.

HTML
Hyper Text Markup Language. Source code that web sites are written in. Web browsers download the source code from web servers and "translate" the code into visual format for the end user to see.

Hub
By definition a hub is a meeting place of sorts. A place of aggregation. In terms of equipment, a hub is a piece of equipment that acts as a multiport repeater.

hybrid fiber coax (HFC)
A network which incorporates optical fiber along with coaxial cable to create a broadband network. Commonly used by cable TV companies.

Hypertext Transfer Protocol (HTTP)
Hypertext Transfer Protocol (HTTP) is a method used to transfer or convey information on the World Wide Web. Its original purpose was to provide a way to publish and retrieve HTML pages.

instant messaging

Real-time communication between two or more people via text or other data.

Institute of Electrical and Electronics Engineers

An international non-profit organization for the advancement of technology related to electricity. It has more than 360,000 members in around 175 countries.

intelligent devices

An intelligent device is any type of equipment, instrument, or machine that has its own computing capability.

interframe gap

Interframe Gap provides a brief recovery time between frames to allow devices to prepare for reception of the next frame. The usual interframe spacing between Ethernet frames is 96 bit times.

intermediary devices

A device that connects directly to end user devices or provides end user routing to other networks. For instance, a router is an example of an intermediary device.

International Organization for Standardization

An international standard-setting organization composed of representatives from various national standards bodies. Also called ISO. There are many ISO standards that span various industries ranging from quality standards to information security standards.

International Telecommunication Union (ITU)

Regulates international radio and telecommunications. Standardizatizes, organizes interconnection agreements between different countries to allow international phone communications and is responsible for allocation of the radio spectrum.

Internet

The Internet is a publicly accessible network of interconnected computer networks that transmit data by using IP, the internet protocol.

Internet Assigned Numbers Authority (IANA)

An organization responsible for the allocation of Internet Protocol addresses to Internet service providers (ISPs).

Internet backbone

A high-speed line or series of connections that forms a major pathway within a network. The term Internet backbone is often used to describe the main network connections composing the Internet.

Internet Control Messaging Protocol (ICMP)

Internet Control Message Protocol. Network layer Internet protocol that reports errors and provides other information relevant to IP packet processing. Documented in RFC 792.

Internet Engineering Task Force (IETF)

Internet Engineering Task Force. Task force consisting of over 80 working groups responsible for developing Internet standards. The IETF operates under the auspices of ISOC.

Internet Protocol (IP)

Internet Protocol. Network layer protocol in the TCP/IP stack offering a connectionless internetwork service. IP provides features for addressing, type-of-service specification, fragmentation and reassembly, and security. Documented in RFC 791.

Internet Service Provider (ISP)

An ISP is a company that provides access to the Internet to individuals or companies.

internetwork

The interconnection of two or more different networks.

Internetwork Operating System (IOS)

Internetwork Operating System. This is the operating system that many Cisco Systems network devices use. Different versions of IOS have different functions for different devices.

interpret as command (iac)

In the telnet application, commands are always introduced by a character with the decimal code 255 known as an Interpret as Command (IAC) character.

intranet

A system internal to an organization such as a web site that is explicitly used by internal employees or students. Can be accessed internally or remotely.

IP address

Unique number that devices use in order to identify and communicate with each other on a computer network utilizing the Internet Protocol standard (IP).

IPv4

Short for Internet Protocol version 4. It is the current version of Internet Protocol.

IPv6

A network layer protocol for packet-switched internet works. The successor of IPv4 for general use on the Internet.

latency

Latency is the time delay between the moment a process is started and the moment the effects of that same process are detected. For instance, when transmitting data, latency is the delay it takes for the data to be sent between the sender and the receiver.

layered model

A model that consists of various layers that enables the development and explanation of technology to be done on a modular basis. This allows for interoperability amongst different technologies within and between the different layers.

limited broadcast

A broadcast that is sent to a specific network or series of networks.

link-local addresses

An IP address in the range from 169.254.1.0 to 169.254.254.255

Linux

A Unix-like computer operating system family. Some versions of Linux are free with underlying source code available for anyone to use.

llc

Logical Link Control is the upper layer of the OSI data link layer. When a host receives a frame and looks in the LLC header it finds out what upper layer protocol is being transported in the frame for example the IP protocol at the Network layer or IPX.

Local Area Network (LAN)

The term Local Area Network (LAN) refers to a local network, or a group of interconnected local networks that are under the same administrative control. In the early days of networking, LANs were defined as small networks that existed in a single physical location. While LANs can be a single local network installed in a home or small office, the definition of LAN has evolved to include interconnected local networks consisting of many hundreds of hosts, installed in multiple buildings and locations.

logical address

A network layer address. An address that can be changed at any time unlike a data-link layer address which is burned in the NIC.

logical topology

The map of devices on a network and how they communicate with one another. Shows the flow of data on a network.

loop back

127.0.0.1 is an IP address available on all devices to test to see if the NIC card on that device is functioning. If you send data to 127.0.0.1, it loops back on itself, thereby sending the data to the NIC on that device. If you get a positive response to a ping 127.0.0.1, you know your NIC card is up and running.

MAC Address

Standardized data link layer address that is required for every port or device that connects to a LAN. Other devices in the network use these addresses to locate specific ports in the network and to create and update routing tables and data structures. MAC addresses are 6 bytes long and are controlled by the IEEE.

mac table

The table that a switch creates in order to know where to forward outgoing frames. The MAC table consists of port number and the MAC address of the host associated with the same port. On a Cisco switch, it is called a CAM table.

mail carrier

A person that delivers mail.

Mail User Agent (MUA)
Mail User Agent (MUA) allows messages to be sent and places received messages into the client's mailbox, both of which are distinct processes.

managed (device)
A device that a user can connect to either a console port or via HTTP to monitor and configure the device.

Manchester encoding
Line code in which each bit of data is signified by at least one voltage level transition.

Maximum Transmission Unit (MTU)
Maximum transmission unit. Maximum packet size, in bytes, that a particular interface can handle.

mbps
megabits (a million bits) per second.

MDI
Medium Dependent Interface. Basically the pinout order on a NIC card on a PC. On Hubs or switches it is also known as an uplink port.

MDIX
Media Dependent Interface Crossover is the pinout of a hub or switch in which the input pins on side correspond with the output pins on the other side.

media
In the context of this course media is the plural form of medium.

medium
A physical medium in which data is transferred. For example, UTP is a form of networking media.

Metropolitan Area Network (MAN)
Metropolitan Area Network is a network that spans a city. The network consists of various buildings interconnected via either wireless or fiber optic backbones.

modal dispersion
The modes of light that enter the fiber at the same time and exit the fiber at different times. This condition causes the light pulse to spread. As the length of the fiber increases, modal dis-persion increases.

most-significant bit
The bit position in a binary number having the greatest value. The msb is sometimes referred to as the left-most bit.

multicast client
A member of a multicast group. Every multicast client in each group has the same IP address. Multicast addresses begin with 224.*.*.* and end with 239.*.*.*

multicast group
A multicast group is a group that receives a multicast transmission. The members of a multicast group have the same multicast IP addressing in order to receive the same transmission (a one to many transmission).

multiplexing
A process where multiple digital data streams are combined into one signal.

ndp
Neighbor Discovery Protocol (NDP) . It replaces ARP in IPv6.

network
A network is multiple computers connected together using a communications system. The purpose of a network is for computers to communicate and share files.

network address
Network layer address referring to a logical, rather than a physical, network device. Also called a protocol address.

Network Address Translation (NAT)
Translation of RFC 1918 addresses to public domain addresses. Since RFC 1918 addresses are not routed on the internet hosts accessing the internet must use public domain addresses.

network baseline
A network baseline is a process that involves monitoring network performance and behavior over a certain period of time allowing for a point of reference when wanting to monitor performance in the future.

network interface card

A piece of computer hardware designed to allow computers to communicate over a computer network.

network segment

A part of a computer network that every device communicates using the same physical medium. Network segments are extended by hubs or repeaters.

Network Time Protocol (NTP)

A protocol for synchronizing the clocks of computer systems over packet-switched data networks. NTP uses UDP port 123 as its transport layer.

next-hop

The next point of routing. When routers are not directly connected to the destination network, they will have a neighboring router that provides the next step in routing the data to its destination.

nibbles

A single hexadecimal digit represented by 4 bits.

node

A data-link layer term describing a device connected to the network.

non-return to zero (NRZ)

Signals that maintain constant voltage levels with no signal transitions (no return to a zero-voltage level) during a bit interval.

nslookup

NSLOOKUP is a service or a program to look up information in the DNS (Domain Name System).

NVRAM

Non Volatile Random Access Memory. Random access memory that, when the computer shuts down, the contents in NVRAM remain there.

octet

A group of 8 binary bits. It is similar, but not the same, to byte. One application in computer networking is to use octet to divide IPv4 addresses into 4 components.

Open System Interconnection (OSI)

Open System Interconnection. International standardization program created by ISO and ITU-T to develop standards for data networking that facilitate multivendor equipment interoperability.

operating system

A software that performs basic tasks such as controlling and allocating memory, prioritizing system requests, controlling input and output devices, facilitating networking, and managing file systems.

oui

Organizationally Unique Identifier. This identifier uniquely identifies a vendor, manufacturer of a network interface card. It is the first 24 bits of a network interface card.

p2p

Peer to peer networking whereupon computers that are part of the same network create a distributed system. Mostly used to share files with other p2p peers. Peer-to-peer computing calls for each network device to run both client and server portions of an application.

packet

Logical grouping of information that includes a header containing control information and (usually) user data. Packets are most often used to refer to network layer units of data. The terms datagram, frame, message, and segment are also used to describe logical information groupings at various layers of the OSI reference model and in various technology circles.

packet tracer

An instructional tool and network simulator developed by Cisco Systems to design, configure, troubleshoot, and visualize network traffic within a controlled, simulated program environment.

pad

A part of the Ethernet frame that fills in the data field to ensure that the data field meets the minimum size requirement of 46 bytes.

pam

Pulse-amplitude Modulation. A form of signal modulation where the message information is encoded in the amplitude of a series of signal pulses. It transmits data by varying the amplitudes (voltage or power levels) of the individual pulses. Is now obsolete and has been replaced by Pulse-code Modulation.

pda
A PDA (Personal Digital Assistant) is a handheld device normally used to help keep a person organized.

pdu
Short for Protocol Data Unit. The term PDU is used to describe data as it moves from one layer of the OSI model to another. In this reference, PDU is often used synonymously with packet.

peer
A host or node that participates in some form of group. For instance peer-to-peer technology defines a group of peers that participate jointly in the same activity, each one have a server and client component.

physical address
A data-link layer address, for example a MAC address.

physical topology
The physical topology of a network refers to the configuration of cables, computers, and other peripherals.

pinouts
The pin assignment that describes which signal may be obtained from some position in the connector.

plug-in
A program that acts as an add-on to a main program such as the flash player that you install in order to view flash animations in your navigator.

podcasting
Podcast is a digital media file or files that are distributed over the Internet using syndication feeds, for playback on portable media players and personal computers.

points of failure
Describes any part of the system that can, if it fails, cause an interruption of required service.

ports
Ports are typically used to identify a certain process or service on a computer. When a remote device wishes to access a certain service on a server, for example, it will direct that data to a certain port which will identify the kind of service that device wants to use.

positional notation
Positional notation or place-value notation system is a numeral system in which each position is related to the next by a constant multiplier, a common ratio, called the base or radix of that numeral system.

Post Office Protocol (POP)
POP (Post Office Protocol) is a protocol used when retrieving an e-mail message.

Power Over Ethernet (POE)
A method of transmitting power to a device by carrying power in the unused 4/5 and 7/8 wires of a UTP cable. It allows access points and other remote devices to be installed where there is no AC power outlet.

prefix length
Number of bits that are used to define the subnet mask. For example the subnet mask 255.255.0.0 is a /16 prefix.

private addresses
An address that is used for internal networks. This address follows RFC 1918 addressing. Not routable on the internet.

privileged executive mode
Privileged Exec Mode is the administration mode for the router or switch. This mode by allows you to view router settings that are considered only accessible to the administrator. This mode also allows you to enter global configuration mode. To get into the privileged exec mode you must use the enable command.

process
A series of progressive and interdependent steps by which an end is attained.

protocol
A set of rules governing communication.

protocol suite
Set of communications protocols that implement the protocol stack on which networks run.

proxy arp
Proxy ARP is when routers respond to ARP requests on one interface with its own MAC address as being responsible for addresses of device addresses on another interface.

proxy server
A server that acts as a kind of relay between the client and the destination server on the internet. The proxy server acts on behalf of the client and the server on the internet. All requests from the clients to the Internet go to the proxy server first. The proxy evaluates them, and if allowed, re-establishes the requests on the outbound side to the Internet. This is also the case on inbound traffic.

public addresses
Public addresses are assigned by InterNIC and consist of class-based network IDs or blocks of CIDR-based addresses (called CIDR blocks) that are globally unique to the Internet.

Quality of Service (QoS)
QoS (Quality of Service) is a control mechanism that can provide different priority to different users or data flows, or guarantee a certain level of performance to a data flow in accordance with requests from the application program.

query
Message used to inquire about the value of some variable or set of variables.

raceway (cabling)
Usually a fireproof external conduit where network cabling is placed in order to keep the physical network organized and the cabling in a safe place.

radix
The number of various unique digits, including zero that a positional numeral system uses to represent numbers. For instance in the binary system (base 2) the radix is 2. In the decimal system (base 10) the radix is 10.

RAM
Random Access Memory is a type of computer memory that can be accessed randomly;meaning any byte of memory can be accessed without concern for the preceding bytes. This is the memory that is available for programs. When the computer is shut down all data that was stored in RAM is lost.

real-time
Events or signals that show output as fast as possible, or as they happen.

Real-time Streaming Protocol (RTSP)
A protocol for use in streaming media systems which allows a client to control a media stream.

Real-time Transport Control (RTTC)
Gathers statistics on a media connection and information such as bytes sent, packets sent, lost packets, jitter, feedback and round trip delay. It is used to provide QoS information to RTP.

Real-time Transport Protocol (RTP)
A standardized packet format for delivering audio and video over the Internet.

redundant network architectures
Network architecture designed to eliminate network downtime caused by a single point of failure.

regional Internet registries (rirs)
Organizations that are responsible for the allocation and registration of Internet number resources within a particular region of the world. American Registry for Internet Numbers (ARIN) for North America, RIPE Network Coordination Centre (RIPE NCC) for Europe, the Middle East and Central Asia, Asia-Pacific Network Information Centre (APNIC) for Asia and the Pacific region, Latin American and Caribbean Internet Address Registry (LACNIC) for Latin America and the Caribbean region and African Network Information Centre (AfriNIC) for Africa.

registered ports
Port numbers that range from 1024-49151. Are used by user processes or programs executed by users.

Requests for Comments (RFCS)
RFCs are a series of documents and memoranda encompassing new research, innovations, and methodologies applicable to Internet technologies. RFCs are a reference for how technologies should work.

reserved link local addresses

An IP address in the range from 169.254.1.0 to 169.254.254.255. It is used to automatically assign an IP address to a device in an IP network when there is no other assignment method available, such as a DHCP server.

resource record

Resource Records (RRs) are the DNS data records. Their precise format is defined in RFC 1035. The most important fields in a resource record are Name, Class, Type, and Data.

RFI

Radio Frequency Interference is noise induced upon signal wires by ambient radio-frequency electromagnetic radiation that causes interference in neighboring wires.

rogue process

Rogue processes are processes that are not started by the end user nor applications on the operating system, sometimes consuming a large percentage of CPU usage.

rollover cable

A null-modem cable that is most commonly used to connect a computer terminal to a router's or switch's console port.

round trip time (rtt)

The elapsed time for transit of a signal over a closed circuit, or time elapsed for a message to a remote place and back again.

router

Network layer device that uses one or more metrics to determine the optimal path along which network traffic should be forwarded. Routers forward packets from one network to another based on network layer information.

routing

Process of finding a path to a destination host. Routing is very complex in large networks because of the many potential intermediate destinations a packet might traverse before reaching its destination host.

routing loop

A network problem in which packets continue to be routed in an endless circle.

routing protocols

Protocol that accomplishes routing through the implementation of a specific routing algorithm. Examples of routing protocols include IGRP, OSPF, and RIP.

routing table

A table stored in the memory of a router or some other internetworking device that keeps track of routes to particular network destinations. A router uses this list of networks to determine where to send data.

runt frame

Any frame that is less than 64 bytes (which is the minimum frame size in an Ethernet network). Runts are caused by collisions and are also known as collision fragments.

scheme

A plan, design, or program of action to be followed. Sometimes an addressing plan is an addressing SCHEME.

scope

The extent of a certain item. For example, an address scope is also known as a range of addresses from the beginning of the range to the end.

Secure http (https)

Uses https a URL that indicates that HTTP is to be used, but with a different default TCP port (443) and an additional encryption/authentication layer between the HTTP and TCP protocols.

Secure Shell (ssh)

Establishes a secure channel between a local and a remote computer. It uses public-key cryptography to authenticate the remote computer and to allow the remote computer to authenticate the user.

selective forwarding

The forwarding of packets where the forwarding decision is taken dynamically, hop-by-hop, based on the conditions of downstream forwarding nodes.

sequence numbers

Used by TCP to ensure that segments are not lost. Each segment will have a sequence number appended to it. This also allows the receiving station to make sure that the data is delivered at the other end in the correct order.

server
A computer that provides services to clients. Servers are the central point in client/server model networks. There exist many services that a server can provide to network clients. For example; DNS, DHCP, File storage, Application hosting, web site hosting.

Server Message Block (SMB)
Server Message Block (SMB) is an application-level network protocol mainly applied to shared access to files, printers, serial ports, and miscellaneous communications between nodes on a network.

session
1) A related set of communications transactions between two or more network devices.

2) In Systems Network Architecture (SNA), a logical connection enabling two network addressable units (NAUs) to communicate.

signaling speed
The speed at which data passes a point in the transmission path of a transmission system.

Simple Mail Transfer Protocol (SMTP)
Protocol for e-mail transmissions across the Internet. Uses port 25.

slot time
Is the time it takes for an electronic pulse to travel the length of the maximum theoretical distance between two nodes. It is also the time that a transmitting station waits before attempting to retransmit following a collision.

smart serial connector
Cisco Smart Serial interfaces have a 26-pin connectors and can automatically detect RS-232, RS-449, RS-530, X.21, or V.35 connectors.

smtp mail relaying
A SMTP mail server that allows anyone on the internet to pass email through it as if the email was originating from it. This used to be a common way for spammers to send spam via another provider's email servers. The recipient of the SPAM would think that it came from the provider's domain and not be able to trace the true origin of the SPAM.

software
Program or codes used by computer to carry out certain functions.

source
The origin of a message.

source address
In communications and networking, the origin of a communications channel.

source device
The sending station of a transmission.

spam
Spamming is sending spam, unsolicited commercial e-mail.

standard
An internationally recognized definition of technical specifications that ensure worldwide consistency.

start of frame (sof)
A field in a data-link frame denoting the beginning a frame transmission.

static routing
Routing that depends on manually entered routes in the routing table.

store and forward
A switching mode where the switch stores the entire frame and processes all the frame's content up until the FCS whereupon after successful FCS calculation the switch forwards the frame through the outgoing port.

stream
The continuous transmission of data from one location to another. For example a streaming video is a continuous, real-time flow of the video being downloaded as you watch the video.

streaming media
Multimedia that is continually downloaded to the receiving host as the end-user views the material. This allows for the end-user to view the material without having to fully download the multimedia file to their computer.

strong passwords

A strong password is a password that is complex and has a minimum of 8 characters. A strong password uses both alpha and numeric characters.

subnet mask

The function of a subnet mask is to identify the network portion, the subnet portion and the host portion of an IP address. Sub netting is a means of dividing the network and breaking a large or extremely large network up into smaller, more efficient and manageable segments, or subnets.

suite

A group of components that work cooperatively. TCP/IP is an example of a protocol suite. The protocols involved in TCP/IP work together to provide communication amongst computer networks.

switch

1) A network device that filters, forwards, and floods frames based on the destination address of each frame. The switch operates at the data link layer of the Open System Interconnection (OSI) model.

2) A general term applied to an electronic or mechanical device that allows a connection to be established as necessary and terminated when there is no longer a session to support.

synchronize sequence number (syn)

A SYN flag is put into the the flag field of a segment by an end-point wishing to establish a TCP session with another end-point.

synchronous transmission

Term describing digital signals that are transmitted with precise clocking. Such signals have the same frequency, with individual characters encapsulated in control bits (called start bits and stop bits) that designate the beginning and the end of each character.

syntax

The rules governing the form of communication.

TCP/IP

Transmission Control Protocol/Internet Protocol. Common name for the suite of protocols developed by the U.S. DoD in the 1970s to support the construction of worldwide internetworks. TCP and IP are the two best-known protocols in the suite.

teletype network service (telnet)

TELNET (Teletype Network) is a network protocol used on the Internet or local area network (LAN) connections.

telnet client application

A terminal emulation program that enables the remote connection of a host to a device.

telnet daemon

The Internet standard protocol for remote login. Runs on top of TCP/IP.

thicknet

Coaxial cable that is 0.4 inches in diameter and has 50 ohms of resistance. Originally used in the first LAN implementations.

thinnet

Coaxial cable that is 0.2 inches in diameter with the same impedance as Thicknet. Easier to install than thicknet.

three-way handshake

A process that establishes a TCP session between two endpoints. The process is as follows. 1. A client wishes to communicate with a server. The client sends a segment with the SYN flag marked. 2. In response, the server responds with a SYN-ACK. 3. The client then sends an ACK (usually called SYN-ACK-ACK) back to the other end and the session is established.

throughput

Throughput is the amount of digital data per time unit that is delivered from one node to another. Throughput takes into account latency variables.

time to live (ttl)

A limit on the time or number of iterations or transmissions in computer and computer network technology that a unit of data can experience before it should be discarded.

token passing

A deterministic network method where a "token" is passed around between nodes that authorizes the node to communicate.

tracert
A tool that shows the path in real-time from the source device to the destination device. It reports the IP addresses of all the routers (or hops) in the path.

trailer
The control information appended to data when data is encapsulated for network transmission.

Transmission Control Protocol (TCP)
Transmission control protocol: TCP is the protocol used as the basis of most Internet services. It is used in conjunction with the Internet Protocol (IP). It allows for reliable communication, ensuring that packets reach their intended destinations.

transparent bridging
Transparent bridging is the learning of source addresses on incoming frames and adding them to the bridging table. After the table has been completed and when a frame is received on one of the bridge's interfaces, the bridge looks up the frame's destination address in its bridging table and the frame is forwarded out the indicated port.

UDP
The User Datagram Protocol (UDP) is a simple protocol that exchanges data without acknowledgments or guaranteed delivery. UDP relies on applications to handle error processing and retransmission.

Uniform Resource Identifier (URI)
A string of characters used to identify or name a resource. Defined in RFC 1630 as the official identifier of web site names.

Uniform Resource Locator (URL)
The name of the web site you type in the name field of your navigator. This term gained popularity before the term URI became an RFC.

UNIX
UNIX is a multi-user, multitasking operating system originally developed in the 1960s and 1970s by a group of AT&T employees at Bell Labs including Ken Thompson, Dennis Ritchie, and Douglas McIlroy. Today's UNIX systems are split into various branches, developed over time by AT&T, as well as various commercial vendors and non-profit organizations.

upload
To transmit data to a server or to another receiving device.

User Datagram Protocol (UDP)
A connectionless transport layer protocol in the Transmission Control Protocol/Internet Protocol (TCP/IP) protocol stack. UDP is a simple protocol that exchanges datagrams without acknowledgments or guaranteed delivery, and requires that error processing and retransmission be handled by other protocols. UDP is defined in RFC 768.

user executive mode
Also known as view mode, this mode is the most restricted on the IOS. The user is only able to monitor and view limited information on the router or switch.

UTP
UTP is a four-pair wire medium used in a variety of networks. UTP does not require the fixed spacing between connections that is necessary with coaxial-type connections. There are five types of UTP cabling commonly used: Category 1 cabling, Category 2 cabling, Category 3 cabling, Category 4 cabling, and Category 5 cabling.

Variable Length Subnet Masking (VLSM)
VLSM is the ability to specify a different subnet mask for the same network number on different subnets. VLSM can help optimize available address space.

virtual circuit
A method in which data is passed to a destination over more than one real communications circuits. End users do not notice the intermediate switching in between the source and destination. Frame Relay is a packet switching technology that uses virtual circuits.

Virtual Local Area Network (VLAN)
A network of computers that behave as if they are connected to the same network segment even though they may actually be physically located on different segments of a LAN. VLANs are configured via software on the switch and router.

virtual terminal (vty)
A command line interface created in a router for a Telnet session.

Voice over IP (VOIP)
Voice data encapsulated in an IP packet allow it to traverse already implemented IP networks without needing its own network infrastructure.

vty password
The password on the VTY lines that is configured on each line or all lines together. When a user attempts to telnet to a router or switch they will be prompted the configured password.

web browser
GUI-based hypertext client application, such as Internet Explorer, Mosaic, and Netscape Navigator, used to access hypertext documents and other services located on innumerable remote servers throughout the WWW and Internet.

web server
A server that responds to HTTP requests and responding with HTTP response data. A web server also holds the directory structure of web sites and their associated images and other media files.

weblogs
A blog is a website where entries are made in journal style. A blog is created by the user and can make changes to the blog via templates or by altering the HTML code of the blog itself. Visitors can leave posts to the blog. Blog is short for Weblog.

well-known ports
Ports that range from 0-1023.

Wide Area Network (WAN)
Wide Area Network. A network that spans broader geographical area than a Local Area Network, over public communications networks.

wiki
A wiki is a website that lets visitors add, edit and delete content, typically without the need for registration. A good example of this is a site called wikipedia where visitors can access the website and add their commentaries to already written articles or create a new article.

Winchester connector
A 34 pin female v.35 serial cable connector.

window size
TCP uses window size to determine the number of segments sent by the sending device before the receiving device sends a confirmation.

wireless technology
Technology that allows for communication without needing physical connectivity. Examples of wireless technology cellular telephones, personal digital assistants (PDA's), Wireless access points and wireless NICs.

Wireshark
A packet sniffing application, used for network troubleshooting, analysis. This program captures packets on the NIC and decodes packet contents for readability.

World Wide Web (WWW)
A large network of Internet sites whose servers provide information on a wide variety of topics and services such as purchasing products or playing games. Entry into the World Wide Web requires a program called a browser such as Internet Explorer or Netscape and connectivity through an internet service provider (ISP).

CCNA Exploration
learning resources

Cisco Press, the authorized publisher for the Cisco® Networking Academy®, has a variety of learning and preparation tools to help you master the knowledge and prepare successfully for the CCENT™ and CCNA® exams.

From foundational learning to late-stage review, practice, and preparation, the varied print, software, and video products from Cisco Press can help you with learning, mastering, and succeeding!

Companion Guides

Companion Guides provide textbook-style support with additional content from leading Academy instructors.

Network Fundamentals, CCNA Exploration Companion Guide	1-58713-208-7 / 978-1-58713-208-7
Routing Protocols and Concepts, CCNA Exploration Companion Guide	1-58713-206-0 / 978-1-58713-206-3
LAN Switching and Wireless, CCNA Exploration Companion Guide	1-58713-207-9 / 978-1-58713-207-0
Accessing the WAN, CCNA Exploration Companion Guide	1-58713-205-2 / 978-1-58713-205-6

Labs and Study Guides

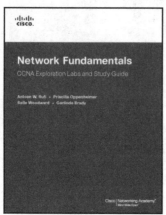

Labs and Study Guides provide study tools and labs, both from the online curriculum and from leading Academy instructors.

Network Fundamentals, CCNA Exploration Labs and Study Guide	1-58713-203-6 / 978-1-58713-203-2
Routing Protocols and Concepts, CCNA Exploration Labs and Study Guide	1-58713-204-4 / 978-1-58713-204-9
LAN Switching and Wireless, CCNA Exploration Labs and Study	1-58713-202-8 / 978-1-58713-202-5
Accessing the WAN, CCNA Exploration Labs and Study Guide	1-58713-201-X / 978-1-58713-201-8

Other CCNA resources

1-58713-197-8 / 978-1-58713-197-4	31 Days Before your CCNA Exam, Second Edition
1-58720-183-6 / 978-1-58720-183-7	CCNA Official Exam Certification Library, Third Edition
1-58720-193-3 / 978-1-58720-193-6	CCNA Portable Command Guide, Second Edition
1-58720-216-6 / 978-1-58720-216-2	CCNA 640-802 Network Simulator (from Pearson Certification)
1-58720-221-2 / 978-1-58720-221-6	CCNA 640-802 Cert Flash Cards Online

For more information on this and other Cisco Press products, visit www.ciscopress.com /academy

Cisco Press   Learning is Serious Business. **Invest Wisely.**